Understanding European Movements

Europe: a social movements have been central to European history, politics, society and culture, and have had a global reach and impact. Yet they have rarely been taken on their own terms in the English-language literature, considered somewhat as counterpoints to the US experience. This has been exacerbated by the failure of Anglophone social movement theorists to pay attention to the substantial literatures in languages such as French, German, Spanish and Italian, and by the increasing global dominance of English in the production of news and other forms of media.

This book sets out to take the European social movement experience seriously on its own terms, including:

- the European tradition of social movement theorising – particularly its attempt to understand movement development from the 1960s onwards
- the extent to which European movements between 1968 and 1999 became precursors for the contemporary anti-globalization movement
- the construction of the anti-capitalist "movement of movements" within the European setting
- the new anti-austerity protests in Iceland, Greece, Spain (15-M/Indignados), and elsewhere.

This book offers a comprehensive, interdisciplinary perspective on the key European social movements of the past forty years. It will be of interest for students and scholars of politics and international relations, sociology, history, European studies and social theory.

Cristina Flesher Fominaya has a PhD in Sociology from UC Berkeley and works at the University of Aberdeen. She is a founding co-editor of the journal *Interface*.

Laurence Cox co-directs the MA in Community Education, Equality and Social Activism at the National University of Ireland, Maynooth. He co-edits the social movements journal *Interface*.

Routledge advances in sociology

Understanding European Movements

New social movements, global justice struggles, anti-austerity protest

Edited by Cristina Flesher Fominaya and Laurence Cox

Routledge
Taylor & Francis Group

LONDON AND NEW YORK

First published 2013
by Routledge
2 Park Square, Milton Park, Abingdon, Oxon OX14 4RN

Simultaneously published in the USA and Canada
by Routledge
711 Third Avenue, New York, NY 10017

Routledge is an imprint of the Taylor & Francis Group, an informa business

First issued in paperback 2013

British Library Cataloguing in Publication Data
A catalogue record for this book is available from the British Library

Library of Congress Cataloging in Publication Data
Understanding European movements : new social movements, global
justice struggles, anti-austerity protest / edited by Cristina Flesher
Fominaya and Laurence Cox. – First Edition.
  pages cm. – (Routledge advances in sociology ; 103)
  Includes bibliographical references and index
  1. Social movements–Europe–History–20th century. 2. Europe–Politics
and government–20th century. 3. Europe–History–20th century.
  I. Flesher Fominaya, Cristina. II. Cox, Laurence.
  HM881.U53 2013
  322.4094–dc23
                                                        2012047901

ISBN: 978-0-415-63879-1 (hbk)
ISBN: 978-1-138-02546-2 (pbk)

Typeset in Times New Roman
by Wearset Ltd, Boldon, Tyne and Wear

Contents

Illustrations

Figures

Tables

Contributors

Kerman Calvo (MA, Juan March Institute, Madrid; PhD, Essex University) is Assistant Professor of Sociology at the University of Salamanca, Spain. His main lines of research are protest politics, LGTB movements and politics, and electoral behaviour, with many publications including *South European Society and Politics* and *Journal of Public Administration Research and Theory.*

Baptiste Colin is a PhD student at the Universities of Paris 7, France, and Bielefeld, Germany, where he is working on a project entitled "Squatting: crossed story of Paris and West Berlin from after Second World War until the end of the 1980s: Aims, perspectives and strategies of a contested housing model".

Laurence Cox is lecturer in Sociology at the National University of Ireland Maynooth, where he co-directs the MA in Community Education, Equality and Social Activism and runs a PhD research programme of participatory action research in social movement practice. He is co-editor of the multilingual social movements journal *Interface* and is an editorial advisor and/or referee for numerous other journals. He has published widely on the alterglobalisation movement, social movements and culture, activist sustainability, working-class community organising, Marxist theories of social movement, research methodology and new religious movements. His work has appeared in *Rethinking Marxism, Ecopolitics online, Irish Journal of Sociology, Sociology Compass, Emotion, Space and Society, Journal of Global Buddhism, Contemporary Buddhism* and numerous edited collections. He is co-editor of the forthcoming *Marxism and Social Movements* and the 2011 *Ireland's New Religious Movements*. Trained in European Studies, he has lived in Norway, France, Germany and Italy and has been active in transnational movement networks since the 1980s.

Priska Daphi has an MSc in Political Sociology from the London School of Economics and Political Science. Currently, she is a PhD candidate at the Berlin Graduate School of Social Sciences (Humboldt-Universität zu Berlin, Germany). She is a founding member of the Institute for Protest and Social Movement Studies in Berlin.

Olivier Fillieule is Full Professor of Political Sociology at Lausanne University and Senior Researcher at CNRS (France). He has published extensively on social movement theory, activism and militantism. He was Jean Monnet fellow at the European University Institute (Florence, Italy) in 1996–1997, and invited researcher at UC Berkeley (2000) and New York University (2009).

Cristina Flesher Fominaya has an MA and PhD in Sociology from the University of California, Berkeley, and a BA *summa cum laude* in International Relations from the University of Minnesota. She has won numerous international merit awards, including the National Science Foundation Fellowship, the German Marshall Fellowship and the Marie Curie Fellowship. She was Assistant Professor in the Department of Sociology and Political Science in the Universidad Carlos III de Madrid and visiting scholar at Georgetown University before joining the Department of Sociology at the University of Aberdeen in 2009. As of September 2013 she will also be Marie Curie Fellow at the National University of Ireland, Maynooth. She has been researching and participating in European social movements since the early 1990s. Her work has been published in *Contemporary Social Science, Sociological Inquiry, Sociology Compass, International Review of Social History, South European Society and Politics* and other journals and several edited collections. She is a founding editor of *Interface* and is founding co-chair (with Laurence Cox) of the *Council for European Studies Research Network on European Social Movements*.

Agnes Gagyi is Assistant Professor at Eszterhazy Karoly college in Hungary. She also teaches Sociology of Communication and Social Movements at Corvinus University and the University of Arts and Design in Budapest. Her dissertation was on the Romanian and Hungarian alterglobalist movement. She was active in the movement between 2003–2008.

Magnús Sveinn Helgason is Lecturer at University of Bifröst, Iceland.

Árni Daníel Júlíusson speaks Icelandic, Danish and English and lived in Denmark between 1992–1996, receiving his PhD from Copenhagen University in 1997. He has been an independent scholar at the Reykjavík Academy since 1997, and has been on the board of Attac Iceland since its founding in 2009.

Ask Katzeff is a Copenhagen-based writer and activist. Currently he is working as a PhD Fellow at the University of Copenhagen on a project on squatting and urban development in Germany, Denmark and England.

Elisabeth Lorenzi is an anthropologist involved in the study of urban transformation influenced by the social movements. Recently she studied the neighborhood movement in Madrid. She currently focuses her attention on two intertwined issues: bike mobility initiatives and the squatters' movement.

Andrea Membretti, PhD in Sociology, is currently Research Fellow at the University of Milan-Bicocca, where he studies urban segregation. He has been Assistant Professor of Urban Sociology at the University of Pavia for the last ten years, working at the same time as a consultant in the field of participation and promotion of active citizenship.

Edouard Morena teaches French history and politics at King's College London and is associate researcher at the CNRS-affiliated Laboratoire Dynamiques Sociales et Recomposition des Espaces (LADYSS, France). His research focuses on the French alter-globalisation movement and peasant mobilisations against neoliberal globalisation.

Pierpaolo Mudu is a geographer collaborating with the Urban Studies program of the University of Washington, Tacoma. The main focus of his research is the development of contemporary Rome in relation to social movements, migrations and the transformation of public space. He has published in *ACME, Antipode, GeoJournal* and *Urban Geography.*

Michal Osterweil is Lecturer in Global Studies at University of North Carolina at Chapel Hill. She received her PhD in Cultural Anthropology and has authored several articles on the Global Justice Movement and the World and regional Social Forums. She is a founding editor of *Turbulence: Ideas for Movement.*

Linus Owens teaches sociology at Middlebury College, Vermont, USA. Having previously written *Cracking Under Pressure: Narrating Decline in the Amsterdam Squatters' Movement* (Amsterdam University Press and Penn State University Press 2009), he is now researching mobilities and material culture in contemporary social movements.

Emmanuel Rivat is doctoral candidate at Science Po Bordeaux, based on a joint supervision with the University of Amsterdam. He was an assistant campaigner at Greenpeace France on the nuclear disarmament campaign (2006).

Eduardo Romanos is a Ramón y Cajal Fellow in Sociology at the Universidad Complutense de Madrid. Eduardo received his PhD in Political and Social Sciences from the European University Institute in 2007. His main research interests are in the areas of political and historical sociology, with a particular focus on social movements and protest.

Christian Scholl is a Brussels-based activist researcher currently working as a postdoctoral research fellow at the University of Louvain. His research interests revolve around globalization, social movements, and social control. He is the author *of Two Sides of a Barricade: (Dis)order and Summit Protest in Europe* and co-author of *Shutting Down the Streets. Political Violence and Social Control in the Global Era.*

Vittorio Sergi graduated in Philosophy, conducting field research on the Zapatistas' communities in Chiapas, in 2002. In 2007 he was awarded a PhD in Philosophy and Politics from the University of Naples and a PhD in Sociology from the University of Puebla, Mexico.

Isabelle Sommier is Full Professor of Political Science at Paris I-Sorbonne University. She has published extensively on social movements theory, political violence, radicalization and terrorism. For her work on the extreme left in France and Italy, she conducted extensive fieldwork in Italy at various locations.

Markos Vogiatzoglou is a PhD candidate in Social and Political Sciences at the European University Institute, Florence, Italy. He studied Sociology at the Panteion University in Athens, Greece, and Social Movements at the University of Crete, Rethymnon, Greece. He was an active trade union activist in Greece.

Acknowledgements

First and foremost we would like to thank the contributors for their engaged and enthusiastic collaboration and in particular for their willingness to meet a tough series of deadlines.

This book was developed in the context of the Council for European Studies' (CES) Social Movements Research Network. We would like to thank the CES, and in particular its director Siovahn Walker, for their assistance with the network and this book.

Cristina would like to thank Jesús and Sofía, and Laurence would like to thank Alannah and Orfhlaith for their support and patience throughout this project.

Introduction

Rethinking European movements and theory

Cristina Flesher Fominaya and Laurence Cox

European social movements have been central to European history, politics, society, and culture and have had a global reach and impact. Yet, European social movements, and social movement theories, have rarely been taken on their own terms in the English language literature, but rather as counterpoints to the American experience. While such comparisons have been fruitful in some ways, they have lacked a sense of history and culture and have failed to take European social movement theory seriously on its own terms.

This has been exacerbated by the failure of Anglophone social movement theorists to pay attention to the substantial literatures in languages such as French, German, Spanish or Italian – and by the increasing global dominance of English in the production of news media, and other forms of media such as the Internet. It is also, of course, driven by the demand for public commentary by well-known intellectuals irrespective of their actual research on social movements, and the pressure on them to make vast generalisations based upon limited personal experience and what little they can glean from a media which struggles to report social movement processes adequately.

This magisterial ignorance is particularly problematic because these same movements – from the European eruptions of 1968, east and west, through to the European marches of the unemployed, East European dissidence, British counter-cultural movements or west European autonomous movements in the 1980s and 1990s – have been central to the construction of the "alterglobalization movement", or Global Justice Movement, which began with alliances between, for example, French ATTAC and Brazilian movement organizations, or between Italian and Spanish radicals and the Zapatistas.

The Global Justice Movement, for its part, has clearly been central in the development and construction of the current wave of global protests. Often the lines of continuity between movements have a markedly national character despite the global nature and impact of mobilizations (e.g. connections between the Spanish experience of the Global Justice Movement and the emergence of the 15-M Indignados movement). Among other things, what is often missing in accounts is the extent to which key European movements represent a continuation of the "New Left" problematic – the experience of a mainly extra-institutional left movement culture in political contexts marked by the institutionalisation of a more moderate left. As the chapters in this book show, contemporary anti-austerity protests and the European *Indignados*/15-M/"Occupy" protests grow out of this same matrix.

This book sets out to take the European social movement experience seriously on its own terms, including (i) the European tradition of social-movement theorizing, particularly in its attempt to understand the development of movements from the 1960s onwards; (ii) the extent to which European movements between 1968 and 1999 became precursor movements for the contemporary anti-globalization movement; (iii) the construction of the anti-capitalist "movement of movements" within the European setting; and (iv) the new 15-M/"Occupy" mobilizations against financial austerity in Iceland, Greece, the UK, Spain, Portugal, and elsewhere.

Overview of this book

In Part I Cox and Flesher Fominaya show the extent to which reflections upon social movements have been constitutive of European social theory, and argues for the latter to be considered more systematically within social movement research. It further shows that the standard rendering of "new social movement" theory reproduced in conventional accounts is more of an origin myth than a serious piece of intellectual history, and examines the actual history of the new social movement debate in order to recover more fruitful lines of enquiry about European movements.

Part II discusses European precursors to the Global Justice Movement. The chapters highlight continuities and disjunctures of movement networks, ideologies, organizing forms and issues in national and transnational European contexts. These case studies and comparative accounts not only provide rich empirical data, but collectively demonstrate the profound differences between configurations of key actors in national expressions of the GJM. As such, these contributions serve as an important corrective to arguments for the radical novelty of the GJM vis-à-vis earlier movements, an insight that can be useful when applied to current analyses of anti-austerity protests.

Osterweil draws our attention to the importance of history and place by tracing the influence of precursor movements, especially autonomous movements, upon the narratives, goals and organizing forms of the Italian Global Justice Movement. At the same time she shows how these place-based movement histories influenced actors, who then influenced and were influenced by other actors in the GJM. In a similar vein, Sommier and Fillieule use a genealogical approach to trace the influence of a diversity of actors upon the emergence of the French anti-globalization movement, demonstrating that most of these actors were organized prior to the emergence of the movement. They show how differences in national political opportunity structures shape the emergence and decline of protest cycles. Their claim that the diversity of actors points to a conceptualization of the GJM as "an amorphous collection of various mobilized groups" rather than a single transnational movement contributes to the ongoing debate over how best to categorize transnational movements. Rivat shows the enduring influence of the anti-nuclear movement upon the contemporary European movement landscape and its close relationship with the transnational Global Justice Movement. His close attention to national variations in relationships between environmentalist groups and political parties over time also shows the enduring tension between the more institutional "old" left and the more autonomous and participatory "new" political identities. Membretti and Mudu trace the historical roots of the Italian *Centri Sociale* (social centres) and their crucial importance in the development of the dynamics, culture and agenda of the anti-globalization movement, not only in Italy but in Europe too. Morena shows how the French peasant organization Confederation Paysanne successfully forged a new alterglobalization collective identity, by drawing on pre-existing popular representations and adapting them to the new neoliberal critical discourse. Flesher Fominaya highlights processes of movement culture continuity and national to transnational diffusion by showing the continuity of five key characteristics of the British anti-roads movement with central features of the GJM.

Part III examines the cultural processes involved in constructing the "movement of movements". Drawing on research on EuroMayDay and climate justice movements, Scholl discusses processes of cross-national diffusion, arguing for the conceptualization of Europe as a "contagious space". Gagyi uses the method of tracking political ideas through historical interactions to compare the ways in which Eastern European activists in Hungary and Romania received and interpreted the concept and practice of autonomy as it was diffused from Western European Global Justice Movement actors. Her analysis calls for careful attention to the ways in which local and national contexts shape the incorporation of key concepts that are all too often theorized in globalizing universalistic ways. Owens, Katzeff, Lorenzi and Colin illuminate the processes whereby activist identities are constructed across space, as activists travel between European squats over time. Their chapter points our attention to the importance of space and mobility in identity processes and contributes to our understanding of transnational diffusion processes. Daphi adopts a narrative approach in order to analyse the relation between collective memories and activists spatial anchoring and collective identity construction in the Global Justice Movement, by comparing Italian and German accounts.

Part IV looks at the new "European Spring" of anti-austerity protests. These chapters represent emerging research that shows the roots of these events in each country's movement history, but also reflects upon the role of transnational networks in shaping them.

Júlíusson and Helgason draw on Gramsci and Badiou in order to trace the roots of the Icelandic revolution of 2008 – which prefigured the later wave of protests from Tunisia to the USA – from the 1930s to 2008. The Icelandic case was small relative to later mobilizations elsewhere, but very successful and influential, being the first mobilizations to directly address the consequences of the global financial crisis. Sergi and Vogiatzoglou show the importance of the mobilization of national symbolic memory on the repertoires of contention in the Tunisian and Greek anti-austerity protests. Romanos traces the processes of collective learning in the Indignados/15-M, highlighting an evolution from and continuity with previous Global Justice Movement networks and mobilizations, as well as noting newer features. In contrast, Calvo draws on empirical survey data on the participants and frames of the 15-M movement, arguing for the novelty of the movement with regard to previous political culture in Spain. Taken together, these two contributions provide us with much food for thought regarding movement continuity and rupture.

The editors' conclusion reflects upon the role of European social movements in the rapidly changing crisis, situating individual anti-austerity and "Occupy" movements and pointing to future avenues for research.

Research context

The 15 chapters of this book include authors based in 11 different countries whose analyses are all grounded in ethnographic and historical research on these movements – in Denmark, France, Germany, Greece, Hungary, Iceland, Ireland, Italy, Romania, Spain and the UK – and, in keeping with the tradition of European social theory, many are active, critical participants in the movements they analyse.

Taken as a whole, the research in this book demonstrates

1   The lasting significance of national movement histories, generating *movement landscapes* which are not reducible to political opportunity structures;
2   The role of cross-national processes of inspiration, learning, alliance and movement which go substantially beyond "transnational advocacy networks" and constitute Europe as an internally-differentiated movement space;
3   The importance of *previous* movement waves and their specific national histories in accounting for the complexities of the present;
4   The particularities of European social movement developments, which, while remaining porous to developments elsewhere, nonetheless deserve reflection on their own terms. This suggests the limitations of quantitative cross-national comparative analysis that fails to incorporate findings from qualitative research and overlooks the national and historical specificities of the cases being compared;
5   The need for theoretical models which are more attentive both to these *historical* dimensions of movement development, continuity and rupture and to the interplay of national, European and local in the formation of complex, differentiated transnational movement cultures.

It is our hope that a reading of the contributions that follow will stimulate new avenues of research and reflection. As scholars and observers struggle to make sense of the current wave of anti-austerity protests, and protests yet to come, we hope this book will serve as a useful and provocative invitation to a historically grounded debate that balances attention to national specificities with the realities of transnational and global dynamics.

Part I

European theory/European movements

1 European social movements and social theory

A richer narrative?

Laurence Cox and Cristina Flesher Fominaya

Introduction

Anyone researching social movements will find themselves hearing or reading a near-identical account, often repeated word-for-word, of how the discipline came to be. It is a tale of the bad old days of collective behaviour theory, followed by the rise of resource mobilization theory, the addition of political opportunity structure, the encounter with ('European') 'new social movement' theory and the arrival of framing theory. Those who reproduce this account are usually doing one of two things: as newcomers to the field, they are affirming their right to belong by repeating its origin myths, or, as established figures, they are underlining the orthodox status of those myths.

We say *origin myths* because this is the actual function of this particular account. Original research is virtually always lacking; even where the author has read the figures cited there is no attempt at rethinking the intellectual history. The closest relatives of this kind of myth are the accounts by Tibetan Buddhist schools of ancient philosophical debates in India, which they understood as predecessors to their own school and as sources of intellectual status – accounts which necessarily relied upon earlier accounts within the same tradition and did so uncritically, producing canons rather than histories.

Our contention is that the *form* of such accounts is that of origin myth – the formulation of a textual canon and the performance of rituals marking membership of a particular group. This is so whether or not the actual content of such accounts is accurate; since they are not critical works of intellectual history but, rather, reproduce the accounts of previous scholars, their accuracy is secondary. As far as the representation of 'European social movement theory' goes, however, the origin myth is at best a very partial and misleading account which confuses a history of transmission, reception and interpretation within a US sub-discipline for actual European debates.

This chapter does two things. It shows that European social theory has largely developed through engagement with movements, in ways which differ from the US experience and which are not represented by 'social movement theory' as a narrowly-bounded subfield of sociology and political science. Second, we explore one aspect of this, which in the standard origin myth is routinely as 'the

European contribution to social movement theory', the discussion of new social movements. Re-placing this debate in its historical and political context, we show that the canonical account severely misrepresents this European scholarship on movements and reduces it to a soundbite which *misses the point*.

The preceding paragraph is polemical, but more in sorrow than in anger. As scholars researching contemporary European movements, we have found the conceptual tools of US movement research helpful on the micro-scale, but incapable of dealing with the macro-questions that are central to European movements (Mayer 1995). An uncritical translation of US exceptionalism (the historical weakness of the political left and labour movements) has been turned into an operating assumption of social movements as a particular 'level' of the political system. This leaves out entirely the European experience, where democratic, nationalist, labour, fascist, anti-fascist, communist and anti-communist movements have repeatedly remade and reshaped states and reorganized whole societies in their own image.

Similarly, the uncritical repetition of a reductionist account of 'European social movement theory' bears no resemblance to the social theorists and processes of movement theorising we encounter within movements and in European writing on movements. This account, regularly reproduced by monoglot writers (in a circular relationship with academic translation processes) is a travesty of the actual debates within which movements have engaged in the last five decades and of the ways in which European intellectuals have engaged with those movements. This chapter is a first attempt at rectifying some of these intercultural misrepresentations and misunderstandings.

A richer narrative

In attempting to provide a richer narrative we first return European social theory to its roots in social movements, showing how well-known figures in social and cultural thought, both classical and contemporary, have shaped and been shaped by movements in their lives, themes, and forms of reflection. Locating them as 'public intellectuals' within a movement society offers a richer understanding of their line of thought and its relevance to the study of movements.

We then use this broader perspective to rethink the category 'European social movements theory'. In place of a selective and misleading canonical account we sketch an alternative history of the complex academic and political theorising around a broader spectrum of movements. European social movement theory was a broader-based reflection upon popular agency in contemporary society, which encompassed strategic as well as cultural elements, the political as well as the economic, working-class struggles as much as others.

Without treating 'Europe' as isolated or bounded, and recognising exchanges between continental western Europe and the English-speaking world, we insist on the need to recognise intellectual context, modes of theorising and relationship to movements if we want a more realistic, and theoretically fruitful, account of European reflections on movements.

European social theory as reflection on social movements

The foundations of European social theory are closely linked to social movements. Saint-Simon, Marx, Weber and Durkheim were all politically engaged with or against movements – as utopian socialist, movement theorist, conservative opponent and party member respectively. De Tocqueville attempted to grasp the American Revolution, while Engels struggled with the Peasant War. The Marx of the *Communist Manifesto* and the historical writings, or the Weber of the *Protestant Ethic* and the analysis of status-groups and parties, were both centrally engaged with theorising popular collective agency and its many different forms in this unstable time.

These were normal concerns for nineteenth-century European intellectuals, in a period in which 'the social question' came to life as 'the social movement' (Cox forthcoming), the plebeian challenge to a society and polity which had no place for them except as 'hands'. Movement took many forms, as did its theorisation: if von Stein's use of the phrase 'social movement' focussed on the French Revolution, this was so characteristic that those who made (Lamartine) and broke (Thiers) later revolutions had themselves written histories of the subject. Elsewhere in Europe, the struggles of German, Italian, Polish and Irish nationalism in particular were central to intellectual life in those areas and resonated internationally. The battle for democracy played a strategic role in a Europe where only a handful of states saw anything approaching full suffrage or the ending of monarchical power before the end of the First (or sometimes the Second) World War.

The late nineteenth-century European political and intellectual experience, then, saw mass popular struggles for power shape the construction of new kinds of state and society, a process which only found a provisional resting-point with the postwar construction, in western Europe, of 'organized' societies combining full formal democracy and corporatist movement involvement in decision-making – and a Cold War which threatened (and which, in Greece and Hungary, delivered) lethal violence to defend superpower control against popular movements which failed to accept their place.

Southern Europe, where dictatorships continued the fascist strategy of mass mobilization around conservative goals until the 1970s, and Eastern Europe, where states supposedly founded by popular movements actively repressed actual movements until the end of the 1980s, were shaped differently again; but in each situation (including their downfalls) social movements were central to the making and remaking of Europe. As Ken Macleod famously put it,

> Our liberties were won in wars and revolutions so terrible that we do not fear our governors: they fear us. Our children giggle and eat ice-cream in the palaces of past rulers. We snap our fingers at kings. We laugh at popes. When we have built up tyrants, we have brought them down.[1]

Unsurprisingly, twentieth-century European intellectuals continued or intensified their concern with social movements, notably in the 'European civil war'

(Pavone 1991) between left movements and fascist counter-movements that shaped the continent in the revolutionary years of 1916–1924, the fascist surge from 1922–1942, and the European Resistance from the Spanish Civil War to 1945 – and which, in many ways, continued to underlie the postwar order in west, east and south.

The generation of engaged intellectuals which flourished from the 1890s to the 1920s – including Rosa Luxemburg, James Connolly, Vladimir Lenin, Leon Trotsky, Georg Lukács, and Antonio Gramsci, among others – is testimony to this. *The Mass Strike, Labour and Nationality in Ireland, State and Revolution, History of the Russian Revolution, History and Class Consciousness* and the *Prison Notebooks* – all profoundly influential on movements far beyond their own traditions – discuss social movements in this perspective of long struggles, revolutionary transformations, or movement defeat and fascist hegemony. Such figures fused organizing practice with theorising about movements and social change in ways that were inspirational for postwar writers.[2]

Lesser, but still influential figures in this generation include Anton Pannekoek, Gustav Landauer, and Karl Mannheim. Politely forgotten today are those Catholic and fascist writers who defended the new European order, and the Stalinists who justified purges and show trials. One generation of engaged social movement theorists died in action or in exile as the processes of social-movements-become-states (nationalist, fascist or communist) turned one-time activists into state functionaries or defenders of the state against movements (Victor Serge, George Orwell).

The post-fascist rethink

The next generations of engaged theorists came of age during the intellectual Resistance against fascism (Wilkinson 1981) and developed in the shadow of Cold War anti-communism in the west and dictatorship in the east and south, brutal wars against Algerian and Vietnamese movements, and the disappointments of national independence and welfare states. E.P. Thompson captured this experience in the words of William Morris' *Dream of John Ball*:

> I pondered all these things, and how men [*sic*] fight and lose the battle, and the thing that they fought for comes about in spite of their defeat, and when it comes turns out not to be what they meant, and other men have to fight for what they meant under another name...
>
> (Morris 1886, ch. 4)

The brutal defeats of movements which nineteenth-century thinkers – including many conservatives – had seen as almost unstoppable; the failure of formal democracy to deliver anything resembling social equality or popular power; the once-inconceivable sight of mass popular action behind programmes to reinforce inequality, strengthen the state, impose conservative religion and expel ethnic minorities; the failure of national independence movements to deliver new societies; the transformation of the Russian Revolution into a monster that ate its own children; the subjugation of a once-revolutionary Europe to fascist power underpinned by mass collaboration, the destruction of movement organizations and industrialised mass murder; and the failure of postwar social democracy and state socialism to deliver either social justice or popular power: all of this changed how European intellectuals thought about social movements.

It is not that nineteenth-century intellectuals were naive; conservative intellectuals often shared left-wing, nationalist and democratic assumptions about the future, because only a fraction of pre-1848 Europe was politicised in the modern sense. The British, Irish and French experience of recent revolution and mass social movement engagement was absent in nations where authoritarian monarchies still ruled supreme. The brief 'springtime of the peoples' was rapidly crushed, and nationalism coopted by constitutional monarchies with middle-class suffrage.

It was only in the 1880s, with new kinds of mass trade union, the Second International, suffragist agitation, and the new nationalisms, that the rest of Europe could be seen as movement societies; and only after the dust had temporarily settled from the battles for formal democracy, national independence, welfare states, socialism and fascism that an adequate balance sheet which did not simply translate polemic into theory became possible.

Intellectuals now had to grapple with four areas of reflection which shaped the subsequent relationship between social *theory* and social *movements*. The first, unsurprisingly, was a reassessment of the state and its relationship to social movements. Previously, movement-becomes-state could be imagined in many different ways, because the examples of more than temporary success were so few. Now it became clear that states made or reshaped by social movements were nevertheless very different from those movements, and had goals and outcomes of their own. Nation states need not be democratic; supposedly socialist states could kill revolutionaries; democracies could enthusiastically seize colonies. The notion of linearity of outcome was radically disrupted.

Second, the idea that some degree of progressive social change was predictable suffered a decisive defeat, whether dated to the rise of fascism out of the defeats of the revolutions of 1916–1924 or to the earlier failure of the Second International to resist the senseless violence of the First World War. The simple organization and mobilization of resources as the articulation of a long-term social trend carried no guarantees of success. Michels and the anti-war revolutionaries drew different conclusions (Barker 2001), but twentieth-century intellectuals were left with a much clearer sense of the importance of *political* choice, as opposed to simply *moral or heroic* choice, and of movements as constructed, rather than automatic.

If in the nineteenth century it was possible to combine a *progressive* historical automatism with an interest in popular agency, by the mid-twentieth century many intellectuals adopted an automatism of despair, in which modernity *inevitably* meant fascism and Stalinism, consumerism, or internalised repression. Those who remained interested in movements had to distinguish structure and agency more clearly, and see ordinary people as agents constrained not only by objective conditions, but also by psycho-social mechanisms of repression that made them active participants in the perpetuation of inequality, including their own.

Third, the capacity of right-wing forces to mobilize popular consent – in populism, nationalism, fascism, anti-communism, and Christian Democracy – was another decisive experience. If Marx had analysed elements of Bonapartism in 1852, still the Vatican had remained deeply hostile to democracy until its post-Second World War acceptance of reality, while a figure like Bismarck struggled to bridge the gap between defeating the democratic elements of 1848 and harnessing its nationalist ones, moving from failed attempts to repress Social Democracy to early welfare concessions. Throughout this period the European Right slowly moved away from the goal of *excluding* popular agency from politics and towards strategies of popular *mobilization* around conservative identities and goals. The mass popularity of war in 1914, and the subsequent fascism, showed the possibilities of this strategy.

Last, if the possibility that popular participation in politics could be a conservative force would have made no sense in 1789, after generations of struggle for democratic rights it was surprising to discover how far popular groups could be captured by a commercial culture of passive participation, even groups which had earlier engaged in radical political movements.

The Frankfurt School's psychoanalytic explanations, French existentialism, and British cultural analysis all, in their own ways, reflected this shock. Many theorists abandoned any interest in popular movements, while others were forced to systematically reconsider their understanding. It is to this powerful learning moment that we owe the writings of Jean-Paul Sartre and Simone de Beauvoir, and of the British and French Marxist historians.

Social theory and social movements

More recent social theorists such as Herbert Marcuse, Michel Foucault, Raymond Williams, Claus Offe, the French post-structuralist feminists, Pierre Bourdieu, Ulrich Beck, and Manuel Castells were similarly shaped by, and shaped, the political movements they observed or took part in. It is curious that this essential fact is forgotten when these theorists are studied, divorcing their ideas from the political motivations and influences which shaped them. Foucault is a prime example: students are taught the technical details of the Panopticon, and the mechanism of surveillance is carefully explained, but there is rarely a mention of his founding of the prison information group, or of his militancy in 1968 and after. Theory does not have to be taught as social history, but to ignore the role of movements in European social theory is to miss its fundamental political motivations and contexts and to misrepresent its purposes, in a provincialism of the present.

Of course, public intellectuals who combine academic work and political activism open both themselves and their work to attacks that are often politically, rather than theoretically, motivated. Sartre, Foucault, Bourdieu, Marcuse, de Beauvoir, and Negri are all examples of this; yet it is strange how *timid* current academic writers are by comparison with those who actively engaged in resistance to fascism, supported the Algerian independence movement in the heart of Paris, or were sacked or imprisoned for supporting the movements of 1968 and 1977.

Simone de Beauvoir

De Beauvoir is a central example of a public intellectual who shaped, and was shaped by, social movements. Her intellectual, political and personal lives were deeply intertwined (Monteil 1997), and her contribution to social movements were manifold. She publicly engaged in prefigurative lifestyle politics, openly rejecting the dominant hetero-normativity and sexual repression and embracing relationships in line with her existential philosophy. Her refusal to marry, her open relationship with Sartre, and her affairs with other men and women were radical departures from the status quo.

Her intellectual contribution to social movements was huge, both through her writings on emancipation, oppression and collective social transformation, and through the concept of the 'appeal' and the dissemination of political ideas through art, in her metaphysical novels. Her most enduring text, only now coming into its own thanks to a much-improved translation, is *The Second Sex*, a founding text of second-wave feminism. It delineates a nuanced, philosophical and political critique of patriarchy and expresses a profound sense of injustice, but also draws clear connections between 'intimate' or 'private' practices and public policies. She develops the idea of freedom as transcendence: subjects are not determined fully by their present circumstances, as these can be transcended. She argues that the radical rejection of values that enslave us, or the embracing of values that liberate us, can only be effective if these actions are taken up collectively. Thus, freedom is only possible through collective action and through an appeal to allies in a political project for social transformation. Her phenomenological approach and focus upon the importance of the body and the embodied nature of oppression are linked to an insistence upon lived experience as the basis for theory.

De Beauvoir's work has clear relevance for social movements, and her influence on feminist theory and epistemologies, and feminist movements, thinking, and practices such as consciousness-raising, has been enormous. In her sixties, she played a key role in furthering the French women's movement, organizing meetings, writing texts, speaking publicly and lending her high profile to movement causes. As a public intellectual her political and intellectual activities were intrinsically linked, as her participation in the *Manifesto of the 343*, which she wrote, attests.

In this 1971 manifesto, 343 women declared that they had had an abortion, illegal at the time. The ensuing public scandal put abortion squarely in the public domain. It was inspired by the *Manifesto of the 141*, produced during the Algerian war of independence and signed by De Beauvoir and Sartre, which asked

French soldiers to desert and refuse to kill Algerians. This manifesto lost many intellectuals their jobs and earned death threats for Sartre and De Beauvoir. Self-incrimination as a political act has subsequently been adopted by a number of movements, and the abortion manifesto was later taken up in Germany and elsewhere as a political tactic. De Beauvoir stands in the frontline of European theorists who have nourished and been nourished by social movements, and her legacy continues long after her death.

Herbert Marcuse

Marcuse is another such public intellectual. Although his rise to fame came much later in life than de Beauvoir's, his activism also brought death threats, hate mail, being hung in effigy, and unceremonious retirement (Katsiaficas1991).

Marcuse was also shaped by Marxism and existentialism. His work highlights many 'movement-relevant' concerns, such as the idea that transcendence relies on a transformation of the inner psyche, without which shifts in objective circumstances cannot take place or have a radical transformative outcome; the importance of art and sexuality in the fulfilment of human species-being; the critique of 'natural' ideologies as perpetuating oppression; and a radical critique of injustice as a means of encouraging collective protest and personal and social transformation through collective action. Marcuse, according to his son, always saw his ideas as best understood in the context of social change (Romano 2011).

Marcuse's work sought to make theoretical sense of National Socialist barbarism, and to create critical theory to illuminate a path to a less barbarous future. His influence on social movements has been great, especially in Germany and the US. He influenced the student movements of 1968, German activists from Rudi Dutschke (a close friend) to the RAF, Green Party co-founder Jutta Ditfurth, and, in the US, his students Angela Davis and George Katsiaficas, among others. *Eros and Civilization* (1955) and *One Dimensional Man* (1964) contributed to the counter-cultural movements of the sixties in both Europe and the US, especially anti-authoritarian student protest in Germany (Jansen 2009; Kellner 1989).

Conversely, the student movement revived interest in the Frankfurt School, and in Marcuse in particular. While Horkheimer and Adorno refused to have their earlier 'radical' works republished and distanced themselves from the movement, retreating into 'pure philosophy', Marcuse engaged with the student movement, speaking publicly and participating in political activism. He saw the student movement, anti-racist movements, and feminism as important actors in the struggle for the creation of alternatives, even if he was pessimistic about the possibilities for revolutionary transformation in advanced industrial society.

The following passage from his controversial essay 'Repressive Tolerance' illustrates the consonance of his writings with European autonomous thought and movements, and the concern with collective transcendence and historicity echoed from Touraine to Katsiaficas, and from Callinicos to Melucci:

Now in what sense can liberty be for the sake of truth? Liberty is self-determination, autonomy – this is almost a tautology, but a tautology which results from a whole series of synthetic judgements. It stipulates the ability to determine one's own life: to be able to determine what to do and what not to do, what to suffer and what not. But the subject of this autonomy is never the contingent, private individual as that which he actually is or happens to be; it is rather the individual as a human being who is capable of being free with the others. And the problem of making possible such a harmony between every individual liberty and the other is not that of finding a compromise between competitors, or between freedom and law, between general and individual interest, common and private welfare in an *established* society, but of *creating* the society in which man is no longer enslaved by institutions which vitiate self-determination from the beginning. In other words, freedom is still to be created even for the freest of the existing societies.

(quoted in Wolff et al. 1969: 87; emphasis in original)

Marcuse's work has inspired generations of activists and scholars. His critique of advanced capitalist society and the possibilities of a long-term striving toward the creation of alternatives give his work a continuing resonance for contemporary progressive movements. Like de Beauvoir, his theory cannot be considered in isolation from the social movements he inspired and was inspired by:

If philosophy is really concerned with existence, it must take responsibility for this existence and fight for truth. The philosopher must know that he or she has not only the right but also the duty to intervene in the very concrete needs of existence, because it is only thus that the existential meaning of truth can be fulfilled. Thus, at the end of every authentic concrete philosophy stands the public act.

(1978: 405 [our translation])

De Beauvoir and Marcuse are only two examples of the relationship between European social theory and social movements.[3] It speaks volumes about the inward-looking character of orthodox social movement studies that, despite the proliferation of texts offering conceptual refinements of orthodoxy, there is not *one* monograph attempting to relate social movement studies to social theory more generally.

Of course, it is not only European social theorists whose work has been informed by political and social movements. Movements are the central mechanism or hope for transformation for a wide range of major theorists, not only scholars of globalization and civil society such as Castells, Giddens, Beck and Kaldor, but also Wallerstein and Harvey on modern world systems, for Butler, Fuss, Seidman and Young in their struggles to understand the possibilities for collective action for critical feminist theory, and for theorists of race and racism Hill Collins and Said. Yet not only has social theory been seen in isolation from the movements that have influenced it, the role of movements *within* those theories has itself been overlooked.

European theories of social movements

Deconstructing the origin myth

The second part of this chapter critiques the canonical account of 'new social movement theory', which the canon equates with 'European social movement theory' *tout court*.[4] It proposes an alternative and more broadly-based understanding of how European theorists actually discussed new social movements in the 1970s and 1980s.

The moral of the story

The 'new social movements' episode of the myth performs three equally important ideological functions. The first is to distinguish the study of social movements from Marxism. What is inevitably repeated is that the 'new social movements' theory came *out of* Marxism (and the purported Marxist search for an agent of history), but went beyond this and is thus legitimately post-Marxist – and can be included in the subdiscipline's genealogy without threatening its academic respectability.

The second purpose is to enable a synthesis between the 'American' and the 'European', the 'strategic' and the 'identitarian', the 'political' and the 'cultural' (and so on), with the former being the dominant term and the lineage into which the latter is absorbed. As Jones (1993) notes, NATO's funding of research on social movements in this period (Diani and Eyerman 1992) symbolises the cultural prestige which US research was then acquiring, and the European search for transatlantic legitimacy.

Finally, this episode denotes the extended theory as thoroughly *academic*, as distinct from the theorisations of movement activists (Barker and Cox 2002) which are simply ignored. This is key in selecting authors to represent 'new social movement' theory (Melucci and Touraine), but equally in the formulation of convergence itself. There is once again *the* literature (to the exclusion of all others), with a canon of its own to which accredited commentators must refer and within which they must situate themselves. The movement participants themselves may not speak.

Extra ecclesia nulla salus, or, more precisely, 'if it isn't social movement studies, it isn't science'. Out go the movement theorists and Marxist scholars; but equally, there go the researchers on 'history from below', the cultural studies writers and the scholars of revolution (though the latter have more recently been offered a place within the Dynamics of Contention fold).

Inventing the 'NSM paradigm'

The 'NSM paradigm' generally claims (1) a particular sequence of empirical developments around movements, namely that the period represented a shift from movements concerned with class/labour to movements with different core actors and modes of organizing; (2) that Habermas, Melucci and Touraine represent a coherent 'school' of European social movement theory; and (3) that these authors are representative of European theory and research on these movements. As we will show, all of these claims are deeply problematic, and as a combined claim they are simply wrong.

Of the three theorists routinely cited as representative of the NSM paradigm, Melucci is the only one who could reasonably be argued to do what the canonical account claims for 'new social movement theory', in that he focussed extensively on what was new in the social movements emerging at the time and saw these as contrasting with the labour movements. Perhaps because of his relative influence in Anglophone social movement studies, and because Melucci's approach is taken to be particularly representative of 'new social movement' scholarship, there has been a misinterpretation of European social movement history of the 'NSM' period as being consistently 'post-Marxist' or post-labour.

It is true – and Melucci's work highlights this – that many European movements emerged in the 1960s and 1970s, such as diverse feminist and autonomous movements experimenting with consciousness raising, autonomous movement spaces, radical direct democracy as an explicit rejection of hierarchically organized movement groups, and environmental movements that were tapping into a range of influences from deep ecology, to romanticism, to anarchism. Many of these movements were indeed rejecting Leninist or social democratic approaches to politics and organizing (e.g. the Leninist critique of spontaneity, the notion of vanguards, patriarchal hierarchical and representative structures, workerist interpretations of Marxism), and instead drew on post-structural, psychoanalytical, radical feminist, anarchist, deep green, anti-authoritarian, libertarian, liberal, romanticist and other sources of inspiration, not least those imported from North America, such as the Free Speech movement, the anti-Vietnam movements and the Civil Rights movement (in all its forms).[5] Second-wave feminist movements rejected 'the patriarchal structure of parties, trade unions, big businesses and the mass media' (Janssen Jureit in Morgan 1984: 251). Feminist theory and feminist and womens' movement texts from this period in particular reflect the wide diversity and range of relations between movements and theory (see, for example, Birnbaum 1986; Moi 1987; Morgan 1984).

In fact, the particular theoretical salience and ideological relevance of different traditions varied greatly by national context. For example, anti-authoritarian students in West Germany initially active in the SDS (the youth wing of the Social Democratic Party) broke with the party in a move towards autonomy and in an attempt to radically renovate a democratic culture they believed was being corrupted by the legacy of a culture of obedience instilled under national socialism (Burns and van der Will 1988). In Northern Ireland, student 'revolt and reform' took on a markedly different character when Catholic university students mobilized in the civil rights movement and for republican nationalist politics. Contemporary US movements (Berkeley Free Speech, Civil Rights, and anti-Vietnam War) were influential in both cases, but in radically different directions. If in the UK the Campaign for Nuclear Disarmament drew on the diverse and combined efforts of 'respectable and apolitical middle-class mothers … perennial protesters, Gandhian pacifists, Labour leftists, and ex-Communists' (Veldman 1994: 125), in Spain the struggles against the Lemoniz nuclear plant were deeply and almost exclusively entwined with Basque nationalist politics (Irvin 1999).

Amidst a diversity of theoretical influences and movement ideologies, the Marxist tradition was also a fertile source of new organizing approaches in this period; while new forms of labour struggle were widespread, these were not always separate from other movements and traditions, nor was there any consensus among theorists as to a break between 'old' and 'new' movements. In the UK, for example, theorists of movements have routinely observed that a plurality of issues, themes and actors has *always* characterized popular protest, and thus have sought deeper commonalities enabling new alliance possibilities.

Thus, for example, the socialist feminists Sheila Rowbotham, Hilary Wainwright and Lynne Segal (1979) argued passionately for the *rethinking* of relationships between feminists and socialists, without proclaiming the death of the latter; Rowbotham's (1973) and Wainwright's (1994) other works continue this approach (see also Rowbotham and Weeks 1977) – and, indeed, Marxist and socialist feminism remain widely taught in gender studies within British universities.

Similarly, the early Birmingham Cultural Studies school adopted a class analysis of what, according to the canon, should be the identity-oriented, expressive subcultures of style, music and deviance, drawing heavily on Gramsci in order to do so (Hall and Jefferson 1993). This history is also familiar to students of cultural studies.

Other massively influential figures such as E.P. Thompson and Raymond Williams also developed important analyses along these lines. Thompson (1977, 1994) argued for a revived alliance between romantic, counter-cultural impulses and political, socialist ones. Williams, for his part, wrote that

> All significant social *movements* of the last thirty years have started outside the organised class interests and institutions [sc. trade unions and Labour Party] … they sprang from needs and perceptions which the interest-based organisations had no room or time for, or which they had simply failed to notice. This is the reality which is often misinterpreted as 'getting beyond class politics'. The local judgement on the narrowness of the major interest groups is just. But there is not one of these issues which, followed through, fails to lead us into the central systems of the industrial-capitalist mode of production and among others into its system of classes.
>
> (1985: 172–173; emphasis in original)

Thus an affirmation of the diversity of movements, past and present, was coupled with a focus on *alliance* between labour and other movements rather than the opposition supposedly central to writing on new movements. Furthermore, *these are not obscure writers*. History from below, cultural studies, socialist and

Marxist feminism are major influences upon the humanities and social sciences in the English-speaking world, and in the UK most of all. A minimal familiarity with any of these perspectives makes it clear that the 'new social movements' episode of the origin myth is a caricature of how actual theorists framed the issue (Cox 2011).

Of course the construction of a self-referential 'literature' is necessarily a process of closure, exclusion and marginalisation – even at the cost of ignoring some of the most significant bodies of writing on movements. Yet given how familiar the perspectives mentioned above are in Anglophone academia, *some* of the writers who endlessly recycled the origin myth must have stopped to ask themselves if their account of theories of movements fitted with intellectual life *outside* their own textual tradition.

Marxist and socialist approaches also continued to play key roles in the thought of movements and theorists all over Europe, yet the canonical account tends to provide a caricaturized view of the labour movement as monolithic, hierarchical, and workerist. Italy is the west European country where this caricature is *least* credible. Since Gramsci, the PCI had focussed on building alliances between different social groups (already central in the Resistance) and had highlighted cultural struggles. Moreover, the 'long '68', lasting up until the movement of 1977, had not only seen the PCI break with Moscow, but had also seen a huge variety of grassroots Left formations (of which the autonomist tradition is the best known among Anglophones), many of which happily engaged in movements around gender, opposition to nuclear power, and resistance to NATO, (Osterweil, this volume, Chapter 2; Membretti and Mudu, this volume, Chapter 5).

Clearly, then, the period under discussion in 'NSM theory' was not only *not* a 'post-Marxist' period by any means, but the canonical account's caricature of labour movements also fails to correspond to their actual diversity and activities. A recognition of the significant shift in many movements away from the centrality of Marxism as the only way to think about social movements should not obscure this.

The second claim involves seeing Habermas, Melucci and Touraine as representing a paradigm or school of social movement theory. This is very difficult to sustain, not only because of the great divergence of theoretical concerns within their respective works, but also because of their relative engagement or theoretical concern with social movements. While Melucci, and Touraine in particular, researched and engaged with social movements to a significant extent, the same cannot be said for Habermas.

Habermas and (West) Germany

As with most Frankfurt School authors, Jürgen Habermas – one of the figures routinely cited (not least by his student Cohen) as being responsible for the 'new social movements' paradigm – was notoriously *distant* from social movements. In Germany, his best-known contribution was to describe Rudi Dutschke's 1967 proposal for a sit-in (in response to the police killing of Benno Ohnesorg and a ban on demonstrations) as stemming from a 'left fascism'. This is not surprising: as Schecter (1999: 33) notes, his political role has been as 'the intellectual conscience of the left wing of the German SPD' and a 'spokesperson for the institutional German left' – the very people against whom the movements of this period were directed. Consistent with this distance, his empirical research on social movements has been entirely absent, and his commentary is of a very general level; indeed, his most-cited comment on social movements (1981) is all of four pages long.

Habermas, then, does not represent German theorising on the social movements of this period. There is no shortage of such literature: a special issue of *Kursbuch* (various, 1977), the collections by Bossell (1978), Brand (1982), Schäfer (1983), and Roth and Rucht (1987) indicate the breadth and complexity of what has been written out of Anglophone accounts of 'European social movement research'.

Finally, but significantly, Habermas does not in fact do what the canonical account tells us 'European theorists' do, and does not propose new social movements as a lever of social change to replace the workers' movement. Rather, his analysis (1987) is of movements as resolutely *defensive* of the lifeworld against the encroachments of the system.

Melucci and Touraine

While there are greater overlaps between Melucci and Touraine (unsurprisingly, given that Melucci was Touraine's student) than between either of the latter and Habermas, their work is very different and cannot be taken as representing a paradigm by any means.

Alberto Melucci is, undoubtedly, the most plausible representative of the 'new social movements' paradigm as it is supposed to have been. He does contrast US and European approaches (1980), and discusses class conflicts as the root conflicts, contrasting them with emerging movements, highlighting the centrality of the body, of identity, of the personalized politics of the everyday and of the centrality of symbolic and cultural movement expressions and activities. He also forms a link between Habermas and Touraine (1989: 182), offering a point of connection between the three. Yet, if Melucci can be argued to adhere, to a greater or lesser extent, to the canonical accounts of 'NSM' theory, the same cannot be said for Touraine, whom we discuss below.

Finally the third 'claim' is that Habermas, Melucci and Touraine are representative of European social movement theory on (new) social movements. Ironically, it may be the role of the public intellectual in Europe and the intrinsic relation between movements and theory that renders less visible the role of movements per se in shaping and being shaped by the theory. Because social movements are so central to European social theory, social movement theory in itself is not readily visible in Europe as a separate field of analysis.[6] Touraine's work is a case in point. Like Marcuse and de Beauvoir, he is a public intellectual, whose theoretical trajectory and political and personal trajectory have been deeply intertwined, with the labour movement, May 1968, the anti-nuclear movement, Solidarnosc, Latin American movements and feminism all having a strong influence despite his desire to maintain a separation between his roles as analyst and activist.

For Touraine, the central goal of sociology should be to study social action, meaning the central conflicts at the heart of society and how social relations are produced and transformed. The purpose of his theory and of his method of sociological intervention is to support transformative social movements, and the problem of action and collective action is central to his work. The concept of historicity, the means by which people deliberately and actively make decisions on the central issues that define their lives, runs throughout his work as a motivating factor for collective action.

His sociology of action claims a central role for social movements, and indeed he sees social movements as *the* central object of study for sociology, not just one of many. While this intertwining of social theory and social movements makes sense in a European context (albeit in contested ways), it stands in contrast to the sharp demarcations of US sociology, where social movement studies has developed as a self-contained subdiscipline, itself strongly shaped by US social movements, and by developments in US sociology. Because of this (and an often monoglot scholarship), the US vision of European social movement theory is narrowed to a handful of authors.

Notably, Jean Cohen's influential (1985) text is often read as a representation of US versus European social movement theory and treated as a definitive demarcation between the approaches. Yet Cohen never set out to provide a survey of either. Her article compares two competing paradigms around a single question: what is *new* about contemporary social movements?

She delineates a strategy-oriented 'resource mobilization' versus an identity-oriented paradigm, seeking to integrate the best of each. For the former she cites a range of theorists, critiquing the resource mobilization approach, and Tilly's political process model in particular. She contrasts this with what she terms an identity-oriented paradigm, within which she places Pizzorno (pure identity model) and Touraine, arguing that a school of research had emerged around his work (with a brief mention of Melucci). Given her emphasis on Touraine, it is odd that she labeled this 'paradigm' identity-oriented, since, as she shows, identity is not as central to his work as it is to Pizzorno's and Melucci's.

Developing Cohen's critique (which was subsequently widely accepted), absent from RMT was a sense of an existential or transcendental motivation for movement activism, a search for authenticity or historicity, attention to cultural politics, and a transformation of consciousness. Also missing were culture, ideology, and emotions. Instead, movements were seen as primarily concerned with issues and goals, political opportunities, recruitment, and as rational actors making calculations about opportunities, frames, audiences, and opponents: strategic in a narrow, lobbying sense, but not in the wide sense of social transformation characteristic in Europe.[7]

Moreover, the general tone of US social movement studies, including Cohen, is one of insufficient attention to the political, cultural, social and historical specificity within which movements unfold – naturalizing its local historical and institutional setting against the radical historicity which has characterized European movements over the last two centuries.

Cohen deploys Habermas (in an interesting move to use social theory instead of social movement theory to overcome the 'gaps' between paradigms) to provide a means of synthesis, pointing to three gaps:

> The first is between theory emerging from within social movements and social scientific theory. The second is between social scientific paradigms based on strategic and/or communicative concepts of action. The third is between macro social theory and theories of social movements.
>
> (1985: 716)

These observations deserve further exploration. Cohen is not responsible for the misinterpretation of her work, but in describing the 'identity-oriented approach' as a paradigm she lent the work of three influential theorists a coherence that is not actually present between them.

To return to the three figures conventionally identified as 'new social movements' theorists, this is an arbitrary collection of authors who were neither strikingly engaged with movements or representative of theorising about movements in this period. Nor do they hold the views officially ascribed to the 'NSM paradigm'. What, then, *did* people researching and engaged in social movements typically think, in this period? No real answer could be as simplistic as the canonical account, but we can explore some characteristic responses to the newer movements of 1965–1985.

New social movements and the New Left: a richer account

Up until the postwar period the phrase 'the social movement' meant, in effect, the agentic aspects of 'the social question': the movements of popular actors which – from the Parisian revolutions of 1848 and 1871 via mass unionisation in the 1880s and the revolutionary wave of 1916–1923 to the anti-fascist resistance – regularly reshaped European states and forced through new power relations between labour and capital (Cox forthcoming). This usage was still widespread in later 1960s discussion of 'the movement' as a unity-in-diversity comprising student activism, the New Left, opposition to the Vietnam War, civil rights, counter-culture, and, for a time, feminism and gay liberation (Barker 2012).

Two important changes in usage emerged during this period, reflecting the developing political conditions. One, up to the end of the 1960s, was the definition of a *New Left*, as opposed to the old. This took many forms (Landau 1966), but a defining feature was hostility, *within* a Left still very much defined around relationships with labour, Marxism and party-building, towards the practices of Stalinism and Social Democracy, centralised and hierarchical forms of organization shaped by close relationships with states, East and West. In its various forms, the New Left challenge was one of a radical, participatory or activist democracy against both bureaucratic and cadre models of political and movement organizing.

Related to this, from the late 1960s on, was the slow emergence of a sense of *movements* rather than *movement*: not of the multiplicity of popular struggles as such, which was always a practical reality facing organizers, but of the growing impossibility of a single strategic organization. This was heightened by a particularist and commodifying 'identity politics', but also by the rejection – by feminists, gay and lesbian activists, internal ethnic minorities, radical critics of industrial development, and others – of the controlling and homogenising role of 'old Left' parties (and some of the new Marxist sects).

Thus, underlying the figure of speech 'new social movements' was a wider figure of thought which stressed the multiplicity of social struggles and their changing historical character. If tightly-defined figures of speech are proper to the canon-building processes of subdisciplines within a positivist notion of science, figures of thought (enabling translation and generative contradictions) are proper to social theory and make it possible to bring *different* literatures into conversation with one another.

An adequate history of the complex theorising around these movements would be a massive undertaking, covering a huge range of academic and political contexts, and what follows will simply indicate some starting-points. We want to underline that these theories are best understood as broad-based reflections on the nature of popular agency in contemporary society. Their primary goal was not to construct a subdiscipline, and this is no doubt why they ignored their exclusion from canon-writing processes in a subdiscipline which was then, in Europe, far from the leading mode of writing about movements.

European theories of the new movements

A general indication of how European political and social theorists actually discussed the plethora of developing movements between 1965 and 1985 might proceed as follows. Firstly, theorists reflecting on this situation moved away from the idea of a central party, in possession of a correct theory, imposing itself upon social movements. Not all authors abandoned party-building per se; in this period, the proposition that a progressive party could have an active relationship to movements and contribute to social change was far more plausible than it may seem in 2013. Rather, the hostility of Old Left parties to movements outside their control, and the limited success of the attempts by New Left groupings to impose themselves, typically led to the conclusion that political organization should grow from movements, and that alliances between movements had to be earned, not imposed.

In a country like Italy the politics of *Il manifesto* and alternative radio, of social centres and neighbourhood organizing, of *autonomia* and grassroots resistance (Balestrini and Moroni 1988), routinely aimed to build alliances between movements; as late as the 2000s *Rifondazione Comunista* drew similar conclusions (Bertinotti 2001). The alliance-building politics of the British New Left (discussed above) pointed in the same direction, in solidarity for the miners' strike and opposition to nuclear weapons, the politics of the Greater London Council and the radical wings of Welsh and Scottish nationalism (Williams 1989). Elsewhere, the understanding of the West German Greens as a party arising out of social movements (most particularly ecology/anti-nuclear power, majority world solidarity, peace, feminism, and gay/lesbian liberation) followed similar lines (Raschke 1985).

This understanding, significant in the early years (Ebermann and Trampert 1984), formed the basis for 'red-green' debates between socialist, ecological and left nationalist parties across western Europe (Blackwell and Seabrook 1988; Goodwillie 1988; Kemp *et al.* 1992; Red–Green Study Group 1995). At an academic level the *Forschungsjournal neue soziale Bewegungen* (*New Social Movements Research Journal*), representing a substantial body of engaged research, drew on similar processes.

A related body of social theory developed, responding to the practical political experience of the diversity and potentially centrifugal nature of social movement issues. This is what was at stake in the development of feminist politics not only in Britain, but also in Germany (e.g. Haug 2008), Italy (e.g. Federici 2004), and elsewhere.

It also underlay the rejection by Ivan Illich (1973), André Gorz (1977), and Rudolf Bahro (1984) of a state-centred productivism shared by the (Fordist) right and left alike, and subsequent attempts around 'red and green' – or, in the third world context, 'sustainable development' – to marry the two and outline a 'socialism with a human face' grounded in workplace democracy, environmental sustainability, feminism, and equitable North-South relations.

Conclusion

What is new?

Between 1965 and 1985, discussions of new movements began with New Left critiques of Stalinism and Social Democracy, representing political common sense in a period where the revolutionary force of labour movements and socialist/communist parties had declined massively under the impact of Cold War power structures, and where student rebellions, anti-war movements, feminism, urban guerrillas and new kinds of labour activism outside official structures were increasingly central to actual movement politics (Sansonetti 2002).

European reflections and debates on new social movements encompassed a range of theoretical approaches, nourished by Marxism, existentialism, anarchism, radical and direct democracy, postmodern, radical, eco, and socialist feminisms, psychoanalytic traditions, deep green ecology, new age religions, and nationalisms. Marxists outside the constraining structures of Stalinist and Social Democratic parties and unions – but routinely including the political and labour components supposedly excluded from the 'New Social Movements' construct – debated the meaning of the new developments. These debates were developed by the movements of 1968 (and, in Italy, 1977), by progressive regional nationalisms and municipal politics in a number of European countries (Castells 1983), and by the later development of Green and other New Left parties as well as by movements such as the anti-nuclear power movement, squatting, international solidarity, East European dissidence, and, subsequently, the anti-capitalist movement.

Flesher Fominaya's analysis (this volume, Chapter 7) of the characteristic features of autonomous or non-institutional modes of organization thus captures themes which run from the early 'New Left' through the uprisings of 1968, the 'new movements' of the 1970s and 1980s, into the anti-capitalist 'movement of movements' (another response to diversity), and on to contemporary *indignados* protests.

Yet the 'new' in 'new social movements' is continually rediscovered: thus, for example, recent work by Juris and Pleyers (2009) discusses the autonomist wing of the Global Justice Movement in the 2000s as representing the emergence of new forms – as if this tradition was not directly linked, organizationally as well as intellectually, to movement struggles going back to the 1960s. Juris and Pleyers are not alone: 'social movement studies' textbooks also transmit a misrepresentation of history which regularly moves the ruptures of 1968 forwards to the period just before the authors' own appearance on the scene.

Is there a European approach?

European theory is far richer than the canonical account allows, but it is also true that European social movement scholarship has not established itself as a separate field or subdiscipline as it has in the US, and this has consequences. The high profile of social movement studies as a consolidated subdiscipline in the US, coupled with the global dominance of English, means that today, in many places (including Europe), US movement theory *is* social movement theory. Of course, in the past 20 years there have been some prominent European movement theorists, but they have often worked predominantly within US social movement scholarship's categories of analysis. European social theory for social movements, in the absence of an articulated *European* movement theory, is largely invisible.

European social movements are also surprisingly under-represented. One key indication of this is the paucity of academic books and readers devoted to European social movements. This invisibility is all the more strange given how central these movements have been to the major political, social, and cultural transformations in European history.

So perhaps it is time to make visible European social movements and European social movement scholarship. At the same time, in both the US and in Europe, perhaps it is time to break free of the idea that it is necessary to use *social movement theory*, as currently defined, to study movements. Social theory, itself deeply shaped by movement history, can also serve this purpose and offers a far richer understanding of movements: resisting the artificially separate analysis of 'politics' and 'culture', seeing different movements not in isolation but as reflecting and shaping a wider social reality, and *contextualising* and *historicising* movements.

More generally, the narrow and self-referential theoretical vision of 'social movement studies' leads to it being widely ignored by movement participants (Bevington and Dixon 2005) and by movement-linked authors (Cox and Nilsen 2007). As an approach, it is more successful at gaining institutional legitimacy than at convincing those most closely engaged with its objects of study. This is a pity; it is valuable to continue research specifically on social movement processes, but disciplinary closure mechanisms which rule out of consideration all theory from outside sources are simply misguided. This chapter is also a plea for a much more open, and theoretically substantive, approach; we hope that this book contributes to that process.

Notes

1 Posting to rec.sf.arts.fandom, 28 September 2000.
2 Presumably the fact that many of the theorists discussed in this section were Marxists and so personae non gratae within US academia contributed to their erasure from the canon.
3 Cox (2011) discusses the relationship of social movement theory to Western Marxism, while Barker *et al.* (2013) does this for Marxism more widely. While there are feminist sociologists of social movements, a reading of feminist *theory* as social movement analysis is lacking (but see Motta *et al.* 2010).
4 There are at least two preceding sources of this account: Diani's (1992) marriage of 'American' and 'European' approaches and Cohen's (1985) article, discussed below. A number of critiques of this account exist, such as those by Mayer (1995) and Jones (1993).
5 For a discussion of postmodern nomadic feminist thought emerging from Italian feminist consciousness raising, see Braidotti (1995). For debates on motherhood and the interpretation of democracy in Italian women's movements of the 1970s and 1980s, see Passerini (1994). See French feminist Irigaray (1993[1987]) for a theoretical treatment of the potential of sexual difference for social transformation. For discussion of the lively debates and complex relation between women's movements and feminist theory in France, see Moi (1987). For a discussion of ecofeminist politics and thought, see Biehl (1991). For a discussion of the importance of the romantic tradition in the development of green politics and movements in the UK, see Veldman (1994). For the multiple theoretical roots of green political thought in Europe see Dobson (2000[1990]). For a treatment of decentered autonomous counter-cultural networks since the 1960s and their enduring influence on the British social movement landscape, see McKay (1996). For a historical comparative treatment of anarchist thought and politics in Europe, see Woodcock (1962). For a discussion of the emergence of autonomous movements in Italy, Germany, Holland and Denmark, autonomous squatter critiques of Marxist-Leninist politics, as well as of workerist understandings of Marxism, see Katsiaficas (2006[1997]).
6 Yet when we founded the Council for European Studies' social movement research network we were astonished to find ourselves with 145 members within a few months. The European members argued that a key task of the network should be to increase the profile of social movement studies within Europe, and of European social movements within the wider academic world.

7 Although it lies outside the scope of this chapter, there are alternative renderings of US social movements that have not adopted the strategic/structural approach – but these have typically been marginalised within the subfield of 'social movement theory', such as the work of Barbara Epstein, Rick Fantasia, George Katsiaficas, Nancy Naples, Peter Linebaugh, and Marcus Rediker.

References

Bahro, R. (1984) *From red to green: interviews with New Left Review.* London: Verso.

Balestrini, N. and Moroni, P. (1988) *L'orda d'oro 1968–1977.* Milano: Feltrinelli.

Barker, C. (2001) 'Robert Michels and the cruel game', in C. Barker, A. Johnson, and M. Lavalette (eds), *Leadership and social movements.* Manchester: MUP.

Barker, C. (2012) 'Not drowning but waving'. Paper to Alternative futures and popular protest conference, Manchester.

Barker, C. and Cox, L. (2002) *What have the Romans ever done for us?* Helsinki: into-ebooks.

Barker, C., Cox, L., Nilsen, A., and Krinsky, J. (2013) *Marxism and social movements.* Amsterdam: Brill.

Bertinotti, F. (2001) *Pensare il '68.* Milan: Ponte alle Grazie.

Bevington, D. and Dixon, C. (2005) 'Movement-relevant theory'. *Social Movement Studies* 4/3: 185–208.

Biehl, J. (1991) *Rethinking Ecofeminist Politics.* Boston: Southend Press.

Birnbaum, L. (1986) *Liberazione della donna: Feminism in Italy.* Middleton: Wesleyan University Press.

Blackwell, T. and Seabrook, J. (1988) *The politics of hope.* London: Faber.

Bossel, H. (1978) (ed.) *Bürgerinitiativen entwerfen die Zukunft.* Frankfurt: Fischer.

Braidotti, R. (1995) 'Feminism and Modernity', *Free Inquiry*, Vol. 15/2: 23–30.

Brand, K.-W. (1982) *Neue soziale Bewegungen.* Opladen: Westdeutscher.

Burns, R. and van der Will, W. (1988) *Protest and Democracy in West Germany.* Macmillan Press: Basingstoke.

Castells, M. (1983) *The city and the grassroots.* Berkeley: UC Press.

Cohen, J. (1985) 'Strategy and identity'. *Social Research* 52/4: 663–716.

Cox, L. (2011) *Building counter cultures.* Helsinki: into-ebooks.

Cox, L. (forthcoming) 'Eppur si muove', in Barker, C., Cox, L., Nilsen, A., and Krinsky, J. (eds), *Marxism and social movements.* Amsterdam: Brill.

Cox, L. and Nilsen, A. (2007) 'Social movements research and the "movement of movements"'. *Sociology Compass* 1/2: 424–442.

Diani, M. (1992) 'The concept of social movement'. *Sociological Review* 40/1: 1–25.

Diani, M. and Eyerman, R. (1992) *Studying collective action.* London: Sage.

Dobson, A. (2000) *Green Political Thought.* London: Routledge.

Ebermann, T. and Trampert, R. (1984) *Die Zukunft der Grünen.* Hamburg: Konkret

Federici, S. (2004) *Caliban and the witch.* Brooklyn: Autonomedia.

Flesher Fominaya, C. (2013) "Movement culture continuity", in Flesher Fominaya, C. and Cox, L. (eds), *Understanding European Movements.* London: Routledge.

Goodwillie, J. (1988) *Colours in the rainbow.* Dublin: self-published.

Gorz, A. (1977) *Ökologie und Politik: Beiträge zur Wachstumskrise.* Reinbek: Rowohlt.

Habermas, J. (1981) 'New social movements'. *Telos* 49: 33–37.

Habermas, J. (1987) *Theory of communicative action vol. 2.* Cambridge: Polity.

Hall, S. and Jefferson, T. (1993) *Resistance through rituals.* London: Routledge.

Hardt, M. and Negri, A. (2000) *Empire*. Cambridge: Harvard UP.

Haug, F. (2008) *Die Vier-in-Einem Perspektive*. Hamburg: Argument.

Illich, I. (1973) *Tools for Conviviality*. New York: Harper and Row.

Irigaray, L. (1993) *Sexes and Genealogies*, New York: Columbia University Press.

Irvin, C. (1999) *Militant nationalism*. Minneapolis, MN: University of Minnesota Press.

Jansen, P. (2009) 'The Frankfurt School's Interest in Freud'. *PhaenEx* 4/2: 78–96.

Jones, T. (1993). 'New social movements'. Paper to Work Research Centre, Dublin.

Juris, J.S. and Pleyers, G.H. (2009) 'Alter-activism: Emerging cultures of participation among young global justice activists'. *Journal of Youth Studies* Vol. 12 (1): 57–75.

Katsiaficas, G. (1991) 'Marcuse's cognitive interest'. Available at www.eroseffect.com/articles/MARCUSE.PDF.

Katsiaficas, G. (2006) *The Subversion Of Politics*. AK Press Distribution.

Kellner, D. (1989) *Critical Theory, Marxism and Modernity*. Baltimore: John Hopkins University Press.

Kemp, P. (1992) *Europe's Green Alternative*. London: GreenPrint.

Landau, S. (1966) *The New Radicals*. New York: Random.

Marcuse, H. (1964) *One Dimensional Man*. Boston: Beacon.

Marcuse, H. (1969 [1965]) 'Repressive Tolerance', in Wolff, R., Moore, B. and Marcuse, H. (eds), *A Critique of Pure Tolerance*, pp. 81–117. Boston: Beacon Press.

Marcuse, H. (1974 [1955]) *Eros and civilization*. Boston: Beacon.

Marcuse, H. (1978) 'Über konkrete Philosophie', in Marcuse, H. *Schriften*. Frankfurt: Suhrkamp.

Mayer, M. (1995) 'Social-movement research in the United States', in Lyman, S. (ed.), *Social movements*. London: Macmillan.

McKay, G. (1996) *Senseless Acts of Beauty*. London: Verso.

Melucci, A. (1980) 'The new social movements'. *Social Science Information*, 19/2: 199–226.

Melucci, A. (1989) *Nomads of the Present*. London: Hutchinson.

Membretti, A. and Mudu, P. (2013) 'Where global meets local', in Flesher Fominaya, C. and Cox, L. (eds), *Understanding European Movements*. London: Routledge.

Moi, T. (ed.) (1987) *French Feminist Thought*. Oxford: Blackwell Press.

Monteil, C. (1997) 'Simone de Beauvoir and the women's movement in France'. *Simone de Beauvoir Studies Journal*, 14: 6–12.

Morgan, R. (1984) *Sisterhood is Global*. New York: Anchor Press.

Morris, W. (1886) *A Dream of John Ball*. Available at www.marxists.org/archive/morris/works/1886/johnball/chapters/index.htm.

Motta, S., Flesher Fominaya, C., Eschle, C., and Cox, L. (2010) 'Feminism, women's movements and women in movement'. *Interface* 3/2: 1–32.

Osterweil, M. (2013) 'The Italian anomaly', in Flesher Fominaya, C. and Cox, L. (eds), *Understanding European Movements*. London: Routledge.

Passerini, L. (1994) 'The interpretation of democracy in the Italian Women's Movement of the 1970s and 1980s', *Women's Studies International Forum*, 17/2–3: 235–239.

Pavone, C. (1991) *Una guerra civile*. Turin: Bollati Boringhieri.

Raschke, R. (1985) *Soziale Bewegungen*. Frankfurt: Campus.

Red–Green Study Group (1995) *What on earth is to be done?* Manchester: Red–Green Study Group.

Romano, C. (2011) 'Occupy This'. *Chronicle of Higher Education* 11 Dec 2011. Online at http://chronicle.com/article/Occupy-This-Is-It-Comeback/130028/.

Rossanda, R. (1968) *L'anno degli studenti*. Bari: De Donato.

Roth, R. and Rucht, D. (eds) (1987) *Neue soziale Bewegungen in der Bundesrepublik Deutschland*. Frankfurt: Campus.

Rowbotham, S. (1973) *Hidden from History*. London: Pluto.

Rowbotham, S. and Weeks, J. (1977) *Socialism and the New Life*. London: Pluto.

Rowbotham, S., Segal, L., and Wainwright, H. (1979). *Beyond the Fragments*. London: Merlin.

Sansonetti, P. (2002) *Dal '68 ai no-global*. Milano: Baldini & Castoldi.

Schäfer, W. (ed.) (1983) *Neue soziale Bewegungen*. Frankfurt: Fischer.

Schecter, D. (1999) 'The functional transformation of the political world'. *Studies in social and political thought*, 1: 33–49.

Thompson, E.P. (1977) *William Morris*. London: Merlin.

Thompson, E.P. (1994) *Witness Against the Beast*. London: Penguin.

Various (1977) *Bürgerinitiativen/Bürgerprotest*. Kursbuch 50.

Veldman, M. (1994) *Fantasy, the Bomb, and the Greening of Britain*. Cambridge: Cambridge University Press.

Wainwright, H. (1994) *Arguments for a New Left*. London: Blackwell.

Wilkinson, J. (1981) *The European Resistance against Fascism*. Cambridge, MA: Harvard University Press.

Williams, R. (1985) *Towards 2000*. London: Penguin.

Williams, R. (1989) *Resources of hope*. London.

Wolff, R., Moore, B., and Marcuse, H. (1969) *A Critique of Pure Tolerance*. Boston: Beacon Press.

Woodcock, G. (1962) *Anarchism*. London: Penguin.

Part II

European precursors to the Global Justice Movement

2 The Italian anomaly

Place and history in the Global Justice Movement

Michal Osterweil

Introduction

On 18–22 July 2001 over 300,000 people – the majority of whom were Italian – participated in protests at the annual summit of the Group of Eight (G8), in Genoa, Italy. The turnout made Genoa the largest mobilization yet in what was then becoming known as the "anti-globalization" movement(s), and what I will refer to as the Global Justice and Solidarity Movement (GJSM). Genoa ultimately came to be considered an important turning point within the GJSM more broadly – partly due to the turnout, but also because the violence used by the police, and the unprecedented alliances present within the Italian and European Lefts pointed to the potential and limits of such a vibrant movement. That Genoa was so significant is perhaps not surprising given that, overall, Italian participation in events of the GJSM – including the counter-summit protests, the World and European Social Forums, and the broader sphere of alter-globalization activism taking place in Europe and the Americas between 1994–2008 – was not only substantial, it was formative. Italians from various organizations on the variegated left – ranging from activists from social centres to members of *Rifondazione Comunista* (Communist Refoundation) and Catholic voluntary associations – were always described as key movers and shakers. Many were central in building some of the core transnational movement networks – including the People's Global Action network, the World Social Forum, and the solidarity movement for the Zapatistas – that cumulatively provided key infrastructure for the GJSM. On whole, Italian organizations and activists consistently played important roles in the global movement.

At the same time, within Italy, the GSJM clearly also had a very strong impact and resonance, transforming the political language, goals, and modalities of much of the institutional and extra-parliamentary left. It also helped to ignite a period of near constant mobilization within the country. Immediately following the events in Genoa, local social forums sprang up in almost every city and even in many towns throughout Italy; in October 100,000 people took to the streets to protest against the Afghan War; in January several hundred Italians attended the Second World Social Forum in Porto Alegre, making Italians third in number of attendees, following Brazilians and Argentineans; March 2002 saw one of the largest protests in European history when three million people converged on the streets of Rome to protest against *Articolo 18* and the increasing deregulation of labour laws; and, in November 2002, Italy was the first country outside of Brazil to host a Social Forum – the first European Social Forum, held in Florence. Importantly, the issues addressed by these mobilizations ranged from global war to Italian-specific labour and immigration laws. Taken together, this complex of movements and actors became known as Italy's "movimento dei movimenti" (movement of movements: MoM) – a movement active in Italy's domestic politics as well as in the more global issues addressed by the broader GJSM.

The pertinent questions are, then, why did the GJSM resonate and receive so much support in Italy, making it one of the most important hubs of European and global activism during the 1990s and early 2000s? And what did Italian-specific issues and politics have to do with a *global* movement ostensibly aimed at opposing neoliberalism and corporate-driven globalization?

In this chapter, based on ethnographic and historical research, I argue that recognizing the role of Italy's particular history and political culture is crucial to understanding both why Italy played such an important role in the global movement, on the one hand, and why the global movement was so resonant in Italy, on the other. Despite commonplace assumptions of the GJSM or global movements as a typology (Guidry *et al.* 2000; Keck and Sikkink 1998), I will argue that it is precisely the Italian context and the ways in which movements have been experienced and thought in Italy that not only make the MoM as an Italian phenomenon possible, but also create the conditions of possibility for its strong resonances with the global movement, resonances that occur at the level of political imaginary, language and form, as much as efforts to oppose neoliberalism.

My argument is multifold. First, it is a statement about the place-based nature of the Italian MoM and potentially other parts of the GJSM. As such, I begin by showing that Italy's MoM was as much a *peculiarly Italian* phenomenon, connected with political critiques of the Italian political system and growing out of past social movements in Italy, as it was a part of a *global* movement, influenced by global networks and events. I go on to describe important elements of that history and what is known as the "Italian Anomaly" – focusing specifically on Italy's unique "anomalous" left, including the communist party and the Autonomist movements of the 1960s and 1970s. I argue that as important as the actual histories and historical connections are the ways in which the legacies and political culture – the background of understanding upon which all politics must act – have been narrated, remembered and understood.

Second, it is an assertion as to the ways in which the political history of Italy and the Italian left in particular yield a politics and set of imaginaries, visions, and theories resonant with the GJSM and the new political imaginary it co-authored or co-created; this points to the place-based nature of the theories and visions which social movements move with. This imaginary includes the political aim of autonomy, a privileging of difference, and an epistemological commitment to partiality and reflexivity. Third, and related to this imaginary, it is an argument about the nature of the political aims and impacts of the GJSM more broadly, suggesting that beyond simply opposing neoliberalism, the GJSM sought to create a "another kind of politics" outside the hegemonic paradigm of liberal representative democracy. Finally, I connect these to the GJSM and point to some theoretical shifts this requires in our treatments of the GJSM and social movements more generally.

The return of politics and the Italian anomaly

When I first began my research on Italy's MoM I was struck by the ways that activists from a variety of backgrounds described the MoM and their participation in it. I had expected people to explain their participation in terms of opposition to corporate-led globalization and neoliberalism, free trade acts, and opposition to the Bretton Woods institutions. However, as I read various primary texts and conducted interviews, I encountered descriptions that spoke about the MoM in particular ways. First, there was a strong emphasis on how the MoM was a refutation of the dominant political modality, and second, these descriptions consistently referred to the cycle of movements of 1968–1979 – a cycle I hadn't heard of – as being crucial to understanding the MoM. In order to understand the meanings of these unexpected framings, I needed to grasp how the history and memory of this period connected to the idea of a new political modality.

In most interviews and texts, people made clear that while many did go to Genoa in 2001 as part of a global movement to protest the G8 and its neoliberal policies, a large number went to express their growing disillusion with the Berlusconi government and official Italian politics more broadly. Even before Genoa, the *popolo della sinistra* (people of the left) had expressed anger with the newly elected Berlusconi government and frustration with the politics of the centre-left, which had been in office for the previous five years. So, rather than discuss the undemocratic policies of the G8, many described the importance of the MoM as a novel "return to politics". For some, this was a very precise reference to a return, after decades of very little that they saw as being real politics (Montagna 2005; Mezzadra 2003). For others, this meant that the MoM posed an alternative to the defunct yet dominant "official politics". As one activist put it,

> While today in Italy and in the world there exists a real crisis of the political … we [the MoM] are the only possible anti-body, the only possibility for a re-thinking of the political in terms of, precisely, *real* political participation.
>
> (interview, Porto Alegre, 2003)

In a widely read article, Toni Negri argued that the presence of this vast and diversely articulated movement – comprising trade unions, university students, immigrants, middle-class intellectuals, peace activists, and many more, potentially representing 20 per cent of the Italian population – was the instantiation of "another, more advanced phase, of the communist revolution". Negri continues:

...the multitudes no longer need social democracy in order to struggle and change the world. The talk in Italy is of a "movement of movements", a process of seeking out new forms of political expression both at the level of theory and in concrete struggles;... The Italian "laboratory" has begun its work [again].

(Negri 2002 [my translation])

This analysis points to the rejection of representative democracy and frames the MoM historically. Notably, many activists I spoke with explained the MoM in explicitly historical terms. For example, when asked "Why do you think Italy has such a strong presence in the global movement?" one activist answered:

F: Why Italy? Italy is an anomaly.... It has always been an anomaly.

It is that which inaugurates the movements for the rights of workers in July of 1960, and that which turns 1968 into a 1968 from which also follows 1969, that becomes the Movement of 1977.... And why is this? In my opinion it is because this is the country of Gramsci, that is the same Gramsci that changed the history of Latin America, who was translated in Latin America and changed its history. It has the strongest communist party in the Western World, with all the good and the bad that this means ... and to whose Left another kind of workers' movement is born. That which is called Laboratory Italy ... that poses the problem beyond the demands based on work – the refusal of work.

(interview with "F.", Bologna, November 2002)

Similarly, when asking about Italy's MoM, I was commonly told:

You see you have to understand our 1977. Whereas in most countries like France and the United States, 1968 lasted only a few months, ours lasted more than ten years!

(group conversation, Bologna, June 2002)

As I began to investigate further, I discovered that both the events of this period and the fact that Italians of various ages were acutely aware of and proud of it (Wu Ming 1 2002) explained a lot about the political nature of the MoM and the GJSM.

In the 1960s and 1970s Italy experienced a period of unparalleled struggle. The years have been referred to as an "earthquake" that "shook [Italy's] foundations" (Lumley 1990: 2; Revelli 1995). Whereas 1968 saw the explosion of "new social movements" and "New Lefts" throughout the globe, Italy's 1968 was unique. Unlike other countries where the high points and massified moments of these movements were rather short-lived – i.e. *May* of '68 – in Italy the events of '68 were only the tip of the iceberg. Kicked off by the anti-authoritarian student movements of 1967–1968, and by a highly conflictual "Hot Autumn" in the Northern factories from 1969–1970, the "great wave" lasted over a decade, reaching its high point in the "Movement of 1977", before enduring a protracted and somewhat a painful end brought on by state repression, the influx of heroin, and burnout among activists (Bologna 1980; Balestrini and Moroni 1988).

As I will argue, the importance of this decade rests in the nature of the political struggles and critiques it asserted, in the ways it has been narrated and remembered, and in terms of the material legacies and infrastructures it left in place – the submerged networks of activists, organizations, practices, ideas, and cultural artifacts – that sustain the horizon and work of movement. Despite the universalized and scientized definitions of social movements which prevail in social movement studies, the ways of thinking – and therefore acting – in pursuit of social change are always both enabled and constrained by the particular historical "backgrounds of understanding" or traditions from which they come (Winograd and Flores 1987: 7). That is to say, how we conceive of the role and potential of movements (or governments, for that matter) has to do with the particular lived histories within which we move; as such, the theories movements move with, and the visions they espouse, are themselves based upon the historical and political backgrounds from which they derive.

While today it is fairly widely known – especially since the publication of Hardt and Negri's *Empire* (2000) – that Italy is home to *operaismo*, which is itself part of a rich tradition of what is alternately referred to as Critical or Autonomist Marxism, we rarely acknowledge that this theoretical tradition is itself culturally specific, and a product of the particular experience of people, movements, and the broader left in Italy. In fact, Italy is often called an anomaly, referring to its rather precarious form of national unity characterized by profound regional differences with uneven economic development, its being the birthplace of fascism, the centrality of the Catholic Church, and the general precarity of the legitimacy of the modern nation state. Perhaps most often the anomaly metaphor refers to the Italian left, which included the largest communist party in the West and some of the most active social movements, based in the working class and the peasantry.

In other words, people spoke of the MoM in the ways that they did because of the historical meaning and experience of social movements in Italy. Understanding how the history of the 1960s and 1970s relates to the MoM means understanding what happened in Italy then, as well as recognizing how those periods are connected. In what follows I argue that the years from 1967–1979 helped to produce a series of political and theoretical innovations in the form of concepts and practices that can be understood as offering a holistic critique of liberal representative democracy and capitalism. The importance of this history has to do with the problems the movements set out to confront, the ideas and practices that were produced as a result, and the material and discursive ways in which the legacies of those movements reached through to the period of the MoM. In other words, it helps to understand how and why certain narratives and theories of politics were produced, narratives and theories that then resonated with the "new" vision of politics promoted by the MoM.

The long decade, Autonomia and the critique of representation

While sharing similarities with the "New Lefts" throughout Europe and the Americas, there are several things that distinguish the Italian New Left and the long decade that yielded the Movement of '77. First, and perhaps most notably, are its deep roots in workers' struggles in the factories, such that it was the workers' movements which informed other struggles and radicalized vast swaths of society, including various sectors not normally seen as protagonists of social change – ranging from more traditional factory workers, peasants and students, to doctors, lawyers, journalists, and others (Bologna 1980, 2001; Lumley 1990). Much like the "new social movements" people associate with 1968, Italy's movements involve a radical rejection of capitalism as an economic, political and cultural system, without, however, ceding the focus on labour and production.

Second, the movements were involved in producing important strategic, political and theoretical innovations that changed the repertoire of workers' and anti-capitalist movements within Italy and beyond. Rather than seeking legal or labour rights *within* the system – i.e. through strikes demanding fewer hours, etc., and expressed in innovative slogans and tactics – these movements rejected the fundamental premises of capitalism, including work, growth and order. Some of the most significant practices and theoretical elaborations included the development of and experimentation with notions such as "autonomy", "the strategy of refusal", and self-reduction campaigns.

Many of these concepts and practices were theorized and elaborated by Italian *operaismo*, a variegated theoretical tradition that, despite numerous differences, was unified in its commitment to the concept of the autonomy of the working class. This meant seeing the worker, rather than capital, as the prime mover of history (Tronti 1966). *Operaismo* also promoted an empirical and horizontal form of research into the actual conditions of workers, known as co-research (Borio *et al.* 2002).[1] *Operaismo* was linked to a strong critique of traditional instruments of representation, namely unions and parties, even though several of its key founders remained party militants.

While in some ways a critique of parties and unions was part of the New Lefts the world over (Cox and Fominaya, this volume, Chapter 1), the tension and break between Italian social movements and the Italian communist party (PCI) was particularly severe. This severity had to do, on the one hand, with specific events in the 1960s and 1970s in which the PCI was pitted against workers and movements, and, on the other hand, it had to do with the particularities of the PCI. Prior to 1968, the Italian left could be treated as a variegated whole with unions and parties representing what movements and society expressed; by the end of the 1960s, and especially from 1973, one had to differentiate quite starkly between the parliamentary and extra-parliamentary left. However, in many ways, the division was always less total than it might appear (Nunes 2007), and it is important to recognize how both the PCI and the movements co-constitute the "background of understanding" necessary for the resonance between Italian movements and the GJSM.

The PCI

Italy boasted the largest and arguably most successful communist party in the West throughout the twentieth century, garnering substantial percentages of the vote, even when US pressure would not officially allow communists to be in the government. There were many reasons for its popularity, size and success. These included its legacy as one of the key structures sustaining the partisan resistance against fascism, as well as the class composition of Italian society. Perhaps most importantly, its particular version of communism combined a sort of pragmatism, autonomy and astute capacity for critique with an able politicking vis-à-vis the Soviet Union. In addition, the influence of Gramsci's particular version of Marxism, in which the concept of hegemony was central, recognized that class power and conflict necessarily took place in civil society and in popular culture (Wu Ming 1 2002; Shore 1990; Ginsborg 2003). Moreover, despite critiques of Gramsci's theories as being too idealist, journals like *Ordine Nuovo*, in which Gramsci first started his political work, were key to fostering a culture of lively debate and critique. Arguably it is this same culture and tradition that led to the founding of key *operaista* journals that were critical to the Autonomia movement, and, later, many of the trajectories that arrive at Genoa.

However, despite this common culture of debate, the severity of the 1970s break between the PCI and social movements was formative. With economic conditions across Italy worsening, and support for the party growing, PCI leaders thought that an alliance with the Christian Democrats and Socialists was the best means of staving off a coup, while providing an opportunity to move from a party of opposition to a party of opposition *and* government. However, this strategy – known as the "historical compromise" – solidified the PCI's unyielding support for the side of order and governance, even to the point of highly repressing workers and movements, and thus further alienating workers and movements from the PCI (Bianchi and Caminiti 1997; Ginsborg 2003).

In addition to the PCI's repression, workers were increasingly at odds with the PCI's approach on the ground. This included the economic and political analyses with which it operated, which didn't address the economic crises of the 1970s. There was also an increasing clash between the more hierarchical culture of the PCI and the workers' associations within the factories. This was aggravated by the tenuous relationship between the PCI and southern Italians – a difficult relationship due to racism, cultural conflict, and historical animosity between the PCI and southerners (Balestrini and Leva 1988; Gramsci and Verdicchio 2005; Tarrow 2012).

Overall, in addition to protests around issues of labour and work conditions, staking out a form of "autonomous" anti-capitalist politics outside, and even against, the traditional party structures and forms became crucial to the movements of those years, hence the term and notion of autonomy.

Autonomia

Autonomia – short for *Autonomia Operaio* – technically refers to the diverse array of autonomous and localized groups, collectives, organizations and practices that were active in the period from 1973 through to approximately 1979, although at times the term gets elided with the whole period of social struggle which began in 1968.

While there is not sufficient space here to go into the full history of the decade or Autonomia in detail, the most important point concerns the ways in which certain ideas and practices of politics, as well as certain cultures of politics, worked to produce certain kinds of movements and politics, largely in response to the failures of politics past – failures that occurred both within movements and parties alike.

One of the most cited texts – still unavailable in English – describes this period as "an authentic labyrinth" comprised of "thousands of ideological and organizational" currents (Balestrini and Moroni 1988: 3). These currents or tendencies ranged from a diffuse cultural Autonomia focused on creative and ironic interventions in public space, to a more militant and organized Autonomia including groups that that could be seen to create a more party-like structure to oppose the PCI. While there certainly were armed groups within the mix, the characterization of the movement as a predominantly armed one is misleading. Some suggest that the more widespread turn to armed struggle and clandestinity was largely in response to state repression (Bianchi and Caminiti 1997; Balestrini and Moroni 1988; Cuninghame 2002). Like most movements there was substantial flow between these various parts, as well as shifts between different tactics and tendencies throughout time.

The peak of *Autonomia* was the Movement of '77. Occasioned by a series of events in which the tensions between the PCI and activists grew, the Movement of '77 saw a massive explosion of activism and the absolute un-governability of cities such as Bologna. According to most, the actual catalysts could not explain the size and energy of the movement, and many have argued that it was better to understand the Movement of '77 not for its immediate demands, but as the ultimate expression of the ensemble of movements since 1968, as well as the ultimate repudiation of the Communist Party, and the system of politics to which it belonged (Berardi 1980; Bianchi and Caminiti 1997).

Ultimately both the fact and the memory of this decade-plus of struggle are crucial for understanding Italy's contributions to and resonance with the MoM. Throughout its tenure the movements produced a series of innovative political practices and strategies which changed the repertoire of workers' and anti-capitalist movements within Italy and beyond. Some of these include the development of and experimentation with notions such as autonomy, the strategy of refusal, the critique of representation, the development of counter-powers, and the valorization of difference. In addition, these were accompanied by epistemological and methodological commitments (and practices) of starting from the messiness and particularities of people's lived experiences – i.e. through co-research – and of paying attention to cultural and regional differences. Taken together these practices were largely the result of, or reactions to, the dominant forms of leftist or anti-capitalist practice prevalent at the time, a rejection of the central model of the communist party and the ways of doing and thinking politics it entailed.

In the following section I describe how the legacy of Autonomia – in terms of the particular ways in which it was remembered, the material practices and infra-structures it left in place, and the political problematics it helped articulate – were what ultimately connected it to the GJSM.

The legacy of Autonomia: the desire for another kind of politics

Without downplaying the tremendous richness and importance of these years of struggle, one of the most important aspects of *Autonomia* had to do with its legacy: what it came to mean, as well as the material, theoretical and other infra-structures it left in place. So today when people speak of Autonomia or the Movement of '77, they are certainly referring to a whole array of diverse move-ments, collectives and projects that worked for a left autonomous from the PCI. However, the reference also connotes something more; it refers to a set of ideas and cultural-political principles which, in many ways, express both a repudiation of politics past, and a desire for "another kind of politics".

The ensemble of practices that *Autonomia* came to denote reflects this search for a better politics through both experimentation and negation. So, for example, the critique of the hierarchy of the party was accompanied by an effort to organize differently. Commitment to "autonomy" meant both rejection of the unions and parties, but also involved the development of place-based counter-powers, the valorization of difference and a commitment to contextual know-ledge and co-research. This also meant rejection of the universalizing, "one size fits all" approach that characterized many versions of Marxist-Leninism, in par-ticular those in communist parties, but also those in movement groups. As a result, it became a common refrain to say that Autonomia in Padua was very dif-ferent from Autonomia in Rome or Naples, because different cities and regions had different social and cultural compositions. As numerous interviewees pointed out, in Italy, "Being rooted in one's territorial particularity was incred-ibly important" (interview, Bologna, June 2002).

In addition to a set of ideas and political notions or principles, *Autonomia* also persisted in various material forms and practices. Key practices that were used in later movements included self-reduction campaigns, free radios, culture-jamming, ironic performances, communication hacking, the practice of squatting or occupying, and the rejection of organisms or mechanisms of representation in their political organizations, among others.

Together, these material networks and legacies of ideas contributed to gener-ating many of the Italian organizational elements that become protagonists in the MoM and GJSM. Remnants of Autonomia remained in what were literally underground networks of autonomous social spaces – what Melucci has termed "submerged networks" (1989).[2] No small matter was also the fact that, in the aftermath of the mass arrests and demise of the movement, social centres were invented, in part to provide prison support (see Membretti and Mudu, this volume, Chapter 5). These "submerged networks" would eventually yield other activist moments and movements, many of which became the politicizing moments for groups and individuals who were later involved in Genoa and the MoM. These included the Anti-Nuclear and Peace movements of the 1980s, the Pantera student movement of 1991–1992, and, perhaps most importantly, the social centres that then formed *Ya Basta!* (Enough Already) and the *Tute Bianche* (White Overalls) and *Disobbedienti* (Disobedients). Throughout the 1980s and 1990s one could find various initiatives including publishing houses, journals, books, seminars, or even articles and conferences assessing the causes of the failure of *Autonomia*, and, more importantly, how to return to the potentialities made visible and articulated in those years.

Overall, this decade-plus of movements mobilized thousands of people and produced infrastructures in the form of free radios, alternative spaces, publishing endeavours, and, most importantly, networks of relationships between people and political cultures, all of which did not end with the end of the movements. The movements of the 1970s remained alive and productive in the form of political practices, theoretical traditions, ideas and political cultures, as well as a series of open questions or problematics. It is these practices, the theoretical innovations they were both based on and generative of, as well the critique of politics they assert, that will be referred to for years on end in Italy and beyond (Deleuze 1988; Guattari 1996; Lotringer and Marazzi 1980).

Not surprisingly, Autonomia has often been treated as offering a potential answer to the core problems of Western politics and capitalism (Lotringer and Marazzi 1980; Guattari 1996). However, that answer itself has as much to do with the critique of politics past, and with the problems it articulates, as it does with providing a set of solutions.

Ironically, when the communist party disbanded and then reformed in 1991 (*Rifondazione Comunista*), it not only acknowledged the divide and problematics left open in the 1970s, it came to play an important role in the MoM and espouse many of the ideas of autonomy. In fact, when Fausto Bertinotti, then head of the more "movementist" faction of Rifondazione, met with Subcomandante Marcos in 1997, he stated that

> The Zapatista struggle is an example not only for indigenous people, but for the whole world ... there is an amazing convergence in analysis and evaluations with Marcos and the Zapatistas ... the workers' movement needs the Zapatista perspective, also the Zapatista point of view on how to refound politics.
>
> (Rosso 1997: 21)

When I spoke to members of the youth league of *Rifondazione*, they actually described theirs as a party whose goal was deeply influenced by the Zapatistas and who sought to make change without taking power (conversation, Porto Alegre 2003; Wainwright 2008).

How actionable and true this rhetoric turned out to be is an important question, but one that I will not engage with here. Instead, what I want to point to are the ways in which both institutional and movement Lefts converge in the *discourse* and political imaginary of the Zapatistas, which in turn coalesce around a principle and political imaginary of autonomy – which entails a political logic of difference and reflexivity (against universalism and ideological dogmatism). Just think briefly of key Zapatista slogans, such as "one world where many worlds fit" (difference), "to walk while questioning" (non-ideological), and "change the world without taking power" (autonomy).

Ultimately, I believe that the importance of the Italian case rests largely in the series of questions it posed to politics that "were not traditionally a part of its statutory domain", so that "now there was a plurality of questions posed to politics rather than the re-inscription of the act of questioning in the framework of a political doctrine" (Foucault 1994: 115). It is because of these particular questions – motivated by a strong diffidence of representative institutions, political parties, and ideological homogenization and universalities – that Italy's importance to the GJSM remains. To understand why Italy responded in such numbers and with such passion to the GJSM, in particular to Zapatismo and the WSF, one must recognize the ways in which their place-based experiences were able to resonate with other place-based experiences, predisposed to understand and desire a political logic of non-party based autonomy.

Conclusion: rethinking globality, theory and movement

Overall, the history of the Italian Left – both the party and extra-parliamentary elements – and the political problems this Left confronted and proposed solutions to, hold many important parallels with, and potential lessons for, the GJSM and even the present moment. In particular I want to highlight the interconnections between economic crises, a critique of capitalism, and representative or party-based politics, and the creative ways in which these political problems were both articulated and addressed outside traditional dogmatic theories or party structures. While certainly the recent frustration with *Italian* political parties was particular to Italy and came from a specifically Italian history, the fact that it paralleled and therefore resonated with similar disillusion with democratic politics the world over was clearly part of the chord struck by the MoM and GJSM. One need not look very far within the experiences most important to the GJSM to see similar disillusionment: for example, the Zapatistas in Mexico, with their opposition to "bad governments", and the popular assemblies and Movements of Unemployed Workers in Argentina who screamed *"Que se vayan todos!"* ("They [politicians] must all go!"). Similarly, the WSF was founded with the commitment to no political programmes and the express rule that political parties could not participate. These all point to significant commonalities with the anti-austerity, Occupy, and other movements that surged in 2011 – and which have insisted on remaining leaderless, horizontal and have refused to valorize the official or electoral political system.

Acknowledging the form of relationship between Italy's particular history and crucial parts of the global movement requires significant shifts in how we think of causality and spatiality in social movements, as well as the nature of social movements, and the GJSM in particular. The emergence of movements may be caused and mobilized by the power of their ideas and their theoretical contributions to larger political problematics, or the problem of politics writ large. These, in turn, are influenced by historical and place-based specificities.

Several authors have written about the importance of recognizing globalization as necessarily "place-based", meaning that it is impossible to imagine a globality that doesn't touch down and become real or territorialized in concrete places (Dirlik and Prazniak 2001; Harcourt and Escobar 2005). Understanding the MoM as a thoroughly Italian – i.e. place-based – movement does not dispute claims that the MoM is global; it is simply an argument for a different way of thinking of globality. This spatial and epistemological reorientation is an important empirical corrective to how we understand local instantiations of various alter-globalization movements and their histories; however, it also contributes to a better understanding of the movements' political aims: for although the GJSM was certainly opposed to neoliberalism, its politics also contested the foundations of liberal representative democracy and worked to develop "another kind of politics" (Santos 2006; Gibson-Graham 2006.)

Within this framework, it is possible to argue that the case of Italy's MoM can be considered exemplary largely because of the presence of a place-based consciousness and framing of events, as well as a specifically Italian modality of understanding movements and politics. By this I mean that both of its components – including their histories, as well as their objectives and impacts – have a notable national inflection, not only empirically, but also because they are explained and thought of in such terms. Their conditions of possibility are structured not by global or universal categories and trends, but by the particular nature of movements and politics in Italy (as well as the rich theoretical traditions developed in close proximity and relation to these).

The sophisticated critique of representative democracy that emerged in Italy in the 1960s and 1970s was itself a product of Italy's particular history – including the *operaista* tradition, the strong presence of peasant and workers' resistance, and the place-based regional differences and consciousness of Italy's movements. The fact that this history remains so present – materially and in memory – speaks to the importance of place, as both a context and structure of meaning.

An additional facet of this argument speaks of the need to recognize that theory and concept-making is part of the work of social movements, and that theories and concepts themselves arise out of particular places and contexts (Osterweil 2010; Casas-Cortés *et al.* 2008; Young 1990). Rather than treat concepts as universal or ahistorical, theories and concepts must be situated in the places, by the people, and under the conditions where they were produced (Haraway 1988) – what we might call "provincializing theory" (Chakrabarty

2000). This stands in strong contrast both to dominant academic practice – including, quite notoriously, social movement studies – but also to certain modes of universalized, de-historicized, and dogmatic forms of theory and knowledge that have accompanied past movements for social change, including many which self-identified as leftist and/or Marxist-Leninist.

I believe that the vision of politics promoted by the MoM – a political imaginary that places a strong emphasis on the constitutive importance of difference, a political vision of autonomy, and a critical and reflexive epistemology and ethos – is itself an outcome of the particular, place-based ways in which theories and practices of social change were experienced in Italy. It is in fact the particular ways that the concepts of the "political" and "movement" are experienced, and therefore theorized and narrated, that then travel and coincide with other particular experiences – such as the Zapatista movement in Mexico.

Notes

1 Operaismo originated as a theoretical and political project or tendency associated with Leftist intellectuals, many of whom were originally members of the Socialist or Communist parties, and who were unified in their critiques of the historical left, orthodox Marxism, and the methods used to understand the struggles of the working class. This was itself part of a rich tradition of worker's and peasant-based research and knowledge production (Montaldi 1971; Borio *et al.* 2002; Wright 2002), and the general practice of intellectual and theoretical production of the Socialist and Communist Left.
2 It should be no surprise that Melucci, who coined this term which is now used as a generic concept throughout SM studies, was Italian and lived through this period of Italian politics.

References

Balestrini, N. and Leva, M., 1988. *Vogliamo tutto* 1. ed., Milano: Mondadori.

Balestrini, N. and Moroni, P., 1988. *L'orda d'oro*, Milano: SugarCo Edizioni.

Berardi, F. ("Bifo"), 1980. "The Anatomy of Autonomy". In S. Lotringer and C. Marazzi, eds. *Autonomia:* 148 171, Los Angeles: Semiotext(e). Los Angeles.

Bianchi, S. and Caminiti, L. eds., 1997. *Settantasette*, Rome: Derive Approdi.

Bologna, S., 1980. "Tribe of Moles". In S. Lotringer and C. Marazzi, eds. *Autonomia*. Los Angeles: Semiotext(e), pp. 36–61.

Bologna, S., 2001. "For an analysis of Autonomia". Available at: http://libcom.org/tags/sergio-bologna, [accessed January 7, 2012].

Borio, G., Pozzi, F. and Roggero, G., 2002. *Futuro Anteriore*, Rome: Derive Approdi.

Casas-Cortés, M.I., Osterweil, M. and Powell, D.E., 2008. "Blurring Boundaries", *Anthropological Quarterly*, 81(1): 17–58.

Chakrabarty, D., 2000. *Provincializing Europe*, Princeton, NJ: Princeton University Press.

Cox L. and Flesher Fominaya C., 2013. "European Social Movements and Social Theory". In C. Flesher Fominaya and L. Cox, eds. *Understanding European Movements*. London: Routledge.

Cuninghame, P., 2002. *Autonomia*, Doctoral Dissertation. Middlesex: Middlesex University.

Deleuze, G., 1988. *A Thousand Plateaus*, London: Athlone Press.

Dirlik, A. and Prazniak, R., 2001. *Places and Politics in an Age of Globalization*, Lanham, MD: Rowman & Littlefield Publishers.

Foucault, M., 1994. "Polemics, Politics and Problematizations". In P. Rabinow, ed. *Ethics: Essential Works of Foucault, Vol 1*, pp. 111–120. New York: The New Press.

Gibson-Graham, J.K., 2006. *A Postcapitalist Politics*, Minneapolis: University of Minnesota Press.

Ginsborg, P., 2003. *A History of Contemporary Italy*, New York, NY: Palgrave Macmillan.

Gramsci, A. and Verdicchio, P., 2005. *The Southern Question*, Toronto: Guernica Editions.

Guattari, F., 1996. *Soft Subversions*, Los Angeles: Semiotext(e).

Guidry, J.A., Kennedy, M.D. and Zald, M.N., 2000. *Globalizations and Social Movements*, Ann Arbor: University of Michigan Press.

Haraway, D., 1988. "Situated Knowledges", *Feminist Studies*, 14(3): 575–599.

Harcourt, W. and Escobar, A. eds., 2005. *Women and the Politics of Place*, Bloomfield, CT: Kumarian Press.

Hardt, M. and Negri, A., 2000. *Empire*, Cambridge, Mass.: Harvard University Press.

Keck, M. and Sikkink, K., 1998. *Activists Beyond Borders*, Ithaca, NY: Cornell University Press.

Lotringer, S. and Marazzi, C. eds., 1980. *Autonomia*, Los Angeles: Semiotext(e).

Lumley, R., 1990. *States of Emergency*, London; New York: Verso.

Melucci, A., 1989. *Nomads of the Present*, J. Keane and P. Mier, eds., Philadelphia: Temple University Press.

Membretti, A. and Mudu, P., 2013. "Where Global Meets Local". In C. Flesher Fominaya and L. Cox, eds. *Understanding European Movements*. London: Routledge.

Mezzadra, S. and Derive Approdi Editors, 2003. "Luoghi Comuni: il movimento globale come spazio de politicizzazione". *Derive Approdi*, (24): 2–6.

Montagna, N., 2005. *Questioning While Walking*, Middlesex University.

Montaldi, D., 1971. *Militanti politici di base*, Torino: G. Einaudi.

Negri, A., 2002. "Un Movimento Sociale Inedito – Rifondare la Sinistra Italiana". *Le Monde Diplomatique*, August 2002. www.ildialogo.org/VerificaEsistenzaCommenti php?f=http://www.ildialogo.org/estero/estero2282002.htm, [accessed December 2009.]

Nunes, R., 2007. "Forward How? Forward Where?" *Ephemera*, 7(1): 178–202.

Osterweil, M., 2010. *In Search of Movement*, Chapel Hill, NC: University of North Carolina at Chapel Hill.

Revelli, M., 1995. "Movimenti Sociali e Spazio Politico". In F. Barbagallo, ed. *Storia dell'Italia Repubblicana*. Torino: Einaudi, pp. 385–476.

Rosso, U., 1997. "Bertinotti e il Subcomandante", *La Repubblica*, p. 21.

Santos, B., 2006. *The Rise of the Global Left*, London; New York: Zed Books.

Shore, C., 1990. *Italian Communism*, London; Concord, Mass.: Pluto Press.

Tarrow, S., 2012. *Strangers at the Gates*, Cambridge University Press.

Tronti, M., 1966. *Operai e capitale*, Turin: Einaudi Editore.

Wainwright, H., 2008. "A Rough Guide to the Italian political situation". www.tni.org/detail_page.phtml?act_id=18131[accessed May 4, 2008].

Winograd, T. and Flores, F., 1987. *Understanding Computers and Cognition*, Reading, MA: Addison-Wesley.

Wright, S., 2002. *Storming Heaven*, Pluto Press.

Wu Ming 1, 2002. "Why Not Show Off About the Best Things?" *Wumingfoundation.com*. Available at: www.wumingfoundation.com/english/giap/giapdigest18.html. [Accessed June 12, 2003].

Young, R., 1990. *White Mythologies*, London; New York: Routledge.

3 The emergence and development of the "no global" movement in France

A genealogical approach

Isabelle Sommier and Olivier Fillieule

Since the end of the 1990s, academic research into the resistance to neoliberal globalization has continued to expand, in step with the many events that can be considered related (such as counter-summits, social forums, so-called transnational demonstrations, etc.), but also consistent with the competition between the academic disciplines concerned, to the forefront of which are the sociology of social movements and the study of international relations. Nonetheless, for a number of reasons, it is not certain that the abundant literature stemming from the antiglobalization[1] protests has been very fruitful. On the one hand, the coming together on the same terrain and the hybridization of subdisciplines as different as the sociology of social movements and international relations have contributed to a permanent blurring of the definition of the object of study.[2] On the other hand, following the example of specialists in new social movements (subsequently referred to as NSM) in the 1970s, doubtless, researchers in the field have succumbed to the pressures of social demands, and, though obliged to accurately report on this movement, have often been inspired by the actors' own discourse on their practices. Thus, they proclaimed the birth of *the* movement, the radical novelty of which was particularly due to its truly "transnational" character, reflecting the emergence of an "international civil society," because it developed concomitantly in various countries, targeted international organizations, was interested in "global" causes, and acted in ways which were in part international or internationalized.

Recently, and partly due to the repeated warnings of some leading researchers, including Tarrow (2001), this fairy-tale version of *the* movement has been subject to some critical questioning. Beyond their vaunted novelty, how did the antiglobalization battles emerge? What were their intellectual, organizational and activist sources? We must go beyond the simplistic idea of the antiglobalization movement arising in response to the transformation of global capitalism. How can we account sociologically for the progressive establishment of a coalition of interests apparently unified in denouncing the harmful effects of globalization on the one hand, and proclaiming the need for solidarity between North and South, and for a genuine participatory democracy on the other hand?

Ultimately, rather than assuming *a priori* that we are dealing here with "a true transnational movement," is it not worth posing the question differently, starting from some possible conditions for protest struggles to spread from country to country, and for dissenting groups to form cross-border relations and eventually to develop new transnational forms of organization and struggle? In short, the transnational character of the movement is a result to be explained, rather than a given characteristic.

To understand how this movement has acquired such a transnational dimension, it is certainly preferable to follow the appearance and development of the antiglobalization movement step by step in a precise location. This is what we propose to do here, based on the French case. The contextualized analysis of the conditions of its emergence and development allow us to resituate it, and thus to render it intelligible, within a cycle of earlier protests (Tarrow 1995) which made it possible. Such a procedure allows us to qualify the two supposed characteristics of GJM. Its radical novelty turns out to be relative, to the extent that it draws upon networks which were largely pre-existing (Agrikoliansky *et al.* 2005). Its transnational essence, upon close examination, seems dubious, the weight of constraints and opportunities particular to the national protest arena determining its emergence and evolution.

In this chapter, we first argue that, in retrospect, some social movements that developed in France appear to be precursors of this movement. At the end of the 1990s, the French were among the first to cultivate this new cause. A genealogical approach allows us to resituate the "no global" movement within the long history of the reconfiguration of activist fields since the middle of the 1980s, with the increasing autonomization of the field of social movements from the Left's political field. Then we will show that, defined as the "movement of movements," the no global movement appears to be a shifting and rather blurred gathering of various organizations, old and new, which, for the most part, already had clear demands and goals. Their unity is strongly related to the multi-organizational memberships of their core activists. We will conclude by examining how, starting in 2005, the pivotal organizations of the amorphous French antiglobalization movement reconcentrated their activist energies domestically, to the point of envisaging an electoral breakthrough in the 2007 presidential elections.

The chapter is based on various field studies, starting from 2003. In particular, two surveys were conducted, one during the protest against the G8 in the spring of 2003 and one during the European Social Forum (ESF) held in Paris that same year.

- a qualitative study: participant observation of the alternative camps and the counter-summit at Annemasse; analysis of the ESF organization's preparation (why and how such different and sometimes competing organizations decided to collaborate in order to organize this event and how they succeeded in doing it); and ethnographic observation during the sessions (how people spoke, what kind of ideological frames were activated, who delivered the talks, etc.)

- a quantitative survey with a questionnaire of about forty questions to determine activists' socio-biological characteristics, political and organizational affiliations, and ideological beliefs. The survey also enables us to understand motivations for participation and participants' contrasting perceptions of the political and economic situation. (On the methodology of INSURA [INdividual SUrveys during RAllies], please see Fillieule and Blanchard 2010.) The questionnaire was translated into Spanish, Italian, English and German. Two thousand people were gathered at the anti-G8 mobilization, and 2,600 at the ESF. It was very revealing to compare these two events because they show two very different types of GJM involvement. The former was probably more costly in terms of time (because of the need to travel during a period of strikes) and risks (alternative villages, demonstrations and blockades) than the latter.

Isabelle Sommier has also been involved with a European survey (the Demos project, 2004–2008, under the direction of Donatella Della Porta, covering five countries) and an ongoing survey on the last World Social Forum, held in Dakar in February 2011.

1 Key moments of the French GJM

European and American activists who identify with the antiglobalization movement claim to read, or at least regularly quote, authors of various nationalities: Noam Chomsky, Naomi Klein, Toni Negri, Pierre Bourdieu, José Bové, Christophe Aguiton, and Arundhati Roy. They also regularly refer to common or unifying international experiences that supposedly make it possible to create a new cause: the Earth Summit in Rio de Janeiro for the environmentalists (1992), Zapatismo (1994), Jubilee 2000 for the cancellation of Third World debt, the battle against the Multilateral Accord on Investment (MAI) in 1998, the Euromarches against unemployment, etc. Yet, at the same time, they refer to their own foundational moments, which they consider to have greater resonance than previous ones, particularly the mobilization in Seattle (1999) which is generally considered *the* seminal mobilization (Losson and Quinio 2002, and also Daphi, this volume, Chapter 10).

1.1 France at the forefront

The new cause arising at the turn of the millennium was a Latin phenomenon appearing in Brazil and two European countries in particular, Italy and France, which contributed to it in two different ways. On the one hand, a powerful umbrella organization, Attac (*Association pour la taxation des transactions financières et pour l'action citoyenne* [Association for the Taxation of Financial Transactions and for Citizen Action]), which brought together the various existing structures under the overarching label of "the fight against neoliberal globalization" was created in

1998. On the other hand, a semi-organizational, semi-activist mode of action – the forum, a renewed form of counter-summit with a unique flavour – was invented.

Attac was clearly the core organization of the amorphous French antiglobalization movement. Its founding fathers came together in June 1998, from different political subfields and activist generations. Unions came first and comprised half of the founders. In addition, there were a number of newspapers, news magazines and intellectual collectives (*Le Monde diplomatique*, Aitec,[3] and Raisons d'agir), organizations of international solidarity (ISO) from the 1960s to the 1980s (Cedetim, CRID[4] in particular), groups coming from some "new social movements" (NSMs) (feminist ecologists with Friends of the Earth), and movements of "those without" (les "sans"; without work, without shelter or poorly housed, without papers, and without rights) from the 1980s (like Dal, and AC![5]). Such a loose and complex network structure is common in the antiglobalization movement. The fact that these diverse organizations have managed to converge under the Attac umbrella gives the organization a central role in national protest politics, in addition to the influence it is rapidly acquiring in the transnational arena.

Indeed, with the creation, in December 1998, of the Attac International Movement (which today includes 38 national Attac groups), Attac is now by far the best known group beyond the French borders. With the Brazilians, it played an essential role in the emergence of the *forum* as a new mode of action and the holding of the first World Social Forum at Porto Alegre in January 2001. It also fills a place left vacant, despite Aitec, in relation to the expert dimension of "no global" activists. Its scholarly orientation is proclaimed in Article 1 of its statutes of this "movement for grassroots education oriented towards action" which sets itself

> as a goal to produce and communicate information, as well as to promote and lead actions of all sorts resulting in the reconquest, by the citizens, of the power that the financial sphere exercises over all aspects of political, economic, social and cultural life in the entire world. Amongst these means is the taxation of market transactions (the Tobin tax).

This role for knowledge is reflected in the existence of an academic council of 108 individuals charged with proposing and conducting research (Article 12) to be widely disseminated by the publishing house. The association was a resounding success: six months after the initial appeal it boasted 5,000 members, then 30,000 at the peak of its glory, before plunging to a mere 10,000 members today following a severe internal crisis in June 2006.

The idea of holding the first World Social Forum at Porto Alegre in 2001, in parallel with that of Davos, was a joint initiative by some Brazilian and French activists, at the forefront of which was Attac, with its director Bernard Cassen, and the Via Campesina, an international peasant organization created in 1993 within the framework of the *Movimento dos Trabalhadores sem Terra* (MST), in which the French *Confédération paysanne* played a significant role. The French delegation was then the most numerous European one; it numbered about 500 activists. At the second meeting in January 2002, under the major influence of the Italians and, once again, the French, it was decided to export the forum configuration to the rest of Europe. The first European Social Forum was held in Florence in 2002, and the second on Ile-de-France in 2003.

The organization of the European Social Forum (ESF) in Paris in November 2003 was another important step for the French GJM. Several months earlier, from 30 May to 6 June 2003, on the occasion of the G8 summit in Evian, a series of demonstrations denouncing neoliberal globalization took place on both sides of the Franco-Swiss border in Annemasse, Geneva and Lausanne, and an alternative summit was organized. Among the French groups participating in the mobilization (38 per cent of the participants were French), trade unions (such as SUD and CGT[6]) still played a central role (Fillieule *et al.* 2004). This was characterized by clearer involvement on the part of NGOs working on development issues, some of them Christian such as Cedetim, as well as associations specializing in grassroots education or immigration issues.

During the ESF, 51,000 participants attended 55 plenary conferences, 271 seminars, and 280 workshops. According to ESF figures, 80,000 people attended the closing session. The ESF provided the opportunity for widely varying organizations that did not traditionally work together to meet, and fostered ties between competing organizations (Agrikoliansky and Sommier 2005: 292). However, differences were also clear. Some groups, such as the young people of "Intergalactics," criticized the institutionalization of the ESF, and two alternative forums were held simultaneously by media activists and anarchists, who always organize separate events in order to differentiate themselves from "reformists," while joining them in the demonstrations. These internal conflict lines were more evident during large-scale gatherings, such as the four-day alternative village organized at the anti-G8 protest, or the major meeting organized under the slogan "The World is not Merchandise" in July 2003 on the 30th anniversary of the struggle of the Larzac farmers against a military camp and in view of the WTO summit in Cancun, Mexico.

1.2 Antiglobalization activism before the "no global" movement: French milestones

While Seattle saw the emergence of the antiglobalization "brand," protests against neoliberal globalization did have forerunners. Organization leaders competed to convince onlookers that they were the first to have mounted protests against the neoliberal order, before any media attention was given to such a thing as the "no global movement." Their aim was to establish their legitimacy as being at the core of the "movement," since the cooperative field of antiglobalization is also competitive. Yet only a few events before 1999 can be considered as truly antiglobalist in that they anticipated the loose network that would, more or less regularly, attempt to mobilize many sectors within the overarching framework of "the fight against globalization."

The struggle against the Multilateral Accord on Investment (MAI) in the winter of 1997–1998 is often presented as the initial mobilization of antiglobalization for a number of reasons:

1 its target: the OECD, which was part of negotiations to continue the liberalization of multinationals' investment conditions;
2 the coalition of actors, individuals (to the forefront, moviemakers mobilized by the recognition of the "cultural exception") and organizations such as SUD (Solidary, Unitary and Democratic), DAL, AC!, and the first ad hoc French group focussed on the critique of globalization, the *Observatoire de la mondialisation* (Observatory of Globalization);
3 the transnational alliances they form (for example, with Lori Wallach and *Global Citizens*);
4 the role reserved for the Internet, in triggering action (it was on the net that the MAI project was discovered), as a catalyst and a standard-bearer for mobilization;
5 its wide range of modes of action, especially centred on awareness-raising (petitions, the rally in April, "the week of actions" in September, and "the citizen summit" in October) and expertise (research, seminars, and a counter-project);
6 its success, in that the withdrawal of the French government from the MAI has been attributed (whether rightly or wrongly doesn't matter here) to the mobilization of opposing forces.

This protest episode is widely considered as the initiative of the GJM because of its evident transnational dimension. Nonetheless, others – more narrowly French or European – contributed to the antiglobalization narrative in as much as they provided, *a posteriori*, ideological frameworks that proved to be useful in the building of a French antiglobalization master-frame. These were the protests for the cancellation of Third World debt (1989), for the defence of the French social model (1995), for the denunciation of unemployment and job insecurity (1997), and for food sovereignty (1999).

Third World supporters are among the most present in antiglobalization mobilization, and also those who generate less division in terms of values (they are the most ecumenical), national traditions (they are driving forces everywhere) or activist traditions since, for 40 years, they have gathered groups of diverse origins, from Marxist anti-imperialists to Christians. Also, they were behind the initial international campaign in 1995, included retrospectively in the prehistory of what Anglophones significantly call "the Global Justice Movement": the "Jubilee 2000" campaign. Thus, as Eric Agrikoliansky (2005) demonstrated, the central themes of this campaign (the cancellation of Third World debt, the denunciation of the policies of international institutions imposed on the developing world, and a fresh approach to North–South relations), had already been placed in the forefront of the celebration of the bicentenary of the French Revolution in July 1989.

Since the mobilization in Seattle, this had been a "citizen" initiative (or at least presented itself as such) *reacting* to the initiative of political authorities who were themselves engaged in a lavish, very formal official commemoration, as this national celebration offered François Mitterrand the opportunity to host the G7 (giving the event a dual dimension, both national and international). This protest initiative concentrated in a few days the entire panoply of modes of action that would soon comprise the "no global" repertoire: a demonstration of 15,000 individuals on 8 July, concluding that same evening with a concert; an "alternative summit" connecting themes which, up to that point, had been considered separate and praising "civil society," with a mixture of expertise and the testimony of "victims"; and, finally, a "Summit of Seven of the World's Poorest Countries." Already we find here "what would become the refrain of antiglobalization: rehabilitate democracy and "civil society" to stand up to the dictatorship of the markets and the policy of the great powers," as well as adopt a formula destined to become famous: "Think globally, act locally" (Agrikoliansky 2005). Organized by the Trotskyite party LCR (Revolutionary Communist League), the mobilization brought together a coalition of disparate groups who would work together again in organizing antiglobalization events: parties (like LCR, the PCF (French Communist Party), libertarians and some Greens), unions (CGT and SUD in particular), groups of activist researchers such as Aitec, and voluntary groups. They reflected the changing character of the Third World circle of influence, through the coming together of its anti-imperialist component, embodied by Cedetim, and its Christian component was leading it to the new field of "international solidarity." This rapprochement was symbolized by the progressive convergence of all of these groups under CRID, one of the central federations of French antiglobalization, and it conferred on it two changes: the development (versus humanitarian) orientation and the importance of expertise. The following year the Comité d'annulation de la dette du Tiers-monde (CADTM – Committee to Cancel Third World Debt) was founded. It was this organization which, in 1994, imported the anglophone campaign "FMI, Banque mondiale, OMC: 50 ans ça suffit" ("IMF, World Bank, WTO: 50 years is enough"), and which then played a major role in the Jubilee 2000 campaign.

The second, solely domestic, act laying the foundation for the French movement consisted of the November–December 1995 strikes against the right-wing pension reform plan. The claim that they constituted "the first revolt against globalization" came, not from activist ranks, but rather from the pen of a journalist from the daily *Le Monde*, Erik Izraëlewicz, in an article published on 7 December 1995. Based on an analysis of 700 leaflets collected during Parisian demonstrations, in one-third of them Jean Gabriel Contamin discovered six "antiglobalization" themes, prior to these being widely disseminated: globalist/internationalist, pro/anti-Maastricht treaty, financial ("denunciations of market rules and those of finance and the stock market"), financial/Maastrichtian "that combine these two anti-subjects," imperialist, and transnational arguments (2004: 245).

Unlike the 1995 strikes, the European marches against unemployment and the lack of job security directly appeared to be one of the driving forces of the antiglobalization movement. They were immediately conceived of as European by the association of unions and organizations of the unemployed, as witnessed by the different points of departure of the marches in April and their point of convergence – Amsterdam, the city where the European Summit was held on 14 June 1997. Fifty thousand people marched there under the banner "Employment is a right; we're entitled to an income." It was AC! that took the initiative in this case, in tune with its initial goal of serving as a bridgehead between the two types of organization and supporting the very radical anticapitalist and internationalist appeal. Sixteen groups from Great Britain, Ireland, Spain, Germany, Belgium, Italy and France answered the call at a meeting held in Florence in June 1996.

The 12 August 1999 dismantling of McDonald's in Millau by the *Confédération paysanne* (CP) is certainly the last episode of the movement's prehistory, and its impact spilled across national borders: The image of José Bové, ostentatiously sporting handcuffs, was shown everywhere and was an illustration of his strategic abilities (and those of his comrades), not so much in initiating action as in ensuring its effect – that is, in transforming local action into a global event (Martin 2005; see also Morena, this volume, Chapter 6).

2   The long history of a new cause

This genealogy of the French antiglobalization movement shows the great diversity of the actors involved (or joining in), most of whom were organized prior to the emergence of the new cause. A comparison of some constituent dynamics of the GJM in five European states (Sommier *et al.* 2008) shows that the pioneering groups or driving forces of the antiglobalization protests differed profoundly from one country to another. Also, if we shift our gaze slightly, to focus, not on the dynamics of the events, but rather on the structural dynamics, we observe that the emergence of the movement in each of the countries studied was related to particular national political opportunities, occasions and dynamics.

2.1   A movement of movements

An examination of the multi-organizational field (Curtis and Zurcher 1973[7]) of French antiglobalization offers a response to the hypothesis of the radical novelty of the new cause. Indeed, if we exclude the few ad hoc organizations, such as Attac, created precisely to denounce the effects of economic and financial globalization, we have to recognize that the so-called alterglobalization movement is actually comprised of the most varied groups, from the perspective of their structural forms (unions, associations, research centres or intellectual clubs and NGOs), their activist cultures, and their longstanding causes. They included unions, movements of "those without," leftist radical groups, ecologists and environmental protection movements, humanitarian and development associations, human rights groups and women's rights groups.

Such a variety is strikingly clear when one considers the founding date of approximately thirty groups chosen on the basis of their regular involvement in this multi-organizational field. A quarter of them were created between 1969 and 1989, and a further quarter after 1995, a pivotal date in the history of contemporary protest politics in France. Approximately one-fifth – 21.8 per cent – appear after 1998 and clearly represent the antiglobalization movement proper – that is, the fight against neoliberal globalization – while the groups created before 1968 constitute 15.6 per cent of the total (Sommier and Combes 2007: 112). Although organizations specializing in the denunciation of neoliberalism and hence, recently created (mainly Attac), constitute the primary pool of activists, they are in the minority among organizations that participate in and even manage GJM events. For instance, the committee that organized the second ESF was made up of 300 groups, including 76 trade unions,[8] 24 humanitarian or solidarity associations, 21 newspapers or think tanks, and 14 environmental groups (Agrikoliansky and Sommier 2005: 291).

This hybrid nature, observed at the meso-sociological level through the study of the social movement organizations, can obviously be found at the micro-level of activists. The multiple memberships at the 2nd European Social Forum revealed one core group structured around antiglobalization associations (such as Attac) and composed of ecological, human rights and development organizations. This collection includes almost half of the memberships declared, so that it constitutes a kind of centre of gravity of the amorphous mass of antiglobalists.

Awareness of the multiple affiliations of activists is essential to understand the networks. They allow people to claim allegiance to a specific organization, while at the same time giving them the feeling of being a part of a homogeneous whole. According to the ESF survey, activists declare they are affiliated with an average of 2.4 organizations, with 22 per cent belonging to none. It was similar for the anti-G8 activists (for an average of 2.7 organizations, and with 25 per cent belonging to no organization) regardless of nationality, with French people being less likely than the British or the Italians to have multiple memberships (Fillieule *et al.* 2004: 41). Of course, the largest organizations in the ESF, such as Attac, are specifically concerned with global justice: 40 per cent of activists are affiliated with one of these organizations, but this is always combined with membership in another, and 35 per cent are affiliated with trade unions, reflecting their predominant position within the French GJM. Humanitarian organizations come next (26 per cent), followed by environmental associations (19 per cent), political parties (17 per cent), pacifist groups (23 per cent), human rights organizations (26 per cent), organizations against racism (16 per cent), and solidarity organizations (16 per cent). For young participants, the hierarchy of the organizations changes drastically: trade unions, second in terms of the overall total of participants, drop to 15th place. Logically, youth and student movements tend to predominate among the young population of our sample, together with the pacifist and "autonomous" groups. In contrast, as Fillieule and Blanchard (2005: 161–162) note, young people are less involved in organizations against racism, solidarity, neighbourhood and religious associations, and political parties.

2.2 *The reorganization of activist fields*

At the beginning of the 2000s, the French antiglobalization network is distinct in that it has a particularly strong social orientation. This can be explained by the profile of the pioneers who, at a key point in the 1980s, revived the social question. These were the so-called associations of "those without" – *les "sans"* – and new radicalized unions (such as the SUDs).

The emergence of the associations of "those without" put the spotlight on the struggles of groups deemed incapable of mobilizing because of their lack of resources, mainly through very visible actions such as the homeless squatting in buildings, or marches against unemployment in the springs of 1994, 1997 and 1999. These groups have in common their recognized position on the "margins," giving voice to those who would be deprived of a voice (and, more broadly, deprived of representation), such as those in a precarious economic and social situation. By their very existence, they highlight the inadequacy of traditional unionism in representing those excluded from paid employment and, more broadly, in defending the most vulnerable, and thus contributing to redrawing the field of unionism, notably by provoking the CGT's reactivation of its committees of unemployed, leading – in parallel with NGOs, and then together with them – the "Mouvement des chômeurs" in the winter of 1997–1998. AC! played an essential role in this linking of the two groups of movements.

The period was also characterized by a profound shift in the union environment due to the appearance of new professional groups, the most significant for our purposes being the SUDs, such as SUD-Post offices, founded in 1988, and SUD-Railway, established in 1996, after the massive strikes of November–December 1995. At the end of the 1990s, approximately thirty SUDs had joined the union group "Solidaires," totalling 80,000 members. The group had a clearly radical set of demands, calling upon "antiliberal forces," condemning the market economy, defending the public service, adopting ecological concerns, etc. Like the *Confédération paysanne*, created in 1987, these new unions could not be seen merely as critics of existing union federations. They intended to renew the union movement by adding activist issues and practices from the "new social movements" that sprang up after 1968, seeking to link the struggles in the workplace and outside the workplace and to renew the range of possible actions to make them more attractive and less humdrum. The priority given to the immediate efficacy of the battles, sensitivity to societal questions, and a more flexible and horizontal organization than that of traditional federations were the keys to their success, amongst young, highly qualified public sector employees in particular. This also gave them a greater capacity to respond and to form alliances with other groups, essential to the development of antiglobalization mobilization.

The interest in the international dimension which these pioneers express seems to correspond to the political positioning strategies of each of the actors, concerned with improving their position and acquiring more resources.[9] Also, it is not surprising to observe that actors central to national protest areas are not as interested in the international domain as actors in marginal positions, with marginal resources, seeking in the opening of European or international arenas a new avenue to express their demands, to develop their specific resources, and to acquire new ones. The *outsiders* in the union movement (salaried employees and farm workers) or in the field of international solidarity (the people of the Third World) find in this new cause a way to navigate around the closing of their respective institutional spaces or to escape from the domination of rival groups who have relegated them to secondary roles.

To be successful, such conversion strategies have to be facilitated by the ongoing transformation of protest arenas and, more generally, of political arenas, which, due to the momentary fluidity they display, offer greater opportunities. Thus, in France, as elsewhere, the taste for the new cause reflects a changing equilibrium and, consequently, alliances between parties of the left, union forces and associations of the so-called social movement. An essential factor in the reshaping of the protest arena, in fact, arose from activists' disappointing experiences with the left in power and the policies adopted, leaving behind – indeed, clearly abandoning – the workers' movement's founding pact between parties (socialist or social-democrat) and unions, the closing off of the partisan terrain on the left under the double effect of the melting away of the communist party (PCF), and the conversion of the socialists (PS) to liberalism. The vibrancy of civil society, as reflected in the increase in social criticism since 1995, is in sharp contrast to the listlessness of the political debate and, curiously, of the Socialist party. This distance illustrates the gap between the movement on the left and the institutional left which opened up following the economic shift of 1983, the social democratic metamorphosis of the PS, and the trivialization of the very idea of political change induced by a series of alternate governments. In this context, aggravated by the social crisis and a nett decline in labour conflicts, the institutional left was in some ways compelled to turn to new protest groups, including those critical of themselves. In this sense, it is certainly the competitive dynamic amongst national movements which is behind the fluctuating appeal of international issues and forms of action.

Conclusion

Beyond the roots of the desire to make "international" demands, both historically and in the short term, we observe significant variations in involvement at this level, again as a function of purely national opportunities. In considering the evolution of the antiglobalization movement country-by-country since its appearance, it seems clear that its transnational orientation is relatively fickle. In Germany and in France, for example, since 2003–2004 the central actors, as well as the themes considered, have neglected international activism somewhat, and have refocussed on domestic activism. Now these shifting scales are, once again, linked to or determined by organizational strategies that are national in character, such as, in Germany, mobilization against the Schröder reform, "Agenda 2010." The "brand" may remain, but it is applied to immediate issues close at hand, and remains strictly within the country's borders. Moreover, therein lies perhaps one of the distinctive features of the cause, the contours of which are sufficiently fluid to allow the actors to navigate from the most "global" to the most "local," with identical actors and an infinitely adjustable framework.

The French case has been paradigmatic in this respect. Since the fall of 2004, activist energies have once again focussed on the domestic arena. An unprecedented electoral mobilization for a "no" in the referendum campaign on the European Constitutional Treaty (ECT) was organized around the PCF, Attac and the Fondation Copernic. It focussed on two central issues: a national one (the revolt of the "people" against the "elites" very widely favourable to the ratification of the treaty); and a European (even global) issue with respect to the "French exception" (France again in the forefront of the rejection of neoliberalism). In total, 63 per cent of French organizations participating in the antiglobalization wave were actively involved in the campaign against the ECT, and 64 per cent of employees in the public sector – the core of "no global" activism – voted against it. The "no's" success (winning with almost 55 per cent of votes cast) gave rise to euphoria in the ranks of activists and led to a controversy over the single candidate of the "left of the left" for the presidential elections of 2007. From that moment, the stakes were strictly national and remained so. Yet, due to the divisions that ensued and to some people voting for the PS for practical reasons, there was a crushing defeat of the six candidates on the left of the PS (10.57 per cent). The defeat provoked a reconfiguration of the "left of the left." Unions and social movements had exhausted themselves in a fruitless resistance to neoliberal reforms throughout Sarkozy's five-year term. The antiglobalization cycle of the French social movement came to an end. Its attractiveness among the young plummeted, as the very limited success of the Occupy movement shows.

This political trajectory of the French antiglobalization protest movement effectively demonstrates that this is not "one" transnational movement, but rather a mosaic, an amorphous collection of various mobilized groups characterized by the history and special nature of their national roots, which come together temporarily under the polysemic label of "the fight against neoliberal globalization" and/or of the battle for "global justice" and, depending on the issues, direct their activities to the local or transnational level.

Notes

1 In this text, we will not distinguish between the terms "antiglobalization movement," "'no global' movement or the 'Global Justice Movement'" (GJM). However, the only term used in France is "alter mondialisation." For a discussion of the labels used and the meanings they convey, please see Sommier *et al.* 2008.

2 On this point, please see the critique formulated by S. Tarrow (2001) and, for an updated version of this critique, J. Siméant (2005).

3 The Association internationale de techniciens, experts et chercheurs (Aitec – the International Association of Technicians, Experts and Researchers) was created in 1983, with the goal of counter-expertise, under the impetus of Cedetim (Centre d'études et

d'initiatives de solidarité internationale – the Centre for Studies and Initiatives in International Solidarity, established in 1966). It brings together university scholars and professionals to consider, for example, such questions as financial institutions and the debt.

4 The Centre de recherche et d'information sur le développement (CRID – the Centre for Research and Information on Development) was created in 1976. Today, it encompasses 51 international solidarity organizations (ISO) including Cedetim, which held the presidency from 1991 to 1998.

5 Droit au logement (Right to Housing, 1990) and Agir ensemble contre le chômage! (Act Together Against Unemployment!, 1994).

6 The CGT (General Confederation of Labour) is the oldest labour union and one of the two main labour unions today. For a long time, it was very close to the communist party.

7 For a cartography, please see Sommier 2003, but also Fillieule *et al.* 2005 and Fillieule and Blanchard 2005.

8 The number of unions is exaggerated because many local unions and professional branches signed the appeal even though their national confederation did too. Nevertheless, unions were then dominant in the French GJM.

9 With an approach similar to that of the "boomerang effect," emphasized by Keck and Sikkink (1998) with respect to the internationalization of NGOs as a means of skirting political obstacles to various causes at the national level. NGOs do not all employ these circumvention strategies in an identical fashion, especially due to the different structure and volume of their resources. There is also competition amongst organizations, observable in the various arenas in which they have a presence.

References

Agrikoliansky, E. (2005). "Du tiers-mondisme à l'altermondialisme," in Agrikoliansky, E., Fillieule, O. and Mayer, N. (eds), *L'altermondialisme en France*. Paris: Flammarion.

Agrikoliansky, E. and Sommier, I. (eds) (2005). *Radiographie du mouvement altermondialiste*. Paris: La Dispute.

Bourdieu P. (1998). *Contre-feux*. Paris: Liber-Raisons d'Agir.

Cohen, R. and Rai, S. (eds) (2000). *Global Social Movements*. London: The Athlone Press Co.

Contamin, J.-G. (2004). "Les grèves de décembre 1995: un moment fondateur?," in Agrikoliansky E., Fillieule, O. and Mayer, N. (eds). *L'altermondialisme en France*. Paris: Flammarion.

Curtis, R.L. and Zurcher, L.A. (1973). "Stable Resources of Protest Movements," in *Social Forces*, 52 (1).

Daphi, P., 2013. "Collective identity across borders," in Flesher Fominaya, C. and Cox, L. (eds) *Understanding European Movements*. London: Routledge.

Della Porta, D. and Tarrow, S. (2004). *Transnational Protest and Global Activism*. Lanham: Rowman & Littlefield Publishers Inc.

Fillieule, O. and Blanchard, P. (2005). "Les altermondialismes entre national et global," in Agrikoliansky, E. and Sommier, I. (eds) (2005). *Radiographie du mouvement altermondialiste*. Paris: La Dispute.

Fillieule, O. and Blanchard, P. (2010). "Individual Surveys in Rallies," in Teune, S. (ed.). *Transnational Challengers*. Oxford and New York: Berghan Books.

Fillieule, O., Blanchard, P., Agrikoliansky, E., Bandler, M., Passy, F. and Sommier, I. (2004). "l'Altermondialisme en réseaux." *Politix*, vol. 17, no.°68. December: 13–48.

Keck, M. and Sikkink, K. (1998). *Activists Beyond Borders.* Ithaca and London: Cornell University Press.

Losson, C. and Quinio, P. (2002). *Génération Seattle.* Paris: Grasset.

Martin J.-P. (2005). "Du Larzac à la Confédération paysanne de José Bové," in Agrikoliansky, E., Fillieule, O. and Mayer, N., *Généalogie de l'altermondialisme en France.* Paris: Flammarion.

McAdam, D., Tarrow, S. and Tilly, C. (2001) *Dynamics of Contention.* Cambridge: Cambridge University Press.

Morena, E., 2013. "Constructing a new collective identity for the alterglobalization movement". In C. Flesher Fominaya and L. Cox, eds. *Understanding European Movements.* London: Routledge.

Reiter, H., and Fillieule, O. (2006). "Formalizing the Informal," in Della Porta, D., Peterson, A. and Reiter, H. (eds) *The Policing of Transnational Protest.* Aldershot: Ashgate.

Siméant, J. (2005). "What Is Going Global?," in *Review of International Political Economy*, 12 (5).

Sommier, I. (1993) *Le renouveau des mouvements contestataires à l'heure de la mondialisation.* Paris: Flammarion, Champs.

Sommier, I. (2009) "The Social Bases of the GJM," with Massimiliano Andretta, in Della Porta, D. (ed.), *Another Europe: Conceptions and Practices of Democracy in the European Social Forums*, pp. 111–127. London and New York: Routledge.

Sommier, I. and Combes, H. (2007) "The Global Justice Movement in France," in Della Porta, D. (ed.) *The Global Justice Movement*, pp. 103–127. Boulder, London: Paradigm.

Sommier, I., Combes, H. and Haeringer, N. (2009) "The Generational Issue," in Della Porta, D. (ed.), *Democracy in Social Movements*, pp. 217–233. London: Palgrave Macmillan.

Sommier, I., Fillieule, O. and Agrikoliansky, E. (eds) (2008) *Généalogie du mouvement antiglobalisation en Europe.* Paris: Karthala.

Tarrow, S. (1995) "Cycles of Collective Action," in Traugott, M. (ed.) *Repertoires and Cycles of Collective Action.* Durham and London: Duke University Press.

Tarrow, S. (2001) "Transnational Politics," in *Annual Review of Political Science*, 4.

4 The continuity of transnational protest

The anti-nuclear movement as a precursor to the Global Justice Movement

Emmanuel Rivat

Introduction

On 12 December 2009, ten years after the protests of Seattle, anti-nuclear activists demonstrated during the climate change summit in Copenhagen.[1] In the months before the protest, they set up a coalition called "Don't nuke the climate" composed of environmental groups such as Greenpeace and global justice groups such as the International Forum on Globalization.[2] They were particularly opposed to the threat of a "renaissance" of nuclear energy projects. During the demonstration, these activists hung banners and distributed stickers in order to increase their transnational audience among the general public and other global justice groups. These efforts have proved successful: the press stated on the day of the demonstration that "nuclear energy, alongside demands against capitalism, has been one of the most important issues in climate change".[3]

This episode of contention shows that the anti-nuclear movement may influence the Global Justice Movement in two different ways. First, anti-nuclear networks have been part of an event identified in the media as a global justice event. Second, they have established alliances with global justice groups that are supportive of the cause. This episode not only shows the visibility of these anti-nuclear demands, it also sketches the transnational convergence of these different groups. This chapter aims to trace the origins of the relationship between anti-nuclear and global justice groups in Europe.

The anti-nuclear movement can be seen as a "new social movement" that emerged at the beginning of the 1970s. At that time, "new" types of movements such as peace, ecological, and gay movements started to receive attention from mass audiences as well as from political allies. In contrast to older forms of organization such as the workers' movement and left-wing political parties, which developed economic claims, the new social movements represented "post-modern" values and cultural claims (Touraine 1980). They were also characterized, in the wake of the student movement of 1968, by their autonomy with respect to the political sphere and political parties (Melucci 1990). As such, these social movements were viewed as a new historical form of protest.

Touraine pushed the argument even further by claiming that the anti-nuclear movement could possibly replace the workers' movement as the main spearhead of social change.

Previous studies have shown that many of the environmental groups which mobilized around the nuclear protest during the 1970s coalesced around the Global Justice Movement in Europe during the 2000s. Passy and Bandler, among others, show that ecological individuals and groups have contributed to a large extent to the dynamic of global justice protests (Passy and Bandler 2003). Sommier and Della Porta underline the fact that ecological and Global Justice Movements share similar demands about participatory democratic decision-making and autonomy with regards to the influence of political parties (Sommier 2003; Della Porta 2007b). All in all, these studies show that social movements are based on previous episodes of contention and are not self-contained. In spite of these strong empirical indications, the question of whether the anti-nuclear movement can be viewed as a precursor to the Global Justice Movement still requires clarification.

One point that makes it possible to analyse this influence is that the anti-nuclear movement is not a homogeneous. According to Rootes, the anti-nuclear movement is particularly interesting because it was the nexus of a power relationship between primarily environmentalist and more left-wing groups (Rootes 2008). Rootes and Richardson also show that political parties that have been involved in the anti-nuclear struggle influenced the formation of the ecological movement (Rootes and Richardson 1995). Hence, we can assume that its inheritance is complex, plural and disputed. Drawing on the insights of Pierre Bourdieu, I propose to elaborate upon the idea that protest groups compete to define the boundaries of social movements as an autonomous social space (Bourdieu 1991).

The main question, therefore, is to understand how the anti-nuclear movement has inspired the Global Justice Movement over time. This implies understanding how the construction of discourse by environmentalist and left-wing groups contributes to shaping acceptable claims and alliances. The first section opens by outlining the emergence and profile of environmental networks in Europe. The second section examines how environmentalist and left-wing groups partly converged on decentralized democratic claims during the 1970s. The third section analyses more specifically how these anti-nuclear groups converged with global justice groups on the basis of new democratic claims during the 2000s. Looking more closely at the impact of political parties on social movements, the last section shows that such historical convergence is hampered by profound national differences between green political parties and the Global Justice Movement.

The emergence and profile of environmental networks in Europe

The anti-nuclear cause is part of a long history of protest and symbols. Despite substantial decline in terms of intensity of protest (Duyvendak 1994), it remains a key feature of the evolution of new social movements. The anti-nuclear movement is part of a phase of "modern environmentalism" which emerged at the end of the 1960s: it contributed to the rise of awareness about the fragility of the earth and paved the way for the emergence of further global concerns such as climate change and sustainable development during the 1980s and 1990s (Carter 2001: 4). According to Rüdig, the environmental movement can be defined around three different poles: conservation groups mainly concerned with nature protection from the end of the nineteenth century, centrist environmental groups which emerged around different issues at the beginning of the 1970s and focused on political change, and radical ecology groups that focused on nuclear energy while pursuing a strong commitment for social change (Rüdig 1988a: 30).[4] This first section will briefly sketch the profile of environmental networks in Europe that have been involved in the anti-nuclear struggle.

The anti-nuclear movement in Europe sprang up at the beginning of the 1970s. The first anti-nuclear demonstrations blossomed at the crossroads of France, West Germany and the Netherlands, and they subsequently developed in various parts of Europe, including Sweden, Austria, Denmark, the United Kingdom, Ireland, and, later, Spain and Italy. They also became very influential in the United States and Japan. It is worth noting that such local protest groups increasingly developed into nationwide social movements shaped by specific political contexts (Kitschelt 1986; Flam 1994; Kriesi *et al.* 1995). National social movements also overlapped and developed using similar claims and repertoires of action due to the flow of communication beyond borders (McAdam and Rucht 1993). The anti-nuclear movement has always, to some extent, been transnational. For instance, Friends of the Earth organized a counter summit against the politics of the AIEA (*Atomic International Energy Agency*) in Salzburg in May 1977. Meanwhile, mass protests have attracted the attention of tens of thousands of demonstrators from multiple countries.

The decline of this wave of protest at the end of 1980s can be partly explained by the shifting position of the main centrist environmental groups.[5] Centrist environmental groups such as Friends of the Earth became increasingly powerful networks in terms of resources and reputation and started to cooperate more closely with political institutions at the expense of protest. The construction of nuclear plants reached a critical level in Europe due to the lack of political opportunities, especially in France, while in other countries such as Germany and the Netherlands, political opportunities became more open to environmental protest groups (Van Der Heijden 1998). Although they continued to mobilize around the nuclear issue from time to time, they mostly moved onto more global issues such as acid rain, climate change, loss of biodiversity, and dealing with the dilemma to "negotiate North–South identity" (Doherty 2006). This shift was not without effect for the transnational dynamic of anti-nuclear protest, because Friends of the Earth, for example, had been influential in coordinating protest beyond borders.

However, radical ecology groups did continue to mobilize against nuclear energy. Certainly, according to Rootes, the environmental movement during the

1980s and 1990s was not mobilized at the transnational level anymore: "not only was there no common pattern, but there was no general trend toward transnational convergence. The pattern of protest was dominated by the particular concerns of the citizens of particular nation-states" (Rootes 2005: 28). However, during the same period of time, environmental networks did continue to mobilize locally against the construction of nuclear waste disposals and, later, waste transport (Hayes 2002). These radical ecology networks became more concerned with transnational protest when they started to identify a worldwide "renaissance" of nuclear energy ambitions at the beginning of the 2000s. They increasingly made connections with groups that had already mobilized during this period. It is therefore not surprising to see that these different ecological and anti-nuclear networks became more visible in the Global Justice Movement, as shown in Table 4.1, below.

As the table shows, anti-nuclear and global justice groups had some strong connections in the 2000s. Passy and Bandler's (2003) study shows several interesting trends. First, to a certain extent the anti-nuclear movement has evolved from being a pole of protest during the 1970s to a component of the Global Justice Movement in the 2000s. It is striking that the ecological and anti-nuclear organizations are the best-represented within the Global Justice Movement, at 18 per cent of organizational affiliations, beyond alter-globalist or North–South solidarity organizations. The global social justice movement presents itself as a "movement of movements" because it transcends the categorical division of anti-nuclear, ecological, or anti-war organizations. Second, the study shows that the so-called "new" protest groups are not completely independent from the influence of political parties, since it scores 10.9 per cent for organizational affiliation. These different aspects are examined more closely below.

This short historical background contradicts some ideas about the knowledge we have of new social movements. It shows that environmental networks have been continuously active beyond borders during the 1970s. It also indicates that the "new" and "old" attributes of social movements appear to be much more intertwined than the terminology of "new social movement" suggests. It is therefore important to understand how these different alliances between centrist environmentalist, radical ecology and global justice groups became possible. Having

Table 4.1 Features of global justice networks at the Evian counter-summit, 2003

Type of organization/ demonstrators	Organizational affiliation (% of total)	Individual affiliation (% of total)
Ecological/anti-nuclear organizations	18.2	10.1
Alter-globalist/North–South solidarity organizations	17.3	6.7
Pacifist organizations	13.5	5.7
Political parties	10.9	11.3

Source: adapted from Passy and Bandler (2003).

emphasized the legacy of anti-nuclear networks, the next section will show how environmental and radical ecology networks learnt how to construct a common discourse beyond borders in the 1970s and 2000s.

Protest and transnational democratic claims in the 1970s

The anti-nuclear movement, as shown here, emerged outside the mainstream political system and formal institutional life. In this respect, Touraine (1980) shows that the movement contributed to the promotion of a new social model of democracy that challenged the control of state over society, including better information about technological risks. It is a "new" movement by contrast with the workers' movement, because activists make environmental and societal demands that differ from typical Marxist-oriented concerns. The main criticism against Touraine's category of "new" movements, however, is that it is far too normative in considering a social movement as a historical actor rather than a complex web of differences (Rüdig 1990; Duyvendak 1994). Social movements are not self-contained, particularly in the case of the anti-nuclear movement: as Bourdieu notes, discourses can hold "the power to make people see and believe, to get them to know and recognize, to impose the legitimate definition of the social world, and thereby, to make and unmake groups" (Bourdieu 1991: 220–221).

Between 1971 and 1976, centrist environmental groups provided the key impulse for the construction of democratic demands. In Western Europe and the United States, they focused on protecting nature and human health and, broadly speaking, nuclear energy was considered as technological "overkill" of pollution and industrialization.[6] Groups such as Friends of the Earth aimed to place environmental issues high on the agenda. Even though they were critical of top-down politics, they were centrist environmental groups because they did not oppose political institutions per se, but rather attempted to cooperate with them in order to achieve greater environmental protection. In 1972, according to McCormick, the United Nations Conference of Stockholm on the Human Environment became a turning point: it gave a strong impetus to new "rational and global" political ways of thinking, in contrast to the first steps of environmentalism of the 1960s (McCormick 1992: 88). In other words, activists maintained a non-ideological style partly in order to be accepted by the various political institutions involved.

Over the course of the decade left-wing groups became increasingly active in the anti-nuclear movement. They were particularly influential in France and West Germany, in contrast to the Netherlands and Scandinavia. In the wake of the student movement of 1968, many young people sought to emancipate themselves from the influence of the "Old Left" political parties, in particular the orthodox Communist parties. These activists, coming from various Maoist and Trotskyst or left-libertarian groups, were driven by Marxist-oriented claims about the domination and emancipation of populations,[7] but they were influenced by ideas of the "New Left" which emphasized decentralized and participatory politics as a way to reconnect with the masses (Kriesi *et al.* 1994; Kitschelt 1988). For them, nuclear energy, and its large capital investment and technological risks, became one of the most exciting opportunities to oppose industrial and political elites. In particular, they focused their demands against the hypothesis of the rise of the "Atomic State" at the expense of basic freedom and the right to demonstrate at nuclear plants.

The spread of anti-nuclear demands resulted in a large coalition of centrist environmentalist and radical left groups. Due to their profound differences, these groups competed for the leadership of the movement in specific places such as demonstrations, conferences, and activist as well as mainstream media. By this point, competition contributed to the cross-fertilization of meaning and symbols in a "spill over effect" (Mayer and Whittier 1994). Activists experienced the lack of democracy that characterized nuclear energy policies. Environmental activists became more aware that dealing with environmental issues was hampered by the power structure of state and nuclear industry interests. Left-wing activists became more concerned about the importance of rural environments and livelihood. As noted by most activists themselves, the environmental movement and left-wing groups borrowed each other's frames, to an extent.[8] Democracy, in this respect, represented a sort of magic slogan for these different groups (Bourdieu 1985: 740). It contributed to the convergence of these political tendencies.

This moment of unification of the anti-nuclear movement is based upon the rise of democratic demands about the autonomy of society. In this respect, Touraine is right about the rising convergence of environmental and left-wing political trends around "new" demands against technology. However, he overestimates the potential of such political change. Centrist environmental groups did not adopt economic claims and did not always manage to gain support from the trade unions and left-wing political parties which traditionally supported industrial development. At the opposite pole, left-wing groups began to develop a sharp critique of liberal democracy against the capitalist and repressive aspect of the state (Tokar 2008). Despite these strong differences, democracy became a transnational point of convergence for these activists, as shown by this representative declaration from the end of the 1970s:

> Opposition to nuclear energy is becoming a world-wide trans-national movement. It is the most advanced manifestation so far of a broad movement of opinion against a technocratic, centralized, authoritarian, undemocratic form of society. It strength and originality lies in the direct involvement of citizens, many previously uncritical or inactive, in deciding about things that affect them. But the forces behind the nuclear option already operate at the international level. It is therefore high time for the movement to organize a flow of information and experience that can enable its action to be more effective and better coordinated.
>
> (World Information Service about Nuclear Energy,
> Declaration of Intent 1978: 2)

In summary, the anti-nuclear movement is not reducible to the "new" environmental movement from the 1970s, but constitutes a locus of transnational power struggles between centrist environmentalist and left-wing political groups. It took a long time for the merging of environmental and economic demands to reshape the landscape of politics and protest in Western Europe during the 1980s and 1990s. On the one hand, the environmental centrist pole slowly converged with left-wing groups and political parties into the formation of European Green parties during the 1980s and 1990s (Rootes and Richardson 1995). On the other hand, radical environmental and left wings groups gave birth to radical ecology groups during the 1990s. This explains why the anti-nuclear movement can be seen as the cradle of political ecology, whether it developed inside or outside political institutions. As we shall see in the next section, in the case of the "Don't Nuke the Climate" coalition, the Copenhagen climate change summit constitutes another concrete step in the convergence of centrist environmental and left-wing groups.

Protest continuity and global democratic claims in the 2000s

A comparison between the anti-nuclear movement of the 1970s and the wave of protest that has emerged following the transnational protest of Seattle in 1999 reveals some interesting aspects of protest continuity. What made the anti-nuclear movement so special was its independence from major political parties, the use of various cultural symbols, and the short term and ad hoc nature of their organizations (Appleton 1999: 16). According to leading scholars, counter-summits and social forums received great media attention as a movement for "global justice", also referred to as the anti-neoliberal or alter-globalization movement (Sommier *et al.* 2007). Most of the research on the Global Justice Movement shows that it encompasses many former "new social movements" and shares similar demands about participatory democratic decision-making and autonomy with regards to the influence of political parties (Della Porta 2007b). The question of how the convergence of the anti-nuclear movement and Global Justice Movement is made possible remains, however. The "Don't Nuke the Climate" coalition sheds light on different, crucial aspects of such cooperation.

The convergence between centrist environmental groups and global justice groups is undoubtedly a striking aspect of the Copenhagen Summit. Since the beginning of the 2000s, these environmental activists have increasingly succeeded in constructing transnational claims that resonate with global issues. In particularl, they pushed forward the argument that new nuclear plants or uranium mining projects shouldn't be built in Southern countries. They established strong connections with local populations from these countries and invited them to come to Europe in order to present reports to the press. They emphasized the fact that such nuclear projects were harming the local populations and emphasized the invisible effects of nuclear industries and radioactive pollution. They also stressed the fact that these populations were not protected by strong national and international environmental safety legislations. This feature is not completely new, when compared with the 1970s, since the effects of nuclear industry in Iran, Brazil, and South Africa was also debated; at that time, however, anti-nuclear claims about technological risks were not presented as a global issue.

Second, such convergence also worked between radical ecology groups and global justice groups. Radical ecology groups insisted that the transnational nuclear industry is akin to the power of multinationals. Their discourse was largely based on the argument that nuclear industries only pursue economic growth, which is a typical Marxist-oriented frame. Radical ecology groups, especially in Copenhagen, presented projects to develop nuclear energy in the South as another form of capitalist "imperialism". This paved the way for further dialogue with other global justice groups, such as Attac, following the Rio Conference of 2002. This frame, however, was not accepted by centrist environmental organizations. This is true for Greenpeace, which defines itself more as an environmental interest group working with political institutions than as a radical ecology protest group. My interview data from Greenpeace activists indicates that, although they sometimes discuss social justice, they are more concerned by risks and renewable energy frames, while they doubt the political effectiveness of the social justice frame.[9] In fact, they can support, but not define themselves as part of, the Global Justice Movement.

Climate change controversy constitutes an important area of convergence between centrist environmental and radical ecology groups. Transnational coalitions have been working for climate justice since the end of the 1990s (Bandy and Smith 2005; Sandler and Peluzzo 2007). Over the last decade, the climate frame increasingly strengthened the image of a worldwide emergency and constituted a global common cause for protest groups from the anti-nuclear and Global Justice Movements. Environmental centrist activists became more aware of the critiques of capitalism, as global warming is produced by the complex configuration of industrial interests. Conversely, left-wing activists accepted that such climate crisis may also increase social inequalities (Flesher Fominaya, this volume, Chapter 7). Climate camps were extremely important in shaping the cross-fertilization processes between environmental and left-wing activists in this respect (Scholl, this volume, Chapter 8). Interviews confirm that such convergence became increasingly important during the 2000s:

> Twenty years ago, I was not ecological at all. I cared about the environment, but I thought that the social issue was a priority. Because I was part of the old model of the workers' movement: there are those who fight for a better distribution of wealth, and those who fight for quality of life, and the latter was considered as a little bit bourgeois. Nowadays, global social inequalities have increased due to wars, climate change, resource depletion and biodiversity. All this. One cannot distinguish the two. You can't have the Earth without people, and people without the Earth.
>
> (Interview with a former campaigner on nuclear energy of Greenpeace France and activist of the French network "Sortir du Nucléaire", 26 September 2011, Paris)

The wind also blew in the other direction, as global justice groups became increasingly interested in an alliance with environmental centrist and radical ecology groups around climate change themes. During the 2000s, global justice events experienced a slow decrease in protests, marked by the difficulty in sustaining global demonstrations and media coverage over time. The formation of new transnational climate networks, such as Climate Justice Action and Climate Justice Now, reflects the concern to include a broad range of groups in making demands on international organizations. They called for direct non-violent actions to celebrate the 10th anniversary of Seattle, including the blockade of the harbour. The symbol of Seattle can be seen as an attempt to expand the boundary of protest and a way to increase the transnational audience of global justice claims. Some anti-nuclear activists from the No-Nuke Coalition declared themselves to be sympathetic to the initiative, even though most of them remained outside the direct action protests.

The Climate Change Copenhagen summit highlights the fact that the convergence between anti-nuclear and global justice groups is mainly based on demands against the power of transnational industries at the expense of local and national populations. It shows that environmental and economic demands have become more integrated within the various transnational networks that fight against the development of nuclear energy. As in the 1970s, "old" and "new" characteristics of social movements are presented under the rubric of "democracy", which works as a slogan for making alliances between environmental and global justice groups possible. This reinforces the hypothesis that, beyond the political diversity of its members, the Global Justice Movement has become a "movement of movements". However, closer scrutiny may show that these similarities are misleading because transnational coalitions are very much "rooted" in specific national conditions (Tarrow and Della Porta 2005: 228). The next section will explore more precisely how the mix of the "new" and "old" divisions plays out differently in specific national political settings such as France, Germany, and the Netherlands.

Mapping the national imprint of global justice protest

The social movements literature has not yet addressed the question of whether alliances of transnational networks are constrained by the influence of political parties. Yet political parties can have significant influence upon the emergence, strength and alliances of social movements, particularly at a national level. For example, the position of the Communist Party on nuclear energy has improved or decreased the influence of ecological groups within national anti-nuclear movements (Duyvendak 1994). In other words, in countries in which the Communist Party has been strong, the anti-nuclear movement has been less important and much less influential upon national politics. This also explains why, in a country such as France, anti-nuclear movements have attempted to enter national politics by giving birth to a Green political party (Rootes and Richardson 1995). As a whole, the strength of Communist parties has influenced how far left Green political parties have stood. Our argument is that understanding the historical evolution of the relationship between Communist and Green parties can help in grasping the different forms of alliances between the Global Justice Movement and the Green Party.

The relationship between Communist Parties and Green Parties in Europe is varied. Three cases can be identified, depending on how influential the orthodox Communist Party was in the 1970s and 1980s. In France, the Communist Party (*Parti Communiste Français*) was highly influential upon the position of left-wing political parties up until the 1980s, and the Green Party (*Les Verts*), as a different political party, clearly exhibits a strong left-leaning structure. In West Germany, the Communist Party (the DKP; *Deutsche Kommunistische Partei*) was rather weak during the 1970s, but most small unorthodox communist groups contributed to the creation of the Green Party (*Die Grünen*). In the Netherlands, the Communist Party (*Niederlandische Kommunistische Partij*) was again rather weak during the 1970s, and merged with other small political parties in the Green party (*GroenLinks*). We might assume *a priori* that when Communist Parties and "old" features are strong, Green parties are more likely to become left-wing oriented and ally with global justice groups. However, this doesn't take into account the specific positions which individual Communist Parties took on nuclear energy.

The Global Justice Movement in France is quite strong, and yet its alliance with the Green party is somewhat weak. The position of the Communist party is a strong explanatory factor here. Since the Second World War, the French Communist Party has taken a strong position in favour of developed nuclear energy on the grounds that it contributes to national independence (Nelkin and Pollack 1980: 131–132). Since its inception in 1996, Attac France, one of the leading organizations in the French Global Justice Movement, has been somewhat influenced by the Communist position regarding the development of nuclear energy in France. As a result, although left-leaning anti-nuclear groups have attempted to initiate discussions about this, Attac have been extremely reluctant to consider nuclear energy as part of the global justice agenda. It was only in 2005, when Attac experienced a political crisis vis-à-vis the communist legacy, that its members began to adopt a more inclusive attitude towards environmental and anti-nuclear claims, albeit rather cautiously.

In the Netherlands, the Global Justice Movement is quite weak and its alliance with the Green party is also quite weak due to the strength of "new" features. As in the case of Germany, the Communist Party adopted a position against nuclear energy during the 1970s and 1980s, thus developing a connection with centrist environmental groups. As a communist party, it has been less aligned to the traditionalist position of the French Communist party and quite open to "new" demands. Similarly, due to the strength of "new" features, the Green Party in the Netherlands became more economically liberal than in France, even though it can adopt claims in favour of social justice. As a whole, the weakness of "old features" meant a lack of energy for the creation of global justice groups. In fact, Attac in the Netherlands only moved closer to the formerly Maoist Dutch Socialist party *(Socialistische Partij) after* its electoral success. But, overall, both the anti-nuclear and Global Justice Movements are rather weak and do not cooperate to a great degree.

In Germany, the Global Justice Movement is strong and its alliance with the Green Party is much more significant than in France. Unlike in France, the Communist Party has been quite active against nuclear energy (Nelkin and Pollack 1980). As in the Netherlands, it also remained fairly weak during the 1970s and 1980s due to the fragmentation of extreme-left groups. However, during this period of time, the "old" features were much stronger than in the Netherlands and small extreme-left groups were influential in the creation of the Green Party. As a consequence, the latter remained quite left-oriented. For this reason, the "old" and "new" characteristics have integrated quite well. We can better understand why the global justice group Attac, since its inception in 1999, has been strong in Germany and "was founded to provide a space for all kinds of actors that are critical to neo-liberal globalization, regardless of their ideological point of view" (Rucht *et al.* 2007: 17). However, according to Rucht, direct contact between the Green Party and the Global Justice Movement is rather weak and informal:

> Whereas these foundations prove to be important alliance partners for movement actors, political parties have lost this connectivity. Compared to the 1980s and most part of the 1990s, when green and social democratic parties were part of or closely connected to new social movements, an ongoing process of alienation can be observed on the side of social movements, since the former partners became members of the federal government in 1998.
>
> (Rucht *et al.* 2007: 10–11)

This brief discussion shows that cooperation between the green political party and the Global Justice Movement is curvilinear (Kriesi 1994). In principle, if "old" features are important in a country, one can expect a greater convergence of ecological and global justice actors, and vice versa where "new" features are prevailing. However, the specific history of anti-nuclear groups offers a more nuanced perspective on how "old features" facilitate or prevent such convergence. Having said this, we must stress the fact that the relationship between political parties and global justice groups is not a strong one, even in Germany. To a large extent, Global Justice Movements remain independent from the influence of political parties. Taking a step back, this may help us to understand why the Global Justice Movement, according to Della Porta (2005a: 201), "finds itself tackling the difficult search for democratic institutions that are not just participatory, but also influencing public policies in the direction of social justice".

Conclusion

The coming together of environmental, anti-nuclear and global justice groups bears witness to the fact that the differences between the first and second wave of protests from the 1970s and 2000s are not clear-cut. First, environmental and anti-nuclear groups mobilized transnational protest and conferences on the basis of democratic claims, but also against the power of transnational nuclear industries with large capital investment. Moreover, the anti-nuclear movement was a pole of attraction during the 1970s for many groups which became involved in the Global Justice Movement. This historical linkage shows a clear continuity of transnational protest over time.

Second, this chapter argues that the anti-nuclear movement's legacy consists of the processes of alliances and conflicts that shape protest. On the one hand, the anti-nuclear and Global Justice Movements share similar demands transnationally about how a democratic participatory approach could change the functioning of social movements and political decision-making. On the other hand, the anti-nuclear movement shapes global justice protest because of the way "new" and "old" collective identities are still polarized. In fact, neither the anti-nuclear nor the Global Justice Movement are "new" social movements. They each form a "nexus" of relationship between environmental and left-wing groups.

However, there are also strong differences between the anti-nuclear and Global Justice Movements which must be underlined. First, transnational networks and counter-summits were much broader in scope during the 2000s than they had been in the 1970s. While the anti-nuclear movement was particularly strong in Europe and the United States, global protests were carried out in Southern countries. Second, Global Justice Movement demands are also more global in scope. While the anti-nuclear movement mobilized particularly against the centralization and repression of the state, global justice demands are much more oriented towards the North–South divide and worldwide social inequalities.

This chapter shows that the anti-nuclear movement has evolved from a centrepoint of protest in the 1970s to a component of the Global Justice Movement in the 2000s. However, this evolution is not true for all of the countries discussed here. Historical analysis reveals that arguments about newness or radical rupture do not stand up to scrutiny, and national contexts influence the strength and development of "global" movements.

Notes

1 This chapter draws on 60 semi-structured interviews with participants from the anti-nuclear movement in France, the Netherlands and Germany, quantitative network analysis, participant observation before and during the climate change Copenhagen Summit from 11–18 December 2009 and the use of archives from Paris, Amsterdam and Berlin. Many thanks to all activists who helped me in the field, and to Kimberly Hagen, PhD student, Open University, Geography Department, for her helpful comments on earlier drafts.
2 The transnational coalition "Don't Nuke The Climate" is composed of the following groups: Greenpeace International, International Forum on Globalization, Women for a Common Future in Europe (WECF), the French network "Sortir du Nucléaire", the Dutch network "WISE Amsterdam", Legambiente from Italy, Women Against Nuclear Power from Sweden, and Urgewald from Germany. All information and data about the campaign can be found on the website of the coalition. URL: www.dont-nuke-the-climate.org/index.php?lang=en.

3 Press release, "Une marée humaine pacifique envahit Copenhague", Reuters, 12 December 2000, author's translation.

4

> In the environmental field, we can generally distinguish among three groups. First, there are the traditional conservation groups which in some cases can trace their origin to the late nineteenth century. Primarily concerned with the preservation of the countryside [...] some of these groups in the 1970s also participated in campaigns on "new" environmental issues including nuclear power. These groups generally do not aim to effect broader political and social change. Second, there are the new environmental groups formed mainly in the early 1970s. Their limitation to single issues, at least initially, was less strict, arising out of a more global ecological concern. While some groups adopted a more radical ecological philosophy and forms of action during the 1970s, others maintained a non-political and non-ideological style, restricting themselves to single-issue campaigning, although they usually span a broader range of issues than conservation groups. Where direct action is used, it is only in an effort to attract media attention. [...]. Third, we have the radical ecology movement. Most of these groups were at first primarily concerned with nuclear energy; their ideological stance is often strongly influenced by New Left thinking. Mass demonstrations, direct action and, in general, grassroots mobilization are seen as the main forms of actions .

> (Rudig 1988: 30)

5 At the beginning of the 1980s, the Euromissiles controversy shifted the attention of anti-nuclear activists towards pacifism, especially in the Netherlands and Germany.
6 Interview with a Dutch activist from a local group, Middleburg, Netherlands, 11 February 2011.
7 Interview with a French activist from an anarchist group of the 1970s, Vannes, France, 9 June 2009.
8 As stated by one Dutch activist:

> The environmental movement has become more politicized and the political parties have become more ecological. The point of view is now that the technological development is actually determined by power relations, and the way the production is organized. [...] The demands for more democracy are resulting from this.

> (Peter Lammers, Friends of the Earth Netherlands, in Cramer 1989)

9 Interview with a campaigner from Greenpeace International, Amsterdam, The Netherlands, 13 September 2010.

References

Appleton, A. 1999. "The New Social Movement Phenomenon". *West European Politics*, 22 (4), pp. 57–75.

Bandy, J. and Smith, J. eds. 2005. *Coalition Across Borders*. New York: Rowman & Littlefield.

Bourdieu, P. 1985. "The social space and the genesis of the group". *Theory and Society*, 14 (6), pp. 723–744.

Bourdieu, P. 1989. "Social space and symbolic power". *Sociological theory*, 7 (1), pp. 14–25.

Bourdieu, P. 1991. *Language and Symbolic Power.* Cambridge, Harvard University Press.

Carter, N. 2001. *The Politics of the Environment.* Cambridge University Press.

Cramer, J. 1989. "The Rise and Fall of New Knowledge Interests in the Dutch Environmental Movement", *The Environmentalist*, 9 (2), pp. 101–120.

Della Porta, D. 2005a. "Multiple Belongings, Tolerant Identities, and the Construction of 'Another Politics'". In D. Della Porta and S. Tarrow, eds. *Transnational Protest and Global Activism*. Lanham: Rowman & Littlefield, pp. 175–202.

Della Porta, D. ed. 2007b. *The Global Justice Movement.* Boulder: Paradigm.

Doherty, B. 2006. "Friends of the Earth International". *Environmental Politics*, 15 (5), pp. 860–880.

Duyvendak, J.W. 1994. *The Power of Politics.* Boulder: Westview Press.

Flam, H. ed. 1994. *States and Anti-Nuclear Movements.* Edinburgh: Edinburgh University Press.

Flesher Fominaya, C. 2013. "Movement Culture Continuity". In C. Flesher Fominaya and L. Cox, eds. *Understanding European Movements*. London: Routledge.

Hayes, G. 2002. *Environmental Protest and the State in France*. Basingstoke: Palgrave Macmillan.

Kitschelt, H. 1986. "Political Opportunity Structures and Political Protest". *British Journal of Political Science*, 16 (1), pp. 57–86.

Kitschelt, H. 1988. "Left Libertarian Politics". *World Politics*, 40 (2), pp. 194–231.

Kriesi, H., Koopmans, R., Duyvendak, J.W. and Giugni, M. 1995. *New Social Movements in Western Europe*, Minneapolis, University of Minnesota Press.

Mayer, D. and Whittier, N. 1994. "Social movement spillover". *Social Problems*, 41 (2), pp. 277–298.

McAdam, D. and Rucht, D. 1993. "The Cross-National Diffusion of Movement Ideas". *Annals of the American Academy of Political and Social Science*, 528, pp. 56–74.

McCormick, J. 1992, *The Global Environmental Movement.* Indiana University Press.

Melucci, A. 1996. *Challenging Codes at the Information Age*, Cambridge: Cambridge University Press.

Nelkin, D. and Pollak, M. 1980. "Political Parties and the Nuclear Energy Debate in France and Germany". *Comparative Politics*, 12 (2), pp. 127–141.

Passy, F. and Bandler, M. 2003. "Protestation altermondialiste". *Annual Conference of the Swiss, German and Austrian political science association*, Berne, 14–15 November 2003, pp. 1–16.

Rootes, C. 2005. "A Limited Transnationalization?". In D. Della Porta and S. Tarrow, eds. *Transnational Protest and Global Activism*. Oxford: Rowman and Littlefield, pp. 21–45.

Rootes, C. 2008. "1968 and the Environmental Movement in Europe". In M. Klimke and S. Joachim. eds. *1968 in Europe*, Oxford: Oxford University Press, pp. 295–305.

Rootes, R. and Richardson, D. eds. 1995, *The Green Challenge.* London, Routledge.

Rucht, D., Teune, T. and Mundo, Y. 2007. "The History and Structure of Global Justice Movements in Germany", *ACI Conference: "Généalogie comparative des mouvements altermondialistes"*, Paris, 30 September–1 October, pp. 1–27.

Rudig, W. 1988. "Peace and Ecology movements in Western Europe". *West European Politics*, 11 (1), pp. 26–39.

Rudig, W. 1990. *Anti-nuclear Movements*. Longman international.

Sandler, R. and Peluzzo, P.C. eds. 2007. *Environmental Justice and Environmentalism.* MIT press.

Scholl, C. 2013. "Europe as Contagious Space". In C. Flesher Fominaya and L. Cox, eds. *Understanding European Movements*. London: Routledge.

Sommier, I. 2003. *Le Renouveau des Mouvements Contestataires à l'Heure de la Mondialisation*. Paris: Flammarion.

Sommier, I., Filleule, O. and Agrikoliansky, E. eds. 2007. *Généalogie des mouvements altermondialiste en Europe.* Paris: Karthala.

Tarrow, S. and Della Porta, D. 2005. "Globalization, Complex Internationalism and Transnational Contention". In D. Della Porta and S. Tarrow, eds. *Transnational Protest and Global Activism.* Lanham: Rowman and Littlefield, pp. 227–246.

Tokar, B. 2008. "On Bookchin's Social Ecology and its Contribution to Social Movements". *Capitalism, Nature, Socialism,* 19 (1), pp. 51–66.

Touraine, A. ed. 1980. *La prophétie anti-nucléaire.* Paris: Seuil.

Van Der Heijden, A, 1997. "Political Opportunity Structure and the Institutionnalisation of the Environmental Movement", *Environmental Politics,* 6 (4), pp. 22–50.

World Information Service about Nuclear Energy, Declaration of Intent, 1978. Wise International, Bulletin, (1), May 1978, pp. 1–16

5 Where global meets local

Italian social centres and the alterglobalization movement

Andrea Membretti and Pierpaolo Mudu

Introduction

This chapter highlights the long-lasting interaction between an Italian political and socio-cultural phenomenon, the *Centri Sociali Autogestiti* (self-managed social centres) and the alterglobalization movement. *Centri Sociali* are significant actors, notably in urban areas, and their history comes directly from the 1970s. Today they involve thousands of activists and their presence characterizes most large and medium-sized Italian cities. It is estimated that there are about 130 around the country, often operating in squatted buildings, offering social services, organizing cultural events and acting as political subjects.

This chapter is organized into two main sections. The first one presents an analysis of the origins and the development of these *Centri Sociali*. The second section explores the link between the *Centri Sociali* and the alterglobalization movement. In the conclusion we highlight the relevance of the construction of space by the *Centri Sociali* in terms of opening new interfaces of opportunities for those looking for alternatives to neo-liberal domination. These opportunities are linked to expanding conceptualizations and tools for networking and communication, supporting new struggles for the commons, and experimenting with alternative decision-making processes.

The development of *Centri Sociali*

Centri Sociali originate through squatting in abandoned buildings and are run, through self-management, by collectives which were originally, in terms of political orientation, radical left, autonomous or anarchist. According to Membretti (2007) and Mudu (2004), and considering the origins of this social phenomenon, it is possible to define a *Centro Sociale Autogestito* as:

- a network of people characterized by a heterogenous socio-cultural and generational composition (although young people often predominate)
- following different leftist ideologies and traditions by participating in a symbolic frame and a repertoire of practices, oriented towards a radical change of society

- sharing the same space, usually an illegally occupied abandoned building (generally in large or medium-sized cities) where they:
  - develop a collective identity;
  - build or enlarge a local and extra-local network of movement relationships (a "movement area");
  - have an internal organization based on non-hierarchical self-management (*autogestione*);
  - mostly focus their actions on the dimensions of non-commodified social relations (that is, the possibility of being together without being in a commercial framework), counter-cultural events and welfare services.

Space plays an important role, as it is the main resource (often contested by different urban actors) both for collective action and for the development of a group identity. In fact, *Centri Sociali* originated as a spatialized actor (they are physical *centres* in defined urban neighbourhoods), and established an ongoing dialectic with other movements and with political institutions, inside a specific and multi-scalar socio-political milieu.

The first generation of *Centri Sociali* emerged in the 1970s, during the long cycle of struggles that animated Italy for a decade, starting in 1969 (Balestrini and Moroni 1997; see also Osterweil, this volume, Chapter 2). *Autonomia Operaia* became a relevant part of this movement due to its strong antisystemic attitude, contesting the legitimacy of the corrupt Italian state (Balestrini and Moroni 1997). The 1970s Italian movement not only employed the full repertoire of working-class struggle, but also sowed the seeds for subsequent new social movements (NSMs) involved in environmental struggles and reclaiming rights and identities.

In Italy NSMs took the form of "urban social movements" with many peculiar aspects. According to the NSM approach (Melucci 1984, 1989; Della Porta and Diani 2006) *Centri Sociali* represented a "movement area" (Melucci 1984), i.e. a network of (g)local actors sharing a common counter-culture and communicating/interacting with each other, even if not unified by a strong ideology or by defined common goals. They represented the territorial and physical expression of a social and cultural milieu, claiming *new rights of citizenship*, as they were defined by NSMs in the 1970s (Melucci 1984). *Centri Sociali* were primarily rooted in their neighbourhoods (mainly blue collar), expressing the needs and the claims of the people living in them, particularly young people. A new generation – deeply involved with the 1977 movement that saw the end of a harsh long-term confrontation with the Italian authorities via a large series of demonstrations, revolts and refusal of the Italian way of life – was facing the risk of social exclusion from both welfare state and labour market, as a consequence of the radical transformation produced by the end of the industrial era and the dramatic transition to a post-industrial one. In the 1970s, animated by this young generation, *Centri Sociali* were mainly born inside the "extra-parliamentary" Left, and were immediately characterized by a particular attention to the spatial dimension of their action and identity. In fact, they called for a bottom-up participation in the transformation of urban power relations, based on the concept of self-representation of interests (a form of direct democracy), which first had to deal with running the physical squatted space as a liberated and participative public place (Membretti 2007). From the beginning, housing, social and cultural services, and non-commodified social relations were the main themes. Moving beyond the local dimension and away from their illegally occupied spaces, *Centri Sociali* contested representative democracy and institutional dynamics, considered to be a means of socially suffocating and integrating any dissent. They proposed a particular approach to the definition of the traditional class conflict, declining it as the contraposition between peripheral/popular spaces and central/bourgeois ones, inside cities that were intended as political fields for building localized forms of "counter-power", within a wider non-local and network perspective.

The birth of *Centri Sociali* also meant a shift in political action from organized forms of activism and militancies to experimenting with alternative ways to form subjectivities resistant to dominant capitalist trends (Foucault 1982). Subjectification – that is, the ways of producing a socially submissive subject – is called into question by *Centri Sociali*, at least for an important segment of relational life. The process of domination is challenged through resisting, with an agency that takes place through the practice and transformation of social relations and activities, in a way that also resembles a development of Marcuse's proposals on radical subjectivity (Marcuse 1964). Marcuse argued that

> the existing society is organized precisely to prevent such a reconstruction of subjectivity and new social relations, prescribing instead a regime of domination, authority, repression, manipulative desublimation, and submission. [...] Instead of the need for repressive performance and competition, the new sensibility posits the need for meaningful work, gratification, and community; instead of the need for aggression and destructive productivity, it affirms love and the preservation of the environment; and against the demands of industrialization, it asserts the need for beauty, sensuousness, and play, affirming the aesthetic and erotic components of experience.
>
> (Kellner 2001: 94)

In *Centri Sociali* people developed the refusal of patterns of domination, being conscious of the failed experience of the 1960s based on love, sensuality and erotic liberation.

The experience of the first generation of *Centri Sociali* finished at the end of the 1970s. The beginning of the 1980s was characterized by the end of the previous period of social mobilization, strongly linked to the transition of western societies to a post-industrial economy and to a radical re-organization of urban regimes. In this context, *Centri Sociali* tended to become increasingly alien subjects inside their changing neighbourhoods, progressively losing their linkages with a social composition that was shifting from the working-class dimension to a white-collar one and to new forms of employment. Gentrification and the spread of heroin pushed out several of these actors; meanwhile, local authorities made an effort towards a generalized eviction of squatted places. *Centri Sociali* became isolated and ghettoized inside the wider society as their capacity to maintain extra-local relationships decreased: the squatted space became the last frontier to be defended by its occupants, in some cases through conflict with the surrounding neighbourhoods.

In the second half of the 1980s a second generation of *Centri Sociali* materialized. Examples of squatting known in other countries of Europe (for example Germany, Switzerland and the Netherlands) were discussed, but the movement was characterized by mixing together a new generation of activists. In big Italian cities, autonomists, punks and underground cultures were intermixed, originating a new wave of *Centri Sociali* (Moroni *et al.* 1995; Dazieri 1996; Mudu 2012). This "contamination" had been built through a conscious spatial strategy where *Centri Sociali* constituted spaces of "amalgamation" for self-management practices (Mudu 2012). In the second half of the 1980s there was a conscious recognition in *Centri Sociali* of a previous condition of ghettoization, and the goal of breaking out of the ghetto was clearly identified, amalgamating the apparently irreconcilable figures of punks, autonomists, students, former leftist militants, and precarious working-class youth. This amalgamation happened through building self-managed projects (to produce non-commercial music, for example) and an intense networking that linked a new disconnected generation at local and national levels (Mudu 2012). This spatial strategy constituted a multiscalar perspective which quickly started to break the ghettoization and sociopolitical isolation and constraints inherited from previous conflicts. Nevertheless, from their origins, *Centri Sociali* represented a complex collective experience with significant geographical differences, when considering the case of northern Italy (Montagna 2006; Membretti 2003), or with Milan (Ibba 1995; Ruggiero 2000) very different from Turin (Berzano *et al.* 2002) and Rome (Mudu 2005) from Naples (Dines 1999).

From the beginning, *Centri Sociali* have kept an international perspective alive, which is linked to two main features: international solidarity (inside an anti-imperialistic ideology), which was mostly a heritage from the 1970s, and the circulation of non-commercial music, mostly punk or ragamuffin.

In 1990, another crucial phase of development of *Centri Sociali* followed the national wave of protest carried out by the student movement against the privatization of universities. This movement, highly diversified and only lightly ideological, represented a great opportunity for *Centri Sociali* to break their socio-political isolation: students, looking for places in which to meet and organize activities, found an important physical and socio-cultural resource in these occupied spaces. Moreover, the student movement carried out a new wave of squatting, creating new *Centri Sociali*, partially inspired by the symbolic horizon of the old ones and viewing the practice of self-management as a crucial point, but attaching different and particular approaches to the meaning of squatting and to the goals to be achieved through it. The squatted space became a resource to invest in a wider arena, avoiding any temptation to localism and

Figure 5.1 1988. Internationalism: the boycott campaign against the South African and Israeli governments.

self-defence. This new attitude contributed to transforming the image of *Centri Sociali* as it was perceived by other socio-political actors and by some aspects of public opinion. *Centri Sociali* started to be considered as public spaces, characterized by a political approach to change reality and, at the same time, to be open to different populations (e.g. migrants) and groups (e.g. students) and open to embrace new political issues such as knowledge transmission or migrants' needs. *Centri Sociali* developed an original music scene of hip-hop bands which became famous all over Italy. New organizational and professional skills were developed by activists, setting the basis for subsequent internal debate about the role of *Centri Sociali* in transforming urban environments and the wisdom or otherwise of accepting legalization and managing them as "social enterprises" –

that is, to organize public activities with an economic dimension in order to provide socially and politically oriented services. In this sense, the original idea from the 1970s – of "spatial networks" organizing a self-managed response to welfare and cultural needs of their surrounding neighbourhoods – was resuscitated and re-invented on a metropolitan scale, attracting people from larger areas: this marked the beginning of new "glocal" identities and practices. In the 1990s *Centri Sociali* animated a strong debate about their possible role in the transition from welfare state to welfare communities. It was also in this period that they participated actively in the building of the alterglobalization movement, both on the socio-cultural and political levels.

In the 1990s it was clear that people participating in *Centri Sociali* were linked by different political networks. *Autonomia* did not exist anymore, and two groups of post-autonomists emerged: the North-Eastern groups (later *Tute Bianche* and then the *Disobbedienti* network), which had civil disobedience and direct actions in their repertoire of conflict, and the rank-and-file radical union of Cobas (Comitati di Base). By the end of the 1990s, the alterglobalization movement in Italy constituted a diversified network of associations, informal groups and political parties, at that time mostly reunited under the name of "*Rete No Global*" (Anti-globalization Network). The three main areas of this wide network included: *Centri Sociali* (with various distinctions), the *Lilliput* network (Catholic groups and environmental associations) and leftist associations and parties (e.g. *Attac*, *Rifondazione Comunista*). To complete the picture it is worth adding that, at the beginning of the century, many *Centri Sociali* had anarchist inclinations, while others had orthodox Marxist influences, or were radical without a particular attachment (Mudu 2009).

At the beginning of the new millennium, political analysis and priorities were changing and some *Centri Sociali* were directly involved in important public campaigns and events inside the alterglobalization movement, based around the promotion of sustainable development, fair trade, and the defence of the commons. For example, *Centri Sociali* organized and hosted meetings and exhibitions of the so-called "new rurality", co-operating with French movements of peasants or with the Italian groups and associations promoting fair trade and the "agriculture of proximity" (e.g. the "*terra/Terra*", "*Genuino Clandestino*", *campiaperti* projects) and the related call for an anti-capitalist approach to the use of the land and to the production/marketing of food. Several *Centri Sociali* supported the recent national referendum in Italy (2011) against the privatization of the commons, particularly water, and offered their spaces and resources to local committees, active in this field, within a wider national and international network of groups, part of the alterglobalization movement.

Some theoretical considerations on the development of *Centri Sociali*

Even though *Centri Sociali* represent a diverse and often divided movement area (Melucci 1984, 1989), for more than three decades they have come together to

Figure 5.2 2008: national event in support of local agriculture and against capitalist land grabs. Centro Sociale Leoncavallo, Milan.

collaborate in building and preserving *situated* and self-organized socio-political networks, autonomous from official institutions and political parties, and acting as alternatives to the cultural and economical mainstream (Mudu 2004). Most of these networks, while coming to terms with past periods of closure and self-defence from external "threats", have increasingly developed an orientation towards their relationship with the space around them – in terms of dialectics and conflict, but also of attempted representation of local issues (Membretti 2007, 2010), as well as with an "outside world" which is increasingly globalized.

The construction of *Centri Sociali* spatiality is the result of a complex mixture of factors: (1) the composition of participants; (2) squatted place; and (3) political context. *Centri Sociali* mirror the composition of society, but a crucial difference is the possibility of exploring the development of radical subjectivities and a range of alternative forms to neo-liberal domination processes (Aaster *et al.* 1995). In particular, they extend decision-making arenas for intersubjective agreement about far more issues than those which liberals recognize as public (Purcell 2008).

The squatted places constitute a long list of abandoned buildings that do not present a common typology, except insofar as they are all post-industrial permanencies, often awaiting demolition or radically transformation by so-called urban regeneration policies. Schools, factories, shops, cinemas: any space can be a *Centro Sociale*. Space can open or limit the possibilities available to these actors: large factories can host dozens of different activities, while a small shop can host just a few. Police repression, particularly in small cities, or attacks by groups of fascists in big cities, can represent serious constraints on action. Squatting – the occupation of an abandoned place – is a space–time transformation, mixing the time of origin and the space to be transformed. Although completely transformed in its social use, the squatted place is usually renamed in continuity with its origins; often the former name is adopted, followed by "*occupato*" (occupied) or preceded by "*ex*" ("former"); in other cases a new name is proposed. This re-appropriation of space through using "ex", proclaims the linguistic break-up of the former social space and a renewed, antagonistic existence (Tiddi 1997). Squatting, graffiti and posters mean the insertion of different signs, different visual stimuli in a neighbourhood (Martínez 2007). The label "*Centro Sociale*" represents the fast and irreversible appropriation of an old label attached to community centres run by local authorities (Sommier 1998). The places of *Centri Sociali* emerge as particular forms of space, ones created through acts of naming as well as the distinctive activities and symbols associated with the people squatting. In this labelling process, the adjective "*autogestito*" ("self-managed"), which all these actors use to describe their spaces and how they organize them, is also very important. *Centri Sociali*, despite their internal and ongoing tensions and ideological differences (Piazza 2011; Mudu 2012), have developed a common background of practices and repertoires. This first concerns their approach to organizing their inner and external spaces. Following Weick's approach (1995), we could say that, if "organizing is sense-making", it can be also an activity of "space-making". Second, there is a common framing of human and inter-cultural relationships operated in this way of organizing through the practice of *autogestione* (self-management).

Political context can be interpreted through scalar strategies. Attention to implicit conceptualizations of space is crucial to practices of resistance and of building alternatives (Massey 2005). Many *Centri Sociali* defy easy categorization, tending to be multifaceted, heterogeneous and open, rather than homogeneous and bounded. *Centri Sociali* have been defined as "virtual communities" (Adinolfi *et al.* 1994), but they refused the idea of community, while virtuality can equally be found in short-term social relations posted on the web. *Centri Sociali* have also been defined as "concrete utopias" (Rampallo and Vaccaro 1993; Tiddi 1997), but utopias are sites with no real place (Foucault 1967). *Centri Sociali* are more similar to "hetero-topias of deviation", "in which individuals, whose behaviour is deviant in relation to the required mean or norm, are placed" (Foucault 1986: 25). In general terms, *Centri Sociali* try to keep the boundaries of their squatted places open and porous: embodiment in the different *Centri Sociali* is the first scale to be considered. In theoretical terms, it is important to consider that places are progressively experi-enced: "a place is a complex of intersections and outcomes of power geometries that operate across many spatial scales, from the body to the global" (Massey 2005). In *Centri Sociali* the experience of placing oneself within a social space happens through different power geometries from the dominant ones. For example, a par-ticular emphasis is put on having people not being passive recipients of events, but taking action and overturning gender dominance. This means operating a conver-gence of practices in order to put the representation of space and its representational forms in close proximity (Lefebvre 1991). Representation of space is operated by all of those who identify what is lived and what is perceived with what is conceived, while a space directly lived through its associated symbols is the space which the imagination seeks to change and appropriate (Lefebvre 1991). In *Centri Sociali* the space of discourses, conceptualizing and planning overlaps with space lived through images and symbols linked to the clandestine or underground side of social life, and to art (Lefebvre 1991). Over the years, the practices of resistance developed by the *Centri Sociali* combined many issues, and made them break out of self-ghettoization and rescale their action (Figure 5.3, next page).

This tension between a desired kind of spatial autonomy[1] and, at the same time, a re-conceptualization of the relationship with the surrounding space, in a glocal approach, has been the basis of the *enactment*[2] (Weick 2003) operated by *Centri Sociali* in relation to their physical and socio-cultural environment. This phenomenon can also be described as a reaction to one of the main aspects of globalization, i.e. the crisis of the dimension of place (Augé 1993), related to a general process of re-organization of space, pushed by the post-industrial socio-economic restructuration (Swyngedouw 1997) and correlated socio-cultural transformations, such as disembedding processes (Giddens 1991).

Two main different approaches to the role of *Centri Sociali* within society faced each other in the movement (Membretti 2007): one focused on the opportunity to develop a network of self-managed cultural and social services in order to attract

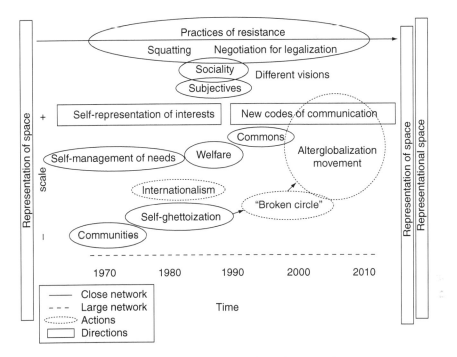

Figure 5.3 Centri Sociali: the rescaling of action through time and space.

more people inside these spaces and to involve them in the construction of a bottom-up political alternative to the privatization of welfare and of the entire society. The other approach connected to the heritage of the 1970s, understood *Centri Sociali* as a kind of political vanguard in an emerging post-industrial class conflict, emphasizing the necessity of building strong political identities and networks, aiming towards a revolutionary process. Other approaches were also developed; for example, many anarchists still considered it possible to disconnect themselves from dominant social trends by building *Centri Sociali* with no local connections but networked among themselves to allow survival and mobility of sympathizers.

The case of Leoncavallo, the most famous Italian social centre, shows, in different ways and at different scales, how several *Centri Sociali* have operated in the last 30 years as providers of self-managed public services (Membretti 2003). These services developed, informally, as a response to two different but intertwined categories of needs: the first concerned with culture and sociality, the second with welfare and social needs. Since the beginning of the 1990s, several *Centri Sociali* have reacted to the growing demand for spaces for the production of an autonomous and non-commodified culture offering opportunities for social exchange, under the banner of non-exploitative relationships between people. Sociality and cultural needs cross traditional class boundaries: some internal surveys, carried out among users of *Centri Sociali* cultural services, show how attendance at concerts, plays, debates and exhibitions is largely diversified according to age, gender, work conditions and place of residence. An increasing number of *Centri Sociali* have been operating in a field that could be defined as "civil welfare" (de Leonardis 1998) – services strongly inter-related with the citizenship dimension, i.e. the concrete response to those basic rights (right to food, clothing, housing, health), without which a human being not only cannot be defined as a citizen, but cannot even possess human dignity. The demand for these services arises from migrants, the homeless, people with mental health issues and, more generally, people below the poverty threshold.

Centri Sociali and the alterglobalization movement: spatialized networks for a glocal action

In Italy, the unofficial birth of the alterglobalization movement is usually linked to the Zapatista uprising in Chiapas, Mexico. On 1 January 1994, the Zapatistas issued their First Declaration of the Lacandon Jungle and their Revolutionary Laws. The day chosen was the day when the North American Free Trade Agreement (NAFTA) came into effect. The Zapatistas immediately received the attention of the Italian radical left activists and *Centri Sociali*. In the history of Italians solidarity movements, Latin America has always been more central than any other part of the world. Furthermore, the Sandinista experience in Nicaragua had ended in 1989, leaving a huge void in the Italian radical left. In 1996 the "First Intercontinental Meeting for Humanity and against Neoliberalism" was organized in Chiapas. Many individuals and groups from Italy participated; most were part of the *Centri Sociali* network. The activities were not only in support of the Zapatistas' struggle, but also involved sharing practices and ideas. An association dedicated to this purpose, called *Ya Basta!*, was created in 1994. It is still operating, mainly in the North of Italy,[3] and for several years it has been hosted inside the Leoncavallo social centre in Milan.

After the Seattle protest of 1999, the 2000 World Bank meeting in Prague attracted thousands of people (many from the *Centri Sociali*) who demonstrated with various tactics (see Figure 5.4, next page). The first World Social Forum was held from 25–30 January 2001 in Porto Alegre (Brazil) and the participation of Italian activists was significant. More importantly, the first European Social Forum (ESF) of the alterglobalization movement was held in Florence in November 2002. *Centri Sociali* immediately tried to provide the political backbone for the alterglobalization movement, but the difficulties of pursuing such an ambitious role were compounded by naïveté in managing the new forms of demonstrations and repression and a problematic dialectical rivalry between the various networks of *Centri Sociali*. In particular, the analyses and proposals of the post-autonomist *Disobbedienti/Tute Bianche* and the *Cobas* differed both from each other and from other components of the movement. The divisions emerged blatantly in Genoa in 2001 (Mudu 2009).

The "movement of movements" was shaped in Italy by these pre-existent actors, by their collective codes/memories/languages, and by their spatially

Figure 5.4 A brochure on anti-globalization initiatives printed by Centro Sociale la Torre, Rome.

rooted repertoires, exemplified in the 2001 Genoa demonstrations against the G8 summit. In Genoa the presence of various blocks oriented towards different uses of space for demonstrating was evident: pacifist, queer/spectacular, or violent.

In the 1980s a famous slogan circulating within *Centri Sociali* was "Smash the ghettos", an indicator of the gated social conditions surrounding past struggles. In less than a decade another famous slogan – "Another world is possible" – certified the re-scaling of vision and action.

More recently, the building of networks involving *Centri Sociali* has happened through mobility (e.g. Intersquat; see Owens *et al.*, this volume, Chapter 11), Critical Mass cycling, and the internet. Intersquat is a network of French squatters and *Centri Sociali* aimed at promoting the exchange of ideas, discussions and artistic exhibitions linked to the squatting experience, organized in 2002. In 2005 the FOU (*Festival des Ouvertures Utiles*), a self-managed festival, was organized in Paris; in 2008 the festival jumped scale to the European dimension, and was held in Brussels. In 2009 Intersquat was organized in Rome at the Forte Prenestino *Centro Sociale*. Music – the organization of gigs and production of records – has been assimilated into a nomadic process which allows multiple identities within single resistant subjectivities.

The circulation of news, building of different images, and direct articulation of their own messages has been a crucial point for *Centri Sociali* and the alterglobalization movement (e.g. setting up Indymedia). The development of media activism represented a long-term shared experience. At the beginning of the 1990s European social centres were already connected through the European Counter Network (ECN). Anarchists saw the internet's potential early on, going online earlier than many other groups on the Left (Owens and Palmer 2003). One reason for this early diffusion of internet practices which many anarchists mention is the convergence between the decentralization of anarchist theory and the decentralized structure of cyberspace (Owens and Palmer 2003). The spread of Indymedia suggests that *Centri Sociali* produced and were embedded in a myriad of inter-linkages and interdependencies with a multitude of places at a global scale. *Centri Sociali* actively and intensely explored networking. Indeed, they constituted active nodes, and new relations were set up from scratch. The use of the Web has three primary goals: (1) connecting adherents; (2) forming coalitions; and (3) spreading their ideas to a wider audience (Owens and Palmer 2003). These goals had a temporal sequence, and the connection of participants was widely used and consolidated during the 1990s (Berzano *et al.* 2002). The formation of coalitions became an issue at the end of the millennium, and the diffusion of ideas to a wider audience is still an issue.

These complex interactions and reflexive processes created a fertile environment, an innovative socio-spatial milieu which, for the alterglobalization movement, represented what we could define, following Koehler and Wissen (2003), as "an infrastructure for a glocalized protest". The main elements of this socio-spatial and cultural infrastructure represent important resources for collective mobilization, as shown in Table 5.1 (next page).

Table 5.1 Centri sociali as an infrastructure of resources for the alterglobalization movement

Resource	Characteristics
Public places	Squatted places, gradually opened to a wider public of "users", mainly through the offering of welfare and cultural self-managed services, and offering a basis for co-ordination/meeting between different actors of the movement
Social networks	Networks were built through socio-political and cultural activities, inside urban spaces and between them, at the national and international scales, increasingly including cyber-space
Decisional processes	Decision-making derived from the practice of self-management, based on non-hierarchical relationships, cluster organization and consensus-reaching methods
Repertoires of action	A new approach was proposed for the symbolic representation and concrete managing of urban conflicts (e.g. demonstrations and protest actions) and the associated collective use of space as a resource for mobilization
Codes of communication	Innovative approaches to the communication of socio-political issues were developed, in terms of languages used, of media activated, and of the construction of collective codes, with a performative power. These codes often derived from the underground culture of previous decades

Due to this creative and spatially rooted interaction between *Centri Sociali* and the alterglobalization movement, a reciprocal contamination and a kind of ongoing *mutual learning* was produced, with a transferring of issues/agendas and of skills, but also of activists. *Centri Sociali* showed, in many cases, a *reflexive attitude* and a consequent change in some of their approaches and goals, starting from the scale of action. For many *Centri Sociali* the scale of action is a combination of both the way their space is operationalized and the possibilities offered by a far-reaching transnational activism. Transnational activism and border crossing are vital for resisting the neo-liberal spatial project (Routledge 2003; Della Porta 2006), and this is not new if we consider the international solidarity history of the working-class movement or the great mobility of anarchists a century earlier (Turcato 2007). The novelty lies in a scale of action that simultaneously embeds multiple scales and provides a continuity that is harder to break by tactics of repression and exile. Transnationalism is a built-in characteristic of many *Centri Sociali*, directly linked to the nature of their tactics and awareness of the role and resources attached to open network organizations. Bodies, young bodies, represented a resource for connecting the alterglobalization movement and struggles all over Europe, and in this kind of movement younger activists are more likely to feel attachments to a global than to a merely local scale of action (Tarrow 2005). Furthermore, *Centri Sociali* considered and deepened the issue of sustainable development (not part of their culture until the end of the 1990s) related to lifestyles representing alternatives to commodification and mindful of caring for place, and also re-thought the question of the representation of interests at a glocal level, as shown in the case of the "NO TAV" mobilization in the Val Susa valley[4] (Della Porta and Piazza 2008).

We can sum up the main areas of mutual learning between *Centri Sociali* and the alterglobalization movement in four points:

- Space/s and squatting
- Networking and communicating
- Commons and shared interests
- Self-management and decision-making

Most *Centri Sociali* today are what we can call, following Laville's definition (1998), "public spaces of proximity" – that is, places open to multiple demands and purposes, often serving different groups and even external users. Within the alterglobalization movement the action of illegal and prolonged squatting in urban spaces in order to liberate and offer them for public use has been recognized as a fundamental tool of conflict and participation. More recently, this has been evident in the actions organized by the "15-M" movement in Spain or the "Occupy Wall Street" movements (e.g. their illegal camps and the squatting of public squares). *Centri Sociali* and the "movement of movements" share the idea (and the concrete practice) that space is tangibly the centre and the node of networks with long and short ties, enhanced and structured by the internet (as a means for trans-spatial connections), but still fundamentally located in its physical, symbolic and face-to-face dimension.

Over time, *Centri Sociali* have shifted from a defensive and identitarian approach to an open network conception of action and communication processes, thanks also to their engagement with the international and boundless dimension of the alterglobalization movement. This process has involved a refusal of any communitarian hypothesis or ideological utopian projects and, on the contrary, has placed the emphasis on networking between different and heterogeneous actors, on the basis of a shared horizon of glocal actions and communication processes. On the other hand, the alterglobalization movement has partially learned and used a set of symbolic codes of communication created by *Centri Sociali* during their long history, adapting them to the new and post-ideological frame of contemporary mobilization.

Due to their changing relationships with their space and "external" society around them, driven by the intersection with other actors in the alterglobalization movement, most *Centri Sociali* have progressively focused their action on safeguarding the commons (soil, water, energy, but also democratic processes and welfare services) and researching alternative glocal models of development, emphasizing a concrete dimension of a set of values that include, for example, direct action and real sustainability of work, human sociability, land control, mutuality, and condivision of resources. The defence/promotion of these concrete values by the alterglobalization movement can rely on the repertoire of actions and symbolic codes developed by *Centri Sociali* during their long history of mobilization (as shown, for example, in the spatial defence/attack strategy adopted by the movement during the demonstrations against the TAV project).

In recent years *Centri Sociali* have explored and widened their decision-making processes (not without inner conflicts), opening up a harsh debate within their networks – and more broadly within the whole movement – about the modality and possibility of self-management in different fields of society (e.g. services, economy, politics). Inside the alterglobalization movement, several collective actors, often structured in more hierarchical relationships, have learned different ways of organizing themselves and managing their public actions, looking at the approach of *autogestione*. At the same time, *Centri Sociali* have had to face the challenge of re-scaling in respect of the concept and the practice of self-management, in an attempt to adapt this approach to wider territorial and communicational arenas.

Conclusion

Ten years after 9/11, after the 2001 Genoa protests and the anti-war demonstrations of the last decade, even if we are in a period of uncertainty about the development of the alterglobalization movement, it has to be recognized that the Italian *Centri Sociali* (or a great part of them) have embedded most of the issues of this movement in their practices.

At the same time, through participation in national and international networks of communication and co-operation, the legacy of *Centri Sociali* has been made available to the future of the movement itself, in Italy and in the rest of the world. *Centri Sociali* pushed for a deconstruction of the North–South divide in Europe in relation to movements and definitions of the "right to the city" (Leontidou 2010). At a national level, *Centri Sociali* have provided an important infrastructure of spaces, repertoires and socio-cultural resources for several glocalized protests/actions and, at the same time, they have maintained many fundamental connections with the alterglobalization movement. The main areas of mutual learning between *Centri Sociali* and the alterglobalization movement include: (1) space/s and squatting; (2) networking and communicating; (3) commons and shared interests; and (4) self-management and decision-making.

We can say that some of the alterglobalization movement's particular themes, such as the demand for new "radical subjectivities", the call for a "civil and bottom-up welfare", and the demand for the "right to the city" cannot be interpreted without reference to the fact that innovative forms of "urban" mobilization, developed by *Centri Sociali*, influenced and still influence the movement's dynamics, cultures and agenda, not only in Italy, but also in the rest of Europe. Furthermore, *Centri Sociali* represent one of the main catalysts of the alterglobalization movement in terms of *spatialization*: due to their direct action and symbolic production, always *situated* although oriented towards a global approach, space has become more relevant inside the movement's agenda and practices, especially at the urban level. Thus, *Centri Sociali* have contributed to the rise of a multidimensional conceptualization of the movement's space, focused on the three main aspects of this concept (Harvey 2006): the dimensions of area (territory), of network (relationships), and of place (identity).

Notes

1 In a few cases this (spatial and temporal) autonomy has been radically pursued, following the allure of the "Temporary Autonomous Zones" theorized by Hakim Bey (Bey 2007).
2 Weick uses the term enactment with regard to the capacity of organizations to create and to give sense to their socio-cultural and physical environment, precisely through their organizational dynamics: "organizing is sense-making" (Weick 2003).
3 It is worth mentioning that between February and March 2001, the Italian post-autonomist "Tute Bianche" (White Overalls) escorted 24 Zapatista commanders during a long march of 3,000 kilometres from the Lacandon Jungle to Mexico City (Becucci 2003).
4 For 20 years the NO-TAV movement has contested a high-speed rail connection between Turin in Italy and Lyons in France.

References

AASTER, C.S. Cox 18, C.S. Leoncavallo, Moroni P. (1995) *Centri Sociali.* Milan: Shake.

Adinolfi F., Bascetta, M., Giannetti, M., Grispigni, M., Moroni, P., Quagliata, L. and Vecchi, B. (1994) *Comunità virtuali.* Manifestolibri, Roma.

Augé, M. (1993) *Nonluoghi.* Milano: Eleuthera.

Balestrini, N. and Moroni, P. (1997) *L'orda d'oro 1968–1977.* Milan: Feltrinelli.

Becucci, S. (2003) "Disobbedienti e centri sociali fra democrazia diretta e rappresentanza". *Quaderni di Sociologia*, XLVII, 33: 5–20.

Berzano, L., Gallini, R. and Genova, C. (2002) *Liberi tutti.* Turin: Ananke.

Bey, H. (2007) *T.A.Z.*, Shake edizioni, Milano.

Dazieri, S. (1996) *Italia overground.* Castelvecchi, Roma.

De Leonardis, O. (1998) *In un diverso welfare*. Feltrinelli, Milano.

Della Porta, D. (2006) *Globalization from below.* Minneapolis: University of Minnessota.

Della Porta, D. and Diani, M. (2006) *Social Movements* (2nd edn). Oxford: Blackwell.

Della Porta, D. and Piazza, G. (2008) *Le campagne contro la Tav in Val di Susa e il Ponte sullo Stretto.* Milano: Feltrinelli.

Dines, N. (1999) "Centri Sociali". *Quaderni di sociologia*, XLIII (21): 90–111.

Foucault, M. (1982) "The Subject and Power". *Critical Inquiry*, (8) 4: 777–795.

Foucault, M. (1986) "Of Other Spaces". *Diacritics*, 16:1, Spring: 22–27.

Giddens, A. (1991) *The Consequences of Modernity.* Cambridge: Polity Press.

Harvey, D. (2006) *Space and Global Capitalism.* London–New York: Verso.

Ibba, A. (1995) *Leoncavallo 1975–1995.* Genova: Costa e Nolan.

Kellner, D. (2001) "Marcuse and the Quest for Radical Subjectivity". In Paris, J. and Wilkerson, W. (eds) *New Critical Theory*. Lanham: Rowman & Littlefield: pp. 85–105.

Koèhler, B. and Wissen, M. (2003) "Glocalizing Protest". *International Journal of Urban and Regional Research*, Volume 27. 4 December: 942–951.

Laville, J.L. (1998) *L'economia solidale.* Torino: Bollati Boringhieri.

Lefebvre, H. (1991) *The Production of Space*. Oxford: Blackwell.

Leontidou, L. (2010) "Urban Social Movements in 'Weak' Civil Societies". *Urban Studies*, 47 (6): 1179–1203.

Marcuse, H. (1964) *One-Dimensional Man.* Boston: Beacon Press.

Martínez, M. (2007) "The Squatters' Movement". *South European Society & Politics* 12 (3), 379–398.

Massey, D. (2005) *For space.* London: Sage.

Melucci, A. (ed.) (1984) *Altri codici.* Bologna: il Mulino.

Melucci, A. (1989) *Nomads of the present.* London: Century Hutchinson Ltd.

Membretti, A. (2003) *Leoncavallo.* Milan: Mamme del Leoncavallo.

Membretti, A. (2007) "Centro Sociale Leoncavallo". *European Urban and Regional Studies* 14 (3): 252–263.

Membretti, A. (2010) "Innovation in the wake of urban movements". In Moulaert, Martinelli, Swyngedouw and Gonzàlez (eds) *Can Neighbourhoods Save the City?* Routledge.

Montagna, N. (2006) "The de-commodification of urban space and the occupied Centri Sociali in Italy". *City* 10/3: 295–304.

Moroni, P., Farina, D. and Tripodi, P. (eds) (1995) *Centri Sociali.* Castelvecchi: Roma.

Mudu, P. (2004) "Resisting and Challenging Neoliberalism". *Antipode* 36 (5): 917–941.

Mudu, P. (2005) "Changing backdrops in Rome". In Wastl-Walter, D., Staeheli, L. and Dowler, L. (eds) *Rights to the City.* IGU – Home of Geography Publication Series Volume III, pp. 265–275.

Mudu, P. (2009) "Where is Hardt and Negri's Multitude?" *ACME* 8 (2): 211–244.

Mudu, P. (2012) "At the Intersection of Anarchists and Autonomists". *ACME* 11 (3), 413–438.

Osterweil, M. (2013) "The Italian Anomaly". In Flesher Fominaya, C. and Cox, L. (eds) *Understanding European Movements.* London: Routledge.

Owens, L. and Palmer, L.K. (2003) "Making the news". *Critical Studies in Media Communication* 20: 335–361.

Owens, L., Katzeff, A., Lorenzi, E. and Colin, B. (2013) "At home in the movement". In Flesher Fominaya, C. and Cox, L. (eds) *Understanding European Movements.* London: Routledge.

Piazza, G. (2011) "Which models of democracy?". Center of Studies on Politics and Society – WP Series, 1,1: 3–54.

Purcell, M.H. (2008) *Recapturing Democracy.* New York: Routledge.

Rampalla, A. and Vaccaro, S. (1993) "Palermo". *A – Rivista anarchica*, October n.203: 28.

Routledge, P. (2003) "Convergence space". *Transactions of the Institute of British Geographers* 28: 333–349.

Ruggiero, V. (2000) "New Social Movements and the 'Centri Sociali' in Milan". *Sociological Review* 48, 167–185.

Sommier, I. (1998) "Un Espace Politique Non Homologué". In CURAPP (ed.) *La politique ailleurs.* Paris: PUF. pp. 117–129.

Swyngedouw, E. (1997) "Neither global nor local". In Cox, K.R. (ed.) *Spaces of globalization.* New York and London: The Guilford Press.

Tarrow, S. (2005) *The New Transnational Activism.* Cambridge: Cambridge University Press.

Tiddi, A. (1997) *Il cerchio e la saetta.* Genova: Costa e Nolan.

Turcato, D. (2007) "Italian Anarchism as a Transnational Movement". *Internationaal Instituut voor Sociale Geschiedenis*, (52): 407–444.

Weick, K.E. (1995) *Sensemaking in Organizations.* Thousand Oaks, CA: Sage.

Weick, K.E. (2003) "Enacting an environment: The structure of organizing". In Westwood, R. and Clegg, S. (eds) *Debating organization: Point-counterpoint in organization studies.* Malden, MA: Blackwell: pp. 184–191.

6 Constructing a new collective identity for the alterglobalization movement

The French Confédération Paysanne (CP) as anti-capitalist 'peasant' movement

Edouard Morena

Introduction: lessons from the Millau 'dismantlement'

On 8 August 1999, at around 10.30 a.m., 100 members and sympathisers of the Confédération paysanne (CP)[1] and the Syndicat des Producteurs de Lait de Brebis (SPLB)[2] invaded the construction site of an unfinished McDonald's restaurant in the small rural town of Millau (close to the Larzac plateau in the Aveyron *département* of southwest France). Their action was in response to the US government's imposition of a 100 per cent tax increase on imports of Roquefort ewe's milk cheese. The US decision was in retaliation to the European Union's (EU) earlier ban on the imports of hormone-infected beef. It produced a public outcry in a *département* where agriculture directly and indirectly employs over 5,000 people. Having invaded the construction site, participants – led by José Bové, spokesperson for the CP and ewe-milk producer – proceeded to 'dismantle' various segments of the McDonald's restaurant and then carried them by tractor to the *sous-préfecture*.[3]

At first glance, the event's repertoire of action – illegal and symbolic – and choice of targets – a multinational corporation and the *sous-prefecture* – were in line with previous trade union actions in agriculture (Duclos 1998). The media's initial coverage tended to highlight this continuity by presenting the *dismantlement* as a violent, destructive, corporatist – and local – trade union action. In the *Midi Libre* newspaper, for example, the significance of the event was downplayed and it was presented 'as a patient and therefore determined, voluntary and methodical rampage' (Martin 2000). It is interesting to note that many of those who took part in the *dismantlement* also stressed this continuity with previous trade union actions. For Jean-Emile Sanchez, Aveyron farmer and CP representative, the event 'was an action like any other'.[4]

It was only from the point when the manager of the McDonald's restaurant took legal action against the perpetrators (with the support of the state prosecutor) and five 'peasant' activists (including José Bové) were arrested that the media revised its initial coverage and gave it a national and international dimension. Having presented it as a 'classic' and localized trade union action, the media now re-assessed the *dismantlement* as a peaceful, non-corporatist and symbolic protest against *malbouffe* (junk food) and, more generally, the economic and social effects of neoliberal globalization. This is particularly evident when looking at the series of articles and television stories that were devoted to the links between globalization, agriculture, and food.[5] In the national media the judiciary system's response was presented as a disproportionate attack on trade union rights. A number of articles also accused the state of unjustly targeting the CP and applying double standards when compared to the CP's main trade union rival, the corporatist and conservative FNSEA.[6] From being a relatively localized and sector-based event, the media played a major role in linking the *dismantlement* to a broader set of issues that transcended agriculture (the threats that globalization poses to trade union rights and French culinary culture). In the process, 'peasants' – and the CP as its newly designated representative – became symbols of resistance to neoliberal globalization.

The *dismantlement*'s re-interpretation as a non-corporatist 'peasant' trade union action was not restricted to the national and international media. Invoking trade union freedoms and the event's non-corporatist character, media commentators, left- and right-wing politicians, and social movement actors (NGOs, trade unions, etc.) were prompt in expressing their support for the incarcerated 'peasant' activists. In so doing, they reinforced the 'peasantry's' position as symbol of resistance to neoliberal globalization and the CP's status as its legitimate representative. For instance, on 23 August, Attac issued a press release in which it expressed its 'indignation' at the judiciary system's decision to jail the CP activists. It presented the *dismantlement* as a 'symbolic action' against 'a multinational company that is emblematic of globalization'. For Attac, far from simply defending their livelihoods, the CP's members sought, through their action, 'to draw the public's and politicians' attention towards the scandal that constitutes the decision by the World Trade Organization (WTO) ... to impose heavy financial sanctions against the European Union'.[7]

The *dismantlement*'s extraordinary resonance can be explained by the way in which its symbolic character, and that of its participants, could be mobilized in support of a variety of activist and political agendas which, in turn, responded to the concerns of French farmers and the wider public. Parallels can be drawn between the re-interpretations of the *dismantlement* and that of the *mouvement social*[8] of December 1995. As Jean-Gabriel Contamin observes of the 1995 strikes, 'it is for very diverse and even contradictory motives that actors, themselves very heterogenous, rallied *a posteriori* to what could appear as a common interpretation' (2005: 259). From being a corporatist action, the *dismantlement* was re-interpreted – and thereby re-appropriated – as an act of revolt against the WTO and the multiple threats that it poses to French agriculture and hence French cultural identity. In the process, the 'peasantry' became a symbol of resistance to neoliberal globalization.

This re-interpretation of the event as an opposition between 'peasants' and neoliberal globalization – two concepts upon which a range of meanings are projected – was centred around the figure of José Bové. As spokesperson for the CP and representative of the SPLB, Bové played a major part in planning and orchestrating the Millau action. His status as trade union representative, personal history (he had taken part in a variety of actions with other social movement groups against the GATT, nuclear testing, GMOs, etc.), Asterix-like appearance, international outlook and rhetorical skills were all used to symbolize the 'peasantry's' resistance to neoliberal globalization and junk food. In other words, Bové reflected various understandings of what 'being a peasant' should mean: variously being presented as the guardian of French culinary culture, protector of trade union rights, and representative of new approaches towards social and environmental justice and international grass-roots solidarity. In the national and international media, Bové was rapidly likened to a series of popular heroes, acquiring nicknames such as 'Robin Hood of the Larzac' (*Le Monde*), 'subcomandante Marcos of the rural cause' and 'Zorro of the Causses' (*Libération*) (Martin 2000). By being likened to 'Gauls at war against *malbouffe*', French 'peasants' – symbolized by Bové – were celebrated as a vital source of 'autonomous cultural production' against an American-imposed cultural imperialism that seeks to impose 'the particularities of a cultural tradition within which commercial logic has been developed to the full' (Bourdieu 2003: 75).

By associating Bové and the 'peasantry' with a variety of positive symbols and ideas (cultural autonomy and diversity, authenticity, 'good food', non-corporatism, international solidarity, Frenchness, regionalism), the media, politicians, and social movement actors re-placed the 'peasantry' – and the farming profession more generally – at the heart of French society and politics. As Paul Ariès explains, 'the *dismantlement* of McDonald's in Millau has created a hero for the modern times in which each and everyone can recognize themselves' (2000: 5). These actors asserted the 'peasantry's' historic status as a 'class-for-others' and effectively encouraged the CP – as the representative of the 'peasants' – to draw on popular understandings and symbols in order to advance its categorical interests (Bourdieu 1977). The union was encouraged to do so for two main reasons. First, it made trade union sense since the projected image of the 'peasantry' increased the CP's legitimacy in professional circles by being in line with farmers' preferred self-presentation (Bruneau 2004). In a survey produced on the eve of the 2000 Paris Agricultural Fair, 39 per cent of those who were questioned identified Bové as the most capable person to defend the interests of French 'peasants'. The survey placed Bové ahead of Jean Glavany, the Minister of Agriculture (17 per cent), and Luc Guyau, the president of the FNSEA (13 per cent).[9]

Second, it enabled the union to reaffirm its non-corporatist approach by strengthening its ties with other social movement groups, groups with which it had previously collaborated (e.g. Attac, APEC[10]). In short, the promotion of its 'peasant' character enabled the CP to respond to the multiple – and sometimes conflicting – demands that arose from its dual status as representative trade union and social movement actor. In other words, the CP's self-presentation as a 'peasant' movement – by drawing on a variety of symbols and ideas – was simultaneously in line with the needs of 'peasant' politics and with the new ways of *doing politics* that characterize contemporary 'opinion democracies'.

What emerges from our brief overview of the *dismantlement* is that the CP's success in media, farming and social movement circles was related to its successful integration of the demands of 'public opinion' (Champagne 2003: 101–102). As Bové himself admitted, the CP's success derives from the successful alignment of the CP's strategy and 'the desires of public opinion'.[11] In addition to being a key feature of contemporary Western democracies, 'public opinion' is characterized by its immaterial and 'de-particularized' nature (Champagne 1990: 47). As Marco Giugni has argued, public opinion plays a facilitating role for social movements in their attempts to obtain a policy impact (2004: 210). It also influences social movement strategies, and their relations with the media in particular (d'Almeida 2003: 71–72; Neveu 2002: 94). Creating 'public' empathy becomes a priority (Riutort 2007: 81).[12]

What distinguishes the CP from other social movement groups is that when it refers to 'public opinion' it draws on popular understandings of what 'being a peasant' should mean. In other words, it does not simply draw on popular beliefs about a given issue – globalization, for instance – but is compelled, as a 'peasant' organization, to connect these issues to popular representations of the 'peasantry'. As the following section argues, historically these representations have been produced by 'non-peasant' actors, and extend beyond the agricultural sector. We shall see how the 'peasantry' became associated with a broad set of ideas and symbols that transcended the field of agriculture. This will lead us, in the second section, to analyse why this made it vital for 'peasant' movements such as the CP to re-appropriate these myths and symbols and adapt their repertoires of action and demands accordingly. In the third and final section, I shall highlight the ways in which the CP, through its references to and re-appropriation of the 'peasant' subject, was logically led to play a leading role in the alterglobalization movement.

The 'peasantry': from social class to symbol

The meanings and symbols associated with the 'peasantry' are the product of historical struggles for the control of the 'peasant' group. Despite its drastic numerical decline, the 'peasantry' continues to constitute a key feature of French society through the meanings and symbols that are associated with it. In the fields of cultural production, politics, and advertising,[13] the 'peasantry' – and ruralness more generally – are often associated with a common set of symbols and ideas (authenticity, tradition, local know-how, nature, Frenchness) which, as we shall see, are historically the product of non-peasant actors. As Annie Moulin explains, the evolution in the meanings that are attached to the word 'peasant' reflects the ways in which the 'outside world' defines, identifies and recognizes the farming population (Moulin 1988).

In late eighteenth-century France the peasantry formed an overwhelming majority of the French population. In view of its particular economic and political status, it could be regarded as a relatively unified social class. While peasant communities varied in size and nature depending on the region, they all shared a common status and fate – as members of the Third Estate – and, because of their geographical isolation, they were, by and large, unaffected by capitalist development (Byres 2009). By abolishing the feudal orders, extending property rights and favouring capitalist incursions into the countryside, the French Revolution accentuated class differences within the peasant group, giving rise to classes of rural labourers, petty-commodity producers, and capitalist farmers.

Yet, despite its progressive – and slow – disaggregation over the course of the nineteenth and twentieth centuries, the 'peasantry' continued to be treated as a unified and largely autonomous social category. In the contemporary French context, where agricultural production is primarily export-orientated and high-yielding and where farmers represent less than 3.5 per cent of the French working population, the 'peasantry' continues to form a central reference point.[14] The reason for this is that the 'peasantry', in addition to being associated with a set of practices and social organization, was, from a very early stage, associated with symbols and values that would serve broader purposes than simply attracting farmer support. By being detached from a specific social category, 'peasant' values and symbols took on an ahistorical character. In other words, while the 'peasant' has, alternatively, been viewed in both a positive and a negative light, the associated ideas and symbols – conservatism, proximity with nature, traditionalism, localism – remained unchanged.

This resulted in the formation of an 'eternal peasant' figure whose characteristics reflect 'non-peasant' understandings about 'what being a peasant means'. Although the 'eternal peasant' does not actually exist, it is 'relentlessly convened and reinvented, [it] takes on a mythical dimension and becomes an ideological construction' (Mayaud 2008: 8). In the nineteenth century, through paintings and novels, French artistic accounts of rural life played a considerable role in shaping and upholding popular attitudes towards the 'peasantry', alternately presenting it as a source of national strength or as a group of savages at the margins of society and of the historical events essential to the French nation's consolidation and definition (Lagrave 1988; Lehning 1995; Ponton 1977). As James R. Lehning argues, the 'peasant' category has 'made and continues to make country-dwellers a distinct part of the French nation' (1995: 3).

Accounts of the 'eternal peasant' were also re-appropriated for political motives: either for the control of the 'peasantry' as a social group, or for the control of the 'peasant' concept as a reflection of French national identity. By drawing on these myths and symbols, political parties rooted them deeper in the popular psyche, blurring the divide between myth and reality in a self-fulfilling 'peasant' prophecy. From the mid-nineteenth century onwards, with the gradual extension of universal manhood suffrage, it became vital to secure 'peasant' support. The 'peasant question' transcended partisan lines, and progressively became a national priority.

In the global economic context of the 1880–1890s, the creation in 1881 of a Ministry of Agriculture and the establishment by *notables* of the first 'peasant' trade unions were intended to secure 'peasant' support towards the bourgeois state. Republican and conservative unions made their material support conditional on the 'peasantry's' loyalty towards them and the ideals that they conveyed. They 'had in common their determination to reinforce existing social structures' (Price 1987: 192). As Wright explains, 'right and left alike favoured undifferentiated organizations uniting all elements of the rural population' (1964: 21).

The development of industry and the growth of urban centres only heightened these 'pro-peasant' discourses and policies. Both moderate republicans and conservatives used the idea of an undifferentiated 'peasant' extensively to offset the threats posed by the proliferation of revolutionary ideas in the industrializing cities (Moulin 1988: 156). By the early twentieth century, following the First World War, in which hundreds of thousands of young rural men lost their lives, the revolutionary left also attempted to attract the 'peasant' masses, even if this meant abandoning its collectivist pretensions for agriculture, recognizing 'peasant' small-ownership, and replacing the Marxist opposition between capital and labour with a more ambiguous opposition between large and small 'peasants' (Lagrave 2004: 14; Lynch 1998).

The emergence, in the 1930s, of agrarian movements such as Dorgères' *Chemises Vertes*[15] or Jacquet's and Le Roy Laduries' *Front Paysan*[16] strengthened the 'peasantry's' position at the heart of French politics (Paxton 1997). In response to these movements, the mainstream left and right celebrated France's 'peasant' heritage through the promotion of folklore and regional traditions.[17] On the left, the Popular Front government cultivated a form of 'national-populist narcissism', extensively drawing on and celebrating 'peasant' folklore (Lebovics 2009: 16). On the right, celebrations of France's 'peasant' heritage culminated in the Vichy regime's extensive use of the 'eternal peasant' to symbolize the continued grandeur of the French nation despite Nazi occupation.

In the immediate post-war years, the national priority was to rebuild a French economy devastated in the war. Yet the reconstruction effort and the tremendous economic and social upheavals that it brought about – combined with France's decline as a colonial power – produced a profound crisis of identity in French society. As Lebovics explains:

> after the massive economic development begun in the 1950s, the decolonizations in the 1960s, the Great Refusal of the young in 1968, and finally the beginning of economic depression in 1974, the fete came to an end. It was time for the French to assess what their society had become.
>
> (2004: 6)

Unsurprisingly, the figure of the 'peasant' would once again be called upon to respond to this national identity crisis, despite the fact that the number of farmers had declined sharply as a result of state economic policies. As Demossier observes, 'the French peasantry is no longer at the core of the republican state, but even if its status is diminishing, it still requires careful handling, mainly because of its deep national resonance' (2003: 268).

The state and mainstream political formations were not the only ones to revive the 'peasant' figure. With the spread of revolutionary and post-materialist ideas in activist and intellectual circles in the 1960s and 1970s, the 'peasantry' became a symbol of resistance to capitalism and of a new, more environmentally sustainable and socially just *modèle de société* (societal model). These changes were accompanied by a resurgence of interest in the 'peasantry' in French academic circles (Mendras 2000). They were also in line with a broader international trend of celebrating 'peasant' values and a 'peasant' way of life grounded on solidarity, reciprocity and egalitarianism (Bernstein 2010: 3).

Over the course of the 1960s and 1970s, the 'peasantry' came to symbolize autonomy and authenticity in a context of growing distrust towards institutional politics, the bureaucratic state, and its 'de-humanizing' policies. Once considered archaic, terms linked to the 'peasantry' such as 'localism' or 'tradition' were now associated with progressive ideas. As Judit Bodnar comments, 'the term "local" no longer had the connotation of "parochial" since "parochialism" [was] in effect redefined as being locked into the production and consumption of global staples such as Big Macs, Coca-Cola, popcorn, Hollywood blockbusters, and so on' (2003: 138). It comes as no surprise that a heterogeneous 'movement of movements' such as the alter-globalization movement should also draw on the 'peasant' figure to promote its ideas.

Having highlighted the 'peasantry's' particular status in French politics, we shall look at the ways in which the CP and the 'peasant' left which preceded it successfully drew upon these popular representations to advance their categorical interests, in the process further reinforcing the 'peasantry's' particular status in French politics and society.

Re-appropriating 'peasantness' for the advancement of sectoral interests

In view of this particular status, the central question becomes whether farmers draw on the 'peasant' dimension of their collective identity to advance their group interests – whether or not the projected image reflects their actual situation – and, if so, how? Before going further, we should remember that in the late nineteenth century the *syndicats agricoles* were not created or managed by 'peasants' but by *notables* and a small elite composed of rich agriculturalists and landowners. Their purpose was to organize and control a farming population, which by the early twentieth century was already heavily dependent upon the state. By the mid-twentieth century, a corporatist system of 'co-management' was in place in which a single union, the FNSEA, acted as the sole intermediary between the farming profession and the state. The emergence of the 'peasant' left in the late 1950s can be seen as a direct reaction to an agricultural system which only benefitted a minority of rich farmers and which was under growing public scrutiny for not addressing the social, environmental and cultural implications of post-war modernization. It was the system's rigidity that led certain farmers to build alliances with left-wing non-peasant groups, even if this meant adapting their discourse to the changing representations of the 'peasantry' and expectations of it.

New left-wing 'peasant' movements took root in share-cropping and tenant farming regions (such as Brittany or Loire-Atlantique) which had been subject to radical transformations as a result of these modernization policies (supported by the government and the FNSEA). It was in these regions that farmers suffered most from these policies (mass migration to the cities, high levels of indebtedness due to investments, highly integrated and 'proletarianized' agriculture). The 'peasant' left also found a positive echo in depopulated and poor agricultural regions (such as the Aveyron, Lozère, Ardèche, Drôme), especially in areas where a new generation of 'neo-rural' farmers had established themselves. Unlike their counterparts in Brittany, these 'neo-rural' farmers often came from educated, urban, non-farming backgrounds and were primarily motivated by a desire to promote an alternative, more environmentally friendly and less state-dependent agricultural model. The 'peasant' term would enable the 'peasant' left – and later the CP – to construct a common identity, which, by being largely grounded on popular ideas and symbols, could accommodate the multiple realities of its members and its target audience.

The emergence of the 'peasant' left and its progressive organization in the form of a trade union in the late 1980s (the CP) thus went against the idea that the 'peasantry' was essentially destined to remain a 'dominated' group, or, as Bourdieu writes, a 'class-for-others' (1977: 4). By selectively drawing on popular representations of the 'peasantry' farmers could hope to advance their group interests and reaffirm their place in society (Champagne 2002: 217). The 'peasant' left's projection, in response to the political discourses of the 1960s and 1970s, of an authentic 'peasant' image represented a useful way of responding to the multiple demands of its members and of attracting non-peasant support, thereby weakening the FNSEA's position as the sole representative of the farming sector.

The Larzac movement (1971–1981) offers a potent example of the 'peasant' left's adaptive strategy and its inclusion of these new 'non-peasant' understandings about what 'being a peasant' should mean. The movement emerged in 1971 when a group of local farmers chose to oppose the planned extension of a military base on the Larzac plateau in the Aveyron. What was initially a 'peasant'-led response to a forced expropriation rapidly attracted the support of a wide array of groups and individuals, from faith-based organizations such as Lanza Del Vasto's *Communauté de l'Arche* to regionalist (Occitan and Breton) groups as well as political parties such as the Parti Socialiste Unifié.[18] As Jean-Pierre Le Goff notes, over 100 support committees were set up across France in support of the Larzac 'peasants' (2006: 248). As a result, the movement, while remaining in line with its 'peasant' dimension – essential to its media success – was framed in relation to a broader set of issues that combined social, cultural and post-materialist demands (anti-productivism, environmentalism, pacifism, regional-ism, third-worldism, etc.). Lebovics comments that the Larzac farmers' 'desire to continue being small peasant farmers in industrializing France led them to invent France's newest modernity', one grounded in a combination of progres-sive ideas and traditional wisdom (2004: 31). At a time when the countryside was increasingly perceived as 'a precious antidote to the negative aspects of the cities' and as an 'ideal terrain for authentic social relations and a direct commun-ion with nature', the Larzac 'peasants' served to symbolize these new approaches (Traïni 2003: 44). Through its use of 'symbols, actions and myth to build a movement', the Larzac movement marks a historical reference point for contemporary social movement struggles (Alland 1994: xxii).

The 1980s diffusion of post-materialist demands and the development of an 'opinion democracy', combined with the growing public interest in agricultural affairs that these changes brought about, encouraged the 'peasant' left to pursue and adapt its self-presentation as the legitimate representative of 'peasants'. The coming together of different left-wing 'peasant' movements and the creation, in 1987, of a single representative trade union – the *Confédération paysanne* – bears witness to the contextual changes taking place and their influence upon the 'peasant' left and the farming sector more generally. This is further supported by the CP's desire to not only defend the interests of 'peasants', but to also promote an alternative model of farming: 'peasant-style agriculture' (*agriculture pay-sanne*) which would not only improve farmers' livelihoods, but would also respond to society's demands for better quality food and environmentally sound agricultural practices (Roederer-Rynning 2005: 101).

As a result of its 'peasant' status, the CP could boast of considerable experi-ence of presenting itself in a non-corporatist manner and of 'widening the cause' (Riutort 2007: 82–83). Long before the wave of alter-globalization protests, the CP had learnt to draw on public opinion for its self-presentation and to construct a common discourse that could respond to its multiple obligations as representa-tive trade union and non-corporatist social movement actor.

'Peasants' against globalization

The wave of protests against neoliberal globalization in the late 1990s – of which the *dismantlement* was an important moment – and their categorization under the 'alter-globalization' label has been regularly presented as the advent of a new approach to social movement activism. Whether or not these mobilizations marked the emergence of a new collective identity has been subject to much debate in academic and activist circles. For some, the alter-globalization move-ment is not radically new, but is an adaptation of pre-existing demands to shift-ing constraints and ways of 'doing politics'. In other words, activists and social movement groups 'connect a heterogeneous series of ills, poverty in the South, exclusion and unemployment in the North, and attribute them to new causes: the globalization of economic exchanges, the retreat of the state when confronted to the markets' (Agrikoliansky *et al.* 2005: 26). For Sommier, the movement's

originality – and therefore its 'newness' – stems from the 'synthesis that it oper-
ates between various historical strata of collective action' (2003: 21). For others,
it marks the rise of an altogether new consciousness, objectives, and action strategies that respond to the radically new and all-encompassing threat posed by
neoliberal globalization (Agrikoliansky *et al.* 2005: 20). Whereas the former
approach tends to view the 'alter-globalization' movement as the logical
outcome of previous mobilizations, the latter focuses on the new circumstances
and the break with previous practices and ways of conceptualising justice that
these have brought about.

What cuts across both approaches is the fact that the concept of 'globalization', like the term 'peasant', is symbolically charged and can be employed in a
variety of different ways. What sets both concepts apart are the interpretations
given to the symbols and meanings associated with them. Whereas globalization
can be associated with standardization, Americanization, and mass production,
the 'peasantry' is often associated with authenticity, cultural diversity, and the
'agrarian question of food' whereby 'food embodies social, cultural and ecological values over and above its material value' (McMichael 2008: 49). In addition to having successfully highlighted the negative impacts of neoliberal
globalization, the CP's prominent position within the alter-globalization movement can also be explained by the fact that, long before the latter, the CP had
framed its demands in terms of an opposition between 'peasants' and 'globalization' and, by doing so, would logically appear as a catalyst for a variety of struggles and experiences. As a result of contextual changes affecting agricultural
production in the 1980s, the CP was led to frame its demands in relation to
supranational trends.

In the early 1990s, in response to the inclusion of farming in international
trade negotiations at a time when agriculture was 'becoming less and less a foundational institution of societies and states, and more and more a tenuous component of corporate global sourcing strategies', the CP set up international
alliances with civil society and 'peasant' groups from across the globe
(McMichael 2000: 134). In the mid-1980s, growing pressures from the European
Commission to open up European agriculture to international trade encouraged
the 'peasant' left to set up the *Coordination Paysanne Européenne* (CPE), an
alliance of twenty-two 'peasant' organizations from across Europe. In 1993, the
CPE, in association with Central, South and North American farmers' groups,
set up the Via Campesina 'in explicit rejection of neo-liberal agricultural policies
and as a direct response to the GATT negotiations' exclusion of the concerns,
needs, and interests of people who actually work the land and produce the
world's food' (Desmarais 2007: 77). Through its calls for greater 'account-
ability', 'democracy', and 'autonomy', the Via Campesina had, long before the
alter-globalization movement, framed its demands in response to what was not
yet termed 'neoliberal globalization'. Its core campaign on 'food sovereignty',
for instance, calls for the right for 'peasants' to 'determine their patterns of food
production and consumption' (Bello 2009: 136). In response to 'unregulated
international trade', the Via Campesina defends local knowledge and cultural

production, and 'peasants' are presented as their natural purveyors. In addition to taking part in the Via Campesina, some CP members also actively participated, along with other civil society groups, in a variety of national and international campaigns against the environmental, economic and social effects of neoliberalism.[19] The CP was a founding member of Attac in 1998, and still holds a seat on its governing council.

The CP was able to secure a prominent position within the emerging movement against neoliberal globalization through its ability to transcend its official status as representative trade union and to integrate a broader set of issues into its activist agenda. French activists and intellectuals referred to the CP's defence of the 'peasant' trade to show that it was possible to accommodate professional and societal demands (Capdevielle 2001). In other words, the CP was used to illustrate a 'return of the social question' in a new form, better adjusted to the new realities and constraints that derive from neoliberal globalization (Aguiton and Bensaid 1997; Confédération paysanne 1996: 2). The CP combined the 'materialist aspirations' and 'post-materialist' values that would be at the heart of the alter-globalization movement (Sommier 2003: 23–24). In the agricultural domain, the CP's presentation of 'peasantness' implied that anyone – including certain farmers who were not legally recognized as such – could be a 'peasant' as long as she/he adhered to the union's overall project. Bové, for instance, insisted that 'any farmer can join the *Confédération paysanne*. It's not limited to those using organic methods or working a certain acreage. You just have to adhere to the basic project' (cited in Mertes 2004: 140–141).

Through its promotion of 'peasantness' the CP was able to fulfil its obligations as representative trade union. This was in line with the alter-globalization movement's adoption of a form of 'self-limiting radicalism', whereby movements express defiance towards the state and institutional politics whilst simultaneously attempting to influence the direction of policy (Sommier 2003). By taking on a variety of meanings and being limited to the symbolic sphere, its critiques of globalization could be combined with negotiations with the state and other social partners. In the mid- to late-1990s, 'the union gained a social recognition which increased its professional legitimacy' (*Confédération paysanne* 2008). The CP was regularly invited by the Ministry of Agriculture to discuss issues such as milk quota distributions, land tenure, and the status of the hors-normes,[20] and a number of their proposals were integrated into the Loi d'Orientation Agricole.[21]

Concluding remarks

In this chapter I have attempted to analyse the CP's position within the alter-globalization movement through an analysis of the 'peasant' concept, its deeper resonances in French politics and society, and its influence on 'peasant' mobilizations. In the first section I showed how, historically, the peasantry went from being an actual social class to a set of meanings and symbols that were the product of 'non-peasants'. The 'peasantry' thereby became a 'class-for-others', upon which a variety of meanings and symbols could be projected. The second section showed how this status as 'class-for-others' had a lasting influence on the 'peasantry's' self-presentation and its strategies for collective organization. Rather than simply reflecting an awakening to new demands, the emergence and evolutions of the 'peasant' left – and later the CP – can be interpreted as a series of reactions to evolving understandings about what 'being a peasant' should mean. In other words, the CP defended its group and organizational interests by aligning its strategies to popular representations of the 'peasantry' and effectively upholding the 'peasantry's' status as a 'class-for-others'.

This has led me to highlight a number of connections between the approaches of the CP and the alter-globalization movement. First, as a movement of movements representing a broad set of demands, the alter-globalization movement's self-presentations and strategies were, as in the case of the CP, shaped and guided by public opinion. Second, like the 'peasant' concept, the term 'globalization' was associated with a variety of meanings and symbols. The issue for both the CP and the alter-globalization movement subsequently became one of re-appropriating both terms in order to advance their strategic interests. Third, both the CP and the alter-globalization movement, by drawing on the symbolically charged 'peasant' and 'globalization' concepts, were able to promote both material and post-material demands. And fourth, when we consider the nature of the meanings and symbols attached to the 'peasantry' and 'globalization', we see that they were in direct opposition to one another. While, on the one hand, the 'peasantry' was associated with the local, cultural diversity, and autonomy, on the other hand, 'globalization' was linked with mass culture, standardization, and anonymity. As a result the CP, as a representative of the 'peasantry', logically appeared to be best-placed symbolically to lead the opposition to neoliberal 'globalization'.

Notes

1 Literally 'Peasants' Confederation'.
2 Ewe's Milk Producers Union (linked to the CP).
3 Local office of the state administration.
4 Extract from the documentary by Damien Doignot and José Bové, le cirque médiatique (2007, 54 minutes).
5 See, for instance, the series of articles by Dominique Pouchin in *Le Monde* in September 1999.
6 Fédération Nationale des Syndicats d'Exploitants Agricoles, France's main farmers' union.
7 www.france.attac.org/articles/cinq-paysans-aveyronnais-emprisonnés.
8 Term used to designate the massive strike movement against the Juppé government's planned austerity measures and pensions reform package.
9 IFOP-Ouest France (28 February 2000).
10 Alliance Paysans Ecologistes Consommateurs.
11 Besset, Jean-Paul, 'José Bové plaide pour une alliance entre les paysans et les consommateurs', *Le Monde*, 9 September 1999.
12 In certain cases, this leads them to set up their own media outlets such as *Le Monde Diplomatique* (Cardon and Granjon 2002: 175–198; Crettiez and Sommier 2006: 503–514).

13 See, for instance, *Perrette et le tracteur: le paysan dans la publicité*, produced for the exhibition at the Forney Library in Paris (September 2008–January 2009).
14 www.lafranceagricole.fr/l-agriculture/panorama-de-l-agriculture/l-agriculture-dans-l-economie-19837.html.
15 Green Shirts.
16 Peasant Front.
17 See, for instance, Edouard Lynch's fascinating account of the Rural Centre during the 1937 International Exposition in Paris (2009; see also Lebovics 1992).
18 Unified Socialist Party.
19 The CP has actively participated in campaigns against nuclear testing/energy, GMO, and free-trade agreements, with groups such as Greenpeace, Attac, Friends of the Earth, Oxfam, etc.
20 'Hors normes' refers to farms that are not officially recognized as such (because of their limited size, production techniques, etc.) As a result, 'hors normes' farmers cannot access credit or financial support, or benefit from the professional social security system (Mutuelle Sociale Agricole).
21 The Loi d'Orientation Agricole (Law on Agricultural Orientation) is a legislative instrument whose purpose is to organize and orientate the French agricultural sector.

References

Agrikoliansky, E., Fillieule, O. and Mayer, N. (2005) *L'Altermondialisme en France*, Paris: Flammarion.

Aguiton, C. and Bensaïd, D. (1997) *Le Retour de la Question Sociale*, Lausanne: Page Deux.

Alland Jr., A. (1994) *Le Larzac et Après*, Paris: L'Harmattan.

Ariès, P. (2000) *José Bové*, Villeurbanne: Golias.

Bello, W. (2009) *The Food Wars*, New York: Verso.

Bernstein, H. (2010) *Class Dynamics of Agrarian Change*, Halifax and Winnipeg: Fernwood Publishing.

Bodnar, I. (2003) 'Roquefort vs. Big Mac', in *European Journal of Sociology*, 44(1): 133–144.

Bourdieu, P. (1977) 'Une class-objet: la paysannerie', in *Actes de la Recherche en Sciences Sociales*, 17–18: 2–5.

Bourdieu, P. (2003) 'Participant objectivation', in *Journal of the Royal Anthropological Institute*, 9(2): 281–294.

Bruneau, I. (2004) 'La Confédération paysanne et le "mouvement altermondialisation"', in *Politix*, 68(17): 111–134.

Byres, T. (2009) 'The landlord class, peasant differentiation, class struggle and the transition to capitalism', in *Journal of Peasant Studies*, 36(1): 33–54.

Capdevielle, J. (2001) *Modernité du Corporatisme*, Paris: Presses de Sciences Po.

Cardon, D. and Granjon, F. (2005) 'Médias alternatifs et média-activistes', in E. Agrikoliansky, O. Fillieule and N. Mayer (eds) *L'altermondialisme en France. La longue histoire d'une nouvelle cause*, Paris: Flammarion, pp. 175–198.

Champagne, P. (1990) *Faire l'Opinion*, Paris: Editions de Minuit.

Champagne, P. (2002) *L'Héritage Refusé*, Paris: Le Seuil.

Champagne, P. (2003) 'Les medias et le traitement des problèmes sociaux', in F. Duschesne and M. Vakaloulis (eds) *Médias et Luttes Sociales*, Paris: Editions de l'Atelier, pp. 91–108.

Confédération paysanne (1996) 'La Confédération paysanne et le mouvement social', in *Campagnes Solidaires*, 93:2.

Confédération paysanne (2008) *1987–2007: Une Histoire de la Confédération Paysanne*, Bagnolet: Confédération paysanne.

Contamin, J.-G. (2005) 'Les grèves de décembre 1995', in E. Agrikoliansky, O. Fillieule and N. Mayer (eds) *L'Altermondialisme en France*, Paris: La Découverte.

d'Almeida, F. (2003) 'La politique entre propaganda et communication', in F. Duschesne and M. Vakaloulis (eds) *Médias et Luttes Sociales*, Paris: Editions de l'Atelier, pp. 63–78.

Damien, D. and Bové, J. (2008) le cirque médiatique (documentary, 54 minutes), Le Plan B.

Demossier, M. (2003) 'Rural France in Europe', in *Modern & Contemporary France*, 11(3): 259–263.

Desmarais, A.-A. (2007) *La Via Campesina*, London and Ann Arbor: Pluto Press.

Duclos, N. (1998) *Les Violences Paysannes sous la Ve République*, Paris: Economica.

Giugni, M. (2004) *Social Protest and Policy Change*, Lanham: Rowman & Littlefield.

Lagrave, R.-M. (1988) 'Mensonge romanesque et vérité des romanciers', in *Etudes Rurales*, 109: 55–73.

Lagrave, R.-M. (2004) 'Le marteau contre la faucille', in *Etudes Rurales*, 171–172(3–4): 9–25.

Le Goff, J.-P. (2006) *Mai 68, l'Heritage Impossible*, Paris: La Découverte.

Lebovics, G. (1992) *True France*, New York and London: Cornell University Press.

Lebovics, G. (2004) *Bringing the Empire Back Home*, Durham and London: Duke University Press.

Lebovics, G. (2009) 'Les sciences divisées, l'humanité partagée', in J. Christophe, D.-M. Boëll and R. Meyran (eds) *Du Folklore à l'Ethnologie*, Paris: Editions de la Maison des Sciences de l'Homme, 13–19.

Lehning, J. (1995) *Peasant and French*, Cambridge: Cambridge University Press.

Lynch, E. (1998) 'Le parti socialiste et la paysannerie dans l'entre-deux guerres', Ruralia. Online. Available at: http://ruralia.revues.org/document54.html (accessed 1 June 2012).

Lynch, E. (2009) 'L'agriculture au Centre rural de l'Exposition international de 1937: entre agrarisme, folklore et modernisation', in J. Christophe, D.-M. Boell and R. Meyran (eds) *Du Folklore à l'Ethnologie*, Paris: Editions de la Maison des Sciences de l'Homme, pp. 64–75

Martin, J.-P. (2000) *La Confédération Paysanne et José Bové*, Ruralia. Online. Available at: http://ruralia.revues.org/document142.html (accessed 1 June 2012).

Mayaud, J.-L. (2008) *Le Paysan dans la Publicité*, Paris: Paris Bibliothèques.

McMichael, P. (2000) 'Global food politics', in F. Magdoff, J.B. Foster and F.H. Buttel (eds) *Hungry for Profit*, New York: Monthly Review Press, pp. 125–144.

McMichael, P. (2008) 'Peasants make their own history, but not just as they please...', in S. Borras Jr., M. Edelman and C. Kay (eds) *Transnational Agrarian Movements Confronting Globalization*, Oxford: Wiley-Blackwell, pp. 37–60.

Mendras, H. (2000) 'L'invention de la paysannerie', in *Revue Française de Sociologie*, 41(3): 539–552.

Mertes, T. (2004) 'José Bové: a farmers' international?', in T. Mertes (ed.) *A Movement of Movements*, New York and London: Verso, pp. 137–151.

Moulin, A. (1988) *Les Paysans dans la Société Française*, Paris: Editions du Seuil.

Neveu, E. (2002) *Sociologie des Mouvements Sociaux*, 3rd edn, Paris: La Découverte.

Paxton, R. (1997), *French Peasant Fascism: Henri Dorgères' Green Shirts and the Crises of French Agriculture, 1929-1939*, New York: Oxford University Press.

Ponton, R. (1977) 'Les images de la paysannerie dans le roman rural à la fin du XIXe siècle', in *Actes de la Recherche en Sciences Sociales*, 17–18: 62–71.

Price, R. (1987) *A Social History of 19th Century France*, New York: Holmes & Meier.

Riutort, P. (2007) *Sociologie de la Communication Politique*, Paris: La Découverte.

Roederer-Rynning, C. (2005) 'France's FNSEA', in D. Halpin (ed.) *Surviving Global Change?*, Aldershot: Ashgate, pp. 91–114.

Sommier, I. (2003) *Le Renouveau des Mouvements Contestataires à l'Heure de la Mondialisation*, Paris: Flammarion.

Traïni, C. (2003) *Les Braconniers de la République*, Paris: PUF.

Wright, G. (1964) *Rural Revolution in France*, Stanford: Stanford University Press.

7   Movement culture continuity

The British anti-roads movement as precursor to the Global Justice Movement

Cristina Flesher Fominaya

Introduction[1]

In 1993, Britain's Department of Transport (DOT) decided to extend the M3 motorway through Twyford Down[2] and the town of Winchester. A group of environmentalists named themselves the 'Donga tribe', after the ancient system of trackways that criss-crossed the downs, and pledged to fight the planned extension. Using non-violent direct action they waged a campaign to prevent the road from being built. Anti-roads protest was not new in the UK, but Twyford came at a time when the environmental movement in the UK was stagnant (Wall 1999a; Doherty and Rawcliffe 1995), public interest in the environment was low, and pressure groups had lost support (Wall 1999a; Wilkinson and Schofield 1994). Locals had been opposed to the scheme since the 1970s, but it was direct action that brought the issue to national attention and re-energized anti-roads protest. The local association had exhausted every possible legal channel, to no avail (Bryant 1996), and some of its members and other locals opposed to the road were receptive to direct action repertoires (Stewart interview, Wall 1999a; *Undercurrents* Vol. 1; Doherty 1998); thus, local opposition and direct action campaigners became linked. The dramatic disruption tactics used by the protesters, the novelty of the 'colorful' alternative lifestyle of the counter-cultural direct action protesters juxtaposed with the participation of 'normal' locals, and the violent eviction of the Dongas' camp generated intense media scrutiny (see also Wall 1999a; *Undercurrents* Vol. 1; Doherty 1998; Rootes 1999).

Over the next four years protesters waged anti-roads campaigns all over Britain. Twyford was followed by protests in Glasgow, Newcastle, East London, and Solsbury Hill. In East London, protesters were joined by local middle- and working-class families who wanted to save their homes from destruction when an extension of the M11 was built to shave eight minutes off the commuter time into London. Protesters occupied the condemned houses on Claremont Road and converted the street into a vibrant community, with two cafés, an art house, and live music on Sundays. In the last weeks of the protest, trade union activists, New Travellers, squatters, and hunt saboteurs swelled the ranks. An estimated 500 protesters faced 200 bailiffs, 700 police and 400 security guards in the final 'battle'. Ultimately, Claremont Road was demolished, but the movement kept going.

'Noisy defeats' led to 'quiet victories' as the threat of direct action protests combined with local pressure resulted in the scuttling of Oxleas Wood (Stewart interview, Stewart *et al.* 1995; Doherty 1998), the widening of the M25, the M1 and M62 link in Yorkshire and the Salisbury Bypass (Wall 1999b). Between 1994–1997 protests were staged in Lancashire, Newbury and Devon, and dozens of smaller protests were waged throughout the 1990s.

The largest of these occurred in 1996, when 14 protest camps dotted a nine-mile stretch of road in preparation for the fight against the Newbury Bypass. Sophisticated communications systems linked the camps (mostly composed of tree houses). Friends of the Earth supported the campaign, local aristocrats and business people pledged their support, and lawyers were available to help the protesters after their arrests. By the time the final 28 campers had been evicted, more than 700 protesters had been arrested. The Newbury Bypass was built, but government policy was shifting, at least partly in response to the growing protests (Stewart interview; Stewart *et al.* 1995; Wall 1999a).[3]

From a proposed 600 road schemes in the *Roads to Prosperity* programme presented by Margaret Thatcher's government in 1989 in an effort to boost the economy,[4] the programme had dwindled to a mere 50 schemes in 1998, many of them minor. Protest activity reflects these shifts, with protests against roads decreasing in response to the cuts. Doherty (1998) argues that it is difficult to weigh the effect of anti-roads protests on the cuts in the DOT programme, because in 1994 there was considerable evidence of opposition to road building from within government. He concludes, however, that the wider debates in the media and by Conservative and Labour governments about the need to rethink transport policy seems unlikely to have moved 'as far or as fast without [anti-roads protesters'] actions'.

The British anti-roads movement was one of the most dynamic, innovative and sustained movements in the UK in the 1990s. Due to this movement, at least up into the 2000s, the proposal of a major road scheme was guaranteed to undergo close public scrutiny, and policing, security, eviction and construction delay costs needed to be factored in. But the movement's impact upon policy is not the only factor to consider. Tarrow (1994) argues that the legacy of protest also lies in the development of new tactics, the mobilization of people who had not protested before, and a shift in public consciousness, all of which can be claimed for this movement. Wall (1999a, 1999b) and Stewart (interview and 1995) point to the importance of the anti-roads movement in re-energizing protest in the UK, and the sheer quantity of anti-roads media coverage and the level of support of locals in the campaigns (see also Rootes 1999) point to a shift in the way roads are viewed. Fiddes (1997) argues that anti-roads protests and the development of a DiY (Do it Yourself) culture may represent the development of an environmental counter-culture on a scale not previously seen in the UK. Anti-roads protests have had a cultural impact as well. From television soap operas (e.g. Coronation Street) to mystery novels (e.g. Ruth Rendell's *Road Rage*), the image of the anti-roads protester has entered the cultural lexicon of the UK.

The movement was itself the product of the confluence of influences from earlier movements and networks in the UK, but also notably in the US, where groups such as Earth First! and other eco-tage direct action groups flourished, as well as Critical Mass, which developed into an important organization in the UK and elsewhere. Reflecting the particular ways in which national contexts translate outside influences, the spiritual deep-green aspects of the US eco-tage movements were less prevalent in the UK, where activists were more likely to make strong connections between environmental and social justice issues, making clear links between what were formerly understood as 'single' issues (environment) to broader critiques of wealth inequality, the effects of capitalism and social justice.[5]

Thus, an important legacy of the anti-roads movement has been its impact upon the development of the anti-capitalist networks that were the precursors to and early participants in what became known as the Global Justice Movement (GJM). Reclaim the Streets and Critical Mass, key actors in the anti-roads movement, were also key organizers of the J-18 protest (18 June 1999) in the City of London, which formed part of the Global Carnival Against Capital, an international day of protest whose slogan was 'Our resistance is as transnational as capital', and which was timed to coincide with the G8 summit in Cologne, Germany (Scott and Street 2000).[6] These protests were themselves inspired by earlier protests organized by the Greenham Common Women's Peace Camp, who in 1983 and 1984 engaged in a Stop the City Campaign to protest against the military-industrial complex, under the slogan 'Carnival Against War, Oppression and Destruction'. This formed one of the many precursor anti-capitalist events which predated the 'Battle of Seattle' against the World Trade Organization, considered to be the moment at which the GJM burst into public awareness.[7]

This chapter draws on ethnographic research on the British anti-roads movement conducted in the 1990s to show that this movement was one important and influential precursor to the anti-capitalist GJM. Many of the features of the GJM (and the current anti-austerity protests) that were heralded as new and unprecedented were in fact already being developed in earlier movements, including this one. There is evidence of organizational and individual actor continuity between the anti-roads movement and the GJM, both in Britain and globally. For example, SchNEWS, an important alternative media collective, founded in 1994, traces a line in their own evolution from anti-roads to anti-capitalism to GJM and beyond:

> From the anti road protests at the M11 in London to the Newbury Bypass to the big Reclaim The Streets events of the nineties SchNEWS was there. From worker's struggles such as the Liverpool Dockers, fights against privatisation of public services to reporting on social centres and sustainable futures – week in week out SchNEWS reported the news from the direct action frontlines. Then in February 1998 some of the crew went to Geneva to the first ever Peoples' Global Action conference. Here we met people

involved in grassroots movements from across the world, swapped stories, made friendships and began to see the bigger picture, and with many others who had been involved in localised direct action campaigns, our attention now turned to also attacking the corporate carve-up of the entire planet while supporting the diverse small-scale alternatives. The first signs of this new shift was in May 1998 when mass demonstrations were held world-wide simultaneously against the G7 Summit in Birmingham, then again on June 18th 1999.

(J18)[8]

Activists involved in RTS were also early members of the PGA network, and their influence is felt in the PGA hallmarks,[9] which closely reflect central anti-roads principles and autonomous principles more broadly.[10] More important than individual or organizational continuity, however, are the ways in which the features of movement culture – which encompasses particular collective identities, repertoires of contention, and philosophies of activism – are transmitted to subsequent movements. Organizational continuity does not necessarily indicate or guarantee cultural continuity. While new movements always translate and somewhat alter this cultural legacy, I hope to show here the high degree of cultural continuity between these two movements, not just nationally, but also in terms of the broader, global influence of the British anti-roads movement. This is not to privilege this particular movement's influence (a similar case could be made for the influence of Italian autonomous movements in Italy, for example[11]) but, rather, to highlight the ways that specific national movement *cultural* trajectories can serve as laboratories which nurture the development of movements beyond their borders.

Through a process of experimentation and practice, the British anti-roads movement articulated five elements that would become central defining characteristics of the Western/Northern manifestations of the GJM:

1   the ideologically heterogeneous nature of its membership;
2   the explicit linking of formerly separate issues (urban social justice and rural conservation) to a broad anti-capitalist framework;
3   the fundamental tension between 'vertical/reformist' and 'horizontal/radical' actors;
4   the centrality of innovative tactical repertoires of direct action; and
5   a markedly anti-identitarian stance.

Movement culture continuity: five features

The ideologically heterogeneous nature of movement membership: an anti-ideological ideology

It can be quite an anti-ideological movement really.

(Jason, anti-roads activist)

Within the core of the anti-roads movement were activists who identified with a range of ideologies: green, deep ecology, eco-feminism, Marxism, anarchism, socialism, as well as those who, on principle, rejected subscribing to any articulated ideology, and those who were simply not bothered about ideology at all (see Plows 2000; Wall 1999a; Dobson 2000; McKay 1998; Aufheben 1998).[12] While such heterogeneity is not surprising to those familiar with the GJM, it was quite a remarkable feature of a movement in the early 1990s and a fertile experimental ground on which to grow movement practices that enabled all those different ideologies to converge into a sustainable, if loosely defined, collective identity.

While it may seem contradictory to state that people who might identify with a range of ideologies were at the same time anti-ideological, this was in fact a core element of movement culture. While *individuals* and *affinity groups* might in fact subscribe to a particular ideology, they did not push these forward in collective spaces or assemblies, or did so at their peril. As with the later pushback in the anti-capitalist globalization movement against the Socialist Workers Party (SWP) (who were accused of 'monopolizing resistance' – in a twist on the GJM slogan 'Globalize resistance'[13] – by trying to convert and recruit members and to dissuade people from direct action), anti-roads activists by and large had little time for people who tried to push their own agendas forward because to do so would (a) fail to recognize the right of others to hold a different view, and (b) be counterproductive to the task at hand, which was, above all, to stop road building by any means necessary.[14]

Of course, the movement was not without internal conflicts and divisions. As Wall (1999a) shows, it was precisely because of disillusionment with groups such as Friends of the Earth, Greenpeace and the Green Party that many activists in Earth First! were inspired to take up direct action and more confrontational politics. Although interviews and later accounts of the movement show that the incidence of cliques and cultural vanguardism did increase over time, manifesting more as protesters became more established and some identities became more fixed (see Wall 1999; Plows 2000; McKay 1998; Monbiot 2000), activists were keenly aware that this was problematic and re-emphasized those aspects of movement culture that served to minimize its impact. In writing about Earth First!, Plows' (1998: 152) declaration 'I should emphasize before I go further that I am speaking as *a* voice of Earth First, not *the* voice' is a typical distinction made by anti-roads activists.[15]

One activist characterized the development of the anti-roads camps in this way:

> As you had at Manchester and Newbury you had people with slightly different views set up different camps. At Manchester there was a camp of the people who had moved up from Exeter, another group were vegans, they had a more travellers style community, one camp was more welcoming for people with children, another was far more single people – it allows for difference, for diversity, even though the overriding issue and aim is the same. There is lots of communication between the bases.

McKay's (1998: 15) argument that the organization of the direct action campaigns is 'intuitively anarchist', rather than explicitly so, connects to this element. This is in keeping with another trend (itself influenced by anarchist principles) to refuse to define or categorize action in explicitly ideological terms. This resistance can have various motivations: historically, the term 'anarchist' has been twisted from its original meaning and deployed as an effective weapon against protesters in the press. But as Hill (1995) notes: 'It is a feature of anarchist ideas that they have often been embraced without their adherents identifying with the term or being aware of earlier movements'. It is also important to note that anarchism was by no means the only influence in the movement.

The highly *strategic* nature of the anti-ideological stance of the movement culture is also very clearly reflected in the culture of the GJM and the more recent anti-austerity movements, and is also often overlooked or misunderstood by observers of all three movements/waves. This approach was summarized in the *One No Many Yeses* slogan and title of a book about the GJM written by Paul Kingsnorth (2004), an activist in the British anti-roads movement.

The explicit linking of formerly separate issues to a broad anti-capitalist framework

Up until the early 1990s, it is fair to say that most movement actors (and observers) saw themselves in terms of mostly single issues (the environmental movement, the peace movement, the anti-nuclear movement) and single or, at best, hyphenated identities (e.g. socialist-feminist). The anti-roads movement is an important example of a movement that began to explicitly make connections between issues that were formerly seen or framed as unrelated, or at least not directly connected. Anti-roads frames ran the gamut from deep-green rural conservational to social justice for urban dwellers whose communities were being destroyed to build bypasses such as the M11 in London. The critique of car culture was linked to a push for affordable alternative forms of transport, and to environmental issues such as smog and car pollution-related illnesses, CO_2 emissions, global warming and the loss of green-belt land. Campaigners began to make connections between relentless advertising for new cars, the push for new roads, developers' proposals for new out-of-town supermarkets, and the construction of bypasses with the destruction of rural and urban communities, the death of the high street, and urban blight.

The vast array of anti-roads frames was remarkable (Flesher Fominaya [Eguiarte] 2000), and perhaps it was precisely this multiplicity of frames that led to one common denominator that stood out for many activists (profit over values), and which paved the way for the anti-capitalist movement that grew directly out of the anti-roads networks. It was a natural progression from the multiplicity of anti-roads frames to a broader anti-capitalist stance and movement and to the building of alliances across issues. The solidarity of RTS with the Liverpool Dockers strike was an important example of early alliance-building within the anti-roads movement, and marked it as a focal point around which the anti-capitalist movement would develop and cohere. This action also prefigures the participation of the Seattle longshoremen in 1999. The diversity of frames and actors led to a common denominator of anti-capitalism for many movement actors,[16] which enabled the forging of alliances across diverse issues and groups. At the same time the explicit commitment to diversity as an organizing principle was a precursor to the establishment of this principle as a fundamental feature of the autonomous wing of the GJM.

The fundamental tension between 'vertical/reformist' vs 'horizontal/ radical' actors

At the start of the movement, the distinction later made in anti-capitalist activist usage between 'verticals' and 'horizontals' had not yet been made. Nevertheless, a fundamental tension between the two approaches to collective action was very clearly present in the British anti-roads movement. Writing in 1999, (Flesher Fominaya [Eguiarte] 2000) I summarized this tension as shown in Table 7.1.

It was precisely the movement's ability to forge alliances and action campaigns across this divide (and across ideological and tactical diversity) that made the movement such a success, again a clear precursor for the types of alliances which were to be seen later in the GJM.

Drawing mostly on data from Spain, I later summarized the differences between the institutional left and autonomous actors in the Global Justice Movement as shown in Table 7.2 (Flesher Fominaya 2007a).

The parallels and overlaps between these two sets of contrasts are significant, and continue to reflect fundamental differences in approaches to collective action in contemporary global justice/anti-austerity movements today. The British anti-roads movement was very successful in bridging these divides, despite conflict and tensions, but the 'concreteness' of the roads issue (no pun intended) may also have played a key role in this. As an issue, roads quite literally cut across

Table 7.1 Two ideal-typical ideological trends within core activists: 'social-expressive' and 'political-instrumental' conceptions of protest

	Political-instrumental	*Social-expressive*
Relation to state	Transform	Resist
Target of protest	State	Society
Relation to mass media	Work closely	Avoid, create alternative
Importance of mass media for movement	Very important	Not important/shouldn't be important
Importance of direct action	A critical method among many forms of protest	The method
Tactics/ideology/culture	Separable	Inseparable
Primary frames/attraction to movement	Environmental/Green	Direct action/communal and alternative lifestyle/ anarchist

Table 7.2 Ideal-typical differences between the autonomous and institutional left political models

	Institutional Left	Autonomous
Political model	Representative	Participatory
Organizational structure	Vertical with clear division of labour and authority	Horizontal, rarely permanent delegations of responsibility
Decision making	Votes, negotiations between representatives	Consensus, assembly is sovereign
Subject	Unitary (worker/citizen)	Multiple identities
Ideological base	Unitary/explicit	Heterogeneous/often left implicit
Legitimate political actor	Collective/party/union	Individual acting collectively
Use of acronyms	Important identifier, symbol of political stance and responsibility	Against acronyms
Political arena	Public/government	Public (streets, public spaces) and private (personal relations, daily life)
Typical repertoire of intervention	Manifestos, protest marches, strikes, legal reforms	Protest demonstrations, direct action, civil disobedience, alternative self-managed collective projects (e.g. social centres), counter-cultural lifestyle politics
Means/ends	Variable	Inseparable, means are ends in themselves if directed at social transformation
Social transformation comes through:	Institutions	Creating alternatives, cultural resistance
Organization is:	Permanent	Contingent, open to continual critical reflection and dissolution

rural/urban and conservative/conservation/progressive divides; roads are visible, as is the destruction they cause. Nevertheless, the movement developed a sustained anti-capitalist critique linked to the roads issue which would lay the groundwork for mobilization against neo-liberal capitalism. The growing influence of autonomous principles and their legitimacy (and, conversely, the illegitimacy of NGOs or more institutionalized groups) within the anti-roads movement was clear in the following quote from a FOE member, himself deeply involved in that NGO's activities:

J: At Newbury FOE got involved again and they were doing a lot of press-release work from London for good or bad. It added a profile to the campaign which may have made a difference as far as media coverage, which I hope it didn't, but it might have.

C: You hope it *didn't*?

J: Yes, it's wrong. You shouldn't have to have an NGO involved – I think it's a valuable news story regardless of who's supporting it. A lot of the staff went down there, but I think it counted as work days for them. It doesn't seem right when everyone else is taking time off and doing it on their own. That causes a lot of resentment among people who are environmentalists because they bloody well believe in it, and people who are on a campaign because they are paid to ... a lot of people believe that highly paid campaigners are just there for the money.

As I have argued elsewhere (Flesher Fominaya 2007a, forthcoming a), the legitimacy of autonomous *principles* in the GJM, despite the continued influence of institutional left groups and NGOs in arenas like the ESF and the WSF, was a notable feature of that movement, and the dominance of assembly style decision-making in the *Indignados* and Occupy camps (2010–2012) is a further testament to their ongoing influence.

Centrality of innovative tactical repertoires of direct action

Direct action has a long history in the UK, from the Diggers in the seventeenth century via mass trespasses against common land enclosures in the late nineteenth and early twentieth centuries and the suffragettes, to the peace camps and anti-nuclear movements from the 1950s to the present.[17] These movements have roots not only in anarchist traditions (see Woodcock 1962), but also in the romantic tradition (see Veldman 1994), the non-violent civil disobedience tradition, and the left-libertarian tradition.[18] For example, Alex Plows, one of the original protesters camping at Twyford Down, made explicit links between the Greenham Common Peace Camp culture and the camp culture at Twyford:

It was very much like Greenham in the sense that we were building community, living on the land, right in the route of the road so it's not like we were just living in our little commune off in the sticks, we have our bodies and our lives on the line right in the middle of this road. We were building community and were living as lightly as we can: we're sharing water, we're sharing resources. It was kind of like post-Greenham. A lot of the lessons had been taken on board and the whole ethic and atmosphere was a lot more an awareness of how patriarchy fucks up men as well as women and basically all of us being more in touch with our male and female sides…

While many people fighting roads in the UK lobbied, pressured politicians, and employed traditional campaigning methods, there is no doubt that direct action had a spectacular role in the movement, not just for its media appeal, which was great, but also because direct action formed such a core element of so many activists' identities, and because shared experiences of direct action, and long weeks, months and even years living together in anti-roads camps, played a key role in forging collective movement identity.

The British anti-roads movement was also tremendously tactically creative. Tactics and creativity were intimately linked, which makes particular sense in a movement where a core of activists were engaged in lifestyle politics. In criticizing the classical idea of society, Alain Touraine (1988: 39) argues that:

> …the unity of modern societies ought not to be defined as a passage from culture to nature, or from passion to interest, but as a movement for the liberation of human creativity. What is new here is the fact that the unity of social life is no longer derived from the idea of society. To the contrary, what is called society is considered henceforth more as a set of rules, customs, and privilege against which individual and collective efforts at creation must always struggle…

Touraine captures an essential aspect of the anti-roads movement: the link between individual sovereignty (the subject), struggle against norms and rules, and the release of creative energy as a means to human liberation. An important benefit of this fluid campaign culture and the freedom of the atmosphere was that it allowed for the release of much creative energy in the form of development of new strategies, symbolic protest through artwork, site recreation, and community building (see also Jordan 1998; North 1998). Anti-road camps and squatted urban areas were protected from eviction by elaborate defense systems designed to delay the evictions, which were developed throughout the movement's trajectory and which varied from site to site. Particularly innovative was the tunneling technique, which involves digging a tunnel into the ground and then moving in. If bulldozers attempt to move over the tunnel, it will collapse, killing or injuring the protester inside. Removing the protesters from the tunnels is time consuming and therefore expensive. The creative energy expended on transforming an occupied site into a protest zone, as opposed to merely organizing a protest at a site, also flowed from this autonomous environment.

Claremont Road, the heart of the 'last stand' against the M11 link road through East London, was declared the Independent State of Leytonstonia. This site was unusual in that it was permanently occupied by protesters for well over a year, and much time and energy was lavished on the site before its destruction by the demolition squads. Artistic expression and symbolic protest were critical features of this site (see also Jordan 1998). RTS street parties, with their combination of occupation of public space, frivolity, deliberate attempts to engage local communities and direct action, were also innovative and were reproduced around the world.[19] The influence of DiY culture in the movement, which also inspired rave culture, also added to the emphasis on creativity (see McKay 1998) While a detailed survey of the creativity of tactics in the GJM and their similarity to those developed in the anti-roads movement is beyond the scope of this chapter, a close perusal of such anti-roads manuals as *Road Raging: top tips for wrecking roadbuilding* (1997) and a look through books such as *We are Everywhere* (Credland *et al.* 2003) will provide substantial visual and written confirmation of the similarities between them. Other examples include the importance of carnivalesque actions such as street parties that are confrontational, defensive *and* fun and occupied autonomous zones. The idea of fun as an intrinsic element of protest, a concept that is now seen as commonplace in Europe, was not so common in the early or even late 1990s, when more staid and 'serious' forms of militancy predominated in many places. The ludic aspect of the movement has by no means been adopted across the board,[20] but the widespread use of samba bands, versions of the Rebel Clown Army, puppets and masks which are now routinely found in protests in Europe has been significantly inspired by British direct action campaigns developed largely in the British anti-roads movement and transmitted in such events as the London ESF in 2004, and has been a significant legacy of this movement in the GJM. The carnivalesque Pink and Silver bloc, first used at the Prague World Bank/IMF counter-summit protests in 2000, was adapted from the RTS street parties (Juris 2005).

A markedly anti-identitarian stance

In addition to the anti-ideological stance of many anti-roads and global justice activists, the British anti-roads movement also had a strong anti-identitarian current. As with the anti-ideological ideology this was at least in part strategic as much as ideological, which again is a central feature of the autonomous sections of the GJM (Flesher Fominaya 2010).

A key point of convergence running through all the activists interviewed, regardless of ideological orientation, was a commitment to individual freedom. Paradoxically, it is this commitment that formed the basis of shared community and emerged as the most outstanding cultural characteristic. The sense of building or creating community was a critical ideological component of the autonomous activists, but this community was conceived of as consisting of individuals who were free to 'be themselves', unconstrained by any organizational membership requirements. As autonomous individuals, no one was in a position to tell anyone else what to do, or to speak for the movement; it left individuals free to sign onto whatever project they felt important or viable. This cultural element developed very strongly later on in the GJM, particularly among activists from the UK, who were often hostile to what they termed 'shopping list identities' (e.g. gay, black, worker) which were seen as static and limiting because they fail to recognize that subjects are not uni-dimensional (Flesher Fominaya 2007a, forthcoming a). Clearly, the point is not to deny the importance of identities, but to reject the idea of single identities being the best basis for collective action. This particular aspect was later more broadly adopted in the autonomous movements in the GJM (Flesher Fominaya [Eguiarte] 2005), and can be seen as a radical departure from the strongly identity-based movements of the 1990s, such as the gay/lesbian movements.

British anti-roads as precursor to the Global Justice Movement

The strong resemblance between key features of the British anti-roads movement and the later development of the anti-capitalist movement is clear, as is a certain overlap of networks that nourished both movements in Europe. While it is not a question of drawing a straight uninterrupted line between movements, even within a national context, what is clear is that movement culture, strategies, frames and tactics developed in the fertile and creative ground of the anti-roads movement evolved and flourished in the GJM. There is no doubt that the movement was an important influence in the GJM in Europe and beyond. The five elements discussed here – ideological heterogeneity; explicit linking of formerly separate issues to anti-capitalist critique; a tension between the institutional and autonomous approaches to mobilization that, nevertheless, was often successfully bridged; the diffusion of innovative and creative tactical repertoires of direct action; and a strategic anti-identitarian ideology – are all clearly reflected in the GJM. The expression of autonomous principles and a rejection of institutional left politics within the GJM is widely documented (see, for example, Davis 2004 and Holmes 2004). Many of the methodologies and principles embraced by autonomous groups today emerged from the laboratories of movements like the British anti-roads movement, which itself drew upon the experiences of earlier movements, both national and transnational.

The success of the anti-roads movement rested in large part not on structural factors (such as strong organizational infrastructure, significant resources, access to political elites, etc.), but on cultural factors. It was precisely the movement *culture*, understood here as a set of meanings and practices, that developed so as to allow the widest array of ideologies, identities and even 'frames' or rationales for fighting roads to co-exist in diversity yet unity around a single goal: stopping new roads. This same approach, deeply rooted in autonomous political culture, is also what nourished the development and sustained much of the success of the anti-capitalist globalization movement. A historical and cultural approach to movements, grounded in empirical data rather than grand narratives, allows us to understand the crucial role of history and culture in social movement success. McKay's work on cultures of resistance (1996) documents the transmission of movement counter-cultures even when many contemporary activists and observers are ignorant of them. As Melucci (1980, 1989) argued, contemporary social movements are cultural laboratories, experimenting with new codes and alternative forms of practice. They may lie latent and submerged for long periods, or appear to do so, but when they become visible they are not bursting forth *de novo*; they are rooted in the movement networks that generate them, however many new recruits they may bring on board when things get exciting. This was true of the British anti-roads movement and of the GJM, and is true of the current wave of global protests against enforced austerity and global financial corruption. Tracing movement continuity is particularly difficult in cases where 'biodegradable networks' (i.e. those made up of deliberately transitory organizations) make organizational continuity difficult to trace. And even organizational continuity is not a sure indication of cultural continuity. A cultural approach to movement continuity offers promising avenues to explain emerging waves of protest that uninformed observers are often too quick to categorize as 'spontaneous', 'new' and 'unprecedented'.

Notes

1 The analysis presented here draws on multiple sources: participant observation at three anti-road sites in June 1994 and July 1998, including 12 in-depth interviews with ten long term activists highly involved in the movement, lasting from 2–6 hours; movement literature: weekly news from 1994–2000 (*SchNEWS*), press releases, flyers, video coverage (*Undercurrents*), alternative books/manuals; anti-roads websites from 1997–2000 (Earth First!, RTS1, Weedslinks, Benjamin's Action Resources); two activist listserves (1998–2000); analysis of over 200 articles on anti-roads in the mainstream British press (primarily from *The Times*, *Guardian*, *Observer*, *Independent*, *Daily Telegraph*, *Sunday Times*, *Evening Standard*, and the *Mirror*, but also some local coverage); and scholarly publications as cited. All quotes come from my interviews or conversations unless otherwise noted. I engaged in ethnographic research on the Global Justice Movement from 2002–2005, mainly in Madrid, but also at ESF encounters and other GJM events in Spain, the UK and Germany.

2 A down is a hill.

3 For specific connections between particular campaigns and changes in government policy during 1995, see Alarm UK (1995). Wall (1999a), in his book on Earth First! and the anti-roads movement, also contends that protests resulted in significant shifts in the government's transport policy, at least in the short term. See also Rowell (1996) for more on the DOT's Roads Programme.

4 The DOT boasted at the time that it was the biggest road-building programme that Britain had seen since the Romans.

5 See also Scholl (this volume, Chapter 8) on the importance of environmental issues in the British GJM.

6 See http://bak.spc.org/j18/site/uk.html#reports. RTS was the contact organization for the London protests.

7 For more on the global antecedents of the GJM see Katsiaficas 2004.

8 www.schnews.org.uk/about_us/.

9 See www.agp.org.

10 Also shared by Italian groups like Ya Basta!, also founders of PGA.

11 Or the the Zapatistas in Mexico, etc.

12 If we look beyond the core to activists in the local campaigns we find every traditional party represented as well: Barbara Bryant and others who were at the forefront of the local campaign against the road through Twyford Down, for example, were members of the Conservative Party.

13 See www.schnews.org.uk/monopresist/monopoliseresistance/index.htm.

14 Of course, the roots of this approach are drawn from earlier movements, and are very similar to other European autonomous movements inspired by anarchism and feminism, among other influences (see Katsiaficas 2006).

15 This was later reflected in the PGA principle of refusing to allow the coordinating committee to 'speak for the PGA'.

16 But certainly not all. The movement very successfully bridged radical direct action activists with conservative rural traditionalists who by no means embraced anticapitalism as a mobilizing ideology.

17 See McKay (1996) for a detailed discussion of cultures of resistance in the UK since the 1960s.

18 Wall (1999a) notes that the decision-making processes and organizational style of Earth First! UK fit all of Kitschelt's (1989: 67) left-libertarian characteristics of European Greens.

19 For much more on tactics in the movement, see Road Alert (1997). For an academic treatment see Doherty (1999a, 1999b).

20 Initially, the use of humour was strongly resisted in some circles in the Spanish GJM (Flesher Fominaya 2007b), which shows that movement culture innovation meets resistance transnationally (see Flesher Fominaya, forthcoming b), but Romanos (this volume, Chapter 13) shows that it has since become an important part of movement culture in the *Indignados* movement, which indicates that the influence of movements like the British anti-roads movement can be felt over long periods of time and across space.

References

Alarm UK (1995) *Roadblock*, London: Alarm UK.

Aufheben (1998) 'The politics of anti-road struggle and the struggles of anti-road politics', in G. McKay (ed.) *Diy Culture*, London:Verso.

Bryant, B. (1996) *Twyford Down*, London: Spon Press.

Credland, T., Chesters, G., Jordan, J. and Ainger, K. (2003) *We are Everywhere*, London: Verso.

Davis, J. (2004) 'This is what bureaucracy looks like', in E. Yuen, D. Burton-Rose and G. Katsiaficas (eds) *Confronting Capitalism*, Soft Skull Press: New York, pp. 347–366.

Dobson, A. (2000) *Green Political Thought*, London: Routledge.

Doherty, B. (1998) 'Opposition to road-building', *Parliamentary Affairs* 51 (3): 370.

Doherty, B. (1999a) 'Paving the way, *Political Studies*, 47 (2).

Doherty, B. (1999b) 'Manufactured vulnerability: eco activist tactics in Britain', *Mobilization*, 4 (1): 75–87.

Doherty, B. and Rawcliffe, P. (1995) 'British exceptionalism?', in I. Blühdorn, F. Krause and T. Scharf (eds) *The Green Agenda*, Keele, Staffordshire: Keele University Press.

Fiddes, N. (1997) 'The March of the earth dragon', in P. Milbourne (ed.) *Revealing Rural 'Others'*, London: Pinter, pp. 37–55.

Flesher Fominaya, C. (2000) 'Ideology and culture among core activists in the British anti-roads movement', Sixth International Conference on Alternative Futures and Popular Protest, Manchester: Manchester Metropolitan University, 1: 1–18 (published as Cristina Eguiarte).

Flesher Fominaya, C. (2005) The Logic of Autonomy, University of California, Berkeley, PhD Dissertation. ISBN 978–0–542–293504 (published as Cristina Flesher Eguiarte).

Flesher Fominaya, C. (2007a) 'Autonomous movement and the institutional Left', *South European Society and Politics*, 12(3): 335–358.

Flesher Fominaya, C. (2007b) 'The Role of humour in the process of collective identity formation in autonomous social movement groups in contemporary Madrid', *Humour and Social Protest*, International Review of Social History, 52: 243–258.

Flesher Fominaya, C. (2010) 'Creating cohesion from diversity', *Sociological Inquiry*, 80(3): 377–404, doi: 10.1111/j.1475–682X.2010.00339.x.

Flesher Fominaya, C. (forthcoming a) *Social Movements and Globalization*, London: Palgrave Macmillan.

Flesher Fominaya, C. (forthcoming b) 'Movement culture as habit(us)', in B. Baumgarten, P. Daphi and P. Ullrich (eds), *Protest|Culture*.

Hill, D. (1995) 'The New Righteous', in *The Observer*, 12 February 1995.

Holmes, B. (2004) 'The Revenge of the concept', in E. Yuen, D. Burton-Rose and G. Katsiaficas (eds) *Confronting Capitalism*, Soft Skull Press: New York, pp. 347–366.

Jordan, J. (1998) 'The art of necessity', in G. McKay (ed.) *Diy Culture: Party and Protest in Nineties Britain*, London: Verso.

Juris, J. (2005) 'Violence performed and imagined', *Critique of Anthropology*, 25(4): 413–432.

Katsiaficas, G. (2004) 'Seattle was not the beginning', in E. Yuen, D. Burton-Rose and G. Katsiaficas (eds) *Confronting Capitalism*, Soft Skull Press: New York, pp. 3–10.

Katsiaficas, G. (2006) *The Subversion Of Politics*, AK Press Distribution.

Kingsnorth, P. (2004) *One No, Many Yeses*, Simon and Schuster: UK.

Kitschelt, H. (1989) *The Logics of Party Formation*. Cornell University Press: Ithaca.

McKay, G. (1996) *Senseless Acts of Beauty*, London: Verso.

McKay, G. (1998) 'DiY Culture' in G. McKay (ed.) *Diy Culture: Party and Protest in Nineties Britain*, London: Verso, pp. 152–173.

Melucci, A. (1980) 'The New social movements', *Social Science Information* 19: 199–226.

Melucci, A. (1989) *Nomads of the Present*, London: Hutchinson Radius.

Monbiot, G. (2000) 'Streets to Nowhere', in the *Guardian*, 10 May 2000.

North, P. (1998) 'Save our Solsbury!', *Environmental Politics*, 7(3): 1–25.

Plows, A. (1998) 'Earth First!', in G. McKay (ed.) *Diy Culture: Party and Protest in Nineties Britain*, London: Verso. pp. 152–173.

Plows, A. (2000) 'Collective Identity through Collective Action', Sixth International Conference on Alternative Futures and Popular Protest, Manchester: Manchester Metropolitan University.

Road Alert (1997) *Road Raging*, Road Alert, Newbury.

Romanos, E. (2013) "Collective learning processes within social movements", in C. Flesher Fominaya and L. Cox (eds) *Understanding European Movements*, London: Routledge.

Rootes, C. (1999) 'The Transformation of environmental activism', *Innovation: the European Journal of Social Science*, 12(2):155–173.

Rowell, A. (1996) *Green Backlash*, London: Routledge.

SchNEWS (2001) *Monopolise Resistance*, Brighton: SchNEWS. Also available at www.schnews.org.uk/.

SchNEWS (2004) *SchNEWS at Ten*, Brighton: SchNEWS.

Scholl, C. (2013) "Europe as contagious space", in C. Flesher Fominaya and L. Cox (eds) *Understanding European Movements*, London: Routledge.

Scott, A. and Street, J. (2000). 'From media politics to e-protest', *Information, Communication and Society*, 3(2): 215–240.

Seel, B., Paterson, M. and Doherty, B. (2000) *Direct action in British environmentalism.* London: Psychology Press.

Starr, A. (2005) *Direct Action*, Zed Books, London.

Stewart, J., Must, E. and Bray J. (1995) *RoadBlock*, ALARM UK.

Tarrow, S. (1994) *Power in Movement*, Cambridge: Cambridge University Press.

Touraine, A. (1988) *The Return of the Actor*, Minneapolis: University of Minnesota Press.

Undercurrents Video Series (1994) Vols 1 and 2, London: Small World Media.

Veldman, M. (1994) *Fantasy, The Bomb, and the Greening of Britain.* Cambridge: Cambridge University Press.

Wall, D. (1999a) *Earth First! and the Origins of the Anti-roads Movement.* London: Routledge.

Wall, D. (1999b) *Earth First! and the Anti-Roads Movement.* London: Taylor and Francis.

Wilkinson, P. and Schofield, J. (1994) *Warrior*, Cambridge: James Clarke and Co.

Woodcock, G. (1962) *Anarchism*, London: Penguin.

Part III

Culture and identity in the construction of the European "movement of movements"

8 Europe as contagious space

Cross-border diffusion through EuroMayday and climate justice movements

Christian Scholl

Introduction

On 14 June 1997 50,000 people participated in a march for social justice at the EU meeting in Amsterdam. Never before had a European mass protest attracted such numbers. Lasting for several days, these EU protests contained elements that became typical of summit protests against the meetings of big intergovernmental organizations such as the World Bank, the WTO, and the G8. The first World Social Forum in 2001 in Porto Alegre inspired a European version under the motto "Another Europe is possible". Counterglobalization networks gained a new arena for converging tactics in constructing alternatives from below.

This chapter conceptualizes Europe as a *contagious space* for the cross-national diffusion of these ideas and tactics. After a brief description of these networks and a conceptual discussion of cross-national diffusion, I argue that (dis-)continuities can best be grasped from a process-centred approach to diffusion. Ideas and tactics can be contagious, *but they need local and translocal networks in order to spread.* This story is told by examining the role and the functioning of international linkages and European networks, but also both the continuities and the ruptures in the construction of a viable European counterglobalization project.

The following two case studies examine the diffusion process of ideas and tactics throughout European counterglobalization networks. I explore the Euro-MayDay movement and the diffusion of MayDay parades and the master-frame of "precarity",[1] and the climate justice movement, specifically the diffusion of climate camps and the master-frame of "climate justice". Based on several years of ethnographic fieldwork in several European countries (Netherlands, Germany, the UK, Spain, Italy, France) covering different types of mobilization (summit protests, EuroMayDay protests, climate justice and Occupy camps), in-depth interviews with key organizers, and text analysis of activist journals and websites, my approach focuses on process-tracing. Centring on the processes of innovation, imitation and adaptation, I explain how learning within and across social movements in Europe occurs, and I examine cross-national differences and similarities in the outcomes of diffusion.

In the following section I elaborate upon the role of cross-border diffusion processes for social movements. A brief overview of the development of counterglobalization networks then sheds light on the historical background of the processes of diffusion discussed here. The third section analyses the diffusion of ideas and tactics using my case studies of EuroMayDay and the climate justice movement. The chapter closes with a discussion of the differences and similarities between the diffusion processes in both cases. I show how counterglobalization networks have opened the way for many movements and mobilizations to diffuse their ideas and tactics more rapidly. The process of diffusion, however – its speed, scope, and continuity – depends upon the linkages of local and translocal activist networks.

Cross-national diffusion

Movements and activists never emerge in isolation. There are always ideas and tactics available from the past or from different contexts. Diffusion is the transfer of ideas or tactics from one site to another across time and space (McAdam *et al.* 2001: 68). This transfer may be within a nation-state, such as the diffusion of the Monday manifestations in East Germany in 1989. This chapter, however, focuses on cross-border diffusion, the transfer of ideas and tactics across national borders in Europe. Cross-border diffusion is not a phenomenon unique to the current global era: the 1848 upheavals, the civil rights movement, and the 1960s student movements all exhibited similar dynamics (McAdam and Rucht 1993; Oberschall 1989). What is notable about the current wave of diffusion, however, is that it connects national contention to transnational conflicts or international institutions.

That ideas and tactics get diffused does not mean that they function in the same way or result in similar effects. In being diffused, repertories are imitated, but are also changed and adapted. For example, the tactic of barricading has undergone significant transformations throughout the centuries (Bos 2005). As Chabot and Duyvendak (2002) point out, diffusion processes can easily result in selective imitation and diminishing effectiveness. This means that only certain parts of an idea or tactic are imitated, while other parts are left out or moulded by other influences. While this may render a specific tactic ineffective, adaptation might also be critical for the successful application of a specific tactic. The Gandhian tactic of nonviolent non-cooperation, for example, was adapted and developed in the US civil rights movement (Chabot 2000; McAdam 1983).

Indeed, seeing activists and protesters as purposeful does not diminish the ways in which tactical repertoires have expressive dimensions that help to build collective identities and submerged networks (Epstein 1991; Melucci 1989). Expressive dimensions are not only important for attracting support and broad participation; they also enable the diffusion of the movement's message through the media (Chabot and Duyvendak 2002). It also helps to build emotional ties among movement participants, solidarity and collective identities. Tactical repertoires thus have instrumental and expressive functions that can be directed internally as well as externally (Scholl and Duyvendak 2009).

In his analysis of the "pace of black insurgency" in the US civil rights movement, McAdam (1983) foregrounds the processes of innovation and adaptation in order to grasp the tactical interaction between insurgents and authorities. Such processes include imitation. As della Porta and Diani (2006) point out, there can be different motivations for imitation in social movements: (1) the success of a specific idea or tactic can trigger imitation (e.g. the 1999 Seattle blockades); (2) style (such as samba bands suddenly emerging during many mass protests in Europe); and (3) traditions of movements (e.g. explicit internationalism).

McAdam and Rucht (1993) break down the diffusion process conceptually into four components: (1) the transmitter/actor initiating diffusion; (2) the adaptor/actor adopting the transfer; (3) the item that is being diffused – here, ideas and tactics; and (4) the channel – i.e. the path via which the process of diffusion unfolds. However, as Snow and Benford (1999) show, in the case of the cross-national peace movement, when cross-national linkages of social movements are very dense and continuous, the distinction between transmitter and adaptor might become empirically impractical. This may well be the case with Europe, given the dense cross-national counterglobalization networks that have flourished throughout the past decades.

In order to understand the different pathways of diffusion, Tarrow (2005: 105) distinguishes relational diffusion from non-relational diffusion, and from mediated (brokerage) diffusion. *Relational* diffusion takes place via an attribution of similarity between two contexts. However, Snow and Benford (1999: 25) stress that similarity always involves social construction because similarities between struggles are never self-evident, but are actively attributed. *Non-relational* diffusion takes the path of theorization – through a book or a manifesto, for example. Finally, *mediated* diffusion relies on brokerage, such as individual activists or organizations actively connecting different sites. One can doubt, however, whether these three paths are empirically distinguishable and whether one "single" diffusion process can so easily be explained causally. Therefore, I suggest seeing diffusion as a process involving attribution of similarity, theorization, and brokerage, which in turn depends upon whether it is ideas or tactics that are being diffused.

Europe as contagious stage: counterglobalization networks in Europe

The formation of counterglobalization networks has long been underway (Pleyers 2010; Starr 2005, 2001), and can be placed on a continuum with the protest wave of the 1960s (Scholl 2012; Maeckelbergh 2009).[2] A number of protests, campaigns, and movements from the preceding decades feed into our present protests:

*   Social movements from the Global South resisting free trade agreements, World Bank sponsored projects, privatizations and other neoliberal policies have been a huge source of inspiration for European activists; in particular,

the anti-dam movements in India, the MST (movement of landless farmers) in Brazil, and, most prominently, the Zapatistas.
- The Peoples' Global Action (PGA) network, which was founded during the second global Zapatista gathering of grassroots movements; a European arm started to organize bi-annual meetings, bringing together important action groups and movements around Europe.
- Earlier campaigns such as STOP MAI, against the Multilateral Agreement for Investment, and the "Euromarches against Unemployment" brought together many counterglobalization activists for the first time, forcing NGOs to leave the terrain of single-issue activism.

These networking dynamics intensified after the 1999 Seattle protests and, for two years, nearly every month a summit protest has taken place somewhere in Europe (see Notes from Nowhere 2003). Important networks that came out of these dynamics include:

- The Attac network, which is particularly strong in France and Germany, and now has thousands of members in national and local chapters all over Europe. A big part of their work goes towards awareness-raising, providing critical information about neoliberal globalization. Attac had a crucial role in the World Social Forum process and often mobilizes towards summit protests.
- The first World Social Forum (2001), which was rapidly imitated at regional, national, and even municipal levels. The European Social Forum created a space for articulating the idea "Another Europe is possible".
- Various networks among larger NGOs ("The world is not for sale", for example), which use social forums for networking and often organize counter-summit conferences next to summit protests.
- The Noborder network of European antiracist activists, which supports migrants' struggles and which has strong ties to counterglobalization networks. Noborder camps have been held almost annually since 1999; during summit protests they frequently have specific action days around migration.
- The Dissent! Network, which was founded for the 2005 G8 protests in Gleneagles (Scotland), and which adapted the PGA principles, and includes many of the groups in that previous network. The name was adapted by German activists to mobilize with a similar network towards the 2007 G8 protests in Heiligendamm.

In the aftermath of the 2001 attacks on the World Trade Center, anti-war protests took off and incorporated many exisiting counterglobalization networks and individual activists (Diani 2005). Social forums and summit protests/counter-summits remained important networking opportunities for counterglobalization movements, enabling the cross-border diffusion of ideas and tactics. However, summit protests also generated intense debates on tactics and strategies, above all around the confrontational practices of black blocs (see Holloway and Sergi in Starr *et al.* 2011). A good part of these networks saw the entire focus on summit protests as a failure, given the intense police repression and the seeming impossibility of disrupting these meetings after the first protests.

This wave of counterglobalization movements has seen the proliferation of networks that transform Europe into a contagious stage of transnational protest. Moreover, due to the availability of relatively cheap flights, geographical proximity is collapsing as a limiting factor. Between European activists within these networks, "continental English" has become the standard language for international meetings. Through EU-funded exchange programs, the biographies of many young people include (sometimes several) international experiences.

Having described Europe as a contagious space is not to say that one can separate it empirically from the rest of the world. The influence of other continents is indispensable, particularly when looking into processes of diffusion. The use of blockading repertoires during summit protests was inspired by the 1999 Seattle protests, the valorization of diversity by the Mexican Zapatistas, and so forth. In looking more carefully at the processes of diffusion within Europe in the next sections, I do not mean to suggest that influences from transnational networks beyond Europe have played no role. Where possible, I make them visible.

Cross-national diffusion of ideas

The diffusion of ideas will be analysed by applying frame analysis focusing on the social construction of problems and solutions and the way movements spread their vision of society (Johnston 2002). For each case, I study the creation, imitation, and adaptation of one master-frame. A master-frame offers a broad interpretation of social reality and functions as an umbrella interlinking various frames as specific elaborations of that master-frame (della Porta and Diani 2006: 79–81).

The diffusion of the "precarity" frame

The starting point of the master-frame of precarity was Italy, which, since the 1990s, has been a laboratory of new forms of struggle that inspired counterglobalization movements. In dialogue with Hardt and Negri's (2000) ideas on the role of immaterial labour in contemporary capitalism in the Global North, the actions of the *Tute Bianche* ("White Overalls") contrasted the invisible service work in precarious conditions of cognitive, flexible and temporary workers with the blue-collar workers (*Tute Blu* in Italian) of industrial capitalism. The Tute Bianche were also an active player within the PGA network at that point.

However, one of the first explicit and visible mobilizations against precarious labour conditions took place by temporary McDonald's workers in France in 2000. While "no" to precarity was the central message in this mobilization, precarity was later affirmed and reframed as a positive identity of a new political subject: the precarious worker (see Raunig 2007). This kind of reframing activity has taken place in important social movements before: for example, the civil rights and the LGBT rights movement. The motto for the 2002 MayDay in Milan captured this message: *il precariato si ribella* ("the precariat rebels"). One important player was ChainWorkers, a radical union for precarious temporary workers in big chains set up in 1999. One chain-worker explains their take on precarity (Foti in Oudenampsen and Sullivan 2004):

> So precarity rallies different people. As Milanese and MayDay people we think that certain young people, women and migrant workers have a special stake here because they are the social categories being most aggravated by precarity. From another point of view, I think that service industry and knowledge industry – technicians, programmers, cashiers and retailers, sellers, cultural operators, truck drivers and pizza delivery boys – are crucially important. These two very polarised categories are statistically the two sectors that have seen the highest growth of employment during the last twenty years of neoliberalism.

Attempting to make 1st May a free day for temporary workers and re-politicize labour relations, ChainWorkers organized their first public MayDay intervention in 2001 in the run-up to the Genoa protests. This was continued in the form of annual MayDay parades in Milan, attracting 100,000 people by 2004.

The master-frame of precarity/precarization consists of four key elements:

* Precarity is an important part and effect of neoliberal globalization
* Precarization is a transversal phenomenon and concerns the totality of social life (e.g. housing, education, affective relations)
* Precarization is a transnational phenomenon, and the struggle against it must be so too
* Precarization creates the class of the "precariat" (as distinct from the industrial "proletariat").

These elements demonstrate how the idea of precarity functions as a master-frame that integrates a number of issues that interconnect easily with counterglobalization frames. The struggle against precarity is, for example, frequently connected to the idea of a basic income and other social rights.

EuroMayDay activists use many forms of creative media activism to communicate the idea of precarity (Hamm and Adolphs 2009), e.g. an online parade, a board game called Precariopoly and "subvertizing" (spoofs and parodies of corporate or political advertisements). These new communication tools diffuse the master-frame of precarity. In a playful variation on the Catholic culture of patron saints, San Precario was launched as the patron saint of precarious people.

The shift towards framing MayDay as a European day of action had already been reflected in the motto for the 2003 MayDay: "la parade del precariato europeo". That year, more and more European groups were involved in preparing for the parade in Milan. In 2005, 19 other European cities organized the first EuroMayDay under the motto "Precarious people of the world let's unite and strike 4 a free, open, radical Europe". Other important moments for diffusing the precarity frame were the 2004 European Social Forum in London and the 2005 G8 protests in Scotland. Marking the discrepancy with old socialist frames of "full employment", the precarity action day in Edinburgh was announced as a "Carnival for full Enjoyment".

Furthermore, activist journals in English such as *Greenpepper, Mute magazine*, the *Fibreculture Journal*, and *Transform* played a key role in diffusing the frame of precarity throughout Europe. These journals were important instruments because in many countries the term "precarity" needed some explanation and the Italian theories about immaterial labour needed contextualization. This shows the close interconnection of linguistic and political translations. These journals became a platform for spreading the ideas which were coming mainly from the Italian context, adapting them to other situations.

The diffusion of the "climate justice" frame

The context for the emergence of the climate justice master-frame was decisively different from the context of the precarity master-frame. Whereas precarious labour and life conditions were hardly present in the public debate in the early 2000s, "climate change" had become the subject of widespread heated debate: various publications, such as the 2006 Stern report, triggered wider coverage and several UN conferences were devoted to finding global solutions. In consequence, the climate justice frame was not so much an attempt to put this issue on the agenda, but rather to redefine the dominant interpretation of the problem and to criticize the proposed solutions. One key slogan of recent protests symbolizes this attempt: "Make system change, not climate change".

The origins of the "climate justice" frame can be less clearly traced back to one context in Europe. Several trajectories and sites were important in this process. In the run-up to the Kyoto protocol, environmental and counterglobalization movements started to protest at UN Conferences of the Parties (UN COP) where global measures against climate change and global warming were supposed to be taken (e.g. in the Hague in 2000). The central critique of the Kyoto protocol was that it applied market mechanisms to nature without enforcing a more sustainable way of production and actual emission reductions. A climate justice assembly has taken place at the World Social Forum for several years, and has made a collective declaration.

Another trajectory developed from the 2005 G8 protests in Scotland, where a day of climate-related action took place. Having a strong environmental focus, a good part of the British counterglobalization networks decided to continue with a major focus on climate change. One of the results, from 2006 onwards, is an annual *climate action camp*, inspiring similar camps in other countries. These climate action camps generally try to combine discussion and information exchange with concrete DiY alternatives and direct action.

At the 2007 UN COP meeting in Bali, broader movements and counterglobalization groups got involved for the first time and organized a parallel

"Solidarity Village for a Cool Planet" (Guerrero 2011). During this event Climate Justice Now! (CJN) was founded, picking up the counterglobalization movements' tradition of horizontal and plural network organization. This network criticized the monopoly of Climate Action Now! (CAN), a platform of moderate NGOs, for being the only one allowed to participate in the negotiations. CJN criticized the UN's focus on technological and alternative lifestyle solutions that failed to address the systemic economic underpinnings of the climate crises.

The 2009 UN COP meeting in Copenhagen became a major focus of cross-border mobilization efforts in Europe. This UN meeting was supposed to reach an agreement on the second commitment period of the Kyoto protocol[3] creating the first worldwide carbon speculation market. Thus far, this mobilization was the most important one, focusing so specifically and extensively on climate justice issues. Networks included CAN, CJN, and *Climate Justice Action* (cooperating with CJN). Entitled "You can't fix a broken system", one Call to Action captures the critique of the UN process:

> The UN climate talks will not solve the climate crisis. We are no closer to reducing greenhouse gas emissions than we were when international negotiations began fifteen years ago: emissions are rising faster than ever, while carbon trading allows climate criminals to pollute and profit. At present, the talks are essentially legitimising a new colonialism that carves up the world's remaining resources. Faced with the profound crisis of our civilisation, all we get is a political circus playing to the interests of corporations.
>
> (Climate Justice Action 2009)

The "climate justice" frame consists of four arguments:

- Climate justice challenges inequalities and social injustice, resulting in differential responsibilities for the Global North and the Global South ("climate debt")
- Climate change and ecological destruction are transnational problems and the struggle against them must be so too
- Climate justice calls into question the limitations of our economic system, which is based on growth and fossil fuel dependence
- Indigenous movements in Bolivia and Ecuador propose "buen vivir" as an alternative to "development".

There were manifold attempts to align the frame of climate justice with other social struggles, such as migration, anti-militarism, and the struggle against capitalism. However, during this mobilization the tension widened between the groups supporting market-based mechanisms to tackle climate change ("The world needs a deal") and the groups that criticize them ("No deal is better than a bad deal"). Moreover, the UN was an ambiguous opponent because some groups still had hopeful expectations from the UN negotiation process. The network dynamics of previous summit protest mobilizations clearly fed into this mobilization. Many activist groups and individuals saw the mobilization towards Copenhagen as a logical continuation of counterglobalization protests. One of the activists involved explains:

> The Climate Justice Action network met from September 2008 onwards. It was a long and complicated process to find a consensus on the form of the major protest action. The main reason was that lengthy debates took place about how to take positions towards the UN. There were people who believed in a "one-foot-in and one-foot-out" strategy and wanted to combine protest inside the UN meeting with protest on the streets. Others did not want to engage with the UN meeting at all and wanted to protest against the root cause of climate change: capitalism.

Still, the climate justice master-frame strongly resonated within certain ongoing struggles, especially those of indigenous communities in Latin America. The Bolivian president Evo Morales was one of the fiercest opponents of the plans presented in Copenhagen, and in 2010 he called for a *People's Summit on Climate Justice and the Right of Mother Earth*. A number of European activists attending this conference collectively produced a booklet to link those discussions back to the European context (Building Bridges Collective 2010). However, except for countries like the UK, where the frame had previously been widely used, "climate justice" after the Copenhagen summit seemed to resonate little in Europe.

Cross-national diffusion of tactics

Tactical repertoires are sites of contestation (Taylor and van Dyke 2004: 268), mirroring the strategic attempts of social movements to create obstacles for their opponents. As Tarrow (1994) points out, repertoires have to calibrate the point between conventional political action and political violence. Ritualization is one danger of tactical repertoires, radicalization/polarization another. The problem might be that social movements need a bit of both: ritualization to be recognizable and innovation to disrupt. The question is thus how to balance this through creative innovation, drawing on past repertoires. For each case I consider one tactical repertoire that introduced a number of tactical innovations and was then imitated and adapted throughout the process of diffusion.

The tactical repertoire of Mayday parades

Mayday parades clearly copy elements of carnival and street parties that were picked up by counterglobalization protesters, such as the British Reclaim the Streets movement and gay pride parades. ChainWorkers innovated the summit protest repertoire by opposing traditional trade union practices in the context of labour struggles on the first of May. On their website it says:

Mayday Parade is the first european self organized demonstration against precarization. Traditionally mayday represented aging unions and the traditional left, both too stale and backward looking to see what the social mobilisations are that society is asking from us. We think that the future lies in developing forms of self-mobilization and production of conflict across wider political spaces, in expressing political and social claims independently – working with existing radical parties and existing radical unions and associations – but as an autonomous force and with new imagery.

(ChainWorkers n.d.)

Five recurring elements now structure MayDay parades as a tactical repertoire. They

- imitate a political march and sometimes picket lines, and hence connect to a familiar repertoire
- utilize colourful and carnivalesque elements, picking up on the earlier Reclaim the Streets tactics
- invite individuals and groups to contribute in their own way
- use popular culture imagery to communicate radical messages, such as superheroes or comic heroes
- allow for a certain degree of "diversity of tactics" familiar from counterglobalization protests.

The 2004 European Social Forum in London constituted an important moment of diffusion of this tactical repertoire. At the parallel alternative forum *Beyond ESF* the "Middlesex Declaration of Europe's Precariat" was drafted:

[…] We have decided to prepare for a common EURO MAYDAY 005, to be held in Europe's major cities, calling for angry temps, disgruntled parttimers and union activists to mobilize against precarity and inequality to reclaim flexibility from managers and bureaucrats, thus securing flexicurity against flexploitation. […] We call onto all our European sisters and brothers, be they autonomous marxists, postindustrial anarchists, syndicalists, feminists, antifas, queers, anarchogreens, hacktivists, cognitive workers, casualized laborers, outsourced and/or subcontracted employees and the like, to network and organize for a common social and political action in Europe […].

(Anonymous 2004)

After the 2004 ESF, national and international preparation meetings were held in several cities, including Paris, Berlin, Hamburg and Milan. In 2005 EuroMayDay parades were held in 19 European cities, and in 22 cities in 2006. In 2007, the EuroMayDay made a first attempt to launch a global MondoMayDay. In 2006 only Tokyo participated, but in 2009 parades took place in nine cities outside Europe.

One successful example of diffusion is Germany. Since 2006, EuroMayDay parades have been held in Berlin, Hamburg, and Hanau, attracting several thousand participants. In Berlin, the fact that "precarity" functions as a master-frame was nicely visualized by distributing posters where protesters could write down their own demands. In Hamburg, another innovation was an action employing "precarious super heroes" copying comic heroes from popular television culture.

However, there were also less successful attempts for EuroMayDay actions – in the Netherlands, for example, where there is neither a strong 1 May tradition, nor a culture of mass demonstrations. Since 2010 a clear limit to the diffusion and expansion of MayDay parades has become apparent, and several cities have stopped organizing them. Endless repetition without significant results in specific protests without innovation can be a dead end for tactical repertoires. Although ritualization was part of the strategy, the EuroMayDay network often aimed at more continuous forms of struggle. Without going into further details, suffice it to say that EuroMayDay has not managed thus far to innovate this tactical repertoire and so move beyond the focus on 1 May.

The tactical repertoire of climate camps

Protest camps have a long tradition in Europe. In the early 1980s the UK *Greenham Common* women's peace camp opposing nuclear weapons found imitation in many places (Harford and Hopkins 1984; Flesher Fominaya this volume, Chapter 7). The early environmental movement also used camps, to protest at construction sites of nuclear power plants or nuclear waste depositions, for example (Barkan 1979). During the counterglobalization wave, the first mass action camp was the 2001 Noborder camp in Strasbourg. From 2003 onwards, the way in which that camp was organized (e.g. in self-organized "neighbourhoods") inspired protest camps opposing summit meetings in rural and remote areas, often with several thousand participants. During the subsequent summit protests in Evian 2003, Gleneagles 2005, and Heiligendamm 2007 an action camp repertoire consolidated into a number of elements:

- Self-organization: people staying in the camps need to self-organize and actively contribute to all collective tasks including, among other things, cooking, washing dishes, running the welcome/information point, cleaning, security, guard duties, or responding to journalists.
- Decentralized structure: normally divided into various neighbourhoods (according to origin, tactical, or other affinities), camps may function as fairly autonomous basic organizational units. They often come with popular kitchens and daily neighbourhood meeting spots.
- Consensus decision-making: this deliberative and inclusive form of decision-making works without voting, using facilitation and hand signals to moderate a complex collective progress of collecting information, proposals, support and objections.

- Multi-functionality: the camps serve to organize protests, to converge, discuss, and get to know each other, and to elaborate and demonstrate (or "prefigure") alternatives.
- Ecological alternatives: activists try to organize their camps in a sustainable way using ecological compost toilets, grey water systems, wind energy, permaculture, etc.

Particularly from 2006 onwards, British activists developed this last-named aspect in their annual climate camps. After the 2005 G8 protests in Scotland, many British counterglobalization activists decided to continue with a major focus on climate change and environmental destruction, and organized their first climate camp. These camps incorporated many of the elements of previous action camps, but also added a definite focus on ecological alternatives. Next to small-scale alternatives, exchange of information and skill, these camps also mobilized for mass direct actions, such as against the extension of Heathrow airport. At the 2009 G20 protests in London, climate justice activists organized a climate camp in front of the European Climate Exchange, which develops financial instruments for carbon trading. Riot police heavy-handedly evicted this encampment.

Along with the fact that an action camp was already a familiar repertoire, the success of the British climate action camps contributed to its rapid diffusion. Climate action camps took place in Germany in 2008, and in 2009 in Denmark, France, Ireland, the Netherlands/Belgium, Scotland, and Wales (as well as Australia and Canada). This explosion of climate action camps in 2009 was in part due to the ongoing mobilization towards the UN climate conference later on that year. The Climate Justice Action network deliberately decided to embed these camps in their mobilization efforts. In the years following the 2009 Copenhagen protests, however, climate action camps persisted only in a few countries, such as Germany and Belgium.

Comparing processes of cross-national diffusion in Europe

The EuroMayDay and the climate justice movements clearly constitute two differing trajectories for the diffusion of idea and tactics. The master-frame of precarity includes the notion of a "precarious class" and thus the projection of a collective identity. The visual and new media practices of the EuroMayDay network feed into this process of identity construction. The master-frame of climate justice is less explicit in defining the central agent of social change. Although the frame is connected to other struggles and social problems, there is no clear political subjectivity emerging from climate justice discourses. Perhaps this helps to understand the *differential* development of the diffusion process within Europe. EuroMayDay networks lasted longer and resulted in a more sustained chain of actions than did the climate justice movement after the 2009 UN protests. Precisely why climate justice movements did not trigger the construction of a collective identity should be subject to another inquiry.

On the level of tactics, too, diffusion processes in each case unfolded differently. Offering an easy way to be imitated, the annual MayDay parades were extended step-by-step to the European and then the global scale. Picking up elements of the previously diffused summit protest repertoire, MayDay parades were also easy to integrate into existing alterglobalization networks. Climate camps, on the other hand, initially triggered a similar dynamic, but this did not continue. One practical reason (amongst others) is the amount of work and the scope of the logistical operations necessary for a climate camp lasting several days, in comparison with the requirements for a one-day parade.

Another difference concerns the danger of ritualization. The MayDay parades purposefully use the ritual of 1 May demonstrations to introduce new radical language and forms of action into labour struggles. Through this focus, however, it has proven difficult to develop other forms of coordinated collective actions. Climate camps, by contrast, faced the danger of ritualization much quicker. Besides this, the annual character of the British camps forced organizers to identify an appropriate action target each year.

Nevertheless, there are also a number of notable *similarities* between these movements. In each case, one country served as an innovator and motor of diffusion: in the case of EuroMayDay, the diffusion of both the idea of precarity and the tactic of Mayday parades was propelled by movements in Italy, but in collaboration with activist networks from France and Spain. In the case of climate justice movements, above all it was the tactical repertoire of climate camps that was diffused throughout Europe from the UK. For these processes of diffusion, cross-border meetings and networks proved crucial.

This corroborates my argument that, in each case, diffusion needs to be understood from the perspective of counterglobalization networks. Ideas and tactics can be contagious, but they need local and translocal networks in order to spread. Brokerage and theorization (see Tarrow 2005) are both important mechanisms, but they can be better understood by mapping and analysing the process of network formation as the backbone of diffusion processes. From the flat ontology of networks, the discussion around transmitter versus adapter (Snow and Benford 1999) becomes nearly obsolete. Granted, it is important for a process-centred approach in order to see where ideas and tactics are innovated; However, the process of diffusion within and throughout counterglobalization networks is far more complex and multi-layered than such analytical categories suggest. As Doerr and Mattoni (2007: 2) argue, it might make more sense to conceive of a "cross-European communicative space in between activists".

Another similarity concerns the continuity of the process of diffusion. In both cases it appeared difficult to sustain and extend this process after the first few years. Diffusion intensified when the new ideas and tactics became successful in the innovating countries. Next to taste and traditions of movement, success thus seems to be a decisive path for diffusion in a context where similarity is generally already attributed. But, as Chabot and Duyvendak (2002) observed, diffusion comes with selective imitation and diminishing effectiveness. Although there were varying levels of success, no country repeated EuroMayDay or climate justice camps as successfully as the innovating countries.

Conclusion

In the cases of the EuroMayDay and climate justice movements, counterglobalization networks have proven to be productive catalysts for later struggles. In this sense the idea that "spin-off movements" (McAdam 1995) capitalize on the advantages and opportunities introduced by initiator movements proves to be correct. In keeping with the broader argument underlying this volume, however, the empirical evidence of my case studies suggests that there is more at stake: the counterglobalization project has fundamentally altered Europe as a political space for contagion. Transnational linkages not only persist, but feed and fuse into new mobilizations and movements. A Europe from below is no longer a claim or possibility; it has become a concrete and rapidly evolving reality.

As I have shown, major continuity exists on the level of ideas connected to counterglobalization: the critique of neoliberal capitalism is central to both the MayDay and climate justice movements. Both movements also continue to develop the counterglobalization movements' tradition of horizontal and network organization, through which to develop a *transnationalism from below*. Even on the tactical level, one can observe ongoing learning processes in transnational meetings, action camps, summit and other mass protests that use civil disobedience and direct action methods.

On the other hand, ruptures are undeniable. Many of the networks that were formed in the past decade had a hard time surviving in the long-term. Several struggles disappeared as suddenly as they emerged. It is too early to judge the cases of MayDay and climate justice networks. It is clear that their continuity in Europe cannot be taken for granted.

But then, maybe we are already witnessing the next transformation of the European counterglobalization project? For example, the recent wave of Occupy movements in response to austerity measures is yet another instance of European cross-border diffusion in which certain aspects of the counterglobalization wave are being employed. The Occupy encampments incorporated and continued important lessons from experiments with democratic self-organization in previous protest camps. The frame of "We won't pay for your crisis" resonates with the counterglobalization frame "Our world is not for sale". We may wonder how far cross-border diffusion from below can help to construct an alternative Europe.

Notes

1 Precarity can be defined as the "interminable lack of certainty, the condition of being unable to predict one's fate" (Neilson and Rossiter 2005). As I show in this chapter, precarity also includes the opportunities for new creative forms of organization.
2 But see Júlíusson and Helgason (this volume, Chapter 12) for the counter-example of Iceland, where a thriving 1968 movement produced no significant GJM mobilization.

3 The first commitment period of the Kyoto protocol started in 2008 and should be followed by a second commitment period in 2012.

References

Anonymous (2004) 'The Middlesex Declaration of the European Precariat'. Online. Available http://libcom.org/library/middlesex-declaration-precariat.

Barkan, S.E. (1979) 'Strategic, tactical and organizational dilemmas of the protest movement against nuclear power', *Social Problems* 27(1): 19–37.

Bos, D. (2005) 'Building Barricades: the Political Transfer of a Contentious Roadblock', *European Review of History* 12(2): 345–365.

Building Bridges Collective (2010) *Space for Movement*, Leeds: Footprint Workers Co-op.

Chabot, S. (2000) 'Transnational Diffusion and The African American Reinvention of Gandhian Repertoire', *Mobilization* 5(2): 201–216.

Chabot, S. and Duyvendak, J.W. (2002) 'Globalization and Transnational Diffusion between Social Movements', *Theory and Society* 31: 697–740.

ChainWorkers (n.d.) 'Mayday'. Online. Available www.chainworkers.org/MAYDAY/index.html.

Climate Justice Action (2009) 'You can't fix a broken system'. Online. Available www.climate-justice-action.org/news/2009/08/14/december-7th.

della Porta, D. and Diani, M. (2006) *Social Movements*, Oxford/Victoria: Blackwell Publishing.

Diani, M. (2005) 'The Structural Bases of Movement Coalitions', paper presented at the American Sociological Association Centenary Meeting, Philadelphia, August 2005.

Doerr, N. and Mattoni, A. (2007) 'The Euromayday Parade Against Precarity', paper presented at the 8th Annual Conference of the European Sociological Association, Glasgow, September 2007.

Epstein, B. (1991) *Political Protest and Cultural Revolution*, Berkeley: University of California Press.

Flesher Fominaya, C. (2013) 'Movement Culture Continuity'. In Flesher Fominaya, C. and Cox, L. (eds) *Understanding European Movements*, London: Routledge.

Guerrero, D. (2011) 'The Global Climate Justice Movement'. In Albrow, M. and Seckinelgin, H. (eds) *Global Civil Society 2011*, Houndmills: Palgrave Macmillan: pp. 120–126.

Hamm, M. and Adolphs, S. (2009) 'Performative Repräsentationen prekärer Arbeit: Mediatisierte Bilderproduktion in der EuroMayDay-Bewegung'. In Herlyn, G., Müske, J., Schönberger, K. and Sutter, O. (eds) *Arbeit und Nicht-Arbeit*, München: Mering: pp. 315–340.

Hardt, M. and Negri, A. (2000) *Empire*, Cambridge: Harvard University Press.

Harford, B. and Hopkins, S. (1984) *Greenham Common*, London: The Women's Press.

Holloway, J. and Sergi, V. (2011) 'Of Stones and Flowers', in Starr, A., Fernandez, L. and Scholl, C. *Shutting Down the Streets*, New York and London: New York University Press: pp. 155–169.

Johnston, H. (2002) 'Verification and Proof in Frame and Discourse Analysis', in Klandermans, B. and Staggenborg, S. *Methods of Social Movement Research*, Minnesota: University of Minnesota Press: pp. 62–91.

Júlíusson, A. and Helgason, M. (2013) "The Roots of the Saucepan Revolution in Iceland". In Flesher Fominaya, C. and Cox, L. (eds) *Understanding European Movements*, London: Routledge.

Maeckelbergh, M. (2009) *The Will of the Many*, London/New York: Pluto Press.

McAdam, D. (1983) 'Tactical innovation and the pace of insurgency', *American Sociological Review* 48: 735–754.

McAdam, D. (1995) ' "Initiator" and "Spin-off" Movements', in Traugott, M. (ed.) *Repertoires and Cycles of Collective Action*, Durham/London: Duke University Press.

McAdam, D. and Rucht, D. (1993) 'The Cross-National Diffusion of Movement Ideas', *Annals of the American Academy of Political and Social Science*, 528: 56–74.

McAdam, D., Tarrow, S. and Tilly, C. (2001) *Dynamics of contention*, New York and Cambridge: Cambridge University Press.

Melucci, A. (1989) *Nomads of the Present*, Philadelphia: Temple University Press.

Neilson, B. and Rossiter, N. (2005) 'FCJ-022 From Precarity to Precariousness and Back Again', *The Fibreculture Journal* 5. Online. Available http://five.fibreculturejournal.org/fcj-022-from-precarity-to-precariousness-and-back-again-labour-life-and-unstable-networks.

Notes from Nowhere (2003) *We Are Everywhere*, London/New York: Verso Books.

Oberschall, A. (1989) 'The 1960s sit-ins', *Researching Social Movements, Conflict, and Change* 11: 31–33.

Oudenampsen, M. and Sullivan, G. (2004) 'Precarity and N/European Identity', *Greenpepper* (October). Online. Available www.metamute.org/editorial/articles/precarity-and-neuropean-identity-interview-alex-foti-chainworkers.

Pleyers, G. (2010) *Alterglobalization*, Cambridge and Malden: Polity Press.

Scholl, C. (2012) *Two Sides of a Barricade*, New York: SUNY Press.

Scholl, C. and Duyvendak, J.W. 'Having/making fun as action repertoire', paper presented at Dag van de Sociologie Conference, Amsterdam, June 2009.

Snow, D.A. and Benford, R.D. (1999) 'Alternative Types of Cross-national Diffusion in the Social Movement Arena', In della Porta, D., Kriesi, H. and Rucht, D. (eds) *Social Movements in a Globalizing World*, New York: Macmillan: pp. 23–39.

Starr, A. (2001) *Naming the Enemy*, London: Pluto Press.

Starr, A. (2005) *Global Revolt*, London/New York: Zed Books.

Tarrow, S. (1994) *Power in Movement*, Cambridge/New York: Cambridge University Press.

Tarrow, S. (2005) *Transnational social movements*, New York: Cambridge University Press.

Taylor, V. and van Dyke, N. (2004) ' "Get up, stand up" ', in Snow, D.A., Soule, S.A. and Kriesi, H. (eds) *The Blackwell Companion to Social Movements*, Malden: Blackwell Publishing: pp. 262–293.

9 The shifting meaning of 'autonomy' in the East European diffusion of the alterglobalization movement

Hungarian and Romanian experiences

Agnes Gagyi

This chapter deals with two Eastern European localizations of the alterglobalization movement in the 2000s, and follows the conceptualization and usage of the idea of civil autonomy in these environments.[1] I will look at 'autonomy' not as a universal idea with a fixed meaning, but as a relational social fact which needs to be understood together with the position and context of its proponents (Bourdieu and Wacquant 1992). In so doing, I will follow the steps of Boltanski and Chiapello (2005), Eyal (2000), Bockman (2011) and Fraser (2009), who track critical political ideas through historical interactions which lead to results not necessarily corresponding with the original political intention of the ideas. Without venturing to present the whole history of the concept of autonomy in the European Left, or to map the internal debates over the independence of civil society within the alterglobalist movement, I will point out two contextual characteristics that have brought the notion of autonomy, as used in the alterglobalist movement, close to a liberal ideal of civil society, conceived as independent from its power context. I will then dwell on the consequences of this notion of autonomy in the two Eastern European cases.

The idea of autonomous global civil society: two remarks on context

The Romanian and Hungarian movements, along with their critical concepts of globalization, were part of the alterglobalization movement from the very beginning. I will point out two characteristics of the movement that I find crucial in explaining the paradoxes of Eastern European alterglobalism. The first is an overlap between the movement's self-definition and the expectations of intellectual commentators. The second is a change in liberal intellectual positions, prescribing support for a 'global civil society', for which the alterglobalist movement was treated as a model.

Movement actors and intellectual supporters: a coalition of 'principle'

The 'birth' of the alterglobalization movement in 1999 was greeted with high expectations on the part of intellectuals. Extensive research projects, such as the LSE Global Civil Society project led by Helmut Anheier (ongoing since 2001), or Democracy in Europe and the Mobilization of Society led by Donatella della Porta (2004–2009) explored the alterglobalist movement as a model for how a global civil society would emerge and bring forth global democracy. Theories of globalization treated what was supposed to be the networked, deliberative, anti-hierarchical, anti-representational, local, autonomous nature of this movement as the embodiment of the best expectations of researchers. The movement was presented as the 'right' social answer to the challenges of globalization. Many of these theories, beyond more political works such as those of Žižek, Chomsky, or Hardt and Negri, belonged to the mainstream of social theory (e.g. Bauman 2000; Beck *et al.* 1994; Castells 1997; Sassen 2000; Appadurai 2000).

There seemed to be a unique correlation between how these theories imagined progressive global politics and how the alterglobalization movement set its ideals. On the margins of the movement, more often than elsewhere, this relationship became one of mutual reassurance. 'These ignorant journalists should read the work of contemporary sociologist Manuel Castells, who says we are living in a NETWORK SOCIETY, and networks are the new organizing principle of human action everywhere', a Romanian Indymedia article complained when an action was interpreted along the lines of actual Romanian political cleavages instead of within an alterglobalist framework (diversi 2006).

One way to understand this relationship is to look at the historical connections between the movement and its research. The alterglobalist movement was constituted by highly educated people (della Porta 2005: 185, Table 8.2) often in direct contact with the lessons of globalization theories.[2] The movement itself was frequently interpreted and theorized by academic intellectuals, whose arguments were in turn fed back to the movement. Intellectual groups such as the French Attac or *Le monde diplomatique* played a significant role in founding the movement. The movement built upon theories and practices of social action that reached back to the tradition of the 1968 movement cycle, just as the interpretative schemes of many of its intellectual commentators did (Boltanski 2002; Graeber and Shukaitis 2007). From this perspective, it is no surprise that the ideals of the movement fit well into researchers' categories. But besides historical links, a further factor that made the movement's claim for 'autonomy' so popular should be considered.

'Global civil society': a position in the globalization debate

The alterglobalist claim for civil autonomy was also connected to a wider debate over democracy and globalization (Held and McGrew 2000), and, within that, to a specific change in intellectual positions on civil society.

In the second half of the 1990s the globalist coalition between political and economic liberals predicting the global victory of political democracy and free-market capitalism broke apart. Seeing the evidence of growing inequalities, political liberals began to speak about an economic globalization that generates inequality, and a civil globalization that generates a democratization of the glo-balization process (Stiglitz 1998, 2002; Kalb 2004, 2005).

The conceptual framework in which the globalization of civil society was imagined here bears the mark of the globalist ideal that preceded it. There, the realm of free market and democracy was imagined in a homogenous global space, irrespective of practical differences in power relations. Similarly, civil globalization was to create the homogenous and universal space of global civil society, independently from the inequalities it criticizes. This global space of civil society was expected to realize itself in the global network of autonomous civil actors (Juris 2004; Sassen 2001; della Porta 2008: 6–7).

The strong intellectual advocacy for the alterglobalist movement cannot be explained without taking into consideration this shift in intellectual positions. The idea of an 'autonomous' civil society provided an intellectual basis for criti-cizing neoliberal globalization on the respectable grounds of political democracy without calling for structural change. It allowed for an intellectual discourse that could remain critical and mainstream at the same time, avoiding a link between the 'autonomous' potential of civil society and existing structures of power relations.

Critics of the global civil society ideal argued that it is erroneous to select successful examples of 'global civil society' and posit them as signs of the birth of an autonomous and independent sphere of global civil action (Chandhoke 2002; Chandler 2005; Axford 2005). It misses the link between the nongovern-mental sphere and economic and governmental power hierarchies. Chandler claimed that the concept of an autonomous civil sphere is rather a gesture of 'normative support' for the actors operating under the slogan of civil autonomy, instead of a realistic image of the complex relationship between governmental and nongovernmental organizations (2005: 238–273).

Supporters of the idea of civil autonomy developed the narrative that civil society is a new collective agent born on the basis of resources created by neo-liberal globalization, and, as such, it is able to counter and control the negative effects of the former (della Porta and Tarrow 2005: 235; Hardt and Negri 2004). By contrast, critics of the idea argued that the growth of civil society follows closely from the neoliberal programme of delegating former state functions to other actors. Chandhoke argued that 'civil society' was the name given to the territory from which the state has withdrawn. From this point of view, the idea that global civil society would tackle global issues solely on an abstract ethical basis, without reference to existing power relations, reflects the confined position defined for it by existing power relations, not the omnipotence of a global civil movement (Chandhoke 2002).

Criticisms levelled against the notion of an autonomous civil society see this independence as a position defined by a wider power structure and tend to construe intellectual support for the idea of civil autonomy as ideological. Axford concludes that the idea of an autonomous global civil society actually works as a theoretical comfort in the face of the withdrawal of the welfare state, as the legitimation of globalist politics despite their negative effects (2005: 187–196). Indeed, there has been a prescriptive element in the way the alterglobalization movement has been raised to the position of a powerful agent in spite of its lack of effectiveness, a fact acknowledged by its supporters as well.[3] The intellectual idea that global civil society can bring forth social change solely on the basis of principles was mirrored in the movement practice, which emphasized principles and prefiguration over practical results. In the context of the two Eastern European cases, this concept of autonomy enabled a detachment of the local movement (as unquestionably relevant in principle) from its practical relationship to its actual context.

How 'global civil autonomy' arrived in Eastern Europe

Although theoretically omnipresent (as reflected in theories of global society as a network, or movement slogans such as 'We are Everywhere'; Notes From Nowhere 2003), the idea and practice of 'global civil autonomy' arrived in Romania and Hungary via specific historical routes. The first waves that reached these countries in 2002 were the Eastern European enlargement programmes of the European Social Forum (ESF), when potential participants and local organizers were being sought.

Eastern European participants did not have a significant influence on the ESF process. As Boris Kagarlitsky (2009), a Russian intellectual involved in the movement put it, the enlargement programme was experienced in Eastern Europe as a mere call for numbers of demonstrators, while the activist elite who defined the movement's agenda remained the same.

This lack of influence meant that the historical experience of 'actually existing socialism' was not reflected in the European alterglobalization movement. Eastern European activists had to deal with the difference between the sensitivities of post-communist societies and the Western left on their own, without being able to articulate this problem on the level of the European movement.

> There were too many red flags [on Western demonstrations]. We believed that with time the Western European wing of the alterglobalist movement would understand and internalize the Eastern European historical experience. That is: red flags yes, Stalin no, red star maybe, but carefully. Because a few decades ago, millions died under those signs. Today we know those hopes were futile.
>
> (R.G., Hungarian activist, 2008)

> I have the impression that the traditional European Left is avoiding the experience of the East European countries.... For some West European leftists, 'Stalinism has nothing to do with us', and socialism, including its

symbols and rhetoric, remains as valid as ever. From such a perspective those who come from the former 'socialist' countries are the only ones who need to 'get over' the collapse of Stalinism.

(Novak 2008)

The identification of local 'items' of global civil society was also problematic. In the search for local players, the 'we are everywhere' framework was not adjusted to the specific environments of post-socialist countries. Also, the possibility of joining a more resourceful Western movement incited competition among local groups.

In both Hungary and Romania the first people to join the ESF process were trade unionists and ex-communists with a political socialization from before 1989. These groups occupied the roles of local representatives of the alterglobalization movement, founded national social forums, and the local branch of Attac. Civil society organizations and informal groups who identified with the anti-hierarchical values of the movement were deterred by the gestures and language of these groups. They associated the former's style with the heritage of communist dictatorship. By 2003, these latter groups had organized themselves in separate networks. I will call this strain of alterglobalist activism the 'second wave' of the local alterglobalization movement.

In Romania the second wave of alterglobalism consisted of punk groups moving towards anarchist alterglobalism, and artist and intellectual groups which internalized the ideas of Western intellectual alterglobalism. Romanian Indymedia, started in 2003 by intellectual media workers, became a collective forum for groups in different cities. Apart from several debates over legitimacy, Romanian second-wave alterglobalist activism did not have significant ties with any of the official local ESF representatives, nor with any big NGOs. In several cases, mostly around specific campaigns, there was a weak collaboration with liberal NGOs. On these occasions alterglobalist activists benefited from the protection represented by their liberal allies, but the frameworks of the two sides did not interact.

Hungary, by comparison with Romania, had a stronger civil tradition from before 1989, accessible to young alterglobalist activists mainly in the form of green NGOs. Second wave alterglobalist activists formed an informal network that organized actions collectively, relying on the infrastructure and legitimacy of big NGOs. In Hungary, the divide between first- and second-wave alterglobalism was perceived as one between 'reds' and 'greens'. This divide, however, although often referred to as an ideological one, did not run between green and red NGOs, but between second-wave alterglobalism, relying on green NGOs, and the first-wave groups that occupied the position of the ESF's local partner. While in Romania the two waves barely interacted, Hungarian first- and second-wave organizations worked together in a conflictual manner. They competed for public recognition and the resources and trust of their western European partners.

By 2003 the second wave had broken with the official Hungarian Social Forum to create the Another World is Possible network (LMVH). Now the two branches of the movement officially became competitors. 'The basic question is, who will be the voice of globalization-criticism', wrote two second-wave activists (Csillag and Scheiring) in 2003.

> Nobody understands this abroad.... When they invite us to the West, they think it is us who are crazy.... [First-wave founders of the Hungarian Social Forum] told us we either join, or they issue a press release anyway, and the Hungarian Social Forum will be formed.... They think in a different way, in an old [communist] way. They appropriated this name, the Social Forum. The people who made up this first Social Forum are almost all above 60, all men, belonging to organizations that have 1,000 members on paper, but it's always one guy who shows up. Yet they tell you they have 120 member organizations, and then you have to compete with them. There really was a competition.
>
> (LMVH organizer, 2008)

Second-wave activism involved more of the horizontal ideals of the alterglobalist movement than first wave organizations did. It conceived of itself as a horizontal, networked movement, part of a homogenous and anti-hierarchical space of global civil society. But, however committed second-wave activists were to applying the alterglobalist ideals correctly, being situated in Eastern Europe left its mark on their endeavours.

Lack of infrastructure, imaginary autonomy, and the East–West slope

The alterglobalist movement rejected the idea of subordinating contemporary struggle to a future revolution. The movement preferred prefigurative politics – that is, to realize revolutionary ideals in the very process of the movement. This technique moved the borderline between the 'old' and the 'new' world from a future historical rupture into everyday practice. This practice was oriented towards producing autonomous spaces and groups where revolutionary life could be realized, and separating these spaces from an oppressive outside world. Activists shuttled between constructing autonomy and destructing the 'old' world, a practice referred to by supporting researchers as 'living between two worlds' (Chatterton and Pickerill 2006).

However, in the case of Eastern European activists, the task of 'living between two worlds' presented itself in a specific way. Activists could neither rely upon a strong heritage of post-1968 social movements, on communicative tropes within public discourse that could be attached to alterglobalist issues, nor on friendly trade unions to support their actions. Even in the peak years of the movement, alterglobalists from Hungary and Romania could not produce a stable network of autonomous infrastructure (squats, people's kitchens, libraries) comparable to that which provided the experience of autonomy in Western European cities. In the Hungarian and Romanian version of 'living between two worlds', the actual experience of autonomy remained mostly the imaginary exercise of cultivating their sense of belonging to a better developed Western infrastructure. Typical forms of cultivating this feeling were speaking about the Western squatters' movement, enumerating demonstrations and squats one had visited, or evoking revolutionary techniques one might identify with, but did not actually practice at home.

This dichotomy served as a juncture connecting Eastern European alterglobalism back to mainstream discourses on Eastern European inferiority. After 1989, 'returning to Europe' and 'catching up' with superior Western levels of civilization constituted a dominant narrative through which Eastern Europe was localized and explained. Hungarian author Attila Melegh (2006) identified this as the East–West slope discourse. He claimed that with the fall of Communism, the classic scale of capitalist modernization, according to which the level of civilization decreases as we depart in space from the Western centre, re-emerged, and replaced the Cold War discourse on competing modernities. It served as the cognitive map of post-socialist transition, as the description and legitimation of Eastern Europe's new geopolitical position, implying economic subordination to Western Europe. Melegh's analysis identifies all post-socialist political positions as self-positionings on the slope.

Theoretically, the alterglobalist movement was aware of the traps of hierarchical geopolitical identification and criticized it from the perspective of the fight for global equality. Budapest activists printed and wore T-shirts with the world map turned upside down, inscribed 'get the system right', to criticize the hierarchical representation of the Global South as inferior. They also rejected simplistic expressions of Eastern Europe as being inferior to Western Europe. However, the difference in movement infrastructure brought the the East–West slope back into their circles as well.

> When I think about the future, you know, I think about the same question everybody does … whether to play the hero and stay here, or play the victim and flee to the West. [This is] from the movement's perspective. If we had a movement as big as elsewhere, I would gladly stay here, and accept this life and these salaries…. But it's about feedback, I mean, if you don't get any feedback, you really feel like you're on the periphery…. And for me the line is very thin now: whether to stay here, like a hero, where I'm needed, where there's no structure at all, or to say 'ok, I'm done, I can't take it any more, I'm not constructive any more, and I'd better go elsewhere, before I turn apathetic, apolitical'. So this is my problem, and I think all of us struggle with that.
>
> (B.B., Romanian activist, 2007)

Identification with the global movement played out on the East–West slope as well. The framework of alterglobalism worked as an alternative strategy for identity construction, through which the hierarchical narrative of post-socialist transition could be circumvented. Instead of the 'bad student' position of the 'catching up with the West' narrative, activists could imagine themselves as equal actors working with the same problems as Western activists. Instead of shameful defects to correct in order to get closer to the West, local issues suddenly appeared as universal problems of a global system. Activists often mentioned how positioning themselves in the framework of a global movement helped them to turn their attention back to an environment they would be running from otherwise.

> A few years ago I lived totally parallel to my country's reality … I feel I stand more firmly on the ground … since I came into contact with my environment, with poverty, with the Roma, 'cause before I had no contact with any of these! Finally I descended into the world that surrounds me, spent my time there, met people there, and began to see things differently.
>
> (P.G., Romanian activist, 2007)

In this context, 'think globally, act locally' meant more than being aware of systematic connections. For local activists it meant that one could be justified in working on one's environment without the feeling of inferiority, through elevating it to a global level. But that elevation required immense imaginative work. Activists judged their actions to be successful insofar as they took place as a symbol of the global movement as a whole. Symbolically these events raised the everyday problems of post-socialist environments to the status of global problems. Documenting actions not only served to fix the movement's 'autonomous' reality and spread information, it served also to inscribe Eastern European actions into the frame of the global movement, in order to prove the existence of a local movement and to gain recognition from Western partners.

In the context of the East West slope discourse, a stronger Western movement served as a symbolic resource for local activism. 'Catching up' with the Western movement was frequently used as an argument and it was widely accepted. As one Budapest squatter explained:

> Wherever I go, they always ask me 'hey, where do you have a squat in Hungary?' And it's so lame to answer 'ok, we are such losers that we don't even have a squat'. So this is a major motivation.
>
> (T.G., Hungarian activist, 2005).

Budapest squats were successfully legitimized by the fact that that the squatters 'speak languages', and follow Western European examples. The East–West hierarchy also served as a tool to compensate for local ineffectivity. When speaking about failures, activists often positioned themselves as an avant-garde immobilized by its 'provincial' 'Balkan' environment.

Even after the internal competition over ESF partnership was settled, the local movement's relationship to the Western movement continued to remain hierarchical. For second-wave activists too, contact with the Western movement kept its function of inauguration, of raising the local movement to the 'global' level, but in a more informal way. The sharpest example of this is the meeting of Romanian and Hungarian second-wave activists with the second wave of the Western movement's attempts at Eastern enlargement: the People's Global Action Balkans Network. In Europe, the People's Global Action (PGA) network functioned as a deliberately more grassroots network, one which criticized the ESF for its formal and hierarchical structure. The initiative for a PGA Balkans network came from an experienced group of Western activists in 2007. They defined the Balkans as reaching from Budapest to Istanbul, leaving aside historical circumstances and local identifications. Their idea was to create a communication platform for collaboration among Balkans groups.

The PGA initiators visited each group they knew of, and, after informal discussions, gathered their 'issues' within a rather pre-fixed system ("Do you have problems with Nazis? Do you have a problem with unemployment?", etc.), and established the Balkan Decentralized Network for Communication and Cooperation website. For most members of the second-wave movement, this was the first and biggest moment of inauguration into the global scene by a Western partner. For new Romanian groups – born as separate groups in separate cities, instead of being sucked up into the Budapest centre as in Hungary – being invited to the PGA meetings counted as a most important gesture of recognition.

The next event coming up in the Balkans on the alterglobalist agenda was the 2008 NATO conference in Bucharest. The newly inaugurated Romanian groups received a call from their Western partners to organize the international anti-NATO demonstrations with this occasion. Romanian groups did not take into consideration their differences from the Western movement centres that usually hosted such events. They did not reflect upon the specificities of local constituency, resources, organizing experience, and the differences in political context. That lack of reflection resulted in the failure of the protest. A national press campaign predicted an armed anarchist attack against the NATO meeting. Activists and their family members were harrassed by the police in the days before the event. Foreign activists were caught and held against their will at the borders. On 2 April almost all of the few dozen activists who took part in the event were attacked, beaten and locked up by police. Finally, with the help of liberal media activists, the action was re-framed as an issue of free speech, the activists were released, and the police over-reaction was criticized by the Romanian and EU authorities. Those repercussions were similar to those experienced at other counter-summits. But beyond this there were no new nett gains for Romanian activists, no local outreach or change in the pro-NATO media agenda. Instead, the event caused a serious crisis for the movement's self-confidence.

'Autonomy' as a position in the local context

The shape which 'autonomy' took also depended upon the position of the alterglobalists among local civil and political players. In Romania socialist dictatorship had not allowed any civic organizations; by the beginning of the 2000s alterglobalist activists could only count on the periodic support of a few big liberal organizations (such as the Open Society Institute, Helsinki Committee, Media Monitoring Agency, etc.), support which was limited to issues of free speech and equal rights. Without powerful allies Romanian alterglobalism remained a coherent but closed subculture, with strong Western ties. By the early 2010s, when a new wave of intellectual leftist critique and social action took root, it only had incidental ties with former alterglobalist groups, and did not use the alterglobalization framework.

In Hungary the second-wave alterglobalist coalition played a much more visible role. 'Grassroots' here meant a dense network of young activists centralized in Budapest, with many working in big NGOs. This network interpreted its achievments as the results of a grassroots, horizontally networked civil society, not represented by any big name or organization. Successful actions, such as the annual Peace Sign demonstrations, the fast-growing Critical Mass bicycle demonstration, or the campaign against setting up a NATO radar station in a national park could be quoted by any network member, irrespective of their actual merits, as a collective achievement, further proof of 'civil society' growing stronger.

The cumulative success of these actions, became a resource upon which organizations involved in the network could capitalize. In 2005, András Lányi, leader of Protect the Future, the green NGO most open to alterglobalization ideas, founded a party called Live Chain. However, young alterglobalist members of the organization did not follow him. In a statement, they claimed that 'Protect the Future is not even informally the party of Live Chain' (Védegylet 2005), and distinguished themselves from Lányi's party in the name of civil society. In 2006, a similar conflict took place when the Humanist Movement, part of the second-wave alterglobalist coalition, decided to use a collectively organized peace demonstration as a platform for the Humanist Party. The Humanists tried to gain acceptance for their party among second-wave activists, emphasizing that it did not seek to be the sole representative of the Hungarian movement, but rather another hub in the collective network. This was more or less accepted, in great part due to good personal relationships. At the same time, alterglobalist activists who distinguished themselves from Lányi's party were already working to frame 'civil society' success along the lines of their own political project. In 2005 the Budapest Critical Mass bicycle demonstration grew to over 25,000 participants. On that occasion, members of Protect the Future spoke about how the bicycle movement should find its place in a general ecopolitical framework (Szombati 2005). In 2007, the same members founded an 'ecopolitical' party named after the alterglobalist slogan 'Another Politics is Possible' (LMP, translated into English as 'Politics Can Be Different').

With the founding of LMP, the series of conflicts and mutual distinctions within the alterglobalist coalition was brought to an end. Drawing on core activists of second-wave activism and its supporting NGOs (especially Protect the Future), the party claimed to be the linear and natural offspring of alterglobalist civil activism in Hungary. On the other hand, it also built upon the conservative base of the green movement. In 2010, LMP achieved 7.48 per cent of the votes.

Partly due to ideological differences between members, it did not follow a coherent leftist alterglobalist agenda, although some of its members continued to cite the alterglobalization movement as a reference point.

The conflicts between big organizations not only influenced the infrastructural base of the alterglobalist network – i.e. the position of its members affiliated to the respective organizations – but also changed the role of members of the alterglobalist coalition who were not formally enrolled in any NGO. These members belonged only to the informal network through a form of membership that accurately corresponded to the alterglobalist ideal of an autonomous, networked movement, where affiliation is voluntary and informal.

While supporting organizations contributed to the discursive umbrella of anonymous civil society with an eye on their own name and resources, informal members of the alterglobalist network identified with it without any restraint. Alterglobalist movement platforms predicted the dissolution of single-issue organizations in the total politics of the global community. The informal members thought of themselves as participating in this dissolution of identifications. For that reason, they were identified as the avant-garde of the Hungarian movement.

This avant-garde position required ceaseless political reflection and radical involvement in prefigurative politics, beyond the compromises formal organizations were bound to make. It was generally this 'avant-garde' who risked illegal actions, frequently as part of a collective action of the alterglobalist coalition. The avant-garde position also required that alterglobalist principles penetrate all fields of everyday life, such as radical democracy within the group, love without 'wanting to own' one's partner, or transcending everyday conceptions of quality of life. People who gave their everyday life to the movement were honoured as living models of the civil society ideal. The avant-garde position, however, depended upon the bigger organizations to sustain the alterglobalist discourse of an anonymous civil society.

When big organizations chose to capitalize upon the movement's achievements, the avant-garde position built upon the anonymity of civil society collapsed. 'Grassroots' activists were left without any immediate external legitimation for their endeavour to imagine themselves as models of an autonomous global civil society. Their efforts to sustain this imagined reality turned into a spiral of critical self-reflection and self-reassurance similar to a nervous breakdown. Minor matters such as conflicts over a love triangle, in the context of the norm that love should not mean possession, could escalate to a questioning of the group's self-definition. Who are we? Do we exist? Do our politics exist at all? Questions such as these, springing out of every corner of everyday activist life, became a pressure that made 'avant-garde' life unbearable, and ultimately led to the flight of members into individual solutions for the challenge of total politics.

Conclusion: positioning autonomy

This chapter has analysed the localization of the alterglobalist idea of civil autonomy in two Eastern European countries. Treating 'autonomy' as an idea shaped
by its context, it mentioned two contextual features which brought the original idea
of Italian or German autonomism close to a liberal understanding of an independent civil society: the specific relationship between the alterglobalist movement
and its intellectual interpreters, and a change in intellectual positions with the
breakup of the globalist coalition between political and economic liberals.

I showed how the idea of autonomy came to be used within alterglobalist
movements in Hungary and Romania. Instead of networking autonomous civil
actors 'everywhere', as the alterglobalist idea would suggest, Eastern European
actors were first integrated into the movement by the hierarchical process of the
ESF's Eastern enlargement, which did not allow the Eastern European experience of existing socialism to inform the movement's ideology, and which
implied a problematic competition between Eastern actors. That competition
split the local movements between groups socialized in communist times who
integrated first into the ESF process, and younger groups who identified more
closely with the anti-hierarchical values of the movement. The latter, second-
wave alterglobalist activism corresponded more closely to the alterglobalist idea
of informal, grassroots civil activity. However, in their case, the idea of autonomy enabled an imaginary elevation to the 'global' level, identified with
Western models, and the subordination of the local context to it.

The final part of this chapter dealt with the local conditions of the construction of 'autonomy'. In Romania, where no network of supporting NGOs was
present, alterglobalism remained a closed subculture with strong Western ties, in
some instances helped out by liberal NGOs. In Hungary, the informal network of
second-wave alterglobalism relied upon assistance from green NGOs. Within the
informal network, those members who were not enrolled in any formal organization, and who identified strongly with the alterglobalist idea of total politics,
were honoured as the avant-garde of the alterglobalist coalition, the living
models of autonomous civil politics. However, when big organizations decided
to capitalize upon the movement's success, the discourse of an anonymous civil
network collapsed, leaving the most 'autonomous' groups without any external
source of legitimation.

By showing how the idea of autonomy allowed for Eastern European applica-
tions that disregarded local context and practical effectiveness, I do not imply that
the ideas of the movement were impossible to transfer to these societies. Rather, I
criticize the movement ideology and research practices which treat the alterglobalist idea of autonomous global civil society as universal. The analysis of the
idea of civil autonomy within the social contexts of its production and application
is crucial – from the perspective both of research and of political action. From
2011, a new international wave of protests took shape in the face of austerity
measures. In the Eastern European region, right-wing framings of anti-
neoliberalism have dominated thus far. The two instances of the alterglobalization

movement presented above did not succeed in challenging that dominant frame. Both movements dismissed the local context in order to identify with the 'global' movement. Whether or not a locally contextualized agenda of democratic civil action can be constructed in the near future might prove crucial to the direction that local movements against austerity would take.

Notes

1 This analysis is based upon MA and PhD research conducted between 2003–2009 in Hungary and Romania, which consisted of systematic participant observation in alter-globalist movement groups, completed by interviews with main movement actors and commentators, analysis of movement and mainstream media, and following activists' international contacts. My observations resulting from the research are not only those of an intellectual commentator, but also of an activist speaking to her colleagues.
2 Anecdotal evidence of direct quotation and application of academic authors is widespread, as is that of activists also active in the academic field – e.g. Biddle *et al.* writing on 'constituent imagination' (2007), Jeffrey Juris (Manuel Castells' PhD student) contributing to Castells' research and writing 'militant ethnography' at the same time (Juris 2004), etc. Such cases are also present in Romanian and Hungarian movement groups.
3 See, for example, how editors of the Global Civil Society yearbook answer practical criticism by retreating to principles: Anheier *et al.* 2001: 38, 25; Anheier *et al.* 2005: 9.

References

Anheier, H.D. (2001–ongoing) *Global Civil Society*. (LSE, London). Online. Available www2.lse.ac.uk/globalGovernance/research/globalCivilSociety/home.aspx (accessed 15 December 2011).

Anheier, H., Glasius, M. and Kaldor, M. (2001) *Introducing Global Civil Society*, in Anheier, H., Glasius, M. and Kaldor, M. (eds) (2001) *Global Civil Society Yearbook*, Oxford University Press, pp. 17–45.

Anheier, H., Glasius, M. and Kaldor, M. (2005) *Introduction*, in Anheier, H. and Glasius, M. and Kaldor, M. (eds) (2004–2005) *Global Civil Society Yearbook 2004–5*, Oxford University Press, pp. 1–22.

Appadurai, A. (2000) 'Grassroots Globalization and the Research Imagination', *Public Culture*, vol. 12, Nr. 1, Winter, 1–19.

Axford, B. (2005) 'Critical Globalization Studies and a Network Perspective on Global Civil Society', in Appelbaum, R.P. and Robinson, W.T. (eds) (2005) *Critical Globalisation Studies*, New York: Routledge.

Bauman, Z. (2000) *Liquid Modernity*, Cambridge, Polity

Beck, U., Giddens, A. and Lash, S. (1994) *Reflexive Modernization*, Cambridge: Polity.

Biddle, E., Shukaitis, S. and Graeber, D. (2007) *Constituent Imagination*, London: AK Press.

Bockman, J. (2011) *Markets in the Name of Socialism*, Stanford University Press.

Boltanski, L. (2002) 'The Left after May 1968 and the Longing for Total Revolution', *Thesis Eleven*, 69: 1–20.

Boltanski, L. and Chiapello, E. (2005) *The New Spirit of Capitalism*, London: Verso.

Bourdieu, P. and Wacquant, L. (1992) *An Invitation to Reflexive Sociology*, Chicago University Press.

Castells, M. (1997) *The Power of Identity*, Oxford, Cambridge, MA: Blackwell.

Chandhoke, Neera (2002) 'The limits of Global Civil Society', in Anheier, H., Glasius, M. and Kaldor, M. (eds) *Global Civil Society Yearbook*, Oxford University Press, pp. 3–33.

Chandler, D. (2005) 'Constructing Global Civil Society', in Baker, G. and Chandler, D. (eds) *Global Civil Society*, London: Routledge, pp. 238–273.

Chatterton, P. and Pickerill, J. (2006) 'Notes towards autonomous geographies', *Progress in Human Geography*, 30(6): 730–746.

Csillag, G. and Scheiring, G. (2003) 'Tiszta vizet a globálba', *Népszabadság*. Online. Available at: www.nol.hu/archivum/archiv-128776 (accesssed 15 December 2011).

Della Porta, D. (2004–2008) 'Democracy in Europe and the Mobilization of Society'. DEMOS (European University Institute, Florence). Online. Available at: http://demos. eui.eu (accessed 15 December 2011).

Della Porta, D. (2005) 'Multiple Belongings, Tolerant Identities, and the Construction of "Another Politics"', in Della Porta, D. and Tarrow, S. (eds) (2005) *Transnational Protest and Global Activism*, Oxford: Rowman and Littlefield, 175–202.

Della Porta, D. 2008. 'Summary of Policy-Relevant Results', in Della Porta, D. and Reiter, H. (eds) (2008) *Democracy in Europe and the Mobilization of Society*, European University Institute, Florence, 6–7.

Della Porta, D. and Tarrow S. (eds) (2005) *Transnational Protest and Global Activism*, Oxford: Rowman and Littlefield.

Desai, M. and Said, Y. (2003) 'Trade and Global Civil Society', in Anheier, H., Glasius, M. and Kaldor, M. (eds) (2003) *Global Civil Society Yearbook 2003*, Oxford University Press.

diversi (2006) *Actiune anti-discriminare in Bucuresti*. Online. Available: http://romania. indymedia.org/ro/2006/11/1742.shtml (accessed 23 May 2012).

Eyal, G. (2000) 'Anti-Politics and the Spirit of Capitalism', *Theory and Society*, Vol. 29, No. 1, 49–92.

Fraser, N. (2009) 'Feminism, Capitalism and the Cunning of History', *New Left Review* 56, March–April, 97–118.

Graeber, D. and Shukaitis, S. (2007) 'Introduction', in Biddle, E., Shukaitis, S. and Graeber, D. (2007) *Constituent Imagination*, London: AK Press, 11–36.

Hardt, M. and Negri, A. (2004) *Multitude*, New York: Penguin.

Held, D. and McGrew, A. (2000) *The Global Transformations Reader*, Blackwell, Polity Press.

Juris, J. (2004) 'Networked Social Movements', in Castells, M. (ed.) (2004) *The Network Society: A Cross-Cultural Perspective*, Edward Elgar, MA, pp. 341–362.

Kagarlitsky, B. (2009) Talk held at the 2009 London Communist University. Online. Available at: http://indy.media.hu/node/13626 (accessed 1 February 2010).

Kalb, D. (2004) 'Time and Contention in "The Great Globalization Debate"', in Kalb, D., Pansters, W. and Siebers, H. (2004) *Globalization and Development*, Dordrecht–Boston–London: Kluwer Academic Publishers, pp. 9–47.

Kalb, D. (2005) 'From flows to violence', *Anthropological Theory*, 5: 176–204.

Kalb, D. and Halmai, G. (2011) *Headlines of Nation, Subtexts of Class*, Berghahn Books.

Melegh, A. (2006) *On the East–West Slope*, Budapest–New York: CEU Press.

Notes From Nowhere (ed.) (2003) *We Are Everywhere*, London/New York: Verso.

Novak, A. (2008) 'European Social Forum', Centre for the Study of Social and Global Justice, University of Nottingham. Online. Available at: http://nottingham-my. academia.edu/AdamNov%C3%A1k/Papers/76061/East-European-participation-in-the-European-Social-Forum–ESF- (accessed 15 December 2011).

Sassen, S. (2000) 'Spatialities and Temporalities of the Global', *Public Culture*, 12 (1): 215–232.

Sassen, S. (2001) 'The Global City', India-Seminar July 2001. Online. Available at: www.india-seminar.com/2001/503/503%20saskia%20sassen.htm (accessed 15 December 2011).

Stiglitz, J. (1998) 'More Instruments and Broader Goals', The 1998 WIDER Annual Lecture, Helsinki.

Stiglitz, J. (2002) *Globalization and its Discontents*, London: Allen Lane.

Szombati, K. (2005) 'The treadly as a tool of ecopolitics', *Népszabadság*, 25 September 2005.

Védegylet (2005) 'Formal statement of organizers of Protect the Future'. Online. Available: www.vedegylet.hu/modules.php?name=News&file=article&sid=304 (accessed 23 May 2012).

10 Collective identity across borders

Bridging local and transnational
memories in the Italian and German
Global Justice Movements

Priska Daphi

Introduction

Social movement scholars have long been enthusiastic about the capacity of
transnational movements to overcome spatial and socio-cultural divides, but
recent studies underline how the local and national dimensions of transnational
activism are also highly significant (e.g. Uggla 2006; Cumbers *et al.* 2008; della
Porta 2005). Instead of bearing witness to a 'disappearance of space' (Harvey
1992), transnational social movements are based on a plurality of intersecting
spaces (Cumbers *et al.* 2008; Pries 2005; Routledge 2000; Sassen 2000). They
encompass different contexts of interaction at the local, national, and transnational levels.

This plurality of spaces challenges social movements in several respects. It
complicates coordination, decision-making and, most significantly, the construction of collective identity. Constructing a collective identity relies upon a spatially concentrated base from which similarities can be drawn, and upon which
dense webs of informal and direct exchanges can be built (Melucci 1996;
Andretta *et al.* 2003; della Porta and Diani 2006; Hetherington 1998). The literature on 'free spaces'[1] has developed this point most elaborately: free spaces
facilitate face-to-face contact and regular interaction and thereby create trust,
understanding, and affection (Taylor 1995; Polletta 1999; Polletta and Jasper
2001). How is collective identity built within transnational movements in which
there is no single physically shared space, but instead various free spaces that
intersect with transnational meetings and networks?

Drawing on a narrative approach to movement identity, this contribution
explores the construction of collective identity in transnational social movements
in relation to collective memory and the spaces to which it is bound. More specifically, it focuses on the construction of a sense of shared experience and space
in the Global Justice Movement (GJM). The narrative approach to collective
identity facilitates insights into processes of collective identity construction in
social movements beyond frame analysis, the predominant method in the field
(Daphi 2011), because of its consideration of how meaning is produced through
temporal ordering. Due to its socio-cultural heterogeneity and geographic complexity, the GJM constitutes a particularly interesting case for analysing the

construction of collective identity (cf. Andretta *et al.* 2003). In particular, this chapter focuses on two distinct national constellations of the movement in Italy and Germany in order to reveal similar processes amongst the different groups of activists.

In the following section, I will first elaborate upon this chapter's narrative approach to collective identity and specify the study's analytical methods. Subsequently, I will introduce the GJM in Italy and Germany, and then proceed to analyse activists' memories in two parts: first, by comparing their accounts of important events of the movement, and second, by showing how these events connect local, national, and transnational levels.

Narratives and collective identity

The narrative approach to collective identity

There are different approaches to the study of collective identity (cf. Polletta and Jasper 2001; Flesher Fominaya 2010). This chapter defines collective identity as a characteristic of a group, rather than an individual quality. Collective identity concerns the internal and external definition of a collective as a group and is continuously reconstructed through interaction with each other and those outside of the collective (Melucci 1996; Rucht 1995; Snow and McAdam 2000; Eder 2000; Daphi 2011).

Furthermore, this chapter focuses on a specific dimension of collective identity: internal narratives. Collective identity draws on a variety of resources, including shared cognitive frameworks, activist networks, and emotional investment (Melucci 1996). Based on a narrative approach, I highlight the role of storytelling in collective identity construction (Daphi 2011). While several movement scholars have stressed the significance of a (fictional) shared past for movement cohesion (e.g. Hunt *et al.* 1994; Sewell and McAdam 2001; della Porta and Diani 2006), only more recently has a systematic approach to narratives been developed, particularly by Francesca Polletta (1998, 2006). Narratives provide information about the networks, frames, and emotions that underlie collective identity; however, none of these elements constitute the narrative approach's primary focus, of highlighting the construction of meaning through the temporal structure of narratives.

Drawing on Margaret Somers' identity theory (1992, 1994, 1995), narratives are understood to play a crucial role in how we come to know, understand, and make sense of the social world (Fine 1995; Eder 2005). Narratives, however, represent reality in a number of different ways than frames do, as Polletta (1998) points out. First, while frames create meaning through analogy and difference, narratives are temporally configurative: they create meaning through ordering experiences into a plot. Second, while the success of frames depends upon the clarity, specificity, and empirical credibility of the account, narratives convince their audience through their openness to different interpretations and the possibility of identifying with the protagonists of the story. Third, narratives are strongly dependent upon an existing cultural stock of plots in order to be intelligible, while frames have more options for 'ideological manoeuvring' (Polletta 1998).

This current analysis focuses on collective memories as a particular type of narrative. Collective memories are narratives about the emergence and development of a group. To understand the significance of memories for collective identity building, it is useful to consider Maurice Halbwachs' theory on collective memory, which has been highly influential on contemporary research in the field.

In the 1920s, Halbwachs established the theory that memory and remembering are not individual, psychological operations, but social phenomena (1966 [1925]). Individuals are only capable of remembering if they place themselves in the present social framework. In his later *La Mémoire Collective* (1980a [1950]), Halbwachs further developed his perspective by arguing that a group is constituted by its collective memory as it provides a sense of cohesion and continuity over time. This collective memory, Halbwachs stressed, is anchored within specific spatial frames because events only settle in collective memory if assigned to a particular place (Halbwachs 1980b [1950]). This attachment of events to places – even places that are remote from a group's lived space – plays a central role in collective identity construction as it facilitates the notion of a coherent shared past (Halbwachs 1992).

It follows from this that collective memory is constitutive of collective identity. Memory provides ways for group members to understand the world, particularly in the sense of defining the group as an entity. A collective memory determines which experiences are shared, and it places these experiences in a meaningful order. In this way, coherent stories of a group's past emerge to form a crucial resource for identifying the boundaries of the group and for empathizing with other members.

Additionally, these narratives are central to the construction of collective identity due to their attachment to particular places. By connecting events into a coherent story, narratives also link the events' locations to each other and thereby merge these places into what is perceived as a shared space of action and interaction.[2] Imagining such shared space allows the identification of similarities with others in the same perceived space. This has been shown with respect to national identity in the sense of Benedict Anderson's *Imagined Communities* (1983), for example.[3]

Consequently, this chapter analyses narratives about the GJM's past in order to explore collective identity construction. In particular, I examine the extent to which activists of the GJM construct a coherent memory of the movement along with a shared space of action. As this contribution addresses the construction of collective identity in *transnational* movements, the question of space involves asking how local, national, and transnational places of action are connected to each other in narratives.

After introducing the analytical method, this chapter analyses activists' memories of the GJM in two parts. The first part provides an overview of the similarities and differences between activists' accounts of specific protest events. The second part entails a detailed analysis of similarities identified in the first step, focusing on the way in which transnational events are narratively connected to local ones and vice versa.

Analysing narratives: merits of combining structural and content analysis

This study considers the structural and content dimensions of narratives. Analyses of narratives in social movement research (as in sociology more generally) tend to focus on the content rather than the structure of the narrative (e.g. Polletta 2006; Nepstad 2001). However, by identifying certain recurrent themes, the original story is often recomposed 'with the coherence and context of each original narrative lost and forgotten' (Franzosi 1998: 548). Consequently, it is important to also consider the *structural patterns* of narratives.

Bearman and Stovel's (2000) study of Nazi life stories provides a fruitful example of combining structural and content analyses of narratives. In a first step, the authors provide a structural analysis of the temporal ordering of narrative elements. In a second step, they distinguish between different types of narrative elements in relation to content (macro-level events, local events and cognition). By combining these two levels of analysis, the authors distinguish between different degrees of self-reflexivity in the life stories. This highlights the fact that the meaning of a narrative is produced both through the temporal ordering of events as well as through non-narrative, i.e. cognitive clauses (e.g. reflections such as 'those were tough times') (cf. Franzosi 1998).

Thus, the following analysis of the GJM will include the narratives' dimensions of both structure *and* content in order to account for meaning produced through both sequence and cognitive association. In this way I consider both the immediate connections between different narrative elements as well as the general context or theme in which narrative elements are situated. Accounting for both of the ways in which narrative meaning is made is crucial in order to examine how the GJM constructs a coherent story of its past as well as a shared space of interaction, and the extent to which this happens. But first a brief introduction to the movement is necessary.

Global Justice Movements in Italy and Germany

While various labels for the Global Justice Movement (GJM) circulate (e.g. alterglobalization movement, no-global movement), those who study these activists generally agree that the movement comprises a network of groups engaged in collective action of various kinds based upon the shared goal of advancing economic, social, political, and environmental justice in opposition to neoliberal globalization (della Porta 2007). Along with national neoliberal policies and transnational corporations, the GJM is opposed to international institutions such as the World Bank (WB), the International Monetary Fund (IMF), and the World

Trade Organization (WTO). A wide range of groups and activists constitute the GJM: its social configurations, sets of mobilizing structures (ranging from trade unions to grass roots groups), and geographic locations are heterogeneous (Andretta *et al.* 2003). This heterogeneity makes it difficult to construct a collective identity for the GJM.

GJM activists in Italy and Germany find themselves in different settings in terms of the constitution of civil society, political opportunity structures, and movement legacies. In fact, Italy and Germany can be identified as typical cases of two disparate constellations of the GJM in Europe (della Porta 2007). Mobilization in Italy – similar to that in Spain and France – entails more disruptive protest dynamics, denser and more decentralized networks, less open political opportunities, and high involvement of oppositional trade unions (in the context of fragmentary system of industrial relations). Conversely, mobilization in Germany – similar to that in Britain and Switzerland – is characterized by more moderate protest tactics, more centralized networks, more open political opportunities, strong involvement of associations and NGOs, and little participation by unions. The timing of mobilization in Italy and Germany also differs: while in Italy the movement lost much of its momentum after 2004, in Germany mobilization continued to the counter-summit in Heiligendamm 2007 (cf. Banse and Habermann 2012).

The following analysis draws from a total of 40 in-depth interviews with Italian and German activists of the GJM (20 from each country) conducted between Spring 2011 and Spring 2012. All of the interviewees have been involved in GJM actions since the movement's inception in the 1990s. The ages of the activists range from 30–78 years. About half are aged between 30–40 years old, with the rest in their fifties and sixties (with a slightly larger proportion aged 50–60 in Italy). In both countries, most of the interviewees have been politically active since the 1980s (about half of the sample). A quarter became active in the 1960s and 1970s, and a further quarter did not become active until the 1990s. The following analysis focuses on answers to an open-ended question about the emergence and development of the GJM.[4] The first part of the analysis includes all 40 interviews, while the second part provides a detailed analysis of a selection of 12 interviews.[5]

Analysis part one: comparing activists' accounts across countries and sectors

The analysis presented in this section compares the activists' memories of the movement with regard to what they identified as starting points, key past events, and turning points. This analysis of similarities and differences provides some initial insights into the degree to which memories are shared.

Activists' accounts differ not only with respect to national contexts, but also with respect to different areas of the movement. Following Andretta *et al.* (2003) and della Porta *et al.* (2006), three sectors of the GJM can be distinguished: an anti-neoliberal sector, an eco-pacifist sector, and an anti-capitalist sector. The anti-neoliberal sector is composed of groups that aim to control the market through politics; it includes trade unions, political parties, Attac and other NGOs. The eco-pacifist sector encompasses environmentalist groups and organizations as well as secular and religious peace and solidarity groups. The anti-capitalist sector is composed of more radical groups, ranging from squatters to anarchist and Trotskyist groups which oppose capitalist structures and often refuse negotiations with institutional politics. Overall, the interviewees are distributed evenly across these three sectors: 13 interviewees are from the anti-neoliberal sector, 14 from the eco-pacifist sector, and 13 from the anti-capitalist sector.

The activists' accounts are similar across sectors and countries in terms of the centrality of certain protest events. All accounts refer to the protests against the WTO Ministerial Conference in Seattle (1999), the first World Social Forum in Porto Alegre (2001), or both as central. However, the extent to which other events and developments are mentioned varies.

First, differences can be found in relation to the national context. Not surprisingly, GJM events that took place in Italy or Germany are more prominent in the accounts of activists from these countries. In the case of Italy this primarily concerns the protests against the G8 summit in Genoa (2001), the European Social Forum in Florence (2002) and the No Global Forum in Naples (2001). In Germany this mainly refers to the protests against the G8 summit in Heiligendamm (2007), against the G8 and EU summit in Cologne (1999), and against the IMF and WB meeting in Berlin (1988).[6]

Second, accounts vary across sectors within each country. Among Italian activists, for example, the beginning of the decline of the movement is understood differently. Activists from the anti-capitalist sector generally consider that the movement declined after Genoa in 2001, but activists from eco-pacifist groups and anti-neoliberal groups identify later points of decline for the movement, namely in the context of the perceived failure of the anti-war demonstrations from 2003–2005,[7] the beginnings of the financial crisis in 2007, and the tension that emerged around the question of supporting the Prodi government in 2006.[8] In a similar vein, the protests against the G8 summit in Heiligendamm in 2007 feature much more prominently in accounts of German activists from the anti-capitalist sector than from the other German sectors.

This first part of the analysis of the narratives reveals the existence of sector- and nation-specific narratives. Not surprisingly, the extent to which events and developments are mentioned depends upon the extent to which the activists, groups, sectors, and national movements were involved in these events. In this way, activists from the eco-pacifist and anti-neoliberal sectors identify a later decline of the movement, mainly due to their strong involvement in the anti-war demonstrations from 2003 until 2005. Similarly, the emphasis on Heiligendamm by German activists from the anti-capitalist sector is mostly due to the central role of radical leftist groups in the preparations for and realization of this event (cf. Teune 2008). However, the reference to certain events in all accounts – despite different degrees of involvement – points to a shared narrative across sectors and nations. The following section will explore this shared narrative in detail.

Analysis part two: remembering Seattle and Porto Alegre

This section examines how activists remember the events in Seattle and Porto Alegre. In particular it explores the ways in which these transnational events are connected to other events, especially at the local and national levels. This serves to explore two crucial conditions of collective identity: it determines the extent to which a collective memory exists, and it also clarifies how events in different places merge into a sense of shared space, as well as illustrating the extent to which this happens. Do transnational events provide the context for local events and developments, or vice versa?

Below is an in-depth analysis of the 12 most elaborate accounts from activists. Due to the early time-frame of the events in Seattle and Porto Alegre, this part of the analysis focuses particularly on the narrative reconstructions of the movement's emergence and its key past events. Following the analytical method developed above, this section considers both structural and content elements: narrative elements have been hierarchically ordered with respect to content as a means to identify the main themes addressed while strictly maintaining the sequential order of these elements so that we can also consider the meaning constructed through sequencing.

All accounts refer to Seattle, Porto Alegre, or both, in order to identify both similarities and differences of events elsewhere as well as to stress changes in the movement. This occurs in two different ways: while the first type of account interprets the events in Seattle and Porto Alegre predominantly as *triggers* for other events, the second sees them as *results* or part of other events and processes. Hence, while the latter account locates Seattle and Porto Alegre within other developments (local/national and transnational), the first type of account does the opposite by locating other events and developments in terms of the encounters in Seattle and Porto Alegre. These two types affect how local/national and transnational activities of the movement are connected. Most of the activists' memories follow the first type of account (eight out of 12); however, no patterns can be found in terms of sector or nation (or regarding age or length of activism). In both types of accounts, activists from all three sectors are represented, and equally in terms of Italian and German activists (see Table 10.1, below).

Triggers vs results

The first type of account presents the protests in Seattle and the gathering in Porto Alegre as turning points that changed the subsequent development of the movement locally, nationally, and transnationally. For example, Andrea, an Italian activist from the anti-capitalist sector, ascribes the development of a 'new language' and transnational ambition to the events in Seattle – a language which facilitated cooperation across borders and sectors:

> We immediately understood that we were witnessing the birth of a new language [...]. The language [...] managed to pull together a social reality,

Table 10.1 Overview of interviewees for analysis part two

Type 1/**Type 2**	Sector	Name*	Age	Politically active since
Italy	Anti-neoliberal	Alessandro	60s	1960s
		Matteo	50s	1970s
	Eco-pacifist	Rebecca	50s	1980s
		Elena	50s	1980s
	Anti-capitalist	**Lorenzo**	50s	1980s
		Andrea	30s	1990s
Germany	Anti-neoliberal	**Hermann**	60s	1980s
		Paul	60s	1970s
	Eco-pacifist	Hans	60s	1970s
		Peter	70s	1960s
	Anti-capitalist	Franziska	40s	1980s
		Matthias	50s	1970s

Note
* All names have been changed.

which was usually very fragmented, very 'molecularized' [...]. For us the Seattle movement was an encouragement: 'let's get out of the extreme-left ghetto' [...]. We wanted to be a different kind of problem and thus, for example, we did things that we had not done so far.

Similarly, Matteo, an Italian activist from the anti-neoliberal sector, recounts the following:

On that occasion [Seattle] a quantum leap was made, from a qualitative point of view. [...] In Seattle the big change was that of posing the problem of democracy. For the first time the movements did not only make some alternative proposals, but they questioned the very fact that a few could take decisions for everybody [...]. This, in my opinion, gave the start signal, also in symbolic terms, to all those movements that globally and locally already existed to begin a real challenge [...].

The second type of account does not single out one event as the starting point of the movement. Instead, Seattle and Porto Alegre are located within general developments of economic change, political change, or both, as well as resistance against it. For example, Paul, a German activist from the anti-neoliberal sector, places Seattle in the context of a growing international critique of the economic reorganization through the WTO and the summits of the G7/G8, as well as related efforts in Germany to build a network of activists:

We [Paul's NGO] said [...] we wanted to do something like France with Attac, and in September 1999 invited those involved in Cologne [protest against the G8/EU summit] to an informal and non-public preparatory meeting. [...], so we already started the preparation before Seattle and then Seattle, of course, was the big affirmation.

More generally, Lorenzo, an Italian activist from the anti-capitalist sector, presents the movement as a global response to the global crisis of capitalism:

> [...] and so, [the incompatibility of democracy and capitalism] along with the financial crisis of capitalism, Seattle explodes in 1999. The failure of the new economy takes place between 2000 and 2002: you can easily see that this Seattle explosion is directly correlated to the first big crisis of the financial dynamics [...].

This shows that the events of Seattle and Porto Alegre are embedded into the narratives differently. On the one hand, they are presented predominantly as triggers for other developments, such as overcoming political divisions and the growing demand for participation in political decisions. On the other hand, they are depicted as results or parts of other more general developments, such as the crisis of capitalism or the growing international critique of free trade agreements. The analysis also reveals that in both types of accounts, Seattle and Porto Alegre have a central function of orientation: other events are frequently compared with them, as the repeated references to these events in the responses show.

Triggers for local events vs results of local events

The differing narrative build-up of the accounts has consequences for how local/national and transnational events are connected. In the first type of account, transnational protest events are predominantly recounted as triggers for local and national events; in the second type, this is largely reversed: transnational protest events are presented as the results of local and national events. For example, for the first type, Rebecca, an Italian activist from the eco-pacifist sector, illustrates Porto Alegre's unifying effect regarding developments in Italy:

> The Porto Alegre spirit gave us the idea that a common front existed. [...] So this was the beginning. And for us [in Italy] the beginning was the mobilization against the G8 [in Genoa]. [...] We chose G8 because for us it was a symbol of the different ways in which we were against what was happening in the world.

Similarly, Matthias, a German activist from the anti-capitalist sector, emphasizes that the events in Seattle facilitated cooperation among different left groups in Germany after the failed attempts to bring together various groups in the mobilization against the G8/EU summit in Cologne in 1999:

> And shortly after this [protests in Cologne] came Seattle and we were laughing up our sleeves because we said 'this is exactly what we had in mind'.

And we had bad luck with relation to Cologne [...] and nonetheless we were right and this is what Seattle made clear [...]. This situation [...] meant that we kept up the communication amongst a broad group ranging from church people, to NGO people and to leftist radicals. This communication did not break down until Heiligendamm.

In contrast, the second type of account largely presents local and national events as triggers of the events in Seattle and Porto Alegre, or rather as parts of larger developments leading up to them. Elena, an Italian activist from the eco-pacifist sector, connects the unifying strength of the international nuclear disarmament movement – ultimately facilitating the cooperation of different groups in the GJM – to developments in Italy:

The big nuclear disarmament movement across the two blocks [...] taught me and many other people in Italy that involvement internationally meant involvement with the peoples in other countries and that this was the best way of overcoming things that we didn't think were right in international politics. Today everyone knows this [...] but in 1980 that was a revelation: the idea that you could work on nuclear disarmament in Western Europe together with people like us who were working on nuclear disarmament in Eastern Europe and in the Soviet Union was revolutionary.

Similarly, Paul cites the internationally growing opposition against the economic reorganization by the WTO and the summits of the G7/G8 – including the campaign against the Multilateral Agreement on Investment (MAI) – to be a prime catalyst for building a network of activists across various groups in Germany:

We [Paul's NGO] participated in the critical guidance of the WTO's trade policy on the way to Seattle. [...] Another development was the process of critical guidance of the G7, and later the G8. Also this started in the 90s and for Germany this materialized at the G8 in Cologne – there was an alternative congress where many of the issues were addressed that were constitutive for the GJM.

First, this shows that all accounts extensively explore the connections between transnational and local/national events. Second, the two types of accounts specify this connection differently. In the first type of account, Seattle and Porto Alegre are predominantly depicted as triggers for local and national events, such as organizing protests against the G8 in Genoa or building up a broad movement coalition in Germany. Conversely, in accounts of the second type, Seattle and Porto Alegre are largely triggered *by* local and national events (as manifestations of transnational developments), such as the nuclear disarmament movement in Italy or the protests against the G8 summit in Cologne.

Discussion of results

This analysis of activists' narratives points to differences as well as similarities in how GJM activists remember the movement. The first part of the analysis not only revealed sector- and country-specific narratives, it also showed that some narratives are shared across sectors and countries despite various degrees of involvement.

Similarly, the second part of the analysis pointed out that, on the one hand, Seattle, Porto Alegre, or both, are located differently within the general story of the GJM – both with respect to the line of causation (triggers vs results) as well as to the connection to local events (triggers of local events vs results of local events). On the other hand, the second part of the analysis highlighted that Seattle and Porto Alegre are central and reoccurring reference points in all accounts extensively connected to local and national events. The places of these events are merged into a small but significant shared space of action. This space does not include all the movement's sites of action, but it does provide a common link between activities occurring in different locations.

Thus, one can conclude that while a single coherent memory of the GJM does not exist, memories do partially coincide and activists share certain narrative patterns. In all narratives, the events in Seattle and Porto Alegre are not only present, they are also similarly remembered. This points to the existence, to some extent, of a collective identity. By determining which experiences were crucial to the group, the narratives specify who belongs to the movement, with whom they empathize (those participating in or sympathizing with Seattle and Porto Alegre) as well as, partly, what central goals unite the groups (e.g. opposition to the WTO). However, as the definitions of shared experiences do not overlap to a great extent, this collective identity is only partial – i.e. it does not cover all areas of activists' sense of belonging. It leaves room for affiliations to other collectives, such as local affinity groups, sector specific organizations, or national movements (cf. della Porta 2005).

Conclusion

Using a narrative approach, this chapter has explored how collective identity is constructed in transnational social movements in relation to collective memories. Accordingly, in order to explore collective identity formation, it analysed activists' accounts of the Global Justice Movement's past by considering the dimensions of both structure and content in their narratives.

Drawing on interviews with Italian and German activists, this chapter showed that while memories differ with respect to content and structure, central narrative elements coincide and allow a partial collective identity to be sustained. It identified differences both in terms of sector- and nation-specific *content* as well as regarding different *types* of narratives independent of sector or nation (as well as activists' age and length of activism). This study revealed similarities in terms of the centrality of the events in Seattle and Porto Alegre and their extensive connection to local and national developments. These overlaps in memory form a basis for a partial movement identity – one that is open to encompass other collective identities.

The focus on collective memories not only allowed for an analysis of the different layers of remembrance; it also enabled an exploration of the dimensions of collective meaning-making beyond diagnostic, prognostic, and motivational framing, which is an analytical approach that may inspire future research into collective identity formation. This chapter showed that movement actions themselves become central resources for the construction of collective identity. More specifically, it revealed *how* collective actions matter – i.e. as parts of a story that tells the orgins of a group, which in this case is the Global Justice Movement. Finally, this study advanced the understanding of how collective identity formation works in large and dispersed entities such as transnational social movements: it builds on certain shared narrative elements to which various other events can be meaningfully connected.

Notes

1 The concept of 'free spaces' has found much resonance among movement scholars (e.g. Melucci 1989; Taylor 1995; Polletta 1999; Routledge 2000). Free spaces are 'small-scale settings within a community or movement that are removed from the direct control of dominant groups, are voluntarily participated in, and generate the cultural challenge that precedes or accompanies political mobilization' (Polletta 1999: 1).
2 This draws on a dual conceptualization of space: space not only influences social action, it is also influenced by these actions through the human arrangement of material objects as well as the interpretation of these arrangements. For details on this approach see Daphi (forthcoming).
3 Though developed with reference to the national context, this argument has been applied to both national (e.g. Taylor and Wetherell 1999) and transnational settings (e.g. Appadurai 1996).
4 Interviewees were asked about the GJM's development in their respective countries and abroad. Hence, the degree to which developments abroad were included into this account was varied and left to the individual interviewee.
5 Six interviews per country were selected based on the two most elaborate narrative accounts per national movement sector.
6 However, most German activists do discuss the protests in Genoa as they significantly shaped the GJM in Europe in Germany and beyond. Conversely, Heiligendamm is not mentioned in accounts of Italian activists.
7 Most activists consider these protests to be failures since they did not stop the war, despite the very high number of participants.
8 These are the three reasons most frequently identified by Italian activists for the movement's decline.

References

Anderson, B. (1983) *Imagined Communities*, London: Verso.

Andretta, M., della Porta, D., Mosca, L. and Reiter, H. (2003) *No Global – New Global*, Frankfurt, New York: Campus Verlag.

Appadurai, A. (1996) *Modernity at Large*, Minneapolis: University of Minnesota Press.

Banse, F. and Habermann, F. (2012) 'Vom Ende der Globalisierungsbewegung'. *Forschungsjournal Soziale Bewegungen*, 25(1): 51–60.

Bearman, P.S. and Stovel, K. (2000) 'Becoming a Nazi'. *Poetics*, 27: 69–90.

Coser, L.A. (ed.) (1992) *On Collective Memory*, Chicago: University of Chicago Press.

Cumbers, A., Routledge, P. and Nativel, C. (2008) 'The entangled geographies of global justice networks'. *Progress in Human Geography*, 32: 183–201.

Daphi, P. (2011) 'Soziale Bewegungen und Kollektive Identität'. *Forschungsjournal Soziale Bewegungen*, 24(4): 13–26.

Daphi, P. (forthcoming) 'Imagining movement space', in B. Baumgarten, P. Daphi and P. Ullrich (eds) *Protest | Culture*.

della Porta, D. (2005) 'Multiple Belongings, Tolerant Identities, and the Construction of "Another Politics"', in D. della Porta and S.G. Tarrow (eds) *Transnational protest and global activism*, Lanham MD: Rowman & Littlefield.

della Porta, D. (2007) 'The Global Justice Movement in Context', In D. della Porta (ed.) *The Global Justice Movement*, Boulder, London: Paradigm Publishers.

della Porta, D. and Diani, M. (2006) *Social movements*, Oxford; MA: Blackwell.

della Porta, D., Andretta, M., Mosca, L. and Reiter, H. (2006) *Globalization from below*, Minneapolis: University of Minnesota Press.

Eder, K. (2000) *Kulturelle Identität zwischen Tradition und Utopie. Soziale Bewegungen als Ort gesellschaftlicher Lernprozesse*, Frankfurt/Main: Campus Verlag.

Eder, K. (2005) 'Remembering National Memories Together', in K. Eder and W. Spohn (eds) (2005) *Collective memory and European identity*, Hants: Ashgate.

Eder, K. (2006) 'Europe's Borders', *European Journal of Social Theory*, 9(2): 255–271.

Evans, S.M. and Boyte, H.C. (1986) *Free Spaces*, New York: Harper & Row.

Fine, G.A. (1995) 'Public narration and group culture', in H. Johnston and B. Klandermans (eds) *Social Movements and Culture*, Minneapolis: University of Minnesota Press.

Flesher Fominaya, C. (2010) 'Collective Identity in Social Movements', *Sociology Compass*, 4(6): 393–404.

Franzosi, R. (1998) 'Narrative Analysis – Or Why (And How) Sociologists Should be Interested in Narrative', *Annual Review of Sociology*, 24: 517–554.

Gamson, W. (1996) 'Safe spaces and social movements', *Perspectives on Social Problems*, 8, 27–38.

Giddens, A. (1984) *The constitution of society: Outline of the theory of structuration*, Berkeley: University of California Press.

Halbwachs, M. (1966 [1925]) *Das Gedächtnis und seine sozialen Bedingungen*, Berlin: Luchterhand.

Halbwachs, M. (1980a [1950]) *The collective memory*, New York: Harper & Row.

Halbwachs, M. (1980b [1950]) 'Space and the Collective Memory', in M. Halbwachs *The Collective Memory*, New York: Harper & Row. Online. Available: http://web.mit.edu/allanmc/www/hawlbachsspace.pdf (accessed 5 July 2011).

Halbwachs, M. (1992) 'The Legendary Topography of the Gospels in the Holy Land', In L.A. Coser (ed.) *On Collective Memory*, Chicago: University of Chicago Press.

Harvey, D. (1992) *The condition of postmodernity*, Cambridge: Blackwell.

Hetherington, K. (1998) *Expressions of Identity*, London Thousand Oaks: Sage.

Hunt, S.A., Benford, R.D. and Snow, D.A. (1994) 'Identity Fields', in E. Laraña, H. Johnston and J.R. Gusfield (eds) *New Social Movements*, Philadelphia: Temple University Press.

Melucci, A. (1989) *Nomads of the Present*, Philadelphia PA: Temple University Press.

Melucci, A. (1996) *Challenging Codes*, New York: Cambridge University Press.

Nepstad, S.E. (2001) 'Creating Transnational Solidarity', *Mobilization: An International Journal*, 6(1): 21–36.

Polletta, F. (1998) 'Contending stories', *Qualitative Sociology*, 21: 419–446.

Polletta, F. (1999) ' "Free spaces" in collective action', *Theory and Society*, 28(1), 1–38.

Polletta, F. (2006) *It was like a fever: Storytelling in protest and politics.* Chicago: University of Chicago Press.

Polletta, F. and Jasper, J.M. (2001) 'Collective Identity and Social Movements', *Annual Review of Sociology*, 27: 283–305.

Pries, L. (2005) 'Configurations of geographic and societal spaces', Global Networks, 5(2): 167–190.

Routledge, P. (2000) ' "Our resistance will be as transnational as capital", *GeoJournal*, 52: 25–33.

Rucht, D. (1995) 'Kollektive Identität', *Forschungsjournal*, 8(1): 9–23.

Sassen, S. (2000) 'Spatialities and Temporalities of the Global', *Public Culture*, 12(1): 215–232.

Sewell, W.H. and McAdam, D. (2001) 'It's About Time', in R. Aminzade (ed.) *Silence and voice in the study of contentious politics*, Cambridge New York: Cambridge University Press.

Snow, D.A. and Anderson, L. (1987) 'Identity Work among the Homeless', *American Journal of Sociology*, 92(6): 1336–1371.

Snow, D.A. and McAdam, D. (2000) 'Identity Work Processes in the Context of Social Movements: Clarifying the Identity/Movement Nexus', in S. Stryker, T.J. Owens, and R.W. White (eds), *Self, Identity, and Social Movements.* Minneapolis: University of Minnesota Press.

Somers, M.R. (1992) 'Narrativity, Narrative Identity, and Social Action', Social Science History, 16(4): 591–630.

Somers, M.R. (1994) 'The narrative constitution of identity', *Theory and Society*, 23: 605–649.

Somers, M.R. (1995) 'Narrating and Naturalizing Civil Society and Citizenship Theory', *Sociological Theory*, 13(3): 229–274.

Taylor, V. (1995) 'Watching for Vibes', in M.M. Ferree and P.Y. Martin (eds) *Feminist Organizations*, Philadelphia PA: Temple University Press.

Taylor, S. and Wetherell, M. (1999) 'A Suitable Time and Place', *Time & Society*, 8(1): 39–58.

Teune, S. (2008) 'Gegen Zaun, Gipfel und Käfighaltung.', in D. Rucht and S. Teune (eds) *Nur Clowns und Chaoten?*, Frankfurt: Campus.

Uggla, F. (2006) 'Between Globalism and Pragmatism', *Mobilization: An International Quarterly*, 11: 51–66.

11 At home in the movement

Constructing an oppositional identity through activist travel across European squats

Linus Owens, Ask Katzeff, Elisabeth Lorenzi and Baptiste Colin

Social movements move. Mobile activists do more than go from one place to another. They also defend, re-imagine, and remake political places and the politics of place. Mobility transforms places, generates new practices and ties within a social movement, and builds new pathways connecting different movements. We investigate activist mobility through a movement that initially appears to not simply desire, but to zealously demand, immobility – squatting. But squatters are more mobile than they first appear. Their defence of home and the local actually relies on moving as much as it does on staying put. In their travels, squatters are more than political tourists. Mobility strengthened and expanded their movement, building a robust network connecting different squatting cities, and opened flows of ideas and activists within it. This network, in turn, became a new place to occupy, one with new demands and identities. Simultaneously cosmopolitan and local, placed and displaced, this structure of movement and relations formed a foundation for developing a European squatters' movement, and later contributed places and place-makings to the emergent alterglobalization movement.

Our argument evolves from efforts to connect separate research projects on different local squatters' movements in Amsterdam, Berlin, Copenhagen, Hamburg, London, Madrid, and Paris from the 1970s to the present. Our individual work revealed diffuse and fluid boundaries around local squatters' movements (Colin 2010; Lorenzi 2010; Owens 2009). Although each movement remained bound to its own location, under the surface, connections between localities proliferated, often built upon contacts made and sustained through travel. Combining our data, we trace the emergence of a European squatters' movement out of the movement of local squatters. Sharing more than ideology and tactics, travelling squatters forged a collective sense of place founded on new identities and solidarities created and nourished through mobility and movement. Even as their networks expanded, these movements remained strongly local, creating new understandings of the local that transcended municipal and state boundaries. This mobile squatting network also helped to create a new relationship to place useful for other movements, who used these political spaces, both squatted and networked, for their own projects. We argue that squatters did more than offer physical spaces; they produced locally grounded networks of mobile activists with a corresponding new sense of political space, what Chatterton (2010) calls "autonomous geographies." This infrastructure contributed to building the alterglobalization movement, grounding a critique of neoliberal visions of mobility, and providing an important resource for mass mobilization.

Mobility defines the modern world (Urry 2007), yet remains underexplored in social movements. Mobility provides a means to occupy and define space and place. McDonald's (2006) study of alterglobalization activists finds communities that are intense, impermanent, and, importantly, mobile. Travel builds new forms of collective identity, fluid but durable – fluid because travel is transient and changing, and durable, since travel is embodied and often structured. Space and place both enable and constrain political action. Movements act in and upon space, often changing it in the process. Cobarrubias and Pickles (2009) show activist map-making as a re-imagining of political spaces, which makes new actions and outcomes possible. Travel can also be its own map; mobile activists re-draw the political terrain, remaking grievances along the way (Featherstone 2003). Summit protests rely upon mobile tactics to build alternative spaces of political contention, with the promise that new spaces bring new opportunities. Eyerman (2006) argues that mobility creates "additional space for education and political and social interaction between activists and with the local community" (206). Fernandez *et al.* (2011) see summit protests as marked by conflicts between police and activists to control space through processes of territorialization. This struggle begins before the actual protest: activists try to move through space to participate, while authorities seek to limit and redirect their movement as much as possible.

Place can be both territorial and relational (Nicholls 2009). Territorial place is fixed and solid. Nicholls finds this understanding alone insufficient for a world defined by mobility and flux, instead treating place as relational and constructed, "where actors with different statuses, geographical ties, and mobilities interact in fleeting and unstructured ways" (2009: 80). Massey (2005) argues that "conceptualizing space as open, multiple and relational, unfinished and always becoming, is a prerequisite for history to be open and thus a prerequisite, too, for the possibility of politics" (59). The mobility of political actors, and the politicization of mobility, complicates space and place, opening them to flows not only of people, but also of ideas and relationships. As Massey notes, "a territorialized space of bounded places provides little in the way of avenues for a developing radical politics" (183). Even as activists struggle for more immediate demands, they resist the closures of space, opening new avenues for action. Understanding how relational place works requires a theory of collective action (Nichols 2009). In this chapter, we examine how activist mobility links local nodes together, forming a broader social movement space, one connected to, but separate from, the individual places giving rise to it. Social movement place-making and mobility cultivate collective ties, increasing the number of possible contact points for diverse actors with similar goals to interact together. Mobile activists spread ideas and identity. In the process, they generate new ideas and new identities.

Mobility is no panacea. It can just as easily reproduce inequality and the status quo as disrupt it. Networks and links built on mobility are often maintained by and oriented towards affluent, elite participants, since they are generally the most mobile. Travel is fraught with access issues. It is gendered and raced (Adey 2009). Nicholls argues that activist mobility can often spark new divisions and political tensions:

> The ability to overcome geographical and cultural obstacles makes it possible for "mobile" activists to forge a coherent social movement space, but in doing this, they introduce new points of antagonism that pit them into conflictual relations with their less mobile and more locally grounded comrades.
>
> (2009: 91)

Thus, mobility is no different from other tactical innovations, creating new opportunities alongside new complications.

Social movement space is the product of the recursive relationship between mobility and stability. Stability makes mobility meaningful. By anchoring place, it enables actors to experience the movement of themselves and others, while creating destinations for travel. Mobility, especially over time, creates stability and formulates attachment – to movement, but also to place. Mobility is not the opposite of stability. Instead, to be fixed and to move are two interrelated components of social movement activity, potentially complementary and contradictory. Therefore, we begin our analysis of squatter mobility through their history of establishing stability.

Staying put

"We will not leave!" For squatters, this slogan is both threat and promise. It is a threat to the landlords and police who want to throw them on to the street. It is a promise to their neighbours and fellow residents of their commitment to maintaining the property and the surrounding community. Squatting is about space: people without enough space appropriate it from others they think have too much. Squatting is also about place – creating, redefining, and defending it. Vacant spaces get turned into meaningful places. To do this successfully, squatters must stay in the buildings they occupy.

Squatting promises a home. Lack of housing is often a driving force behind squatting efforts. Beginning in the 1960s, Dutch activists targeted vacant housing stock for those without adequate shelter. Critiques of the housing shortage, and the real-estate speculation that kept places empty, helped build public support for their cause. Squatters sought homes for themselves, but also argued for remaking the city as less of a market and more of a home for all (Owens 2009). Similar housing struggles occurred in London in the 1970s (Wates and Wolmar 1980). Alternatively, other squatters' movements, such as in Spain (Martinez 2007), Italy (Mudu 2004), Germany, and Denmark, focused more on developing new forms of collective communities and mutual support through squatting social centres.

But there is a problem. In most European countries squatting is illegal, and even where it is legal (such as in the Netherlands until 2010), squatters are constantly threatened with eviction. Successful political projects require stability – something property owners and authorities rarely provide without a fight. Yet public support often requires commitments to the long term – to being good neighbours and good caretakers of buildings. In the mid-1970s, Amsterdam squatters vigorously differentiated themselves from squatting tourists, who vacationed in empty buildings, usually leaving them in a worse state than they found them. In solidarity with their neighbours, activists framed their squatting as the defence of a very fixed and stable conception of place, rejecting touristic mobility as a threat to the local (Owens 2008). Stability is seldom given; it must be demanded and defended. Squatters' movements across Europe became notorious for their struggles with police to resist evictions in the 1980s. In Amsterdam in the late 1970s, after years of leaving buildings willingly to avoid confrontation, squatters decided it made more sense to stay and fight. Following an eviction order in 1979, they transformed a threatened building, the Groote Keijser, into a fortress. Unexpectedly, the conflict came elsewhere. After successfully retaking another evicted building, squatters beat back the police and occupied the entire street for the weekend, until the city government called in tanks to crush the barricades. Despite losing the street, they kept the building, gaining international media coverage in the process (Duivenvoorden 2000). While particularly dramatic, this case is far from unique, with large squatter riots occurring in such cities as West Berlin, Zürich, and Copenhagen during the early 1980s.

Emergent squatters' movements emphasized stability. Being a good squatter meant staying. Being a successful movement meant staying. The movement sought to balance the tensions of place-making – the differences between public and private space, and between protecting and changing place – while facing external threats of eviction. Establishing itself made the movement both more stable and more volatile: more stable, because squatters were able to remain in and more fully remake their places, yet more volatile, because a stable movement can expand and develop its politics and tactical repertoire. This newly-won stability also encouraged a dramatic increase in squatter mobility, making travel not only possible, but, in some cases, absolutely necessary. Mobility was a defence of stability, and product of it, too. A successful squatting action keeps certain bodies in place, while setting others in motion.

Taking off

Staying is one way to resist. Moving is another. Squatter mobility generally took three forms: defending buildings from eviction, sharing skills with other activists, and expanding the movement's boundaries. Together, they encompassed a broad range of motivations for mobility, making activist travel attractive to people with many different levels of political commitment and interest, from the staunch radical spreading the word to a more casual participant just looking for a change of scenery.

Staying put often requires a willingness to move on the part others. Resisting eviction, an explicit demand to remain in place, relies on mobility. Travel to defend threatened buildings is as old as the movement itself. Christiania, the squatted "free state" in Copenhagen, called for sympathizers to travel there in order to help combat eviction as early as 1975. Amsterdam squatters frequently travelled to Germany in the early 1980s to defend buildings targeted for eviction. Their visits to West Berlin brought episodes of fierce fighting between squatters and police. Eviction defences provided many teachable moments for tactical sharing: "German police reports pointed not only to the presence of Amsterdam squatters, but also to the fact that the fighting methods employed seemed to be transplanted directly from the Netherlands" (Duivenvoorden 2000: 180). New mobile actors were launched. German police travelled to Amsterdam to learn counter-tactics from their Dutch colleagues. Calls for help continue to cross borders, including efforts to save the Kalendarpanden in Amsterdam in the 1990s, and Copenhagen's Ungdomshuset (Youth House) in the 2000s.

After their much-publicized victory in 1980 the Amsterdam squatters achieved celebrity status among European activists, who were eager to bring similar successes to their own cities. Capitalizing upon their fame, Amsterdammers hit the road, travelling to England, France, Spain, Italy, Switzerland, and Germany (Owens 2008). They held public meetings in numerous cities, sharing strategies and organizing principles, and sometimes did a bit more. That same year, Amsterdammers introduced political squatting to Madrid. As one Spanish activist remembers, "The squatter event marked a break in time. Their approach to personal life, the alternative occupation of flats ... like water in the desert" (Lorenzi 2007: 57). Mobile activists shared their local knowledge in new places, creating new local knowledges in the process.

Travellers wanted to learn as well as teach, bringing new ideas back home. Such exchanges proved valuable in developing the movement at both the local and translocal levels. In 1982 the Parisian squatters' collective called "*occupants-rénovateurs*" adopted the configuration of West Berliner's "*Instand-besetzer*" (both mean "occupy to restore"), in doing so hoping to gain in legitimacy and to develop squats in Paris. Educational exchange soon became formalized through international squatters' conferences, bringing together squatters from across Europe to meet and discuss strategies, tactics, and political goals, not to mention building stronger personal networks within the movement. The summer of 1981 saw the *Tuwat* festival in West Berlin: initiated by squatters, it brought together activists from alternative movements from all over Europe to meet and share knowledge. International meetings remain important, taking place in cities in France, Germany, Spain, and, in 2012, in Brighton (UK). Such meetings proved particularly useful for smaller movements to learn from larger ones. In 1986, for example, Danish squatters returned from a congress in Frankfurt with stronger international ties and an organizational structure taken from West German and Italian autonomous groups. Sometimes bringing back new information is the explicit intent of travel: in 1994, the Rozbrat social centre in Poznan (Poland) was constructed by local activists following their return from an inspiration-gathering trip through Europe. Although squatters often confronted very specific local property laws and different protest and policing cultures, the movement of activists and the flows of information they opened quickly diffused general tactics and practices, culture, and identities across Europe during the 1980s and beyond.

Not all travel was formally organized. In fact, most commonly, activists visited other squatting cities on an informal basis. Sometimes these trips were little more than activist vacations, visiting the city in order to stay in a squatted house for a while and experience the local scene. Some trips were more permanent, with activists moving to new cities via the access provided through squatting: Londoners moved to Amsterdam; Berliners to Barcelona; New Yorkers to Rome. Newcomers sometimes squatted their own place (Duivenvoorden 2000), but more frequently they moved into existing squats. By providing low-cost housing, squatting can lower barriers for activists relocating to a new city (Ryan 2006).

Relocation usually meant moving to cities with existing scenes, but some squatters sought new challenges, pushing the movement's boundaries outward. Historically, squatting in New York City looked very different from squatting in Western Europe. When European squatters came in the mid-1980s, they brought with them the tactics and organizational structures of their home countries, establishing a form of political squatting new to the city and unique in the United States (Pruijt 2003). Connections spread across the Atlantic, generating new routes for the squatters' movement and the movement of squatters. The fall of the Berlin Wall opened East Berlin to a flood of occupations – some by locals, but many by West Berliners, alongside others from across Europe – drawn by the abundant vacant buildings and the city's frontier qualities (Ryan 2006). Travel also flows in the other direction. As older squatters' movements decline, travellers sometimes replace locals. Currently, for example, many squats in Amsterdam are home to Eastern Europeans.

Travel defended buildings, spread new ideas from the local to new localities and the wider social movement space, and extended the movement's borders. While information also circulated through the exchange of newspapers and 'zines, activist travel played a significant role in diffusing local innovations and identities across many squatted spaces. Before easy access to online information and communication technologies, physical presence offered one of the better guarantees for meaningful learning and participation. Even today, despite ubiquitous communication and information flows, the importance of travel has not diminished. In fact, as Nicholls (2009) argues, access to more information and more contact often encourage more travel, not less.

Growing up

Successful place-making can disrupt a coherent sense of place. To make a place worth living in is to make a place worth keeping and worth defending, but also a place worth visiting and worth reproducing. A stable squat can thus destabilize the places around it, even while committed to protecting the local. For example, squatters claim to defend the neighbourhood, yet often contribute to significant neighbourhood transformation, bringing in new people and practices, as well as new ties to the outside. Mobile activists reaffirm and reproduce the local while simultaneously drawing it further into networks of non-local forces and influences, producing a local defined by openness and flows, not just stability and solidity (Colin 2010). Ironically, in their efforts to "fix" the local, squatters frequently employ strategies that "unfix" them from that very same local.

Once set in motion, squatter mobility continued to grow throughout the 1980s. Early squatter mobility sought primarily to stabilize squatting at the local level, but the increasing reach and depth of squatted stability facilitated mobility, making it attractive and accessible. No longer sporadic and rare, travel became more frequent and normalized. Over time, the movement of multiple activists to and from multiple locations produced a broad network of inter-connecting nodes and pathways. A network born from ongoing interactions between mobilities and places assumed its own sense of place, with its own solidarities and identities.

Social centres are important places in the squatting world. The practice, originally from the Italian tradition (Membretti and Mudu, this volume, Chapter 5), has been embraced across Europe, proliferating in England, Germany, the Netherlands, Spain, and more. Often (but not always) squatted, they furnish public spaces for activist communities. Chatterton (2010: 1205) describes them as "semi-permanent, self-governing, not-for-profit place-bounded political projects which promote grassroots activism, politics and culture and which largely rely on volunteer labour." They offer a broad range of services, including offices, concerts, cafes, archives, and more. Here, politics intersects with the everyday, encouraging cross-movement pollination and the politicization of everyday life. Social centres' stable, physical presence provides a vital touchstone for activists, furnishing a primary point of contact and engagement. Social centres blur the boundaries between public and private, offering a place where insiders welcome outsiders, where political activism meets cultural innovation.

Unsurprisingly, when squatters travel, social centres provide an organizing framework. Because of their relative openness, they serve as an excellent entry point into new locations, offering a convenient orientation into a city's activist and counter-cultural layout. Social centres' public function means they are generally easier to find and enter than other squats. Their relatively greater longevity (for example, Leoncavallo in Milan, which has existed since the 1970s; Mudu 2004) provides clear destinations and stable moorings, important due to the fleeting nature of much squatting. Activists' travel narratives describe moving through Europe's underground, with frequent stops in the social centres of the cities they visit (Ryan 2006). Stability, coupled with publicness, facilitates mobility by reducing the risks and costs of travel. Hospitality helps make this system work. Norms of reciprocity create an open door policy for travellers. In some cases, hosting systems developed, with guestrooms and dormitories in squatted buildings for visitors. In Spain, despite few formal hosting systems, an informal structure of hospitality means that once one has a connection, it is possible to find a place to stay. This principle also applies locally, where evicted squatters and social centres are temporarily rehoused with others. Importantly, these connections form organizational and tactical links along with affective ties and friendships. Exchange helped build an imagined community among squatters, with every squat a potential home. Making initial contact could prove difficult, especially before easy and inexpensive electronic communication, which is why social centres proved to be such important ports of entry for travellers. For example, the now-defunct 121 Anarchist Centre in Brixton, London, received numerous visits from people from Europe travelling through the city for the first time, many of whom had read the same article about the centre in a magazine, providing them with one location where they could learn how to navigate the rest of the London scene.

The social centre as a port has some historical reference for radical politics. Tchen (1999) describes port culture as "hybridizing" and "challenging authority, wealth, and … normalcy" (72). Ports are places of exchange, difference, and innovation, created out of the flux of interacting individuals, some stable, some mobile. Linebaugh and Rediker (2001) studied the working class politics of seventeenth to nineteenth century North Atlantic sailors, showing how ports and routes interact to create new political identities based on mobilities. They argue that this new political consciousness emerged from experiences of mobility and corresponding forms of confinement. It combined local traditions, fostering a dynamic relationship with place and others. Their experiences of mobility and rapid change revealed the possibilities of other worlds, forming the basis of their politics.

Social centres bring a variety of social, political and cultural currents together, mixing them under one roof. Bike workshops in Madrid's social centres provide an interesting example of the overlap between local users, activists, and travellers. Travellers seeking transportation rely upon these services, which they often know from back home. Using these facilities integrates travellers into local networks, drawing them into related local politics, such as Critical Mass activism, itself part of a global networked movement (Lorenzi 2010). Local outreach extends the centre's reach into the community. Chatterton's research on UK social centres found that their primary goal was "to create spaces for engagement and new political potentials and alliances that could not have been conceived before" (2010: 1217). Overlapping with so many social worlds, connecting mobile activists to local activists, activists to non-activist locals, social centres provide both a launching pad into mobility networks and a landing strip into local worlds.

Opening up

The European underground music circuit offers a significant example of how mobility and openness strengthen network ties, even when not explicitly political. The role of social centres within the music circuit is well-documented

(Dunn 2008). Bands used this network for the same reasons squatters and other activists did: a low-cost infrastructure of travel and easy access to locals with shared interests. In return, concerts supply financial stability to social centre projects (Martinez 2007). Music can attract new people into a social centre, both from the local community and, via travelling bands, from outside. As musicians made use of places and connections originally created by activists, the music circuit reinforced these same connections and extended them, increasing the network's usefulness for all users.

Strong nodes and repeatedly reinforced ties produced a very robust and dynamic network. Sometimes this network structure and membership became formalized, linking active members together in order to share resources and information, usually at either the national level, such as the UK Social Centre Network and France's Intersquat (which connects artists' squats), or more locally, as found in Amsterdam and West Berlin. Although independent and separate, they only needed one link between them, often secured and sustained through travelling activists, to pull them all into a broader web. Sometimes new political issues would encourage the connecting together of different networks. In the 1980s Copenhagen squatters incorporated solidarity with Palestine and anti-apartheid activism into their politics, binding them closer to other squatters across Europe, particularly those from Amsterdam and Hamburg, in order to plan and perform coordinated actions against South African embassies, Shell gas stations, and companies trading with South Africa.

In practice, however, this network is neither formal nor singular; rather, it is the aggregation of the overlapping and inter-relating travel and communication paths of different activists and movements. Established to defend and celebrate the local, the network eventually became its own place. Although mobilized to defend individual local squats, it becomes less and less dependent upon specific places in the network. In a large network, losing an individual node would have little effect on individual mobilities, as itineraries can be re-routed to other destinations. At the same time, defending one place in the network became equivalent to defending them all. When German solidarity protesters chanted, alongside similar protests in France, Italy, and elsewhere, "We are all the Ungdomshus!" when Copenhagen's Ungdomshuset was evicted in 2007, they expressed the critical interdependence of squatted places and a shared identity born out of ongoing interactions. Conflicts around one place in the network could be "re-placed" into a different local context. As nodes in separate but overlapping networks, social centres bridge political and cultural activists, extending the network's reach and flexibility, deepening its sense of place. Exchange, informal and formal, temporary and long-term, formed a squatting circuit in Europe, one that could be mobilized to help threatened squats, as well as facilitating the mobility of squatters, along with others, during less heightened moments.

A network is greater than the sum of its parts. Mobility launches new mobilities. Place makes new places. We identify this network as a trans-urban social movement space, one that establishes and defends difference locally, while simultaneously producing trans-local sameness. Locally, the social centre and squatting scene display and defend a marked form of difference. With their links to both radical politics and underground music, squatting scenes act as counter-cultural bases. Squatting worlds can be quite insular – whether from preference or necessity. Squatted spaces provide more than housing; they also accommodate entertainment, food, and even retail. It is possible, therefore, to live almost entirely within a squatted world. While this difference is often expressed as oppositional to the larger city, a space of freedom and experimentation against the forces of capital and the state, it is not impervious to co-optation and recuperation. For example, in Amsterdam in the late 1990s, the city sought to incorporate large squatted social centres into its efforts at self-branding, turning "squatter chic" into the basis for tourist economies (Owens 2008).

From the network level, however, things look different. Building a collective identity of shared practices and beliefs creates internal homogeneity. The more information, tactics, and cultural practices that flowed through the network, the more it developed as its own place, tied to but separate from the local places from which it emerged. This space of flows brings together radical politics and counter-cultures, which grew more similar to each other and more different from others. Homogeneity makes travel easy; heterogeneity makes it worth it. In other words, travel helped produce sameness as well as protect difference. Enter a social centre in any major city and you will likely experience a sense of déjà vu. Although every centre is unique, most have common features quickly recognizable to anyone familiar with the genre, sharing politics, services, and cultural trappings (Wakefield and Grrrt 1995). To travel within this network is to move through physical space without necessarily leaving one's social space. No matter where they go, they are always at home. This highlights a curious tension in the network: the infrastructure intended to protect difference relies upon a process of building and strengthening internal sameness. "Squat the world" is more than a slogan: it also imagines the movement as a world in itself.

Movement connects people to people, people to places, and places to places. The building of this network contributed to developing a broader European squatters' movement, and fed the growth of autonomous movements in the 1980s (Katsiaficas 2006). Networks allow for mobility; meaningful places encourage travel. Together, they formed a new local, one un-fixed from a specific physical place. This network does not require large-scale participation in order to work effectively. Although not all squatters travelled the network, the squatting circuit minimized costs and risks, which helped open travel to the "masses" within the movement. Those who did travel did not need to go everywhere in the network to support it, nor did they need to go far. A robust network can scale-up small movements into large effects, which in turn can make it easier for users to travel more and further, minimizing the costs of distance. In the 1990s, for example, Copenhagen was "closer" to Milan for many squatters than nearer cities such as Amsterdam, due to the high number of Italians who had moved to the city. From this foundation emerged new place-based identities, ones loosened from existing local and national identities, but more grounded than an abstract global cosmopolitanism. The network requires a new form of activist, one who is not simply mobile, but whose activist identity arises out of and depends upon it. Mobility is not just one tactic among many, but a primary basis for politics and action. These activists are actually "at home" in this movement. Mobility is an extension of where they live, and should be defended with the same vigour.

Moving on

The creation of this network returns the story to the beginning. A new-found place brought equally new-found demands to protect and maintain it. While the original threats of landlords and authorities remained at the local level, new ones arose at the network level, namely European integration and neoliberal globalization. Mobility sits at the heart of new European spatial visions, which depend upon new flows of capital, consumer goods, and people. But this mobility excludes some actors, primarily non-European immigrants (Adey 2009), while constraining the internal movement of others, such as oppositional political actors (Fernandez *et al.* 2011). Such mobility conflicts directly with the kind practised within squatter networks. Squatting provided an explicit critique of neoliberal urban planning (Mudu 2004). The movement was equally defiant at the transnational level. In this section we examine how the efforts of squatters' movements to engage place and mobility contributed to how the alterglobalization movement emerged, providing not just territorial spaces but also new conceptions and practices of making and relating to places.

Summit-hopping – travelling to and between large summit protests – is one of the more recognizable new tactics which arose from the burgeoning alterglobalization movement during the late 1990s and early 2000s. The practice was not without controversy. Even while providing a dynamic way both to protest neoliberal globalization and to practise an alternative relationship to place and mobility, not to mention increase participation levels at events, this tactic came under fire. Marco (2001) criticized activist mobility as an expression of privilege which undermined the larger goals of the movement. Some activists sought to distance themselves from the politically problematic aspects of travel, leading to a rediscovery of the local and the need to protect it (Thompson 2010). But the local that activists returned to was not the same local that others had mobilized around before, despite sharing the same name. To set the local against the mobile misreads how place works. It also neglects the history of experiments with place, mobility, and movement that had been occurring amongst activists in Europe in the period leading up to the "sudden" appearance of these protests.

The history of squatter mobility helps place this debate in context. By the late 1980s squatters had already mobilized their networks against threats to their practices of place-making and mobility. In May 1989, Danish, Dutch, and West German squatters briefly occupied the EU headquarters in Brussels. Throughout the 1990s, social centres mobilized opposition against the economic integration of the European Union. At the 1998 EuroTop summit in Amsterdam local squatters provided organization, infrastructure, and resources, bringing together activists from across Europe to disrupt the meetings (Duivenvoorden 2000). In the early 2000s, squatters from many localities joined other activists in the No Border network to challenge new European migration policies (Walters 2006). Social centres were central in this network, providing solidarity for asylum-seekers, and hosting information and outreach events (Chatterton 2010). Strategically, however, squatting proved to be limited. While useful for defending specific places at the local level, squatting buildings alone did little to defend the trans-urban networked places threatened by neoliberal globalization. The limits of squatting called new movements into being.

Solid ties between squatters, social centres, and the alterglobalization movement existed throughout Europe, including Spain (Martinez 2007), Switzerland (Eggert and Guigni 2007), Italy (della Porta *et al.* 2006), the Netherlands, and Germany. In Genoa, during the G8 protests in 2001, the city's robust social centre infrastructure was essential to the organization of the event (Mudu 2004). Most studies, however, leave the impression that social centres and squatters simply provided planning spaces and bodies on the streets (Juris 2008). We believe that squatters did more for the alterglobalization movement: they also contributed to forming new conceptions and practices of place, one based upon activist bodies in motion.

The alterglobalization movement also focuses on creating and propagating new forms of space and place. Research emphasizes the spaces coming out of the movement, primarily the more temporary forms. Lacey argues that protestors generate more than "tangible, albeit fleeting, physical protest spaces," they also produce "rhetorical and emotional spaces" (2007: 247): less a location than a set of social interactions. What such studies share is an emphasis on novelty. These spaces, however, should be considered as extensions of existing forms of place, rather than new inventions. The alterglobalization movement does help create new places, but it is itself a creation of existing new political places created by other movements. Social centres offered space for activists to organize; they also offered a network and ideology of locally grounded, trans-urban mobility. Squatters provided bodies in the streets; they also provided mobile bodies, bringing an expansive vision of both place and mobility which could ground resistance, including local infrastructures of action, translocal infrastructures of mobility, and new understandings and identities of place. Many celebrate the networked nature of the alterglobalization movement, attributing it to the rise of the internet and new communications technologies (Van Aeist and Walgrave, 2002). It is not that squatters did not care about the internet – squatters have included dynamic computer activists, including the Chaos Computer Club and a vibrant hacker community, since the 1980s, as well as current projects providing access to computers and the internet. But the physical network matters, and we argue that there is also an underlying structure with a longer history at work here, the product of mobile bodies.

Understanding the history of the squatters' network and infrastructure of mobility provides an important example of how activists get from one place to another, and how this can lead from one movement to another. The network of social centres that developed out of the local squatters' movements of the 1970s, 1980s and 1990s provided a new model of place and belonging. This model of mobility and movement reinforced the meaningfulness of the local, while simultaneously establishing connections to a trans-local identity, one grounded in a real network of moving bodies and ports of entry and exit. And just as the local place, once created, needed to be defended, so too did the trans-local. While squatters' movements continued to struggle over making and defending place, the tactics that worked at the local level required innovation at the network level. In defending not just the specific network, but also the networked way of life, squatters made common cause with the more radical forces of alterglobalization, sharing their spaces of occupation, both territorial and relational. This networked place proved valuable in activists' efforts to "jump scale" – where "political claims and power established at one geographical scale are expanded to another" (Smith 2000: 726). Local actions seeking to resist global processes required a jumping-off point. We believe that this trans-urban social movement space provided one such point, creating a middle ground which linked global and local in an oppositional space. Although simply one strand of a larger phenomenon, squatter mobility places the "newness" of the alterglobalization movement and mobility into an important context. Summit-hopping is not an act of free-floating movement which erases the local; rather, it is an extension of existing practices of mobility within long-lasting networks which connect trans-urban and transnational social movements spaces. Social centres are "inspiring examples of radical politics" (Chatterton 2010: 1220) because of the kinds of places they are, but this kind of place is more than four walls and a roof. It is a network connecting flows of people, information, and identity, providing access to both the local and the global. Squatters provided alterglobalization activists with places to organize, but also an organizing understanding of place.

Conclusion

In this chapter we make two arguments about place, mobility and movements. Our primary argument is that the squatters' network, forged from the combination of stabilizing the local and increasing activist mobility between localities, created a new political place. This trans-urban social movement space produced new solidarities and responsibilities, maintained local differences alongside translocal identities, and helped produce a dynamic, open political movement, at once cosmopolitan and strongly local. Our second argument involves the ties between squatters' movements, their networks of mobility, and the politics of place in the alterglobalization movement. While we can show no direct path from one to the other, we rely on multiple interactions and a shared sense of place, which did not come from nowhere – or, should we say, "no place". Rather, we argue that it is the product of an embodied space of movement, one that arose in resistance to neoliberal forces of urbanization, which was then translated through the movement of activists into resistance to neoliberalism at the transnational scale. Certainly, this is only one of many pieces of the puzzle of explaining the origins of the alterglobalization movement, but we believe it is one worth recognizing.

Place matters for social movements. Because place matters, mobility matters, too. In fact, they are so highly dependent upon each other, they are best studied in tandem. Stability both facilitates and constrains mobility; mobility, in turn, both stabilizes and destabilizes place, and, with it, any social movement with a politics organized around defending or defining place. Mobility and networks move activists within movements and between movements, and sometimes even transform one movement into another.

References

Adey, P. (2009) *Mobility*, London: Routledge.

Chatterton, P. (2010) "So What Does It Mean to be Anti-Capitalist?", *Urban Studies*, 47(6): 1205–1224.

Cobarrubias, S. and Pickles, J. (2009) "Spacing Movements", in Warf, B. and Arias, S. (eds) *The Spatial Turn*, New York and London: Routledge, 36–58.

Colin, B. (2010) "'Pas de quartier pour les squatters!'", in Aiosa, B., Naït-Bouda, F. and Thévenon, M. (eds) *Repères et Espace(s). De la pluridisciplinarité à la polysémie*, Grenoble: Presses universitaires de Grenoble, 252–266.

Della Porta, D., Andretta, M., Mosca, L. and Reiter, H. (2006) *Globalization From Below*, Minneapolis: University of Minnesota Press.

Duivenvoorden, E. (2000) *Een Voet Tussen de Deur*, Amsterdam: Arbeiders Pers.

Dunn, K. (2008) "Never Mind the Bollocks", in Constantinou, C., Richmond, O. and Watson, A. (eds) *Cultures and Politics of Global Communication*, Cambridge: Cambridge University Press, 193–210.

Eggert, N. and Guigni, M. (2007) "The Global Justice Movement in Switzerland", in Della Porta, D. (ed.) *The Global Justice Movement*, Boulder, CO: Paradigm, 184–209.

Eyerman, R. (2006) "Performing Opposition or, How Movements Move", in Alexander, J., Giesen, B. and Mast, J. (eds) *Social Performance*, Cambridge: Cambridge University Press, 192–217.

Featherstone, D. (2003) "Spatialities of Transnational Resistance to Globalization", *Transactions of the Institute of British Geographers*, 28(3): 404–421.

Fernandez, L., Starr, A. and Scholl, C. (2011) *Shutting Down the Streets*, New York: NYU Press.

Juris, J. (2008) *Networking Futures*, Durham, NC: Duke University Press.

Katsiaficas, G. (2006) *The Subversion of Politics*, Oakland, CA: AK Press.

Lacey, A. (2007) "Forging Spaces of Justice", in Shukaitis, S. and Graeber, D. (eds) *Constituent Imagination*, Oakland, CA: AK Press, 242–250.

Linebaugh, P. and Rediker, M. (2001) *The Many-Headed Hydra*, New York: Beacon Press.

Lorenzi, E. (2007) *Vallekas, Puerto de Mar*, Madrid: Traficantes de Sueños.

Lorenzi, E. (2010) "Centro Social en Movimento", in Dominguez, M., Martinez, M. and Lorenzi, E. (eds) *Okupaciones en movimiento. Madrid: Tierradnadie Ediciones.*

McDonald, K. (2006) *Global Movements*, Malden, MA: Blackwell.

Marco (2001) *S-Top hopping!* Online: www.ainfos.ca/01/jul/ainfos01075.html (accessed 29 May 2012).

Martinez, M. (2007) "The Squatters' Movement", *South European Society and Politics*, 12(3): 379–398.

Massey, D. (2005) *For Space*, London: Sage.

Membretti, A. and Mudu, P. (2013) "Where Global Meets Local", in Flesher Fominaya, C. and Cox, L. (eds) *Understanding European Movements*, London: Routledge.

Mudu, P. (2004) "Resisting and Challenging Neoliberalism", *Antipode*, 36(5): 917–941.

Nicholls, W. (2009) "Place, Networks, Space", *Transactions of the Institute of British Geographers*, 34: 78–93.

Owens, L. (2008) "From tourists to anti-tourists to tourist attraction", *Social Movement Studies*, 7(1), 43–59.

Owens, L. (2009) *Cracking Under Pressure*, Amsterdam and State College, PA: Amsterdam University Press and Penn State University Press.

Pruijt, H. (2003) "Is the Institutionalization of Urban Movements Inevitable?", *International Journal of Urban and Regional Research*, 27(1): 133–157.

Ryan, R. (2006) *Clandestines*, Oakland, CA: AK Press.

Smith, N. (2000). "Scale", in Johnston, R.J., Gregory, D., Pratt, G. and Watts, M. (eds), *The Dictionary of Human Geography* 4th ed. Oxford: Blackwell, 724–727.

Tchen, J.K.W. (1999) *New York Before Chinatown*, Baltimore, MD: The John Hopkins University Press.

Thompson, A.K. (2010) *Black Bloc, White Riot*, Oakland, CA: AK Press.

Urry, J. (2007) *Mobilities*, Cambridge: Polity Press.

Van Aeist, P. and Walgrave, S. (2002) "New media, new movements?", *Information, Communication, & Society*, 5(4): 465–493.

Wakefield, S. and Grrrt (eds) (1995) *Not for Rent*, Amsterdam: Evil Twin Productions.

Walters, W. (2006) "No Border", *Social Justice*, 33(1): 21–39.

Wates, N. and Wolmar, C. (eds) (1980) *Squatting*. London: Bay Leaf Books.

Part IV

Understanding the new "European Spring"

Anti-austerity, 15-M, Indignados

12 The roots of the Saucepan Revolution in Iceland

Árni Daníel Júlíusson and Magnús Sveinn Helgason

The protests in Iceland between October 2008–January 2009 (popularly called the Saucepan Revolution) were the first events in what would later become a worldwide uprising against the neoliberal order. They were caused by the collapse of the Icelandic banks, which was the result of the international financial crisis of September 2008. The protests in Iceland led to the fall of the Icelandic government and new elections to parliament. They also toppled the leadership of the Central Bank of Iceland, and spelled an end to the hegemony of neoliberalism in Iceland. In this sense, Iceland was the weakest link in the neoliberal chain (Collerson 2011; Wade and Sigurgeirsdóttir 2010).

The protests also prefigured the later riots in Tunisia, Egypt, Spain, and the USA, amongst other countries, in that they focused on one urban location where the movement unfolded. There was a lot of other activity, but the act of taking one central official space and using it as a continuous meeting place for developing the movement was initiated in Austurvöllur in the centre of Reykjavík, the capital of Iceland. This tactic was used again, to similar effect, in Tahrir Square in Egypt in February 2011, in Spain in May 2011, and in many cities in the US in the autumn of 2011. It was a new way of organizing protest, a development that seemed to correspond to possibilities for the creation of movements of anti-capitalist subjectivity not directly based upon workers' organizations suggested by Antonio Gramsci in his writings in the third and fourth decades of the twentieth century (Gramsci 1971).

The dramatic resurgence of an active phase of class struggle which these events represent, of the masses initiating protest and riots because of the capitalist crisis, demands analysis on an equally massive scale by the activists and scholars associated with the movements. The scale of the present article is limited, of course; it is not possible to include in this analysis anything remotely approaching a full analysis of the Icelandic protests and their historical and social contexts, but an attempt will be made to indicate some positions which will hopefully be developed in further analyses.

Some notes on theory

As is well known, Antonio Gramsci outlines two kinds of social power. One is the power inherent in police forces, armies, and so on: the naked power of the state. The other is inherent in what Gramsci calls civil society: the power of the ideology of the ruling class as it is interpreted and practised in institutions, media, businesses, families, and associations of all kinds. He refers to this power as hegemonic, ideological power. It is the reason why a ruling class can control a society even if the interests of the great mass of people in that society are contrary to the interests of the ruling class (Gramsci 1971: 45). The concept of civil society was central to Gramsci's explanation of why there was a revolution in Russia and not in the rest of Europe at the end of the First World War. The ideological influence of the ruling class was distributed and maintained in Western Europe by means of all kinds of institutions, as mentioned before, but not in Russia.

Gramsci argued that it would be necessary to establish a counter-hegemonic movement, where subaltern groups and their organic intellectuals would produce a counter-hegemonic ideological movement – intellectual, cultural and moral – in civil society in preparation for revolution. This Gramsci termed a war of position (Gramsci 1971: 108). Since all social relations and interactions between individuals, groups, and nations are 'historically produced', they are consequently 'politically contestable' (Rupert 1995: 27–28). It is possible for a revolution to take place during what Gramsci called an organic crisis of the bourgeoisie.

This organic crisis – such as losing a war, financial meltdown or an economic crisis – would then expose the ideological hegemony of the ruling class, hitherto accepted by society as the eternal truth, as empty and meaningless. Even so, it is possible that the ruling class might still be dominant but not leading, meaning that it would have completely lost its ideological dominance but still rule by the power of the police and the armed forces. In Gramsci's well-known words: 'The crisis consists precisely in the fact that the old is dying and the new cannot be born' (Gramsci 1971: 210).

The French Marxist Alain Badiou talks of a similar occurrence in different terms: the event or the truth event when the hegemonic structure is revealed by the event and the truth suddenly appears (Snæbjörnsson 2007). Badiou provides a useful discussion of the nature of early twenty-first century riots. Discussing the riots in Tunisia in 2010–2011, Badiou defines riots as the street actions of people who want to overthrow the government 'by means of varying levels of violence', and he immediately points out what makes the Tunisian riots rare: the fact that they were victorious (cited in Collerson 2011 [online]). This redefines the regime, secure in place for 23 years and now overturned by popular action, as the 'weakest link' – like the Icelandic neoliberal regime in 2008, another example of a weak link. Such an overthrow is a rare event, and Badiou goes back 30 years before he can find a comparable precedent, namely the Iranian Revolution of 1979. (Badiou excludes the East European revolts because the USSR allowed them to happen).

During this period the dominant conviction was that such events were no longer really possible. The thesis of the 'end of history' did not mean that nothing more would happen, but that the period where the organization of power could be overthrown in favour of, as Trotsky said, 'the masses entering the stage of history', had ended (Collerson 2011). The normal course of things was the alliance of the market economy and parliamentary democracy, the only tenable norm of general subjectivity or global subjectivity. Thus, the fascinating thing about Tunisia, for Badiou, is the historicity of the events. They demonstrate that the capacity to create new forms of collective action is intact.

Badiou goes on to explain the characteristics of what Gramsci calls 'the organic crisis', i.e. the reason for riots. There is the systemic crisis of capitalism that became visible in 2008 and 2009 with

> its procession of social impasse, poverty and the growing feeling that the system is not viable nor as magnificent as was previously said. The vacuity of political regimes having become manifest with their only purpose to service the economic system and "save the banks", and at the same time taking dramatically reactionary measures in more and more areas (railways, post, schools, hospitals ...)
>
> (cited in Collerson 2011 [online])

Badiou then proceeds to locate these phenomena in the framework of a historical periodization. 'In my opinion', he says,

> the rioters' disposition arises in *interval periods* [*périodes intervallaires*]. What is an interval period? There is the sequence in which revolutionary logic is clarified and where it explicitly presents itself as an alternative, succeeded by an interval period where the revolutionary idea has not been passed on to anyone [déshérence], and in which it hasn't yet been taken up, a new alternative disposition has not yet been formed. During such periods the reactionaries can say, precisely because the alternative is impaired, that things have returned to the natural course. Characteristically, this is what happened in 1815 with the restorers of the Holy Alliance. In interval periods, discontent exists but it can't be structured because it is unable to draw its force from a shared idea. Its power is essentially negative ('make them go away'). This is why the form of mass collective action in an interval period is the riot. Take the period 1820–1850: It was a grand period of riots (1839, 1848, the revolt of the Canuts of Lyon); but it doesn't mean they were sterile, they were haphazard [*aveugle*] but very fertile. The great global political orientations that were the hinge [*vertébré*] of the next century emerge from that period.
>
> (cited in Collerson 2011 [online])

According to Badiou, the particular problem of the riot, inasmuch as it calls state power into question, is that it exposes the state to political change (the possibility of its collapse), but it doesn't embody this change; what is going to change is not prefigured in the riot. This is the major difference with a revolution, which in itself proposes an alternative. That is the reason why, invariably, rioters have complained that a new regime is identical to an old one. The party of the type created by the Bolsheviks is a structure explicitly designed to constitute itself as an alternative power in the place of the state. There is a contrast between the 'real' revolution in Russia in 1917 and the 'riots' in Tunisia and Egypt in 2011.

In this context the Icelandic riots of 2008–2009 probably appear akin to the kind of riots Badiou describes: interval riots without the benefit of an oppositional bloc having prepared a counter-hegemonic assent of civil society for a revolution. The hegemony of the neoliberal state is exposed as essentially vacuous and collapses, but at this point there has been no 'war of position' in the preceding period, the counter-hegemonic forces being so weak as to have been unable to create a force capable of utilising the 'organic crisis' in order to replace the former power with an alternative one, and 'the new cannot be born'. The state also retains the element of force, and the rioters are not creating an alternative.

The context: an Irish treatment

A look at the context of the Icelandic protest movement 2008–2009 is necessary here. Laurence Cox has written on the context of social movements in Ireland in his 'Gramsci in Mayo', and as the situations in Ireland and Iceland have important parallels, it is a useful point of departure (Cox 2011).

In his very suggestive treatment Cox points out that Ireland is one of the few states in the world where peasant struggles succeeded in producing a land reform which transformed rural class relationships and land ownership structures. He also notes that an analysis of Irish social movements in terms of ethnicity and empire has been central to Marxist writing on Ireland for over a century.

Cox points out that a big gap in the studies of popular mobilization after independence in Ireland is movements in favour of the new state and Catholic supremacy. According to Cox

> a combination of the victorious social classes together with subaltern groups such as women and labour held power together with enormous levels of popular participation in the dominant religion and its various sodalities and voluntary organisations and the years of political and cultural repression of sexuality, writers, republicans, communists, atheists and so on.
>
> (2011: 3–4)

Organized public opinion was supportive of the elite-sponsored, nationalist and religiously authoritarianisms of Spain, Portugal and Italy. Irish social movement history is not simply post-colonial history, in Cox's view: it is also a history shaped by popular collaboration with authoritarian cultural nationalism.

Cox has little to say about the effect of 1968 on Irish society. The key moment in the history of the context of Irish social movements after independence appears to be entry into the EEC. This changed the strategies of movement elites, leading them to develop strategies geared towards legal and media activism '(and hence professionalised, middle-class modes of organizing at the expense of popular struggle and alliance-building) not only in the women's movement but also in environmentalism...' This was followed by the success of the rhetoric of civil society, active citizenship, and so on in political discourse as a cover for neoliberal 'consultation' and 'participation' of the most contained and constrained kinds (Cox 2011: 3–5).

A hegemonic alliance in Ireland of national capital, large farming, and the church, with the subordinate support of small farmers, small business, organized labour, and women, gave way what is now recognisable as the beginnings of neoliberalism, a shift to multinational interests with national capital and (even more so) small business definitely subaltern. The church was dropped from this hegemony in the long term in order to make a 'liberal', modernizing alliance with the new service class. Cox discusses how social movements from below should be thought of: namely, that it is more accurate to think of them in terms of proto-hegemony than anything else. A broad social alliance around issues such as women's rights or environmental issues are an aspect of the 'war of position', the putting in place of a possible coalition which may be able to fight a 'war of manoeuvre', to actually shift the main lines of power. Nuclear power in Ireland was defeated and church power partially dislodged. Such alliances between the working class left, poorer rural interests, and culturally radical social movements hold significant potential (Cox 2011: 10–11). Cox's conclusion is that

> a Gramscian analysis of Ireland would need to study the ways in which the remarkable levels of self-organisation visible in the Land War, the cultural nationalist project and the dual-power structures of the War of Independence were channeled, contained and ultimately demobilised in the process of the long Irish Revolution (say 1879–1924), as well as the ways in which the working class, women and small farmers in the 1910s were split by nationalism and the First World War, used as footsoldiers for the nationalist cause and by the mid-1920s put firmly back in their various boxes. It would have to highlight particularily the dramatic scope of the popular struggle for land reform and the achievement of political independence, and the way in which these energies were contained within an ultimately conservative political project.
>
> (2011: 13)

Cox talks of Ireland as at one and the same time a 'conservative province', with a party system consistently skewed far to the right and closely tied to religious and rural conservatism, and simultaneously capable of real progressive achievements such as the destruction of an aristocratic land-holding system by popular direct action, the breaking apart of the core state of the world's then-largest empire, and the defeat of nuclear power. There is, though, the possibility that many Irish people have moved from an unthinking loyalty to the church to an unthinking loyalty to consumerism (Cox 2011: 12–17).

The context: Iceland

It is similarly possible that, in about 1980, many Icelandic people moved from an unthinking loyalty to the nation state to an unthinking loyalty to consumerism, and with it the whole gamut of neoliberal phenomena: financialization, privatization, globalization. Many of the things Cox mentions are familiar from Icelandic history, expecially the core of the narrative, where a successful peasantry defeats a land-owner class, breaks apart a very old kingdom (even if it is not the core state of the world's strongest empire) and creates a nation state. Other things are not as familiar – the place of the church is not the same – but there is a conservative period in the history of the state (Matthíasdóttir 2004), where women were 'put in their place' and nationalism was the unquestioned faith of the people (about 1930–1960).

As in Ireland, there is a dearth of writing on the context of social movements and no real tradition of Marxist writing about Iceland, with Marxism being constantly suppressed in academic circles and the few attempts at Marxist analysis begun in the 1970s being mostly abandoned in the 1980s. The main outline of such a narrative has been traced out, however, especially for the period before 1940 (Ísberg and Júlíusson 1993; Guðmundsson 1997). The analysis of the new social movements which appeared in the 1960s is not as well developed.

Iceland was a part of the Danish empire until 1944, but by about 1850 an anti-feudal peasant movement had already effectively established itself, turning Iceland into an emergent nation state. The peasant movement then became one of the most important elements of the new hegemony, a state-building element along with the old feudal bureaucracy, which now allied with the new capitalist class of fishing enterpreneurs to create a viable capitalist economy in Iceland. Culturally, Iceland was never entirely subaltern in the empire, with the national language always dominant in the Icelandic culture, both official and private, and the Icelandic cultural heritage an important part of the common heritage of the Danish–Norwegian state. But in the eighteenth and nineteenth centuries some Danes (and Icelanders) regarded Iceland as a colony of Denmark, and Danish merchants dominated trade with Iceland until 1855. This did not prevent fast economic growth from about 1820, all the way until 1929 and beyond (with some setbacks) (Júlíusson forthcoming 2013).

According to Gestur Guðmundsson (1997: 269–270, 275–283), the key to understanding social hegemony in Iceland, along with the other Nordic countries, is to be found in the new social alliances which were forged in the period 1930–1940. The first traces of the Nordic model appeared in Denmark after the start of the global crisis in 1929. The social-democratic government there attempted to temper the impact of the crisis by strengthening social support and supporting the business community, as opposed to the austerity policies implemented in the other Nordic countries. In January 1933 a far-reaching social contract was made, where peace between labour and capital, the organization of a social welfare system, and support of agriculture were agreed upon. A similar contract was made in Sweden in the same year, and in 1934 a new government consisting of the farmers' party (Framsóknarflokkurinn) and the Labour Party (Alþýðuflokkurinn) implemented a similar policy. Norway followed in 1935, and Finland in 1937.

In Gramscian terms the social movements in the Nordic countries entered the state and became part of the hegemony of the Fordist period. There was probably little space for a meaningful development of civil society outside of the alliance of the state, the workers' movement, and the farmers' movement, all of whom were subordinated to the goals of the nation state.

These governments created solutions to the economic crisis situation that benefitted both workers and peasants. Preventing the peasants from bankruptcy meant that bankrupt peasants did not compete with workers chasing what little work there was to be found, and by supporting the growth of industry in towns the urban demand for fish and agricultural products such as milk and meat grew. The subsequent increase in taxation did not affect these groups. The result was a broad consensus, a social peace settlement. This settlement can be seen as a result of the partial capitulation of the ruling elite of these countries to the power of the social movements of town and country, the workers' movement and the peasant movement. These movements united in a social contract with the capitalist state, creating the famous Nordic model, with a strong welfare state and relative social peace. This social model was only strengthened by the experience of the Second World War. Another factor in the strength of these social movements was the threat of revolution, which had already occurred on the doorsteps of these societies at the end of the First World War, in Russia and (unsuccessfully) in Germany.

There were some differences between the Nordic states in terms of the degree of the strength of the welfare system, and in some ways Iceland was a conservative province in this group, its welfare state being the least developed of all the Nordic countries. Parts of the hegemonic alliance created in the 1930s still remain in place, perhaps to the extent that to say it was ever fully replaced by a neoliberal hegemony is perhaps misleading. This is because so much of the basic compromise between social movements and the capitalist state in the 1930s is still in place, possibly to a degree where the 'organic crisis' of neoliberalism is not an organic crisis of the 'underlying' Fordist hegemony.

One interesting point to note is that during the period 1930–1960, when left-wing authors unquestionably dominated the cultural scene in Iceland, and when the moral high ground was quite definitely in the hands of what Gramsci would call an alternative hegemonic cultural agenda to the one propagated by the capitalist elite, there was a strong counter-hegemonic cultural current in society. But, in many ways, it was frozen because of the Cold War. The 'war of position' was a war where the fronts did not move. Also, this counter-hegemonic culture was a rather conservative one, with patriotic undertones of the working class and peasants forming the real nation, with its poetry and sagas as the real culture of the Icelandic people, now threatened by American cultural influences. This dialectic was behind the large and extremely symbolic riot against NATO in Reykjavík on 30 March 1949. This riot happened in the very same square where the protest movement of 2008–2009 later based itself, not without good reason.

A change

Then, in 1968, everything changed. It was a period of riots, protests and revolution. It was a period of general revolt. There was an organic crisis of the ruling class because of the war in Vietnam. The biggest imperial power was fighting a losing war, and parts of its ideological hegemony were exposed as being very problematic. There was also a crisis of hegemony in the communist world, leading to the pyrrhic victory of closing down the Prague Spring with state force. The '68 movement had almost equal criticicism for that part of the post-war settlement that had its background in the Soviet Union, the unions and the farmer's movement, as for the part that originated in the capitalist discourse. It even criticized the achievement of the Fordist consensus, the increasing prosperity of the working classes, the triumph of social democracy, as an empty piling up of useless goods (Judt 2005). There was also the widespread sense of a deep shift in cultural hegemony, towards a looser culture with different sexual moralities and a different place for women in society.

This was the most important background to '68 in Iceland, as elsewhere (Guðmundsson and Ólafsdóttir 1987: 67–107). In Iceland more and more women were engaging in formal economic activity. Women, along with the farmers, were drifting from the countryside to work in the towns, moving out of the domestic sphere and into the workplace. There was also a big increase in the number of young people completing high school and university education. The revolt resulted in a new feminist movement, which became very strong, very fast. A woman was elected president in 1980, the first democratically elected female head of state anywhere. A women's list was elected to parliament, and held seats there throughout the 1980s (Guðmundsson and Ólafsdóttir 1987: 223–261).

After 1970 Marxism gained many followers and new Trotskyist and Maoist parties were founded. These criticized the old Communist Party, now a part of the social contract created in the period between the wars. They maintained that this party was now co-operating with the bourgeoise and that the workers' movement had to be radicalized (Guðmundsson and Ólafsdóttir 1987: 261–295). There was also a significant increase in criticism of American imperial power, which had military bases in Iceland.

A Gramscian theoretical frame becomes even more relevant here than in the treatment of the social settlement of the 1930s, because the new counter-hegemonic forces were only loosely tied to old socio-economic groups such as the working class or the farmers. A whole new group of activists became active. Now a social war was waged against a hegemonic alliance which included organizations of the working class and the farmers. Feminists, gay activists and Marxists all sought to restore some earlier moment of popular struggle, or to extend the liberation front to new groups such as gays and women. Other parts of the movement – especially the environmentalist movement, the hippy/punk counter-culture and the Marxist critics of the Soviet Union – actively opposed the earlier consensus of popular movements: the social democrats, the communists, and Fordist hegemony in general.

There were moments when the population actively supported movements initiated by the Fordist state with goals in harmony with this hegemony. In 1968 an organic crisis developed in Iceland because of a fall in fishing catch. There was a great fall in the national income and a surge in unemployment, with a large number of people emigrating to search for work. In 1971 a new government consisting of centre-left parties took power and decided to expand the fishing limits, with the aim of pushing British and other foreign trawlers out of the Icelandic fishing grounds. This led to the Cod War, wherein Icelanders united against the foreign power. Internationally, it was regarded as a victory over one form of colonialism. All the existing social movements supported the Icelandic state against the British state – the radical youth movement, the unions, and the farmers.

After the 1970s, there was never to be such a moment again. Now neoliberalism entered the stage. In an development analogous to Ireland, the working class and farmers' movements were dropped from the hegemonic alliance, and the organic intellectuals who had been engaged within the earlier discourse were replaced by hundreds and thousands of MBAs, economists and people educated in business administration (Júlíusson 2009). There was an enormous increase in higher education in the areas of law, business studies, and so on, while the traditional academy languished. However, the feminist movement, the gay liberation movement, and the environmental movement all survived and remained active in the period 1980–2008. The punk movement became the signature cultural movement of this period, in a very ambiguous role. The post-modernist discourse enabled these movements to ally themselves to or co-exist within the dominant neoliberal hegemony. These movements now appeared as a kind of an alibi for neoliberalism.

The punk subculture intertwined with social change in ways that are too complex to be accounted for here, being both a prop to neoliberalism and contributing to the 'charm' of neoliberal hegemony, which has been described as follows:

> It is clear that a great deal of the success accorded the neoliberal bloc involves its 'intellectual leadership' and the attraction of liberalism as an ideology in shaping the wants, desires, and tastes of the masses. This is especially true regarding its focus on the individual as the key actor within society, and the prominence of the consumer as subject in terms of freedom, choice, and individual autonomy.
>
> (Butko 2006 [online])

In this context the punk subculture had an ambigous role, both as a context of individualism and 'progressive' or 'culturally interesting' consumption, and as a site of negation, resistance and an initiating site for anarchist and cyberpunk activity. In many ways the success of the Icelandic punk scene (internationally as well as domestically) was symbolic of neoliberalism and the new values it sought to advertise vis-à-vis Fordist hegemonic values, but at the same time it was at least a potential Achilles' heel, because of the grounding of punk ideology in essentially anti-capitalistic values.

The women's liberation movement was originally very strong in Iceland, as was the environmental movement, but by the 1990s it was as if the war of position initiated by the '68 movement had died down. In the thaw at the end of the Cold War the trenches seemed to melt away. When, from 1994, a new movement arose in the world against globalization, nothing happened in Iceland. It was as if the left had wholly capitulated to fighting only the kind of social movements 'allowed' in the neoliberal context, and that the struggle against globalization was interpreted as not being relevant in the Icelandic context.

The weakest link

If Iceland was the weakest link in the neoliberal chain, it was partly because, as a state, it was too weak to bail out the banks when they collapsed. There is not enough space here to trace the slow build-up of neoliberal hegemony, but in essence the neoliberal onslaught was an attack on Fordist hegemony, but from the right, and not from the left as with the '68 movements.

The 'economically destructive' power of the unions' strike weapon, the 'costly agricultural system', the growing 'burden and expense' of paying for the welfare state – these were some of the arguments used to attack the gains of the social contracts from the 1930s. These were all attacks upon elements of the Fordist hegemony which the 1968 left had supported; indeed, the educational, health and welfare system was perhaps the main social base of this revolt, but the '68-ers wanted to expand the social elements of the 1930s social contract to include women, gays, etc. This was not the aim of neoliberalism. The economy was to be invigorated and streamlined for participation in globalization by cutting the bloated state bureaucracy (Helgason 2010).

But why was Iceland the weakest link, to the extent that it was the scene of the 'end of the end of history', in the sense Badiou talked about, where the masses entered the stage of history for the first time in 30 years? To be sure, something similar had happened in Seattle in 1999, and in Argentina in 2001–2003, so Iceland was only the weakest link at precisely the moment of the collapse of the world economy in 2008–2009. It was not only the weakest link in the sense that the collapse of the neoliberal order was total, but also in the sense that the uprising against it was victorious. How was it that the uprising developed, and why was it able to topple the government? Only tentative answers will be given here. It should be noted that the anti-globalization movement was not very strong in Iceland at this point. There was no branch of the international Attac organization, but several activists from Iceland had attended the yearly World Social Forum prior to 2008.

The eve of the Saucepan Revolution

On the eve of the Saucepan Revolution, the government consisted of the right wing Independence Party, with its leader Geir Haarde as Prime Minister, and the social-democratic Samfylkingin. The leader of that party was Ingibjörg Sólrún

Gísladóttir, a historian and activist who had earlier been a leader in the feminist/women's liberation movement. Samfylkingin had only recently joined the government, but the Independence Party had previously ruled with the Progressive Party for 12 years, from 1995–2007. This earlier coalition had been responsible for the implementation of the neoliberal policies of the Washington Consensus. It had also involved Iceland in its first war: the invasion of Iraq in 2003. Furthermore, it was responsible for the monstrosity of the Kárahnjúkar hydropower project in eastern Iceland.

The fourth party, the Left Greens, had never participated in government. It had been somewhat critical of the neoliberal policies of the last 20 years. The Left Greens was the rump of the left socialists, formerly communists, who did not enter the Samfylkingin (Alliance) when it was created in the late nineties by a merger of all three left parties: the Women's List, the Social Democrats, and the Socialists. The other parties were all heartfelt neoliberalist parties, and in the event the leadership of the Left Greens were to prove that their anti-neoliberal stance consisted mostly of so much hot air. But their activists were very active in the 2008–2009 protests, as were social-democratic activists (Bernburg 2012).

Other groups besides the Left Greens articulated dissent with the ruling hegemony, most of them with some ties to older oppositional movements. Among them was the Nýhil collective of poets and philosophers, involving a number of neo-Marxists, which organized publication of poetry and discussed the works of Slavoj Žižek, Hardt and Negri, and Alain Badiou. Feminists were also very active, with Internet discussion boards and many different social initiatives defending women, while in the northern town of Akureyri a group of people discussed left politics in a society called *Stefna* or 'Direction'. Some communist activists were organized in an organization called *Rauður vettvangur*, or 'Red Arena'.

There was a group of anarchists publishing books and organizing protests against the construction of the gigantic Kárahnúkar hydropower project in eastern Iceland. These and other activists organized themselves in the Saving Iceland organization, which confronted the police on a number of occasions – or, rather, the police confronted the environmentalists when they were protesting at the site of the project and in Reykjavík. A sort of liberal centre of discussion had been established in the citadel of post-modernist academia in Iceland, at the Reykjavík Academy, a collective of independent scholars, but in the context of this Gramscian analysis it should be termed counter-hegemonic because it was explicitly aimed at countering the neoliberal goal-setting of the educational system (Júlíusson 2009). A group of Internet activists also formed a little-known dissident community. There were perhaps other centres of discussion, organization and activity, possibly entirely apolitical, that were transformed into centres of political activity by the fall of the financial system.

So, there was indeed a war of position waged by some activists, but it was very much below the surface. It was substantial enough in that when the organic crisis came it transformed into a war of manoeuvre, producing the uprising of 2008–2009.

These groups were essential in organizing resistance to the regime at the time of the collapse. Gay activists, dissenting or heterodox economists, internationally respected authors, environmentally active intellectuals, Internet anarchists, punk anarchists, neo-Marxists: these became the people who led the movement to its eventual victory (Júlíusson 2008).

The events of October 2008–January 2009

On 29 September 2008, a Monday, it was announced that the situation was serious. The government bought 75 per cent of the shares in the Glitnir bank in order to prevent its collapse. This proved to be of no use. During the next week the banks all fell, despite the best efforts of the government. Emergency laws were implemented, laws which were long-prepared because, as far back as February, the two leaders of the government already had full knowledge of what was about to happen. These laws guaranteed the savings of Icelandic citizens in the collapsed banks. Those with money in the foreign branches of the Icelandic banks, such as the Icesave branch of the Landsbanki in Great Britain and the Netherlands, were not as fortunate and lost their money. In reality, Icelanders were not much more fortunate. They watched in horror as the Icelandic króna plummetted; by mid-October it had reached about half of its pre-collapse value. Unemployment began to rise, reaching catastrophic proportions by the end of 2008. The IMF was consulted and took over the economic administration of the country.

A fog of horror descended upon the country. The nation was stunned during the week of 29 September–6 October, but by the next weekend a protest was organized in Austurvöllur, at three o'clock on Saturday 11 October. These demonstrations continued at three o'clock every Saturday for the next five months or so. The demands were that the government should resign, that parliamentary elections should be held, and that the leadership of the Central Bank of Iceland should resign.

Many more centres of activism soon developed. A group of people started to organize citizens' meetings every Monday. Persons regarded as responsible for the collapse were called upon to answer for their actions. Bankers, politicians, media figures, and government officials all received a call to meetings where they were questioned by the public. One of these meetings, on Monday 24 November, was held in a large cinema, and was broadcast to the whole country by state television. The organizers called upon the government to attend and defend their actions, and, to the surprise of many, some ministers did turn up.

The anarchists organized their own preparatory meetings, and then met up at Austurvöllur. These meetings were well-attended by the younger generations (Árnason 2008). Masked anarchists (of the black bloc variety) soon became a staple of every protest.

The enormous tension in Icelandic society subsided somewhat as people prepared for Christmas, but in January the protests resumed. On 15 January 2009, people at the weekly demonstration in Austurvöllur were asked to show up at the opening of parliament at one o'clock on 20 January, with pots and pans, and to make noise which would then be heard all across the nation via television sets. The police surrounded the parliament building and fought the protesters, attacking them with pepper spray. As night fell, fires were started at Austurvöllur. Thousands of protesters stayed and continued the banging.

The next day the Reykjavík chapter of the Social Democrats held a meeting and agreed to call upon the party to leave the government. This proved decisive; the uprising had triumphed (Jóhannesson 2009).

The protest movement had indeed succeeded, in just four months, in establishing a new and effective tradition of protest and democratic activism by the common people. It had also intervened in the political process in a way that exposed the alienation of the political elite and the media from the lives of ordinary people. The movement had also reinvented and kickstarted the politics of the left by taking to the streets.

Was the Saucepan Revolution in any way rooted in earlier movements?

We agree with Badiou about the interim character of the post-crisis riots. They were not a revolution because a revolution is carried out by a revolutionary force that then takes and holds power. This did not happen in Iceland. However, the riots mark a definite break with the preceding period of conservatism. It was the end of the end of history. The masses, who were supposed to be watching the stage of history from their comfortable seats in the audience reserved for each individualized consumer, stood up, left their seats, and invaded the stage of history.

It is clear that the war of position initiated in 1968 by counter-hegemonic forces had largely been lost in Iceland in about 1990, the frozen trenches melted away at the end of the Cold War. However, in Gramscian terms, when the organic crisis hit the bourgeoisie, a war – not of position, but of manoeuvre – was initiated by some of the earlier counter-hegemonic forces, organic intellectuals of the multitude, in alliance with the masses, resulting in a very important victory for the counter-hegemonic forces fighting neoliberalism.

It is difficult to disentangle the exact level of influence of each kind of oppositional group on the course of building this alliance, be it '68 Marxists, environmentalists, anarchists, hippies, punks, feminists, etc. Indeed, anarchist youth acted as a vanguard to a much more eclectic riot crowd, with a large number of middle-aged women among them, which Alain Badiou regards as the hallmark of the 'historical riot' (Badiou 2012). Badiou also remarks that what he labels an historical riot is generic in that it breaks down all of the identities used by the state to control the multitude, and the Icelandic Saucepan Revolution was indeed a very fine example of such a collapse of divisive identities.

References

Árnason, Ari Júlíus, personal communication December 2008.

Badiou, Alain 2012: *The Rebirth of History*. London, Verso.

Bernburg, Jón Gunnar 2011: Interview in Víðsjá, RÚV, 14 December 2011.

Butko, Thomas J. 2006: Gramsci and the "Anti-Globalization" Movement. *Journal of the Research Group on Socialism and Democracy*, Online. http://sdonline.org/41/gramsci-and-the-%E2%80%9Canti-globalization%E2%80%9D-movement-think-before-you-act1/, downloaded 20 May 2012.

Collerson, Jonathon 2011: Alain Badiou on Tunisia, riots & revolution. *Wrong+ Arithmetic*. http://wrongarithmetic.wordpress.com/2011/02/02/alain-badiou-on-tunisia-riots-revolution/, downloaded 20 May 2012.

Cox, Laurence 2011: Gramsci in Mayo, In: *New Agendas in Social Movement Studies Conference*, September 2011, National University of Ireland, Maynooth.

Gramsci, Antonio 1971: *Selections from the Prison Notebooks*, Quintin Hoare and Geoffrey Nowell Smith, eds. New York: International Publishers.

Guðmundsson, Einar Már 2009: *Hvíta bókin*. Reykjavík, Forlagið.

Guðmundsson, Einar Már 2011: *Bankastræti 0*. Reykjavík, Forlagið.

Guðmundsson, Gestur 1987: "Endalok Norðurlandanna?" *Saga Norðurlanda 1397–1997. 10 ritgerðir*. Copenhagen, pp. 267–294.

Guðmundsson, Gestur and Ólafsdóttir, Kristín 1987: *68 hugarflug úr viðjum vanans*. Reykjavík, Tákn.

Helgason, Magnús Sveinn 2010: *Íslenskt viðskiptalíf Aðdragandi og orsakir falls íslensku bankanna 2008 og tengdir atburðir*. Reykjavík. Rannsóknarnefnd Alþingis.

Ísberg, Jón Ólafur, Kjartansson, Helgi Skúli, Júlíusson, Árni Daníel (eds) 1993: *Íslenskur söguatlas 3. Saga samtíðar – 20. öldin*. Reykjavík, Iðunn.

Jóhannesson, Guðni Th. 2009: *Hrunið. Ísland á barmi gjaldþrots og upplausnar*. Reykjavík, JPV útgáfa.

Júlíusson, Árni Daníel 2008: Minutes of meetings of activists in Reykjavík November 2008. Personal Archives.

Júlíusson, Árni Daníel 2009: *Fræðimenn í flæðarmáli. 10 ára afmælisrit ReykjavíkurAkademíunnar 1997–2007*. Reykjavík, ReykjavíkurAkademían.

Júlíusson, Árni Daníel 2013: *Landbúnaðarsaga Íslands 2. bindi. Bændur og nútími. Saga sveitasamfélagins 1800–2012*. Reykjavík, Skrudda.

Judt, Tony 2005: *Postwar. A History of Europe since 1945*. London, William Heineman.

Matthíasdóttir, Sigríður 2004: *Hinn sanni Íslendingur. Þjóðerni, kyngervi og vald 1900–1930*. Reykjavík, Háskólaútgáfan.

Rupert, Mark 1995: *Producing Hegemony*. Cambridge: Cambridge University Press.

Snæbjörnsson, Magnús Þór 2007: Er Draumalandið sjálfshjálparbók handa hræddri þjóð? *Skírnir*, 464–497.

Wade, Robert and Sigurgeirsdóttir, Silla 2010: Lessons from Iceland. *New Left Review*, September–October 2010, pp. 3–29.

13 Collective learning processes within social movements

Some insights into the Spanish 15-M/ Indignados movement[1]

Eduardo Romanos

On 15 May 2011 protest marches called by the *Democracia Real Ya* [Real Democracy Now] digital platform with the slogan 'We are not products in the hands of politicians and bankers' managed to draw tens of thousands of people all over Spain.[2] In Madrid some of the protesters decided to continue the march with a 'reclaim the streets' type activity, blocking traffic in the centre of the city with a sit-down protest. After confrontations with police, which led to some arrests, a group of about 40 people remained at the Puerta del Sol in order to, among other reasons, 'support the detainees and continue with the demonstrations'. From this meeting there arose an assembly 'with the main idea of creating and maintaining a permanent camp'.[3] Thus was born *acampadasol.*

The story of events up to the holding of municipal and autonomous region elections on 22 March is well known. *Acampadasol* grew around various committees that worked on the maintenance of the camp and the logistics of the assembly process, as well as various working groups concerned with generating discourse related to the emerging protest movement. The support received by the movement grew as well, both on the internet and at the Puerta de Sol. The hashtag '#spanishrevolution' became a worldwide trending topic on Twitter. More and more people turned up at the 'mini-republic' established at the Puerta de Sol (Elola 2011). The website www.tomalaplaza.net gathered information relating to what was happening in the square and other locations where protestors had gathered, including those outside Spain. The behaviour of the authorities and some elements of the mass media assisted in the growth of the process, specifically:

- the violent expulsion by police of the first protestors to occupy the square at dawn on Tuesday 17 May;
- the prohibition of assemblies by the Provincial Electoral Committee of Madrid; and
- the cover of *The Washington Post* of Thursday 19 May.

As a result, at midnight on Friday 20 May, 25,000 people broke into applause at the end of a symbolic minute's silence, in an act of civil disobedience the impact and size of which had had no precedent in the recent history of Spain.

Figure 13.1 The Puerta del Sol on the night of 20 May 2011 ((cc) J. Albarrán).

One of the objectives of this chapter is to dismantle the idea of the spontaneity of the movement that arose from this protest. Though to some degree a surprising phenomenon, especially in terms of how it sprung onto the domestic social and political scene (and has managed, so far, to stay there), the so-called 15-M movement does not appear to have been a spontaneous one. The success of the demonstrations on 15 May would not have been possible without the previous work carried out by various groups and organizations. Furthermore, these and other actors contributed participants, collective action frames, communications networks and mobilizing structures to the subsequent development of the protest movement.

Neither did these mobilizing actors appear from nowhere. Leaving to one side those factors more related to the political and social context, both domestic and international (see Calvo, this volume, Chapter 15), this chapter makes use of a perspective of analysis situated at the meso- and micro-levels, from which to observe possible changes and continuities between the 15-M movement and some other movements, mobilizations and campaigns that have arisen at the local level in recent years. In doing this, I will focus on events in Madrid, the epicentre of the protest of 2011. My hypothesis suggests the existence of a learning process which, on the basis of certain collective experiences, both failed and successful, links past and present social movement developments.

Exploring this learning process enables a better understanding of certain key elements which help to explain the early success of the 15-M movement in terms of its geographical extension, intensity, and continuity of social support and participation. Some of these elements, specifically the movement's inclusiveness and moderation, distinguish it from other recent anti-austerity movements in Europe. The Spanish movement has managed to involve a large number of people without previous or recent active experience in civil society groups and organizations, while participants have shown their strong commitment to non-violence, paying particular attention to diverting any attempt at escalation.

This chapter has three main sections. It begins with a brief presentation of some of the most visible actors involved in the emergence of the 15-M movement in Madrid. It then looks at some recent initiatives and mobilizations which have taken place in the city. In the third section I discuss the echoes of these experiences in the new movement. My intention is to offer a general overview of the evolution of the social movement sector in Madrid. This is a preliminary examination of the subject and the tone of the chapter will be fairly descriptive in nature, due in part to the complex nature of the available data. In this chapter I will make use of participant observation and analysis of various documents and websites, as well as of interviews, currently in progress, with key informants.

Mobilizing actors in the *Madrid Spring*

To tell the story of how the 15 May 2011 demonstration was prepared is in large measure to tell the story of *Democracia Real Ya* (DRY – Real Democracy Now: democraciarealya.es). This protest campaign, which over time has become a social movement organization, has its origin in a small group of young people who at the end of 2010 decided to form a Facebook group, *Juventud en Acción* (Young People in Action) (Elola 2011). Influenced by what had happened in Iceland (Júlíusson and Helgason, this volume, Chapter 12) and contemporary events in North Africa, the members of the group soon identified a series of problems which they wished to protest about: the distance between formal politics and the people, the stranglehold of the two main parties on the system of representative democracy, and the subjugation of politics to the markets. They also identified those responsible for these problems: political representatives and those with economic power, united in a coalition to protect their privileges. These views would eventually be condensed into a slogan which gave its name to the movement itself: '*Democracia Real Ya*: We are not products in the hands of politicians and bankers'.

The group set up a website to organize the protest, a protest to which more established organizations such as *Plataforma de Afectados por la Hipoteca*, (Platform of those Affected by Mortgages), *Asociación Nacional de Desempleados* (ADESOR – National Association of the Unemployed), Attac España, and Intermon-Oxfam gradually came to offer their support. Other groups, either newer or with a lesser degree of internal structure, also offered their support, among them *Estado del Malestar* (State of Discontent), *No Les Votes* (Don't Vote For Them), and *Juventud Sin Futuro* (Young People With No Future). These more loosely structured actors organized a series of protest campaigns which helped prepare the way for what was to occur on 15 May. Thus, DRY can be seen as a 'mesomobilization actor' whose protest campaign managed to integrate and, to some degree, coordinate other 'micromobilization actors' who, in turn, managed to motivate and mobilize individuals both inside and outside the micromobilization groups themselves (see Gerhards and Rucht 1992).

The participants in the pre-15 May protest campaigns had certain characteristics in common: they felt emotionally united, regardless of ideological differences, they shared a similar emotional state, and they identified similar problems and similar parties as being responsible. From the beginning of 2011 *Estado del Malestar* (malestar.org) organized a series of peaceful and imaginative flash mobs every Friday evening – 12 up to 6 May – in the main squares of various cities. Participants said that they were united by the 'indignation and rage' produced by the deception of the financial and political systems which, in their view, had promised them wellbeing, but which had in fact left them without a future. This initiative began in Seville, on the basis of a call posted on Facebook to participate in the first of the events. Within two months this phenomenon had spread to 50 cities. The number of those participating in the flash mobs varied greatly. They rejected any party, trade union or business sector identification. According to one organizer it was important, 'to leave ideology at home in order to be able to come together on the street' (quoted in Letón and Paratcha 2011: 5). Many local groups (and many individuals participating in them) participated in the call for a demonstration on 15 May. Three days prior to that key date DRY carried out a flash mob in the style of *Estado del Malestar*: at the Puerta del Sol in Madrid, a group of 'victims of the market' momentarily collapsed onto the ground while holding placards calling for people to participate in the demonstration scheduled for the 15th.

No Les Votes (nolesvotes.com) was an electoral boycott campaign, in its own words a 'grassroots anti-campaign', aimed at the parties responsible for the passing of the Sinde law on internet piracy (*Partido Popular, Partido Socialista Obrero Español* and *Convergència i Unió*)[4] which at the same time called for people to vote for alternative parties at the municipal and autonomous region elections on 22 May 2011. The campaign was founded by a group of bloggers committed to the defence of freedom and the neutrality of the internet. The call from the *No Les Votes* campaign to participate in the 15-M demonstration criticized the corruption of political organizations (especially in the three parties mentioned above), the power of media and business lobbies, and the closure of the political system to the demands of citizens. It also identified the electoral law as being a mechanism for the perpetuation of this system and demanded that new mechanisms for citizen participation in decision-making be found (see Galli 2011). On its website the group claimed to have 80 working groups throughout the country.

Finally, *Juventud Sin Futuro* (JSF: juventudsinfuturo.net) was a grouping led by various associations of university students (Rubiño 2011) which launched a call for protests against several government measures in early 2011. Its main objections were to the reform of employment legislation and pensions and 'the commodification of public education'. In its manifesto the group recognized the influence of recent similar protests in Europe (Italy, France, Greece and Iceland) and particularly those in the Arab world, which caused a kind of 'cognitive liberation' (McAdam 1986) by showing them the vulnerability of the authorities. Various intellectuals and academics signed the manifesto, a document which by the eve of 15 May had collected a total of 9,000 signatures. On 7 April the JSF organized demonstrations in various Spanish cities. According to the organizers the Madrid protest drew more than 6,000 people (Errejón 2011: 67).[5] This protest ended with the arrests of several activists who had confronted the police. On the day of the demonstration the group published an editorial on its website which announced its support for the DRY's call for a demonstration on 15 May and which ended with a declaration of intentions: 'the spring, our spring, has only just begun'.

Frames, actions and infrastructures in contentious Madrid, 2003–2011

> 15-M was something that was always going to happen because it is an accumulation of those irritations suffered by the people and their being fed up with them, but also because it is also the sum of many things that have happened over many years: the Arab Spring of course but also March 13th, 2004, the *V de Vivienda* [H for Housing] sit-ins, the Iraq War, the evictions and a whole load of people from different movements who suddenly found themselves in this mixture and we brought together the synergies and this sprang out of it.[6]

As has been shown by the extensive literature on the matter, the emergence of social movements is a more complex process than is indicated in this quote. However, the testimony of this 15-M activist is still relevant in the context of what we are discussing here because it mentions three specific and recent mobilizations, each of which seems to have left its mark on that mobilization which we here call the 'Madrid Spring' and which later became the 15-M movement. The first was the protests that were held on 13 March 2004. On that day thousands of people protested outside the headquarters of the *Partido Popular* (the then-governing party) and demanded the truth about the terrorist attacks two days previously, in which 192 people were killed and around 2,000 wounded when a dozen bombs went off on commuter trains in Madrid. The demonstrators accused the leaders of the party of manipulating information about the attacks for electoral purposes by accusing the Basque terrorist group ETA of being responsible for them. As Flesher Fominaya has pointed out:

> [The action] was initially organised by a nucleus of activists who drew on contacts developed through previous mobilisations, used new ICTs to disseminate the call, and made a conscious decision to engage in civil disobedience on the day of reflection, making the protest historically unprecedented

in Spain. The strength and importance of the protests, however, extend far beyond the social movement network that initiated them, and reflect public support for the protest's critique.

(2011: 291)

The second mobilization mentioned above was the series of sit-ins organized by *V de Vivienda*, a name used by various local assemblies that were formed by the movement campaigning in favour of access to decent housing (Blanco 2011: 20). The first of these assemblies, and one of the most active, was the *Asamblea Contra la Precariedad y por una Vivienda Digna* (ACPVD – Assembly against Precarity and for Decent Housing), founded in Madrid in June 2006. The coming into being of this organization involved a radicalization of the movement that had been campaigning for access to decent housing since 2003. This happened after a series of protests in the form of sit-ins, the first of which used e-mail and the internet to bring together 5,000 people in the city centre. A week later the second sit-in ended with the intervention of the police and several arrests, which partly motivated the creation of the ACPVD for the defence of the movement. Along with sit-ins and their continuation as city centre marches blocking traffic, the ACPVD also carried out other forms of protest such as theatrical performances mocking the authorities, a sit-in on a university campus which coincided with the municipal and autonomous community elections of May 2007, and an unsuccessful campaign to occupy vacant buildings. The movement organized itself internally on the basis of committees dealing with specific issues and tried to decentralize by creating various neighbourhood assemblies (Blanco 2011).

Aguilar and Fernández (2010) hold that the social basis of the movement for decent housing was predominantly formed and led by unemployed young people and students with experience of other protest campaigns, such as those against the Spanish participation in the Iraq War and against the Bologna Plan. Among the factors identified by these authors as being responsible for the lack of political and social results produced by the movement – in spite of the fact that it seemed to have been operating in a favourable context given that Spanish public opinion recognized the problem of access to affordable housing – the one that stands out is the construction of a radical, exclusive and poorly functioning mobilization frame which tended to drive away potential allies in conventional politics and the media, but also among immigrants, workers and women.

The third mobilization mentioned above was that organized against the Iraq War, more specifically the demonstration that was held simultaneously in many cities around the world on 15 February 2003 (Walgrave and Rucht 2010) and which was the most significant and visible event arising from the so-called Global Justice Movement which had sprung up around the turn of the century (see, for example, della Porta 2007). In Spain the rise of this movement meant the 'integration of the Spanish political struggle' into a broader, transnational cycle of protests which would go on to affect other representative democracies (Jiménez and Calle 2007: 97). This somewhat attenuated the historical singularities which had, up to then, characterized the development of social movements in Spain (see Romanos 2011a). This integration or 'Europeanization' was the work of a new generation of activists formed in the context of a set of shared experiences (volunteering and multi-movement campaigns) which had fostered the gradual development of cohesive identities and a rising degree of inter-organizational coordination. To all of this may be added the influence exerted by participation in global campaigns, and access to the new forms of interconnectivity provided by the internet (Jiménez and Calle 2007; see also Jiménez 2006).

Jiménez and Calle (2007: 88) identify the 2003 protest against the war in Iraq as marking the initial phase of a period of decline in the Global Justice Movement in Spain. Among the different factors that help in understanding this tendency is the decline in the scope of the activities carried out, among them the protests, oriented to an ever-greater degree towards having an impact at the local level (though there were still flows of solidarity resources and coordination of activities between groups and organizations in different territories). Both the demonstrations held on 13 March 2004 and those held by the ACPVD fit this pattern.

Another local-level initiative also seems relevant when it comes to considering the subsequent development of the 15-M movement. This initiative is the creation and maintenance of a network of self-managed social centres in Madrid. These social centres – which some activists refer to as 'second generation' or 2.0 – represent an evolution from the dynamics of the squatter movement as it had developed in Spain since the middle of the 1980s:

> There is an attempt to abandon what was an inbred, ghetto logic and a clear and well defined aesthetic, in favour of an attempt to develop a more open field of work and political action which any citizen of the city might feel themselves addressed by, and to have socially squatted buildings seen not as spaces closed in on themselves but rather open to everybody.[7]

This statement may be more of an expression of intent than a reflection of reality, but in any case it represents a change with regard to previous experiences. Some activists sought to transform the occupied and/or self-managed space from being an end in itself to being a resource for the construction of a broader and more enduring project of social change. As well as their strongly inclusive discourse, these centres represented, in Madrid's alternative scene, the building of bridges to social and artistic criticism and the encouragement of deliberative democracy with the power to make decisions as a management model for all that affects local residents in general (Tabacalera 2011).

The network of social centres has to some degree compensated for the scarcity of infrastructures which Flesher Fominaya (2007a, 2007b) noted in the autonomous activist movement in Madrid. The consolidation of this kind of resource has also reduced the dependence of the local autonomous movement on the institutional left, with which it has always maintained tense relations within the anti-globalization movement (a phenomenon common to other countries, as noted by

Flesher Fominaya 2007b). Autonomous groups and networks have equipped themselves with new resources and physical spaces, thereby constructing a 'new *institutionality*', as some activists call it, which has opened up new opportunities for the development of its political practice. Even the legal framework has changed, with new relationships established with political institutions, as in the transfer of the former tobacco factory in Madrid (*La Tabacalera de Lavapiés*).[8]

According to Flesher Fominaya (2007a, 2007b) autonomous political practice was still 'relatively new' in Madrid. In fact, her research showed evidence of the process of creation of a new political identity – different and distinct from that of the institutional left – by autonomous local groups within the anti-globalization movement in the early 2000s. A key tool in this process was humour, a factor which activists used to integrate new and marginal group members, release tension and negotiate conflict, while at the same time conceptualizing direct actions whose intended audience was the general public.

Changes, continuities and learning processes in the 15-M movement

The protests on 13 March 2004 and 21 May 2011 have a number of elements in common. Both were misinterpreted by some observers and media outlets as either spontaneous demonstrations or as being in the service of the PSOE. Both were acts of civil disobedience held on the eve of elections (general in the first case, municipal and autonomous region in the second), when Spanish law forbids political demonstrations. And both were organized and disseminated primarily through mobile phones and the internet. Flesher Fominaya in 2005 (2011) points out the novelty of the 2004 protest in this respect: it was the first protest on the day of reflection prior to an election and the first 'political flash mob' in Spain, in the sense of being organized as a response to an urgent situation or crisis. Thus the 2011 protest represents an improvement in the organization of such protests.

In relation to the mobilizing frames, the message of inclusiveness and moderation of the mobilization actors taking part in the 'Madrid Spring', and a similar message coming from the 15-M movement itself, contrast with that of the *V de Vivienda* movement. Some accounts by JSF activists link both experiences as a learning process. In the creation of their mobilization messages the JSF activists chose to make vague and general reference to the losers in the crisis (visible in the generational call to 'young people with no future') by contrast with more specifically identified winners, a decision which in some way helped to construct a recognizable dividing line between 'us' and 'them'. They were careful with the definition of 'who are we' and 'what we want', and in the process they took into account experiences arising from previous movements and mobilizations, especially those of *V de Vivienda*.

The influence of this movement can be seen both in the way of communicating messages and in the message content. JSF activists tried to 'recover [*V de Vivienda's*] style'; this was visible not only in the use of the same colour, the same font and similar rhetoric in their stickers and posters, but also in the use of social networks for the design and dissemination of these materials, in the coordination of symbolic actions, and in the calling of press conferences (Raboso and Merino 2011; see also Haro and Sampedro 2011).

In terms of the content of the mobilization messages, the influence of the *V de Vivienda* on the JSF can be seen in the 'demands which are presented as those of all citizens and therefore above left-right divisions'. At the same time, the JSF recognized what they had learned from the earlier movement, given that '*V de Vivienda* was a bit more weighed down by the dynamics of the left'. In this way JSF took a step towards overcoming traditional cleavages:

> [Our aim is] to draw a line not between the left and the right but rather in such a way that any young person, of whom there are thousands in this city, between the ages of 20 and 35, who is being a paid a shit wage and has no home of their own, could identify with you. To do this the problem has to be brought closer and this must be done in very simple language.[9]

In the area of infrastructure, social centres played an important role in the 15-M movement. As in previous cycles of protest (see Flesher Fominaya 2010), these centres hosted activists' meetings and assemblies. They also provided material resources, for example the tents that covered the Puerta del Sol as well as the public address systems for the assemblies. However, their most important input was probably their contribution to activists' know-how in the areas of the techniques of deliberative democracy. The Global Justice Movement has applied the principles of this new concept of democracy to the heart of its internal networks and the development of its decision-making processes. In this way, its activists have constructed an 'organizational culture' based on the values of diversity, subjectivity, transparency, open confrontation oriented to decision-making, and placing 'ideological contamination' ahead of dogmatism (della Porta 2005a, 2005b). In Spain this organizational culture has shown itself to be effective in the creation and management of certain infrastructures like the '2.0' social centres (for other 'laboratories' of deliberative democracy see, for example, Nez 2012).

As I have indicated elsewhere (Romanos 2011b), the practices and discourses of the 15-M movement show a profound commitment to the deliberative concept of democracy. Deliberative democracy, or empowered deliberative democracy, seems to a considerable degree to be a response to the call for 'real democracy', made during the 15 May and subsequent demonstrations, as possible solutions to the problems of democratic deficit and institutional hostility identified by the activists. One of the novel aspects of the 15-M movement was the way it placed experiments with new forms of democracy in the centre of public space. In this way, the movement brought practices of deliberative democracy – previously confined to more or less limited spaces such as social forums, social movement headquarters, peace camps and social centres – out into public squares, where passers-by were invited to join in. This seems to be an important difference from the practices of previous movements and mobilizations.[10]

Figures 13.2a JSF poster

Figures 13.2b V de Vivienda poster (detail), photographed by (cc) Álvaro Minguito.

Finally, as noted humour played an important and particularly visible role in the 15-M movement. The power of humour in the framing of political protest is certainly not new (Hart 2007); many social movements have used it in the past. However, it seems more central and strategic in recent cycles of protest (e.g. the pro-democracy movements in Eastern Europe, the Global Justice Movement, or the case under review here) than in previous ones. In the context of the 15-M movement the use of individually handwritten placards provided a space for the use of imagination and the display of irony. Already-familiar texts such as poems, advertising slogans, film and song titles, public statements, and the language of signs in public spaces were subverted to identify and communicate problems, name those responsible, and make demands (see Minchinela 2011).

The protests also included ironic performances organized by specific groups. Some, such as the funeral for democracy or the aerobics assembly (which used humour to communicate the methodology for general assemblies) served to cool tempers at moments of great stress caused by the intervention of the police or internal arguments (e.g. about the decision to abandon or maintain the camp). These performances also served to facilitate emotional union within the group and to attract media attention, as the activists themselves recognize in their documents.[11]

Humour is also present in internal documents. One of the most notable cases of this was the *Proyecto Acta* drawn up by the World Extension Team of *acampadasol* (in charge of disseminating the movement internationally). This committee decided to draft the minutes of its meetings in a fun way, as if they were a story incorporating elements of what was going on around them:

Figure 13.3 The performance of the assembly aerobics team, 19 June 2011 ((cc) Eduardo Romanos).

We have to find another language. What we want is to be read. What gets read? The stories we are told – stories are read, minutes aren't.... It has something to do with the atmosphere created in the committee. Making humour part of your tone, removing the pompousness, the heaviness [from things] ... was what made it a committee in which we had fun and where we wanted to be.... Getting together wasn't an obligation.[12]

In this case humour helped lower the fatigue-related costs of activism. It helped make participants read the minutes and get involved in one of the most boring movement tasks: writing them.

Although not all activists were favourably disposed to the use of humour (for example, *Proyecto Acta* provoked anger amongst those who thought that 'minutes are something serious'), its widespread use within the movement has contributed to the creation of a distinctive style that sets it apart from other movements and forms of collective action, also within the Left (recognizable in a phrase repeatedly heard in the comments of participants, 'we even laugh at ourselves', which might be followed by, 'while you take yourselves very seriously'). If, as claimed by Flesher Fominaya (2007b), the recognition of humour's potential for subversion in political activism was a relatively new concept in Spanish movement circles in 2005, what we have learned from our study of the 15-M movement leads us to think that this is no longer the case.

Recently, new opportunities to use humour have been provided by means of social networks. The Spanish *indignados* have been prolific in their creation of false accounts which supplanted the identities of certain people and parodied the behaviour of the police and the authorities. One of these was *@acampadapolicia*, created at a particularly tense time when the Puerta del Sol was closed off by the police at the beginning of August. Some activists with experience in social networks started to tweet 'as if the police were encamped in the centre of the square, with their problems, their celebrations, their demands and necessities'. This account received a rapid and positive response. Asked about the usefulness of the account, one of the creators stated that

It's useful for disseminating a lot of information, in a different way, with humour.... Laughter produces 'I likes' and comments and produces exponentiality. The laughter multiplies and you can communicate the same thing with a funny message as with a serious one but you reach more people.[13]

Conclusion

There is no doubt that activists' ability to use new technologies for organizing and coordinating protests with a high level of media impact contributed decisively to the success of the demonstration on 15 May 2011 and that of the social movement that grew out of it. However, the geographical extension, intensity and continuity of social support and participation seem to have relied equally upon certain internal dynamics of the movement which reflected its strongly inclusive and moderate character. Among these were:

1   the creation of mobilization messages aimed at the construction of general demands and easily identifiable actors responsible for particular grievances;
2   respect for the principles of deliberative democracy in decision-making processes; and
3   the use of humour to facilitate communication and internal cohesion and to lower the tensions and costs of activism.

This chapter has tried to show the degree to which these social movement developments may be connected with recent local experiences. In the case of Madrid these experiences were:

1   the construction of mobilizing frames which did not obtain enough support to sustain the mobilization and achieve satisfactory results, as had happened with the movement for decent housing;
2   the consolidation of an deliberative organizational culture which has been shown to be efficient in the creation and maintenance of certain kinds of infrastructure in the alternative milieu, as had happened with the new network of social centres; and
3   the consolidation of an alternative political identity where humour has played an important role, which differentiates it from the practices of the institutional Left, as had happened with autonomous groups within the anti-globalization movement.

Social movements have important consequences for one another. This type of social movement outcome has been considered extensively in the specialized literature (see, for example, Meyer and Whittier 1994; Whittier 2004). Social movements do not have to re-invent everything with each step they take. Their forms of action, frames, collective identities and organizational cultures accumulate and spread to other movements across time and space. This chapter underlines the need to take into account lived experiences at a local level when analysing the processes of learning and diffusion within social movements. In the case of Madrid, these experiences marked a trend towards the development of more open and public initiatives by movements increasingly concerned with attracting adherents from people with no previous involvement in such groups or in civil society organizations. In my view, awareness of this trend helps us to better understand the rise of the Spanish 15-M movement. This movement has, in turn, created valuable knowledge that some activists have sought to transmit to other countries:

> Our goal was basically this: extend this [from] here to other places and try to create a sort of 'how to', something we are learning here, then quickly send it to other places and replicate this and get the entire world to rise up. Everything we learn – translate it and move it.[14]

However, this remains a tentative argument, based on limited observation of the phenomenon, the analysis of some documents, and a few interviews. A more exhaustive study would be required in order to explain in detail the conditions and implications of the possible learning processes sketched out in this chapter. Such a study could analyse the careers of activists, based on in-depth interviews and life stories, with a view to finding out the degree to which individuals who participated in previous movements and mobilizations participated in activities connected to the 15-M movement as well, and in what ways. An additional tool might consist of an analysis of networks which would include a temporal dimension, in order to probe the network of exchange and flow of resources between the various groups and organizations over time.

Notes

1 I wish to thank the editors of this volume as well as the participants and organizers of the workshop Social Movements in Times of Financial Crisis (Florence, May 2012) for their feedback and criticism of an earlier draft of this chapter.
2 The number of participants varied according to the source: 20,000 (according to the police), 80,000 (according to *El País*), or 130,000 (according to the organizers).
3 '1ª noche'. Available at: http://madrid.tomalaplaza.net/2011/05/16/ (accessed 20 December 2011).
4 A controversial article of the Ley 2/2011 de 4 de marzo de Economía Sostenible related to the regulation of websites and the protection of intellectual property known as the Sinde law after Ángeles González-Sinde, Minister of Culture at the time.
5 A month before a similar protest was held in Portugal, called by the self-styled *Geração à Rasca* (Desperate Generation), which, in Lisbon only, attracted 300,000 people (according to the organizers).
6 E. Romanos' interview with Stéphane M. Grueso, 17 October 2011, Madrid (Romanos 2012).
7 Statement by an activist from *Patio Maravillas*. Available at: www.youtube.com/watch?v=08NK6j4CjHU (accessed 11 January 2012).
8 The Ministry of Culture temporarily ceded the space to activists in 2010. At the end of 2011 it renewed the agreement for two years, with the possibility of a further renewal.
9 E. Romanos' interview with R.M., 12 January 2012, Madrid.
10 The European Social Consulta and the Consulta Social organized by the *Red Ciudadana por la Abolición de la Deuda Externa* (RCADE – Citizens' Network for the Abolition of the External Debt) at the early 2000s can be seen as earlier but failed attempts to do this (see Flesher Fominaya 2010).
11 'Grupo de Teatro 15 de Mayo' minutes, 13 June 2011. Available at: https://n-1.cc/pg/groups/171971/teatro-quince-de-mayo/ (accessed 21 May 2012).
12 E. Romanos's telephone interview with C. (8 April 2012).
13 Stéphane M. Grueso's interview with Zulo. Available at: www.15m.cc/2011/12/conversaciones-15mcc-zulo.html (accessed 15 February 2012).
14 E. Romanos' interview with M.A., member of the World Extension Team of *acampadasol*, 6 March 2012, Madrid.

References

Aguilar Fernández, S. and Fernández Gibaja, A. (2010) 'El movimiento por la vivienda digna en España o el porqué del fracaso de una protesta con amplia base social', *Revista Internacional de Sociología* 68(3): 679–704.

Blanco, R. (2011) *¿Qué pasa? Que aún no tenemos casa*, Madrid: Fundación Aurora Intermitente.

Calvo, K. (2013) 'Fighting for a Voice', in C. Flesher Fominaya and L. Cox (eds) *Understanding European Movements*, London: Routledge.

della Porta, D. (2005a) 'Deliberation in Movement', *Acta Politica* 40: 336–50.

della Porta, D. (2005b) 'Making the Polis', *Mobilization* 10(1): 73–94.

della Porta, D. (ed.) (2007) *The Global Justice Movement*, Boulder: Paradigm.

Elola, J. (2011) 'El 15-M sacude el sistema', *El País*, 22 May.

Errejón, I. (2011) 'Algo habrán hecho bien', in Juventud Sin Futuro (ed.) *Juventud Sin Futuro*, Barcelona: Icaria.

Flesher Fominaya, C. (2007a) 'The Role of Humour in the Process of Collective Identity Formation in Autonomous Social Movement Groups in Contemporary Madrid', *International Review of Social History* 52: 243–58.

Flesher Fominaya, C. (2007b) 'Autonomous Movements and the Institutional Left', *South European Society and Politics* 12(3): 335–358.

Flesher Fominaya, C. (2010) 'Creating Cohesion from Diversity', *Sociological Inquiry* 80(3): 377–404.

Flesher Fominaya, C. (2011) 'The Madrid Bombings and Popular Protest', *Contemporary Social Sciences* 6(3): 289–307.

Galli, R. (2011) 'Sobre el nacimiento del #nolesvotes … o el nolesvotes.com', *De software, Internet, legales.* Available at: http://gallir.wordpress.com/2011/02/17/sobre-el-nacimiento-del-nolesvotes-o-el-nolevotes-com/ (accessed 24 January 2012).

Gerhards, J. and Rucht, D. (1992) 'Organizing and Framing in Two Protest Campaigns in West Germany', *American Journal of Sociology* 98(3): 555–596.

Haro Barba, C. and Sampedro Blanco, V. 'The new social movements in Spain', paper presented at the 6th ECPR General Conference, Reikjavik, August 2011.

Hart, M.T (2007) 'Humour and Social Protest', *International Review of Social History* 52: 1–20.

Jiménez, M. (2006) 'El movimiento de justicia global', *Revista de Estudios de Juventud* 75: 29–41.

Jiménez, M. and Calle, A. (2007) 'The Global Justice Movements in Spain', in D. della Porta (ed.) *The Global Justice Movement*, Boulder: Paradigm.

Júlíusson, Á. and Helgason, M. (2013) "The Roots of the Saucepan Revolution in Iceland", in C. Flesher Fominaya and L. Cox (eds) *Understanding European Movements*, London: Routledge.

Letón, H.R. and Sanz Paratcha, D. (2011) '¿Quién es quién en las protestas en la red?', *Diagonal* 149 (28 April–11 May): 4–5.

Maestre, R. and Aldama, C. (2011) 'Sin miedo', in Juventud Sin Futuro (ed.) *Juventud Sin Futuro*, Barcelona: Icaria.

McAdam, D. (1986) 'Recruitment to High-Risk Activism', *American Journal of Sociology* 92(1): 64–90.

Meyer, D.S. and Whittier, N. (1994) 'Social Movement Spillover', *Social Problems* 41(2): 277–298.

Minchinela, R. (2011) 'Lemas y consignas del movimiento 15M'. Available at: http://vimeo.com/27147951 (accessed 12 February 2012).

Muñoz, A. (2011) 'Del síndrome Wikileaks a la democracia 2.0', in J.M. Antentas, A. Fernández-Savater, A. Muñoz, A. Requena and E. Vivas (eds) *Las Voces del 15-M*, Barcelona: Los libros del lince.

Nez, H. (2012) 'Among Militants and Deliberative Laboratories', in B. Tejerina and I. Perugorría (eds) *From Social to Political: New Forms of Mobilization and Democratization*, Bilbao: Universidad del País Vasco.

Raboso, A. and Merino, A. (2011) 'Y nosotros qué', in Juventud Sin Futuro (ed.) *Juventud Sin Futuro*, Barcelona: Icaria.

Romanos, E. (2011a) 'Retos emergentes, debates recientes y los movimientos sociales en España', in D. della Porta and M. Diani, *Los Movimientos Sociales*, Madrid: CIS-UCM.

Romanos, E. (2011b) 'El 15M y la democracia de los movimientos sociales', *Books and Ideas*. Available at: www.booksandideas.net/El-15M-y-la-democracia-de-los.html?lang=fr (accessed 18 November 2011).

Romanos, E. (2012) '*Esta revolución es muy copyleft*. Entrevista a Stéphane M. Grueso a propósito del 15M', *Interface* 4(1): 183–206.

Rubiño, E. (2011) 'Salvan los bancos, destruyen la educación', in Juventud Sin Futuro (ed.) *Juventud Sin Futuro*, Barcelona: Icaria.

Tabacalera (2011) *La Tabacalera*, Madrid: LTBC.

Walgrave, S. and Rucht, D. (eds) (2010) *The World Says No to War*, Minneapolis: University of Minnesota Press.

Whittier, N. (2004) 'Consequences of Social Movements for Each Other', in D.A. Snow, S.A. Soule and H. Kriesi (eds) *The Blackwell Companion to Social Movements*, Malden, MA: Blackwell.

14 Think globally, act locally?

Symbolic memory and global repertoires in the Tunisian uprising and the Greek anti-austerity mobilizations

Vittorio Sergi and Markos Vogiatzoglou

Introduction

This chapter presents the findings of a comparative examination of two movements that developed in the Mediterranean area during a common time frame,
the winter and spring of 2010–2011. In Tunisia, the suicide of the 27-year-old
street vendor Muhammad Bouazizi on 17 December 2010 in the town of Sidi
Bouzid sparked a popular revolt which ended up overthrowing a long lasting
political regime and inspired other mobilizations, rebellions and regime changes
in the Arab world, notably in Egypt and Libya. This mobilization also encouraged social movements and popular resistance on the northern side of the Mediterranean region. When the public debt crisis exploded in the EU, the protests in
response to the austerity measures imposed upon the Southern European countries found a source of inspiration in the outcomes of the "Jasmine Revolution",
which were seen as successful (Eltahawy 2011).

In Greece the "*Aganaktismenoi*", the local version of the *Indignados* movement, managed to mobilize more than 25 per cent of the country's population
against the harsh austerity measures imposed by the Greek government and its
creditors, and spearheaded the anti-austerity protests for several months (aler-
thess.gr 2011). If the Tunisian insurrection of January 2011 was described as the
spark of a complex chain of political events in the Arab world, the Greek mobilization against the austerity measures and financial speculation has brought into
the territory of the European Union an unprecedented degree of social contention
and criticism against the mainstream economic and political models.

Several authors have begun to analyse the nature and characteristics of this
chain of events (Arditi 2012; Kneissl 2011). According to some, the new Mediterranean movements are considered to be part of a worldwide "Facebook
revolution" (Crook 2011, Naughton 2011), which can provide movements with
innovative means (see for example, Olsson 2007), but also imposes new challenges and constraints (Chadwick 2006). Others have raised methodological
concerns regarding a potential comparison between the two sides of the "Mediterranean Spring" (Kennedy 2011), or have even claimed that the differences
between the North and the South are so extensive that there is no point in search-
ing for movement similarities on a cross-national level (see Hilleary 2011).

Should there be any apparent similarities, they are attributed to a sort of meta-physical "domino effect" of collective action (Brown 2011). We argue that, despite the obvious contextual differentiations, the Tunisian and Greek cases do present some similarities worth investigating. However, the most important amongst them are not to be traced to the common digital networking platform per se, but to the *rationale* behind its use and the outcomes this has produced.

We will present the main events that led to the insurrection against the *Rassemblement Constitutionel Democratique* (RCD: Democratic Constitutional Association) government in Tunisia, as well as the socio-political background of the Greek version of the *Indignados*, which culminated in the occupation of Syntagma Square in Athens. In both countries movement members utilized frames, slogans and mnemonic constructions bearing strong symbolic connotations in order to frame their grievances and claims. They re-appropriated strategic places closely associated to each country's movement past, namely Syntagma Square in Athens and Kasbah Square in Tunis. Participants re-shaped the meaning of nationally recognized symbols – flags, emblems and national anthems. Their discourse addressed local issues but was, at all times, framed as an attempt to challenge the political and economic hegemony of neo-liberalism, both at the national and the global levels. Whilst exploring this rich movement repertoire and analysing its rationale, we shall point out the contradictions and controversies it sparked among the participants.

We argue that the multilevel intertwinement of the "global" and the "local" is perhaps the most important trait of the movements under scrutiny. What we encountered in our research is a new generation of activists who have inherited the alter-globalization movements' famous slogan "Think globally, act locally", and is in the process of developing and implementing it.

Methods

Our broad research field being what we defined above as the "Mediterranean Spring", we approached the cases of Greece and Tunisia with a comparative perspective (Gerring 2004), through a most-different, case-oriented research design (della Porta 2008).

The empirical data for the research project were gathered during three separate periods: first, from February to March 2011, participant observation was conducted and interviews were undertaken in various Tunisian cities, particularly in the Kasbah occupation in Tunis; second, from May to August 2011 we visited Greece and participated in all of the main events of the Greek *Indignados* movement; and finally, in December 2011 we visited Greece again and interviewed several participants. In sum, we filled dozens of pages of field notes, recorded 13 interviews, filmed or participated in the shooting of many hours of video footage, and gathered a – more or less – complete archive of the printed material (announcements, press releases, leaflets, etc.) which was available at the time. Data were also retrieved using the rich archive of digital movements which is still available on the net, on various websites and blogs. The people we interviewed were protesters from different social, geographical and political backgrounds. During the sample selection process we took into account the interviewees' role in the protest and their vision of how the political movements they participated in should develop. Our top selection priorities were to achieve a pluralism of political standpoints and a variety of viewpoints in relation to the different ways our interviewees participated in the complex movements we are examining.

Tunisia's movements under Ben Alì and the emergence of the anti-Ben Alì movement

The political regime that ruled Tunisia until January 2011 began in 1987 through a "soft coup" led by Zinedine Ben Alì. Most opposition parties were proclaimed illegal at the beginning of the 1990s and the few parties that maintained their legal status had no access to power due to direct repression and electoral manipulation at all levels. By the end of the 1990s the Tunisian government had implemented a neo-liberal agenda within a model increasingly based upon the off-shore factories of European and Asian multinational enterprises, third sector development, financial marketing, and a black economy mostly fuelled by smuggling and immigrant remittances from Europe (Palidda 2011).

The political opposition to the RCD government was pluralistic and was characterized by various degrees of activity and contention. Its role in the recent uprising should not be underestimated, although the regime was toppled by a social movement which was not identical to the pre-existing political organizations. As massive scholarization policies were implemented by the Tunisian government, vast numbers of youngsters entered secondary and third-level education, although the weak competitiveness of the Tunisian educational system made them barely employable in the national labour market. In this context social mobilization in Tunisia seems more dependent upon exclusion and increasing social inequality than upon material deprivation (see United Nations 2009: 12–13). The increased restrictions in the EU's border policy put further pressure on "the escape valve" of social tension – international migration (Palidda 2008). As the repression of political Islam and growing unemployment and inflation diminished the people's loyalty to the regime, the rise of social contention over the past ten years was a fact which scholars analysed from both a global and regional perspective (Harrigan and El-Said 2011).

Mohammed Bouazizi set himself on fire on 17 December 2010, in the city centre of Sidi Bouzid, the capital of one of the most marginalized regions of Tunisia. On the same day a small group of parents and relatives of the young man protested in front of the government building, but were dispersed by the authorities. During the next few days the protests expanded to other cities of the central region, this time supported by the grassroots committees of the UGTT (Tunisian General Labor Union). Strikes, demonstrations, and sit-ins also began in Tunis, Kef, and on the tourist island of Djerba. The spreading protests were organized by the newly formed "Unemployed and young people's defence committees" and the slogans ranged from the openly anti-government *"Ben Ali, voleur!"* (Ben Alì, thief!) to *"Travail, Liberté, Justice sociale"* (work, freedom and social justice). and, the best-known, *"degage!"* (piss off!/get out!) (Sergi 2011). The level of police violence increased, with live ammunition being fired at the protesters: by 8 January, Amnesty International was reporting that 60 people had been killed in Kasserine, seven in Regueb and six in Thala.[1] After several days of street battles the police withdrew, leaving the ground to the army and to the local assemblies of citizens.

The army, led by General Ben Ammar, refused to obey the presidential order to open fire on the protesters and took control of strategic positions all over the country. Martial law was declared. Despite this, on 14 January the UGTT union called for a general strike. Large demonstrations took to the streets of Tunis and several groups of protesters moved towards the Ministry of Interior and the presidential residence in Carthage. In an effort to control the situation, the army gave Ben Alì and his close relatives permission to flee by plane to Saudi Arabia. On 17 January a provisional government was formed by the President of the Republic Fouad Mbazaa, led by Mohammed Ghannouchi, former Prime Minister of Ben Alì. The interim government did not gain much popular support since the demand of the majority of the people was a complete regime change and dissolution of the RCD. Up until the end of January the protests became more intense and radical than ever. In every mobilization women were present in considerable numbers and, as had also been noted for earlier protests and strikes which took place in Redeyef in 2008 (Seddik and Dahmani 2008), in the male-dominated Tunisian political scene, female participation in the demonstrations represents a good indication of the amplification of the protests. Non-coordinated strikes, factory squats, mass avoidance of work, and retaliation against bosses and landlords were reported by the international press (Lowe 2011). As a young UGTT member in Kasserine noted:

> … many workers, especially women, stopped going to work. Because of the insecurity, but also because you had to keep on working for nothing … this is the revolution; it's better to stay with your people even if you don't have any money.[2]

Three elements should be emphasized in relation to the Tunisian insurrectionist movement: the first was the cooperation of the urban and rural young unemployed to stage a lasting protest using the strategic combination of a complex electronic media and communications arsenal, urban guerrilla tactics, and traditional strikes. The second was the asymmetrical power of social network communication and its influence upon the mainstream audience. The third, as previously stated, was the activation of mnemonic constructions bearing strong symbolic connotations. Those constructions were rooted in strongly symbolic places such as the Kasbah historical square in Tunis, the streets as public spaces, "immaterial" representations such as the figure of the "martyr" (prevalent in the Islamic subjectivity), the anti-imperialist movements' slogans, and the demand for the "*karama watanya*" (national dignity) which, as we shall demonstrate below, added new symbolic content to national items such as the flag and the national anthem.

Greece under IMF rule: the anti-austerity movements and the Greek *Indignados*

The Greek movements we examined are part of Greek society's response to the explosive combination of austerity measures and administrative reforms imposed by the Greek government and the "troika" of its international creditors since May 2010.[3] The Memorandum of Cooperation (MoC) signed at that time obliged the government to adopt harsh measures in order to reduce the public sector deficit, in exchange for a series of bail-out loans financed by the international community. Two years after the initial implementation of the rescue plan, the expectations raised at that time have not been met. Greece is still on the verge of default; the recession is getting deeper and deeper each year; unemployment, social inequality and poverty indicators have peaked at an unprecedented level (INE-GSEE 2011).

The Greek social movements' response could be classified into three broad categories (or periods), in relation to the movement repertoire chosen by the actors and the types of organizations which spearheaded the mobilization:

1   [April 2010–April 2011] *The "traditional" mobilization*. During this period, the movement behaved in a similar way to mobilizations in the recent past. The repertoire included the usual general strikes, demonstrations, clashes with the police and protests in the majority of Greek cities.

2   [May–August 2011]: *The Indignados movement*. Inspired by the Arab Spring and adopting the organizational patterns of the Spanish *Indignados*, the "occupy the squares" movement began in Thessaloniki and Athens, and spread in a few weeks to the main squares of all Greek cities.

3   [September 2011–May 2012] *Labour mobilization and civil disobedience*. The third phase of the anti-austerity movement is characterized by the massive participation of workers' organizations, and by the widespread discontent amongst various social groups, mostly expressed through acts of civil disobedience: refusal to pay newly-imposed taxes, verbal and physical attacks on politicians in public spaces, protesting in previously non-politicized settings (such as football stadiums, and military and school parades) are some examples of this (Insider 2012; Karatziou 2012; to vima 2011).

The Greek version of the *Indignados* movement was launched on 25 May 2011. The initial calls to mobilization were circulated through Facebook pages, but then the news of the forthcoming protest began spreading outside Facebook; e-mails were sent in large numbers, articles appeared on blogs and news sites, hashtags were introduced on Twitter.[4] This was not the first time that calls to occupy Syntagma Square had been issued, [5] yet it was the first time that a truly bottom-up mobilization was attempted. As Antonis states,

> It was clear to everyone that all parties should stay out. If they [the party members] wanted to come, they should come as citizens, as individuals, not to gather their votes or sell their newspapers.[6]

On the designated day, around 50,000 people showed up in Athens and some 5,000 in Thessaloniki, according to media reports.[7] In Athens, whilst on the upper side of the square thousands protested against the government and the international creditors, on the lower side hundreds participated in the popular assembly in an attempt to "trace a common path for their struggle".[8] The decision taken was to form an *"acampada"* camping in the Square, to occupy it and to call for daily demonstrations to be followed by popular assemblies.[9]

The daily assembly was the main organizational and decision-making apparatus of the mobilization, during the months that it lasted. The assembly operated as follows:

> In the beginning [...] we would decide on which issues to discuss. Those who wanted to speak would take a paper with a number, then we had a "lottery", and the numbers drawn would speak.[10]

Apart from the assembly, another characteristic inherited from the Spanish *Indignados* was the formation of working groups, which would undertake specific tasks and provide constant feedback to the assembly.

We can distinguish four important characteristics of the protests that subsequently took place, in May and June 2011.

1   Their frequency and duration: the protests occurred on a daily basis (every evening at 18.00) and lasted until late at night (occasionally after midnight).
2   Their explicitly non-violent character: for the first time in recent years, there was consensus amongst the protesters to avoid direct confrontation with the police forces.
3   The use of innovative means, at least with regard to the traditional repertoire of Greek movements: laser pointers, choreographies, improvised banners, and so on, were all used. But the most significant innovation, at least for this generation of activists, was the use of the Greek flag as a uniting symbol of all Greeks for the first time since the fall of the military dictatorship (1974).
4   Finally, as regards the participants' socio-political characteristics, the crowd which attended both the demonstrations and the assemblies was significantly diverse, compared with all other mobilizations of the post-dictatorship era. If present, party and traditional organizations' members were obliged not to refer openly to their political identity. This gradually changed in time as the movement became more and more politicized. During the demonstration

peaks, when maximum mobilization was an explicit goal, all potential participants were welcomed.

The peak of the Syntagma Square mobilization were two general strike days (28 and 29 June), when yet another set of austerity measures was discussed in the Greek Parliament. Practically all of the Athenian social movement organizations (SMOs) joined forces in and around Syntagma Square in order to implement the Parliament blockade plan proposed by the *Indignados* Assembly. What followed was 48 hours of street blockades, barricades, failed attempts to invade the Parliament, counter-offensives by the police forces, fierce clashes, and destruction of property. The "battle for Syntagma Square" left almost 800 people injured and caused millions of euros in damages. Yet, the proposed legislation was finally approved by the Parliament. Despite an unprecedented "unity in action" spirit evident in the majority of the Greek SMOs during those two feverish days, and despite the recapturing of the square by the protesters after an evacuation operation by the riot police, the movement now lacked a clear and achievable goal. It did not manage to reach the mobilization peaks of the previous period and slowly faded.

A "Facebook revolution"?

In January 2011, shortly after the protests in Tunisia turned into riots and then into a rebellion across the country, mainstream media such as Al Jazeera, Al Arabiya, France 24 and the BBC started reporting the widespread use of social networks both as mobilization tools and as sources of direct and uncensored news from the social grassroots (Miladi 2011). As previously stated, Tunisia had witnessed an increase in internet use and mass formal education over the past decade (United Nations 2009). Even if the patterns of electronic media usage and diffusion were not equal to that of western countries, they had reached significant levels in a relatively short time. In the Greek case, use of the internet and other digital tools for movement purposes had been relatively common since the beginning of the 2000s (Vogiatzoglou 2009). The Facebook platform, though, was not too popular among the Greek activists. The main tools used up until the *Indignados* protest included alternative news portals, mailing lists and blogs, but for movement purposes Facebook remained relatively unexplored.

In Tunisia the political opposition to the RCD regime on the web encompassed various political and cultural options, but the majority of those were included in a "universal citizenship" frame (Bennani-Chraïbi and Fillieule 2003; Ozdalga and Persson 1997). Much evidence and many observers link the growing number of educated young people and the diffusion of radical arts and music to the political mobilization across the whole Arab world. This phenomenon had been neglected and often categorized as youth sub-culture, yet it was shaping a whole generation of trans-national activists and artists whose impact upon the Arab democratization movement deserves further examination (Skalli 2011).

During our research, we observed that the instrumental and conscious use of social networks derives from face-to-face practices and interactions in the physical world, towards establishing counter-hegemonic regimes of truth, as well as mobilizing a virtual audience within public space. Our interviewees noted how the production of news was the result of a chain of symbolic and physical exchanges. Most of the people interviewed asserted that Facebook held a key role amongst other social media, namely for its diffusion, usability and horizontal networking capacity:

> The revolution of 14 January took place really thanks to Facebook. If we hadn't had this medium we wouldn't have reached this point, because the mainstream media didn't have this direct diffusion. Such information was not available on our computer screens and television.[11]

Filippos, a 25-year-old student who participated in the Syntagma assemblies, admits that Facebook also proved useful in multiple ways for the Greek *Indignados*:

> ...you would see videos and news, for example police brutality videos, spreading in zero time, thousands would click and share and distribute their own material.... I don't like it [Facebook], yet it was used in a good way, I must admit.[12]

Yet the most relevant characteristic to our research is how Facebook, and internet-based communication tools in general, were simultaneously perceived by protesters as encompassing global and local traits. Activists were fully aware that the platforms they used were "border-less", in the sense that the basic procedures ("like", "tweet", "share") would be used in completely different settings across countries and continents. The claim they expressed was *locally* oriented, yet its audience and sources of potential solidarity could emerge from the other side of the world. Both in Tunisia and Greece hashtags were introduced to disseminate information in French, Spanish and English. In Greece several alternative or movement-friendly news portals devoted parts of their website to non-Greek speaking readers (RadioBubble 2012). One difference from the alter-globalization movement was that such globally oriented campaigning was neither formulated to facilitate direct involvement in the events (as in the case of websites for trans-national protests), nor did they simply aspire to raise consciousness on a specific subject.

All in all, although Facebook, as well as digital social networking platforms in general, were undoubtedly an extremely important tool for the development and the publicizing of both movements, they still maintain their *tool* status, as constituent parts within a wider repertoire which also included more traditional movement means as well as innovations, or, most importantly, innovative ways to approach the movement tradition in each country. In the following paragraph we will explore the latter, focusing on the use of national symbols.

Mnemonic constructions at the service of movements (1): innovation and renovation

Based on a large corpus of inter-disciplinary research, scholars addressing the issue of social memory construction have produced a significant theoretical work both in a general sociological perspective (for a brief overview, see Kansteiner 2002; Olick 1999) and, more specific to our research questions, a social movement one (Edy 2006; Harris 2006). As Gongaware eloquently put it, movement memory construction is a complex process which "allows participants to consider new ideas as though they are extensions of what the movement is already doing or has already done" (2011: 41). Yet, as Harris warns, during this process the members "may actually consciously or unconsciously block out some events of the past while privileging others that are more favourable to their experience" (2006: 20).

The combination of these two assumptions is relevant to the analysis of the movements under scrutiny. In the case of Tunisia, the promotion of national symbols already carried a strong and direct link to the country's anti-colonial past. The use of national flags was widespread during all of the demonstrations and protests of December and January. In the interviews, this shift was contrasted with other social events, namely the Tunisian national football team's matches:

> ...the flag was a symbol we had especially used [when playing] against the French [national team], but now it means that the politicians have no right to wave it, it has come back into the people's hands.[13]

In the Greek case, the flag and national anthem had been absent from the movement repertoire for more than three decades, due to their strong association with the right-wing, nationalist regime which had triumphed in the Greek civil war (1946–1949). Unsurprisingly, more experienced activists raised strong concerns when the first Greek flag appeared during the Syntagma Square demonstrations:

> When I first saw the flags, I felt sick, I said, this cannot be happening![14]
> I freaked out in the beginning, they would even sing the national anthem in front of the parliament.... I said, we must be surrounded by nationalist monkeys, fascist chimpanzees![15]

As the days passed, however, and the "fascist chimpanzees" did not appear on the horizon,[16] our interviewees realized that what they were facing was a much more complex phenomenon:

> [the people with the flags] they are members of our society, they are part of the people who will revolt when the time will come ... In the very end, we were struggling for the same purposes and goals.[17]

> We came to realize that the flag-carrying people were members of the ex-middle class, those whose life had literally been crushed by the crisis. Those

people, when looking for a banner of resistance to identify themselves with, opened their closet and what they found inside was the Greek flag. Therefore, they took the Greek flag and came out on the streets.[18]

Thus, the flag turned out to symbolize both the re-emergence of the threatened middle class on the streets of Greece and national unity, national mobilization with the same goals. We can note a significant similarity between Greece and Tunisia at this point. The major transformation that occurred, with respect to the previous experience these two countries had of the symbolic connotations of national flags and anthems, was that this time there was no obvious *external* enemy whose threatening behaviour could be repelled if the people united under the national symbols (Anderson 1991). This time the enemy was *internal*; it was each country's own elites, be they political or economic. For precisely this reason we argue that this common development was an innovative tool in the movement repertoire rather than a direct reference to the mnemonic constructions of the movement.

The "internalization" of the conflict – and its symbolic portrayal in the use of national symbols – is yet another indicator of how the Greek and Tunisian protesters perceived their mobilization to be simultaneously local *and* global. This is especially relevant in the Greek case; Tunisian's international references were by definition more limited, as they were the ones who initiated the "Mediterranean Spring". A few days before the launching of the Syntagma Square occupation, a false rumour was circulated via several media outlets. Supposedly, the Spanish *Indignados* had raised a banner in Puerta del Sol reading "Ssshhh.... The Greeks are sleeping" (Sapouna 2011). This initiated extensive discussion amongst the future protesters. As Filippos recalls:

> Yes, I got really angry. I said 'these stupid Spaniards, who supported Franco for fifty years and were only dancing flamenco and eating tapas, they are mocking us. And now they gather in their thousands, and what are we doing? Nothing. They are mocking us for doing nothing.'[19]

Just a couple of days after the occupation, a banner was raised in response to this false rumour. The banner portrayed a Spanish flag and stated: "We have woken up. What time is it? It is time for them [the governments of Greece and Spain] to go!"[20] During the demonstrations, one could see protesters waving Spanish, Italian, Egyptian and Tunisian flags. The identification with national symbols was not perceived as an attempt to construct barriers to the neighbouring Mediterranean nations, but rather as a symbol of the Greek people participating in the common effort to overthrow neo-liberal policies at the global level.

Mnemonic constructions at the service of movements (2): the Kasbah and Syntagma Square occupations

The first occupation of the Kasbah took place on 23 January 2011, after the "March of Freedom" which brought thousands of people from the rebel town of

Sidi Bouzid to the capital. A few days later the sit-in was dispersed by the police. The second occupation of the Kasbah in Tunis lasted from 20 February to 9 March 2011. The Kasbah is located in the middle of the historic centre of Tunis and hosts the most important palaces of the colonial authorities, as well as the Ministries of Defence and Financial Affairs, the Municipality of Tunis, the Prime Minister's office and an important mosque. Nevertheless, the Kasbah, as the name suggests, is also close to the old city's commercial and popular neighbourhood. Syntagma Square, in Athens, Greece, is the central city square, situated in front of the Parliament, and close to many ministries, the Presidential Residence, the Prime Minister's office, and the city's commercial centre. In summary, the spatial and socio-geographical configuration of the two sites is strongly linked to the representation of political authorities, as they had been distributed in the past, and as they are in the present. When protesters took over these squares with a permanent sit-in they were openly inspired by the Tahrir Square sit-in in Egypt, and the Puerta del Sol occupation in Madrid, respectively.

Both movements gained political momentum through the occupation of a symbolic place that worked as a catalyst for collective representations and memories of struggle (Olick and Robbins 1998: 113). The centrality of the Kasbah introduced a direct challenge to the regime, and in fact the state tried to respond to the challenge – succeeding at first in evacuating the occupation, failing a second time (at the end of February), and then blocking it again (during the October 2011 electoral process for the Constituent Assembly). The same process of defiance and resistance was noted in the Greek case: the main challenge for both the protesters and the riot police was to secure their presence in the square. This became evident during the violent clashes of June 2011 and continued until the final eviction of the occupation.

The occupation of historical and central places in capital cities may also be interpreted as a strategic choice by the movements in their attempt to build a direct link to previous instances of the struggle for democracy. In the case of Tunisia, the reference to democracy was rooted in two apparently distinct iconic events of the past: the liberation struggle of the Fellagha,[21] and in the contemporary "open society" culture and rhetoric. In both cases the democratization process was the political project chosen to challenge authoritarianism, although one could identify various political visions amongst the protesters, even the most radical ones:

> We speak of revolution when the majority of the people takes part in a struggle and achieves its aims. This is not what we have now in Tunisia; we can talk about a minority that started the revolt, defended it and continued. We see that our revolutionary aims are far from being reached. That's why we talk about revolt and not revolution.[22]

In Greece the most prominent banner decorating Syntagma Square quoted the final article of the Greek constitution: "Observance of the constitution is entrusted to the patriotism of the Greeks who shall have *the right and the duty to resist by all possible means* against anyone who attempts the violent abolition of the Constitution" (Hellenic Parliament 2008: 134–135, emphasis added). The reference – or threat – was obviously directed at the government and the deputies overlooking the occupation from the windows of Parliament. Yet it had an additional connotation: in English "Syntagma" means "Constitution". The name was given to the square after the 1843 popular revolt against the King, the epicentre of which was the square, and which ended in the approval of the first Greek constitution. Thus even the name of the site chosen for the mobilization was a reminder to participants, by-standers, and those addressed that the struggle for democracy (as perceived by the protesters[23]) drew from the past but also involved the active provisions of the nation-state's founding texts.

Conclusion

The movements we have examined were characterized by an, often contradictory, linking of what is usually perceived as "global" and "local". The Tunisian activists used a globally uniform platform to spread the word that their state leader should fall. Their Greek counterparts based their argumentation as to why locally oriented austerity measures should be abolished on a fierce critique of worldwide neo-liberalism. The more militant amongst them condemned the Western-style representative democratic models, counter-proposing a direct democracy which drew on their own experience as they had applied it to make their assembly work. Both countries' movements simultaneously employed their own interpretations of "universal citizenship" by means of national symbols, re-configured in terms of symbolic content to suit the needs of the mobilizations. The activists found inspiration in and asked for the solidarity of the neighbouring countries' version of the movement, whilst simultaneously fearing that over-involvement by the traditional entities of their own country would undermine their cause.

Similar – and perhaps even clearer – hostility was identified during the alter- or no-global mobilizations, especially amongst the autonomous and anti-capitalist protest groups (Juris 2005). Flesher Fominaya explains that whilst the institutional left conceives of the collective, the party, and/or the union as ideal-typical political actors, autonomous groups promote a model of the "individual acting collectively" (Flesher Fominaya 2007: 338). This was also the case with the Tunisian and Greek movements. However, anti-capitalist groups arrived at this conclusion after a well-elaborated critique of the institutions of representative democracy as a whole. To claim that this elaboration was present in the case of Greece and Tunisia would be an exaggeration. It is possible that the majority of the participants in the Kasbah and Syntagma Square occupations were not even aware of this debate. Giorgos' reflections on this issue are very interesting:

> Our [i.e. the more militant activists'] big illusion was that we believed that we had suddenly persuaded hundreds of thousands of people to reject

democracy, that they were ready to go to the "next step" [...]. They [the protesters] cursed the politicians, all politicians indiscriminately, yet they remained in front of the parliament all day, as if they were expecting something from their representatives. Their claim was addressed exactly to the people they were shouting against. This, we did not see at that point.[24]

What Giorgos confirms is that the contradictory nature of all the above did not pass unnoticed by the participants themselves. We have witnessed and discussed the controversies and doubts the complex repertoires and organizational schemes created amongst the protesters. Perhaps one could describe the above phenomena as inherent in the conflictual consequences of the neo-liberal policies imposed upon those societies. In the same way that we perceive and analyse the importance of neo-liberalism in shaping national and regional policies, we could also consider it as a complex procedure which has had multiple effects upon the subjectification of peoples and their cultures. If this is the case, movement memory should not only be perceived as a potential source of movement repertoires and identities of resistance (Scott 1990), but also as its opposite, as a wounded memory requiring reconstruction.

It is true that further research (and perhaps, a more extended temporal distance from the events) is required for a more detailed analysis. However, a final comment related to the above should be made: both the Tunisian and the Greek movements lacked a hegemonic organizational entity or a charismatic leader. According to popular rhetoric it was the multitude of social subjects, those who have neither public voice nor public face, who took the initiative. As a popular Tunisian poet wrote:

> It is the unemployed and the vagabonds,
> the beggars and the hobos,
> It is the barefoot,
> the sons of the scarred women,
> it is the street vendors
> who made this revolution!
> It's the children of Thala,
> Kasserine, Regueb and Jelma,
> of Bouzaiene, Sidi Bouzid and Meknassy
> the forgotten children of the hinterland.[25]

Notes

1 A full report of Tunisia uprising's casualties can be found on Amnesty International's website special section: www.amnesty.org/en/region/tunisia.
2 Interview with Ahmed, a 33-year-old graduate in mathematics, and a member of the UGTT in Kasserine. 12 March 2011.
3 The international creditors, referred to as the "troika", are the International Monetary Fund (IMF), the European Central Bank (ECB) and the European Union (EU).
4 See www.enet.gr/?i=news.el.article&id=281752.

5 See, for example, the call issued by the editors of the left-wing newspaper "Dromos tis Aristeras", on 15 February 2011.
6 Interview with Antonis, 20 December 2011.
7 www.enet.gr/?i=news.el.ellada&id=278585.
8 Interview with Alexandros, a 55-year-old unemployed architect, participant in the Assembly and member of the Communication working group of the Acampada. 10 December 2011.
9 www.tanea.gr/ellada/article/?aid=4632926.
10 Interview with Filippos, 10 December 2011.
11 Interview with Fatima, 8 March 2011.
12 Interview with Filippos, 10 December 2011.
13 Interview with Abdi, 6 March 2011.
14 Interview with Giorgos, 16 December 2011.
15 Interview with Alexandros, 21 December 2011.
16 Extreme right-wing organizations did make several attempts to participate in the Syntagma Square demonstrations, but were forcefully pushed away by anarchist and anti-fascist militia-like squads.
17 Interview with Filippos, 10 December 2011.
18 Interview with Giorgos, 16 December 2011.
19 Interview with Filippos, 10 December 2011.
20 A photo of the banner, as well as similar Syntagma Square messages to European people, can be found here: http://ksipnistere.blogspot.it/2011/05/blog-post_2744.html.
21 Originally, this Arab word refers to highwaymen and bandits. Fellagha fighters were the partisan guerrillas who fought against the French colonial occupation of Tunisia during the most intense period of the anti-colonial struggle, from 1952 to 1956.
22 Interview with Rafik, 27 February 2011.
23 It is interesting to note that in the case of Greece, the "Democracia Real Ya!" ("Real Democracy Now!") slogan of the Spanish *Indignados* was immediately transformed to "Direct Democracy Now!". Some observers noted that this choice, apart from the demand for a much more specific content of what we're referring to when talking about "democracy", is strongly related to the ideals of the Ancient Greek democracy model (Lieros 2011).
24 Interview with Giorgos, 16 December 2011 (emphasis added).
25 Excerpt from: *Qui a fait la Révolution?* ("Who made the Revolution?") Poem in the Tunisian dialect by Wala Kasmi, quoted and translated into French in January 2011, at http://revolisationactu.blogspot.com.

References

alerthess.gr. (2011). MRB issues new poll on the "Indignados". *www.alerthess.gr*. Retrieved 31 December 2011, from www.alterthess.gr/node/8839.
Anderson, B. (1991). Imagined Communities, London: Verso.
Arditi, B. (2012). Insurgencies don't have a plan – they are the plan. *Journal of Journalism, Media and Cultural Studies*.
Bennani-Chraïbi, M. and Fillieule, O. (2003). *Résistances et protestations dans les sociétés musulmanes*. Paris: Presses de Sciences po.
Brown, J. (2011). Algeria's Midwinter Uproar. *Middle East Research and Information Project*.
Chadwick, A. (2006). *Internet politics*. New York: Oxford University Press.
Crook, E. (2011). Tunisia: The facebook revolution. *The British Council Voices*.
della Porta, D. (2008). Comparative Analysis. In D. della Porta and M. Keating (eds),

Approaches and methodologies in the social sciences: A pluralist perspective (pp. 198–222). Cambridge: Cambridge University Press.

Edy, J.A. (2006). *Troubled pasts*. Philadelphia: Temple University Press.

Eltahawy, M. (2011). Tunisia's Jasmine Revolution. *Washington Post*, 15 January.

Flesher Fominaya, C. (2007). Autonomous Movements and the Institutional Left. *South European Society and Politics*, *12*(3), 335–358.

Gerring, J. (2004). What is a Case Study and What is it Good for? *American Political Science Review*, *98*(2), 341–354.

Gongaware, T. (2011). Keying the Past to the Present. *Social Movement Studies*, *10*(1), 39–54.

Harrigan, J., and El-Said, H. (Eds). (2011). *Globalisation, democratisation and radicalisation in the Arab world*. Basingstoke: Palgrave Macmillan.

Harris, F.C. (2006). It Takes a Tragedy to Arouse Them. *Social Movement Studies*, *5*(1), 19–43.

Hellenic Parliament. (2008). The Greek Constitution. Athens: Hellenic Parliament.

Hilleary, C. (2011). Arab Activists, *Voice of America*.

INE-GSEE. (2011). *Greek economy and employment – annual report 2011*. Athens: INE-GSEE.

Insider. (2012). The fans of PAO and the controversial banner. *Insider.gr*. Retrieved 4 June 2012, from www.theinsider.gr/index.php?option=com_content&view=article &id=16157:the-angry-supporters-of-pao-and-the-controversial-banner&catid=34: football&Itemid=88.

Juris, J.S. (2005). Social Forums and their Margins. *Ephemera*, *5*(2), 253–272.

Kansteiner, W. (2002). Finding Meaning in Memory. *History and Theory*, *41*(2), 179–197.

Karatziou, N. (2012). Am I not paying or I cannot afford to pay? *MONO*. Retrieved June 4, 2012, from http://monopressgr.wordpress.com.

Kennedy, M. D. (2011). Arab Spring, Occupy Wall Street and historical frames, 2011. *Jadaliyya*, 23 October.

Kneissl, K. (2011). Elements For A Scientific Analysis Of The Arab Revolutions In Spring 2011. *Social Anthropology*. Vienna.

Lieros, G. (2011). *Thoughts on Direct Democracy*. Athens: Ekdoseis ton Synadelfon.

Lowe, C. (2011). Tunisia struggles to tame revolutionary spirit. *Reuters*, 15 February.

Miladi, N. (2011). Tunisia: A media led revolution? *Al-Jazeera*, 17 January.

Naughton, J. (2011). Yet another Facebook revolution, *Observer*, 23 January.

Olick, J.K. (1999). Collective memory. *Sociological Theory*, *17*(3), 333–348. Wiley Online Library.

Olick, J.K. and Robbins, J. (1998). 'Social memory studies: From "collective memory" to the historical sociology of mnemonic practices', *Annual Review of Sociology*, *24*, 105–140. Retrieved from www.jstor.org/stable/10.2307/223476.

Olsson, T. (2007). An indispensable resource, in P. Dahlgren (Ed.), *Young citizens and new media*. New York: Routledge.

Ozdalga, E. and Persson, S. (Eds). (1997). *Civil society, democracy and the Muslim world*. Richmond: RoutledgeCurzon.

Palidda, S. (2008). *Mobilità umane*. Roma: R. Cortina.

Palidda, S. (2011). La rivoluzione inimmaginabile. *alfabeta2*, 7.

RadioBubble (2012). Radiobubble news in English. *Radiobubble.gr*.

Sapouna, Z. (2011). Ssssh … the Greeks are sleeping! *Skai.gr*. Retrieved 4 June 2012, from www.skai.gr/news/opinions/article/170412/sss-tha-xupnisoun/.

Scott, J. (1990). *Domination and the Arts of Resistance*. New Haven: Yale University Press.

Seddik, O. and Dahmani, I. (2008). *Leila Khaled, la Tunisienne*. Comité national de soutien à la population du bassin minier, Tunisia, 34 min. Retrieved from http://vimeo.com/14090526.

Sergi, V. (2011). Appunti etnografici dalla rivolta tunisina. *Etnografia e ricerca qualitativa*, *3*, 447–465.

Skalli, L.H. (2011). Youth and the art of protest in North Africa. *Al-Jazeera*, June 27.

To Vima (2011). Riots and cancellation of the parades all over the country. *tovima.gr*. Retrieved 4 June 2012, from www.tovima.gr/society/article/?aid=427388.

United Nations. (2009). *Arab Human Development Report*.

Vogiatzoglou, M. (2009). Burning, looting, falling in love. *16th panhellenic conference for PhD candidates: Methodological issues in social sciences*. Rethymnon.

15 Fighting for a voice

The Spanish 15-M/Indignados movement

Kerman Calvo

On 15 May 2011, responding to the calls by a number of internet-based 'platforms', more than 70 Spanish cities hosted demonstrations that demanded a 'real democracy'. Participants demanded solutions to the financial and debt crisis, zero tolerance to corruption, and also a broad reform of the political system in the direction of strengthening citizens' engagement with politics. Few among the network of politicized activists that engineered the 15-M demonstration ('m' standing for *Mayo*, 'May' in English) expected that these demonstrations would turn into mass and highly visible events. Estimates of the participants in Madrid alone talked about more than 20,000 demonstrators (El País 2011a).

The so-called 15-M movement takes its name from this founding protest event. In the aftermath of the 15-M demonstration a group of protesters remained in the *Puerta del Sol* square in Madrid: 'nobody wanted to leave' (Rivas 2011: 50). Harassed by the police on the nights of the 15th and 16th, the following day a large group of citizens responded to the calls launched on several online platforms to peacefully 'resist' by remaining, and purposely occupying, that very same urban spot ('*toma la plaza*', as the banner read in Spanish). In the words of one of the occupiers, 'citizens' peaceful invasion of public squares is a symbol of how public spaces can be 'regained', and also of how 'real' and 'deep' politics can be made' (Freire 2011: 53; emphasis mine). As activists persisted in the occupation, provisional infrastructures started to emerge that soon resembled a living 'camp' (*acampada*). Life in those camps revolved around daily assemblies that debated a wide array of political issues. Participants discussed, among many other things, the meaning and goals of participation, but also corruption, social injustice, electoral politics and the excesses of capitalism. Activists in Madrid set an example that was rapidly emulated by like-minded activists in Spain's other large cities, including Barcelona, Valencia, Bilbao, Seville, Granada and Salamanca.[1]

The main aim of this chapter is to discuss empirical data on participants in the 15-M movement. First and foremost, the analysis draws on my own data on protesters in Salamanca, collected during the first wave of protests in May 2011. Salamanca is a thriving university town of roughly 150,000 inhabitants, plus approximately 50,000 students registered at its two sizeable universities. The Salamanca 15-M movement was among the most active and visible in the country. This chapter also draws on later work done on Bilbao by Arellano *et al.* (2012) and on Madrid by Likki (2012). In the three cases we have samples of roughly the same size (around 250 participants) that provide data on profiles and motivations; the questionnaires were of similar (though not identical) orientation. The three projects included questions about access to new technologies, evaluations of the economic and political situation, the reasons behind the occupation of public spaces, and so forth. The presentation of the empirical material reveals striking similarities among the samples, in terms of relevant socio-demographic indicators as well on the issue of goals and priorities.

The chapter is organized as follows: the first section introduces the 15-M movement and argues for its conceptualization as a novel form of collective action that disrupts negative patterns in Spanish political culture.[2] The discussion then moves to a basic analysis of socio-demographic profiles, where questions relating to the gender, age and educational backgrounds of participants are discussed. The third section argues for the need to distinguish between two types of 15-M participants: occasional participants and active participants. Finally, the issue of the goals of participation is explored.

The 15-M movement and changes in political culture

From the beginning, Spanish society liked the 15-M movement. According to one poll nearly 80 per cent of Spaniards thought that the 15-M movement pursued just and legitimate causes (Metroscopia 2011). For the most part, this boiled down to a declared interest in the movement. More than half the population had followed the evolution of this social movement with 'quite' or 'high interest', and an additional 27 per cent had some interest in it. Of those declaring at least some interest, only 8 per cent had developed negative views. As expected, a positive opinion about the 15-M movement was clearly associated with other important variables: namely, ideology, age and 'political satisfaction'. In all of these cases the associations are statistically significant: younger, leftist and, consequently, more dissatisfied respondents were much more likely than older, conservative and politically satisfied people to have developed positive inclinations towards the 15-M movement. An illustration of this is provided in Figure 15.1 below, where the mean of a variable measuring individual satisfaction with democracy (0 to 10) is charted (following an ANOVA analysis) along levels of interest with the 15-M movement: those more interested in the movement were those with more critical views on the quality of Spanish democracy.

The combined reading of the available survey data, therefore, gives weight to one of the leading and most popular arguments circulating around the 15-M movement; namely, that it emerged from a generalized and widely shared feeling of discontent with fundamental elements of the political and economic systems. Before proceeding, it should be noted that this social movement was the site of interesting naming practices. Feelings of rage and indignation were certainly quoted by the organizers of the founding 15-M demonstration; these resonated well with the then recently published book *Indignez-vous* by Stéphane Hessel

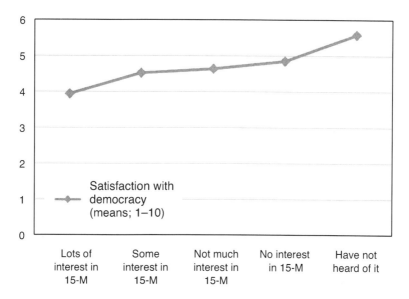

Figure 15.1 Satisfaction with democracy and interest in 15-M Movement (source: data from Centro de Investigaciones Sociológicas (CIS) study number 2905 (June 2011)).

(Hessel 2011). The activists, however, have also defined themselves in other terms: as members of *Acampada Sol* (Camp in Sun Square), participants in the 15-M movement, or even as part of the '#Spanish revolution', for instance. The references made in this chapter to the 15-M movement are thus to be taken as a way to simplify the presentation, acknowledging that naming practices do indeed have political meaning.

This chapter discusses data taken at different stages in the evolution of the 15-M movement. The first and more vibrant wave of protest lasted from mid-May to early July 2011 (Hughes 2011). These were the weeks of unremitting street-based political debate and consciousness-raising. Urban camps started to decline right after the local and regional elections of 22 May 2011;[3] in fact, they would have disappeared by the beginning of June if local authorities in Barcelona had not decided to end the occupation of Plaza Cataluña by force on 26 May 2011. Images of unjustified police brutality sparked new enthusiasm amongst campers that added further continuity to the movement (El País 2011b). Still, by early July most forms of continuous occupation had been called off. After that date the 15-M movement took a different profile, defined by the absence of continuous occupation of public spaces and, also, by the hybridization with pre-existing social movements (for instance, neighbourhood civic associations and trade unions in public education). It is true that the Spanish 15-M movement contributed heavily to organizing the October 2011/Global 15O demonstrations, and also to launching initiatives to take street-based protesting to the

European Parliament. On the other hand, during the second stage the movement lacked the continuity and consistency associated with daily work in urban camps (although regular assemblies were organized and the necessary structures of mobilization for collective action remained).

The first anniversary of the 15-M movement (May 2012), celebrated yet again by mass occupations of public spaces in Madrid, Barcelona and other large cities, signals the beginning of the third (and current) stage. Activists in Spain already possess a markedly global perspective following the media successes of the so-called 'occupy movements' in the United States and United Kingdom. The goals and modes of protesting largely remain the same. However, a year after the birth of the Spanish 15-M movement, the movement is starting to suffer from the internal tensions associated with political incorporation. *'Democracia Real Ya'* [Real Democracy Now], one of the 15-M movement's most recognizable members, suffered a dramatic internal rupture during May 2012 (ABC 2012): key members within that organization, including some of the best-known spokespersons of the 15-M movement, were perceived as seeking access to the political system and political moderation. This led to angry debates and, ultimately, to their replacement.

This is not the place to discuss the future of the 15-M movement; while many envisage a long and prolific political existence for it, others – particularly right-wing commentators and influential bloggers – have always seen the 15-M movement as an episodic quasi-revolution, a media 'trending topic' without real substance (see, for example, Galindo 2011). From the perspective of the social sciences, however, the emergence of the 15-M movement must be seen as a remarkable disruption of the existing patterns of political culture. Spanish political culture is defined by significant apathy and lack of involvement in anything political, including social movements (Morales and Geurts 2007; Bonet *et al.* 2006). Such maladies are particularly notorious among young people (García and Martín 2010).[4] Discontent is seldom translated into sustained collective protest. Most of the traditional social movements are currently unable to bring protesters to the streets; this includes LGBT rights and women's movements, but also environmental and even labour movements. These 'traditional' movements survive 'in the doldrums' thanks to some regional and local public funding, with membership numbers that are very low in comparative terms. Traditional yearly events of protest, such as the 1st May demonstration, have also lost most of their punch. This is clearly acknowledged by students of Spanish social movements who, while underscoring the rise of internet-based forms of 'online participation', have lamented the decline of traditional, 'off-line', mass forms of participation and collective action. The 15-M movement's immediate 'off-line' precursor – namely, the so-called movement for decent housing (Aguilar and Fernández 2010) – was a small-scale, prone to radicalism, episodic social movement whose existence is barely acknowledged by the general public.

The 15-M movement offered something new that helped the involvement of large groups of previously demobilized citizens. In the first place, the 15-M movement adopted organizational strategies commonly associated with the so-called autonomous/alternative social movements (see, for instance, Juris 2005). Autonomous movements are keen on non-hierarchical, horizontal, stubbornly participatory understandings of involvement that depart from formal organizations, defined leaderships and representative modes of action. The 15-M movement has given a much larger resonance to this mode of organization, which was hitherto limited to less visible networks of goal-specific activism (Juris 2008; Flesher Fominaya 2007). A second contribution has been an expanded repertoire of mobilization that revolves around the long-term and peaceful occupation of urban spaces. Third, a dialectic relationship has been established with society at large that skips traditional connections between movement organizations and social constituencies. Fourth, this is not a social movement against a well-defined opponent: the whole establishment is to blame. And, last, and related to the former, the 15-M movement proposes a departure from constituency-based modes of defining collective identity; it has established itself as a social movement with a universalist appeal that seeks to make connections across social groups in order to activate basic feelings of discontent, injustice and rage.

Wondering about the purpose of the 15-M movement, one activist argued that 'what truly matters is how the mental structures of those who have participated in all this have changed' (Alvarez 2011: 22). One explanation for the formidable success of the 15-M movement among educated, left-wing and mostly unemployed young people (see below) lies in the capacity of new structures of mobilization and modes of protest to liberate political voice. Observation of the assemblies reveals how much participants in the Spanish 15-M movement have relished the discovery of a personal way of reacting to changing political and economic circumstances. The 15-M movement, thus, takes the form of a consciousness-raising laboratory with a contribution that is highly praised by (some) political philosophers: citizens acquire political information, critical thinking, and a taste for political participation. This, eventually, might lead to better democratic processes, improved forms of decision making and, of course, more efficient and fair public policies (Pettit 2011).

Who are they?

This section discusses empirical data on participants in the 15-M movement.

Three samples are explored, although in different ways. The first relates to my own data on Salamanca (N=253; May 2011). It draws on a questionnaire distributed to occupiers of Salamanca's 'Constitution Square', who camped for almost four weeks, beginning on 18 May 2011 (around 50 respondents), and also to participants in the daily evening assembly (200 valid respondents). Only those who had participated in at least one assembly were considered in this analysis. This invalidates the responses of around 40 respondents. The Salamanca questionnaire included more than 90 variables. All together this sample resembled the size of a standard assembly (around 300 participants). Of course, participation in these events followed a cycle: considering the case of Salamanca alone, between 18–20 May, according to my own personal estimation as an observer and participant, more than 500 people gathered for the 9 p.m. assembly. After that date, participation rates declined to an average of 300 participants. On 29 May, as a reaction to the violent clashes between activists and security forces in Barcelona, a new wave of support for the 15-M movement boosted participation, which reached its peak with a general assembly of more than 2,000 people. In June the speed of decline accelerated: the movement evolved from a two-per-day to a three-per-week system of assemblies, until the original camp was finally abandoned on 12 June.[5] The second sample was compiled by Arellano *et al.* (2002) (N=222; May 2011) and provides data on participants in the 15-M movement in Bilbao. The questionnaire was relatively simple, including only 12 questions. The third and more recent sample draws on the work of Likki (2012) in Madrid (N=230; November 2011). This involved a complex questionnaire of around 85 variables with theoretically guided indicators. In all three cases the researchers had similar goals: namely, a basic exploration of socio-demographic profiles and, also, an identification of the reasons leading to the engagement with collective action. Likki's questionnaire, drafted once the 15-M movement had already entered its second stage of evolution, included more specific questions, particularly in relation to the reasons underpinning participation.

According to the data presented in Table 15.1 below (Salamanca sample), only 43 per cent of participants in the 15-M movement had actually demonstrated on 15 May 2011. There is, however, a convincing explanation for this (see, for instance, Arellano *et al.* 2012: 22–23). The 15-M demonstrations were organized by like-minded 'cyber activists' networked through previous online protest events (see also Haro and Sampedro 2011). Encouraged by the unexpected success of the demonstration, calls for further engagement were launched through several online platforms; these calls reached people who either had not heard of, or had decided not to participate in the demonstration, but who found new meaning in the strategy of the occupation of public spaces. Note that Likki's work on Madrid includes a similar question on participation which produced, however, somewhat different results (Likki 2012: Table 15.1). In this case, 82 per cent of respondents claimed to have participated in the 15-M demonstration; note, however, that the Madrid data was collected in November 2011, when the 15-M movement was no longer aiming to occupy public spaces. It is therefore likely that, as the weeks passed, only the initiators of the 15-M movement (who

Table 15.1 Participation in protest events (Salamanca; multiple answers)

	N	%
15-M demonstration	106	43
Camping before local elections	134	54
Camping after local elections	127	51
Assemblies, but no camping	177	71
None	7	3

had presumably participated in the organization and marketing of the event) continued to be involved.

Turning to the question of participants, the core of the 15-M movement is made up of young (but not adolescent) men and women, well-educated, and with a left-wing political orientation. Most of them are enrolled in university degrees or have completed university education. They are, moreover, what is commonly referred to as 'digital natives' (Prenski 2004). Politically, 15-M movement participants share a collective urge to change things and are imbued with a well-developed understanding of the problems of social exclusion, but, at the same time, are unsure about how to develop their ambitious political agenda, or are unwilling to do so. Participants in the 15-M movement have a suspicious approach to political negotiation, fearing the 'corrupting' effect of bargaining with existing political institutions.

Neither in Salamanca nor in Bilbao was gender found to have a meaningful effect upon the profiles or attitudes of participants, with the samples having virtually the same number of men and women. As shown in Figure 15.2

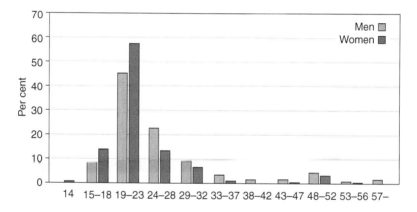

Figure 15.2a Age and gender (Salamanca).

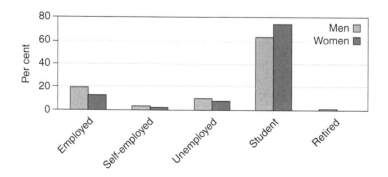

Figure 15.2b Occupation and gender (Salamanca).

(Salamanca), only slight gender differences are identified when breaking down the sample by age group or occupation. In the case of Bilbao (Arellano *et al.* 2012: chart 1) women were only slightly younger than men.

That gender is not perceived as a key issue for the 15-M movement movement is of some interest. Most of the internal divisions that afflicted participants in *acampada Sol* (the largest 15-M movement camp) actually had a gender dimension. Defying the view that previous identities and alliances should not be incorporated into 15-M movement frames of mobilization (Botella-Ordinas 2011), feminists in Madrid organized autonomously and defined themselves as 'outraged feminists'. In stressing a particularist identity, feminists and the other activists camped at *Sol* square established a very difficult relationship, which resulted in accusations of sexism, intolerance, and even sexual assault (La Vanguardia 2011).[6]

The 15-M movement is a gender-balanced social movement of young peoples. The age dimension of participation was readily observed by some early commentators, who stressed the fact that this was not an *adolescent* social movement (see, for instance, Taibo 2011). In Salamanca, as is shown in Figure 15.2b above, most participants fitted in the 19–30 age range (70 per cent). Participants in Bilbao and Madrid, however, were slightly older. While the bulk of participants lay in a similar age range (20–35 years in Bilbao; 20–35 in Madrid), in both cases there was a greater number of mature participants. In Madrid, for instance, 15 per cent of participants were aged between 50–68 years (Likki 2012: 4).

Participants in the 15-M movement are qualified, but they are out of work. As shown in Figure 15.3, 70 per cent of participants in Salamanca had either completed or were currently studying for a university degree. In Bilbao this rate was lower, at 50 per cent (Arellano *et al.* 2012: 29[7]). The figure for Madrid was close to that for Salamanca, at 66 per cent (Likki 2012: 4). In all cases the rate of

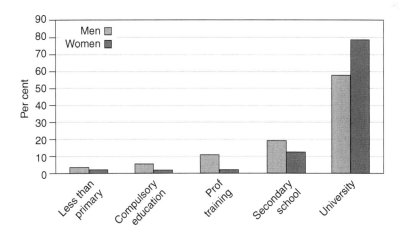

Figure 15.3 Education and gender (Salamanca).

participants with no education or only basic primary education is low, at around 18 per cent. A strong educational background, however, does not guarantee labour market access. In Salamanca only 16 per cent were working at the time of responding (as shown in Figure 15.2). In Madrid and Bilbao – richer regions, and with a higher proportion of older respondents – the rate of employment increased significantly. In Madrid, half the sample group reported being in paid work (Likki 2012: 4).

Opinion makers have often defined the 15-M movement as an anti-system movement, against politics and against ideology. In this reading, participants would be unwilling to understand political reality through conventional ways, instead adopting a reactive, hostile approach to anything political. Spanish society shared this view: in June 2011, 50 per cent of respondents to the Metroscopia survey believed that the 15-M movement had no defined political orientation (Metroscopia 2011).[8] However, this is not what the data tells us. Participants in the 15-M movement in Salamanca had no particular difficulties in finding a location in the conventional 1 to 10 ideological scale; this is interesting as, on average, 20 per cent of Spaniards cannot do so (Martínez and Orriols 2011). In Salamanca, as shown in Table 15.2, only 12 per cent of respondents could not or did not want to find a place on the ideological scale. Also, ideological identities are clear: the mean for ideology in Salamanca was 2.84 (when the mean for ideology in the post-electoral survey of 2008 was 4.5, for instance).[9] Table 15.2 gives detailed information on the distribution of ideology in Salamanca, with an explicit comparison to the distribution of the same variable in that post-electoral survey. While, on average, most respondents in national surveys tend to define themselves as centre-leftist (positions 3, 4 and 5), in Salamanca half the sample were in positions 2 and 3. Likki's data for Madrid is similar to that for Salamanca: a similar rate of non-response (12 per cent) and a clearly leftist

Table 15.2 Ideology of 15-M movement participants

Ideological scale	%	Ideology in post-electoral survey 2008*
1	10 (25)	3.7%
2	20 (48)	5.0%
3	35 (88)	17.1%
4	13 (32)	17.9%
5	5.0 (14)	20.4%
6	0.8 (2)	8.9%
7**	1.2 (3)	6.6%
8**	2.0 (2)	4.5%
9**	1.2 (3)	1.0%
10**	0.8 (2)	0.9%
Ns/Nc	12 (27)	27
Total	100 (257)	257

Notes
*   CIS study number: 2757, March 2009.
** Not included in the analysis.

ideological orientation among participants. In her case, however, the ideological mean leant more evidently towards the left, with a score of 1.62 (Likki 2012: 6).

The existing data, however, is still too poor to assess the previous mobilization trajectories of participants in the 15-M movement. Recent journalistic and/ or biographical accounts on participation relate the 15-M movement with previous episodes of unrest, including the 'movement for decent housing', internet activity against government plans for regulating copyrights on the web, protests against the so-called 'Bologna reforms', and so on (Haro and Sampedro 2011; Romanos 2011). That participation in the 15-M movement is a logical extension of a previous trajectory with social and civic participation would explain Likki's data on Madrid (2012: 7). In her sample, 99 per cent of respondents had previously participated in demonstrations, and 82 per cent had been involved in some form of political action and/or organization. This data, however, contradicts the analysis by Arellano *et al.* (2012: 33–34): only 33 per cent of participants in Bilbao declared any previous involvement with NGOs, social movements or other associations (unfortunately, respondents in Salamanca were not asked about previous associational involvement).

Participants in the 15-M movement are 'political' activists, and they do engage with electoral politics, but not in the ways that dominate in Spanish politics. The Bilbao dataset included a question in relation to voting intentions (general elections, scheduled for November 2011). More than 70 per cent of respondents said that they were going to vote (Arellano *et al.* 2012: 19; for a discussion of the electoral impact of the 15-M movement, see Jiménez 2011b). In the case of Salamanca only 56 per cent had participated in the local elections of May 2011; 79 per cent of these voted for a small party, and 8 per cent spoiled their vote.

A movement with two souls

The 15-M movement has loose mobilization structures. In this particular case it is difficult to decide who participates and who does not, as horizontal structures of decision-making are preferred to hierarchical ones. The data used in this chapter assumes a participant in the 15-M movement to be mostly anyone who declares themselves to be; in practice, this tends to mean anyone who has attended at least two assemblies or similar gatherings with a 15-M theme. Assemblies, of course, stand at the heart of the workings of the 15-M movement. They are highly valued by participants, and more so by those more actively engaged with movement activities. Analyzing the Salamanca data, 95 per cent of respondents valued or highly valued the fact that assemblies resulted in decisions being taken by everyone. Similarly welcomed aspects of assemblies were, for instance, the forging of feelings of belonging or their capacity to incite individual thinking on issues of general interest. However, participants were also aware of important limitations associated with horizontal structuring. As reported in Table 15.3 (next page), members of the Salamanca 15-M movement thought the lack of fluidity in decision-making was the most serious limitation.

Table 15.3 Problems with assemblies (Salamanca; respondents invited to select two) (%)

	Total	Work in commission?	
		Yes	No
Slow decision-making	60.2	54.2	63.5
Hampers remote coordination	30.9	15.7	39.7
Give voice to only a few	20.1	16.9	21.8
Debates do not move on	7.6	2.4	9.6
Arguments constantly repeated	43.0	43.4	42.3
No problems!	11.6	18.1	9.0
Other	8.4	14.5	5.1
No reply	4.0	6.0	2.6

The table distinguishes between actively committed and occasional participants (see below); this is done on the basis of whether or not people participate in specialized working groups (*comisiones*) outside their daily appearance in a general assembly. This is a helpful distinction that reveals, for instance, that those actively committed are generally more tolerant of the workings of assemblies than are those whose only participation is in those gatherings.

Still drawing on the Salamanca data, Table 15.4 shows that around 34 per cent of respondents worked in one of the many specialized groups working on specific needs such as logistics, legal relations or communication. Interestingly, the percentage of participants having slept in camps is similar (33 per cent); similarly, those considering themselves to be 'active' members constituted 39 per cent of the sample, while 37 per cent spoke in assemblies. Statistical tests (not shown here), plus some applied common sense rightly suggests that we are seeing the same people across these different indicators: namely, a core of mobilized activists who slept overnight '*en la plaza*', actively contributed to assemblies and, of course, gave flesh to the *comisiones*. These are the 'actively committed' activists mentioned above, and can be said to represent between 30–40 per cent of 15-M movement participants. Thus, by 'occasional participants' we mean people who more or less regularly participated in some of the daily assemblies organized by their local 15-M movement. This division into

Table 15.4 Intensity of participation in the 15-M movement (Salamanca)

Have you got involved in any *comisión*?	Yes 34%	No 64%
How often have you slept in the camps?	At least once 33%	Never 67%
Do you speak in assemblies?	At least once 37%	No 63%
How would you consider yourself?	As an active participant 39%	Occasional participant, sympathizer 61%

committed participants and occasional participants gives some substance to Taibo's early claim about the twofold 'soul' of the 15-M movement (Taibo 2011: 34): one inclined to moderation, the other inclined to a libertarian way of thinking and acting.

'Active' and 'occasional' participants exhibit interesting differences. Going back to the issue of ideology, active participants – the hardcore of the 15-M movement – are more leftist than the occasional participants. Table 15.5 (below), displays the ideological means for men and women, and also for occasional and active participants. The table also displays the result of a simple t-test of comparison of means. The table confirms the leftist identity of committed activists: it also shows that this difference is wider in the case of women (0.5 points between the two types of activists). In the case of women, but also in the case of occasional participants, the differences in means are statistically significant. An additional benefit of this table is the light it sheds upon the differences in ideology identified between the Salamanca and Madrid samples: as noted above, activists in Madrid have an even more defined leftist ideology than their peers in Salamanca. The Madrid sample consists of 'surviving' activists, who found a way to navigate from the first stage to the second stage of movement development. We also saw that, in Madrid, most participants had a strong record of social and civil involvement. All combined, this suggests an evolutionary reading where the original 'committed' activists of the first wave sustained and engineered the transformation of the 15-M movement that took place after the summer of 2011. By contrast, occasional participants, who participated in some assemblies and responded to the calls for big demonstrations, largely abandoned the 15-M movement after July 2011.

The goals of participation

Participants in the 15-M movement are 'digital natives' (Prenski 2004); they belong to generations whose educational and socialization experiences are defined by being embedded in digital forms of knowledge and communication. Table 15.6 (next page) summarizes the information included in the Salamanca database in relation to the role of digital media in the dissemination and circula-

Table 15.5 Ideology, gender and participation in the 15-M movement

Do you participate in a commission?			*Mean for ideology*
	Yes	Male	2.66
		Female	2.51**
		Total	2.58**
	No	Male	2.96
		Female	3.02**
		Total	3.00**

Note
** Statistically significant.

Table 15.6 How did you hear about 15-M (Salamanca; several answers possible)

From Facebook/Tuenti[10] (% of group)	From a friend (% of group)
88.9	38.9
57.1	35.7
51.4	100.0
100.0	27.3
80.0	30.0
83.3	33.3
41.7	16.7
101	101

tion of information about 15-M protest events. Most respondents stated that they heard of the 15-M demonstration through digital means, with only 35 per cent of respondents giving a primary role to off-line contacts as a fundamental means for obtaining relevant information. Digital media have been the channel for the further production and dissemination of relevant information (data not shown here).

The results for Bilbao were somewhat different: there, 52 per cent of respondents mentioned the internet as the primary means of accessing information about the 15-M events. This is a much lower percentage than that identified in Salamanca. Nevertheless, this result makes sense considering the differences in sample composition, with educational levels being higher in Salamanca than in Bilbao. In both cases, only 30 per cent of respondents obtained information through personal contacts (Arellano *et al.* 2012: 32). In the case of Bilbao 38 per cent of respondents accessed information through TV and radio; in Salamanca only 14 per cent mentioned traditional media as the primary source of information.

What were the aims of participants? At a very general level, Arellano *et al.* (2012: 34–35) claim that 15-M movement participants are mostly driven by an urge to 'change things' (65 per cent of Bilbao sample), instead of merely 'protesting' (19 per cent). Likki (2012: 9) suggests three basic categories of reasons for participation: (1) 'concern for public services'; (2) 'concern about inequality'; and (3) 'concerns about markets and corruption'. The first one is clear and speaks of concerns based around the shrinking of the welfare state. The second one is less homogeneous, and includes obvious concerns about inequality along with more generalized concerns about the lack of democracy or the manipulation of ideas. The last one includes issues such as housing, banks, and corruption. A comparison of the Salamanca and Madrid samples offers the chance to test the effects of time in the definition of goals and priorities. Table 15.7 (next page) explores a fourteen-item list of goals that participants in Salamanca were asked to evaluate according to perceived relevance (using scale of 1 to 10).

Presenting this array of descriptive statistics is important in order to show how difficult it was for the early participants to prioritize. In all cases the most popular value (i.e. the mode) is value 10. In other words, most respondents said

Table 15.7 Goals of the 15-M movement (Salamanca; 1 to 10 scale)

	Mean	St deviation	Median	Mode	N
Concerns for public services					
Labour market reform	8.69	1.88	9	10	246
Educational reform	8.7	1.86	10	10	247
Protection of environment	8.12	1.99	9	10	247
Defence of welfare state	8.32	2.2	9	10	245
Improving quality of urban life	7.51	2.3	8	10	244
Lowering of military spending	7.9	2.34	8	10	237
Concerns about inequality					
Tranformation of democracy	8.83	1.91	10	10	245
Punish big political parties	7.78	2.41	8	10	246
Gender equality	8.07	2.38	9	10	245
Achieve neutral media	8.72	2.77	9	10	248
Concerns about markets and corruption					
Fight against corruption	9.16	1.75	10	10	246
Control of financial markets	8.86	1.84	10	10	245
Bring those responsible for the crisis to justice	8.53	2.97	9	10	248

that all items in the list were of the utmost relevance. Thus, the median scores in all cases are very high, with only three items scoring less than 8 points (improving urban life, lowering military spending and punishing big political parties). The table shows that, in Salamanca, the fight against corruption and the controlling of financial markets were the most important goals pursued by participants in the 15-M movement.

Respondents in Madrid were asked about a similar (but shorter) list of reasons for participation (Likki 2012: 8). In November 2011, when the Madrid data was collected, the fight against corruption and the need to regulate financial markets were again leading goals for movement participants. However, it is interesting to note that concerns for public sector reform were more important in Madrid than in Salamanca: in fact, a 'concern for the educational system' topped Likki's list with a score of 6.66 (on a scale from 1 to 7). This undoubtedly reflected the evolution of political events: protests against spending cuts in public education resulted in a series of demonstrations between September and December 2011 generally referred to as the 'green sea' (*marea verde*).[11] This was one of the episodic causes that counted on the support of the 15-M movement during its second phase.

However, it appears that participants in the 15-M movement are not merely following an instrumental logic of action. Participation can be a goal in itself, inasmuch as plenty can be gained by the simple experience of engaging in collective action. Returning to the Salamanca data, Table 15.8 (below) shows a range of personal benefits associated with participation. Most participants see the 15-M movement as a good vehicle for showing their indignation. The movement is also credited as having had an educational influence upon participants: it has taught them about systemic injustices. Other consequences of a personal nature, including the expansion of circles of friends, seem to be of lesser relevance. Note, however, that 'meeting interesting people' is given a high value by the most committed activists.

One of the striking features of the 15-M movement is the central role that emotional displays play in its very fabric. Emotions such as anger or moral outrage are a critical aspect of social movements as they may energize mobilization. It is therefore not surprising that the participants of the 15-M movement are

Table 15.8 Personal consequences of participation in 15-M movement (Salamanca)

	Mean	Participate in Comisión?	
		Yes	No
I can show my indignation	8.6	8.45	8.62
I learn about injustices	7.8	7.64	8.03
I meet interesting people	7.0	8.13	6.32
I learn about working in social movements	7.5	7.50	7.44
I learn about consensus	7.6	7.66	7.54

called the 'indignados', or the 'outraged'. In the Madrid study participants were asked to indicate the extent to which they felt different emotions when thinking about economically disadvantaged people: morally outraged, angry, sad, guilty, or hopeful. The general picture that emerged from the results was clear: the key emotion was moral outrage, but two other negative emotions – anger and sadness – also rated highly. The 15-M movement is a movement characterized by anger at social injustice. As discussed in Likki (2012: 10–11), the mean for the positive emotion of hope was low – only 3.18 on a scale from 1 to 7 – suggesting that despite their active participation in the protests, the participants were reserved in their hopes that economic inequality would be resolved soon.

Conclusion

The aim of this chapter has been to discuss some empirical data on 15-M movement participants. It has shown that young people with a leftist political orientation stand at the core of this social movement, there are not significant gender differences, and levels of education are very high. Sadly, this has not opened the gates of the job market for these people. This is a good explanation for the overt emotional element associated with the 15-M movement. Participants are furious; they are outraged at the closure of opportunities to which a whole generation of highly qualified people has been condemned.

The 15-M movement is expanding the repertoire of mobilization in Spain in a significant way: new strategies, new themes, new goals and new people are giving flesh to a different way of engaging with collective action which is defying categorization by experts and bystanders alike. In getting involved in alternative forms of participation, Spanish younger generations might be showing a new disposition to break with established patterns of political apathy and discontent: a radically leftist ideology co-existing with peaceful modes of protesting as well as with very sophisticated strategies of knowledge production and dissemination.

All of this might lead to a fundamental question: what sort of political contribution is the 15-M movement? A great deal of the political debate on this social movement has tried to establish whether the movement sought to break the system or, rather, to fix and improve it. Interestingly, 62 per cent of respondents in Salamanca thought that this was a reformist social movement, not an anti-systemic one. Close attention to this social movement could well give us new clues to reconcile ideas about change and continuity that are increasingly relevant in dealing with a systemic political and economic crisis that is shaking all elements of the social fabric.

Notes

1 See http://tomalaplaza.net/lista-de-ciudades-que-ya-han-tomado-la-plaza/ [accessed 1 March 2012] for a list of towns that at some point hosted a camp.
2 See Romanos in this volume for a more nuanced discussion of patterns of continuity and change in the cycle of protest in Spain.

3 A participant in the 15-MM Madrid described the tensions and dilemmas associated with decay and steady demobilization in Rivas (2011: 58–60).

4 It is true that the number of demonstrations more than doubled between 1985 and 1999; the total numbers of people involved with them have also increased (Jiménez 2011a: 20). Note, however, that these findings are not indicative of the strength of the left-leaning social movement sector. For instance, a great deal of the increase in protest has to do with the engagement of right-wing groups, as well as the Catholic Church, with collective action.

5 Further information on assemblies, places and related background data can be found in Salamanca's 15-MM 'official' web site: http://acampadasalamanca.blogspot.com. es/ [last accessed 20 June 2012].

6 The 'feminist manifesto', in Spanish, can be found at the following web address: http://old.kaosenlared.net/noticia/manifiesto-feminista-de-sol [last accessed 3 July 2012].

7 Note that in this case respondents had to state *completed* levels of education, leaving current university students classified as secondary education or professionally qualified.

8 The wording of the question went as follows: 'would you say that (the 15-MM) is closer to the left, closer to the right or, perhaps, without any specific political orientation?'

9 Centre for Sociological Research (CIS) study number 2757, March 2009.

10 A Spanish social networking site.

11 Further information can be found at the following address (in Spanish): http://mareaverdemadrid.blogspot.com.es/ [last accessed 6 July 2012].

References

ABC (2012). 'Las tensiones que dividieron Democracia Real Ya'. 14 May. www.abc.es/20120511/espana/rc-tensiones-dividieron-democracia-real-201205110219.html.

Aguilar, Susana and Alberto Fernández (2010). 'El movimiento por la vivienda digna en España o el porqué del fracaso de una protesta con amplia base social'. *Revista Internacional de Sociología* 68(3): 679–704.

Alvarez, Klaudia (2011). 'No hay vuelta atrás; vamos a más y mejor', in Klaudia Alvarez, Pablo Gallego, Fabio Gándara and Oscar Rivas. *Nosotros los Indignados*. Madrid: Destino (9–23).

Arellano, Javier, Iziar Basterretxea, Cristina de la Cruz and Santiago Yaniz (2012). *15-M Bilbao*. Colección *Gazteak*, 5. Vitoria: Servicio Central de Publicaciones del Gobierno Vasco.

Bonet, Eduard., Irene Martín and José Ramón Montero (2006). 'Actitudes Políticas de los Españoles', José Ramón Montero, Joan Font and Mariano Torcal, eds, *Ciudadanos, asociaciones y participación en España*. Madrid: CIS (105–132).

Botella-Ordinas, Eva (2011). 'La democracia directa de la Puerta del Sol'. Books and Ideas.net: www.booksandideas.net/La-democracia-directa-de-la-Puerta.html.

El País (2011a). 'Miles de ciudadanos "sin casa, sin curro y sin miedo" exigen "un futuro digno"'. 16 May. http://politica.elpais.com/politica/2011/05/15/actualidad/1305495860_450894.html.

El País (2011b). 'La carga policial desata la indignación en Barcelona'. 27 May. http://politica.elpais.com/politica/2011/05/27/actualidad/1306489864_137130.html.

Flesher Fominaya, Cristina (2007). 'Autonomous Movement and the Institutional Left'. *South European Society & Politics*, 12: 3: 335–358.

Freire, J. (2011). '¿Volverán los políticos a hacer política?'. #spanishrevolution# y el.

resurgimiento del espacio público', in VV.AA.: *Indignados*, Madrid: Mandala Ediciones, 52–54.

Galindo, Jorge (2011). 'El 15M no existe'. *Politikon*: http://politikon.es/2011/12/05/el-15m-no-existe/.

García, Gema and Irene Martín (2010). 'La participación política de los jóvenes en perspectiva comparada', in Mariano Torcal (ed.) *La ciudadanía europea en el siglo XXI*. Madrid: CIS.

Haro, Carmen and Victor Sampedro (2011). 'Activismo político en red'. *Teknokultura* 8 (2): http://teknokultura.net/index.php/tk/article/view/14.

Hessel, Stéphane (2011). *Indignaos!* Madrid: Destino.

Hughes, Neil (2011). 'Young People Took to the Streets and all of a Sudden all of the Political Parties Got Old', *Social Movement Studies*, 10:4: 407–413.

Jiménez, Manuel (2011a). *La normalización de la protesta*. Madrid: CIS.

Jiménez, Manuel (2011b). '¿Influyó el 15-M en las elecciones municipales?', *Zoom Político* 2011/04. Madrid: Fundación Alternativas.

Juris, Jeffrey (2005). 'The New Digital Media and Activist Networking within Anti-Corporate Globalization Movements', *The Annals of the American Academy of Political and Social Science* 597: 189–208.

Juris, Jeffrey (2008). *Networking Futures*, Duke: Duke University Press.

La Vanguardía (2011). 'Las feministas de Sol denuncian agresiones sexuales', 3 June. www.lavanguardia.com/politica/20110603/54164947089/las-feministas-de-sol-denuncian-agresiones-sexuales.html.

Likki, Tiina (2012). '15m Revisited', *Zoom Político* 2012/11. Madrid: Fundación Alternativas.

Martínez, Alvaro and Lluis Orriols (2011). '¿Cómo votan los que no tienen ideología?' *Zoom Político* 2011/05. Fundación Alternativas.

Metroscopia (2011). 'Opinión de los españoles sobre el 15M'. 22 June.

Morales, Laura and Peter Geurts (2007). 'Associational Involvement', in J.W. van Deth, J.R. Montero and A. Westholm (eds) *Citizenship and Involvement in European Democracies*. Routledge (135–157).

Pettit, Philippe (2011). 'Republic Reflections on the 15-M Movement', Books and Ideas. net: www.booksandideas.net/Republican-Reflections-on-the-15-M.html.

Prenski, Mark. (2004). 'The death of Command and Control?', *SNS*, 20 January. www.marcprensky.com/writing/Prensky-SNS-01–20–04.pdf.

Rivas, Oscar (2011). 'La democracia real acampó en Sol', in Klaudia Alvarez, Pablo Gallego, Fabio Gándara and Oscar Rivas (eds) *Nosotros los Indignados*. Madrid: Destino (50–61).

Romanos, Eduardo (2011). 'El 15-M y la democracia de los movimientos sociales.' Books and Ideas.net: www.booksandideas.net/El-15M-y-la-democracia-de-los.html.

Romanos, Eduardo (2013). 'Collective Learning Processes within Social Movements', in C. Flesher Fominaya and L. Cox (eds) *Understanding European Movements*. London: Routledge.

Taibo, Carlos (2011). *Nada Será como Antes.* Madrid: Catarata.

Conclusion

Anti-austerity protests in European and global context – future agendas for research

Cristina Flesher Fominaya and Laurence Cox

Over the past three years, a series of protests rooted in demands for economic and political inclusion have taken place across diverse parts of the globe. The mass mobilization in response to a perceived disenfranchisement in both the economic and the political realms, and the greater fairness and representation demanded by protesters in Iceland during the 2008 "saucepan revolution" appear to be features echoed in a string of subsequent protests, from the Arab Middle East, to the Euro-American "core" of the global economic system. In Tunisia, the harsh security crackdown against protests triggered by the self-immolation of a street vendor sparked an uprising which, between December 2010 and January 2011, successfully overthrew Ben 'Ali's seemingly solid authoritarian regime.

Protests were immediately echoed in Egypt, overthrowing President Mubarak in under three weeks (25 January–12 February 2011), then spreading to Syria (26 January), Yemen (27 January), Bahrain (14 February) and Libya (15 February). While the Tunisian uprising is the first and thus far most successful case of popular uprising in the Middle East, the Egyptian case is probably most significant, containing strong social movements pushing for regime change, but also a more entrenched regime, and a degree of sectarian divisions and violence aimed at protesters, albeit not to the extremes reached in Libya, Syria and Yemen.

Within Europe, countries that have been particularly hard hit and/or whose governments have been required by international financial institutions to impose austerity measures include Iceland, Spain, Greece, Ireland and Portugal. In all of these countries, citizens have responded by public protest, although to greatly varying degrees. Protests have targeted national political and economic elites for failing to adequately address internal structural problems, and for failing to protect citizens against the effects of the global financial crisis (Shihade *et al.* 2012). They have protested the external imposition of budgetary austerity measures, which, in their opinion and those of a number of scholars (Krugman 2012; Fishman 2012), threaten to worsen both cyclical and structural economic problems. Underlying these protests has been a deep critique of policy-making processes and a strong sense of injustice.

Understanding the roots, development and implications of these protests is a critical challenge not only for several social science disciplines, but also for a range of stakeholders in the public arena, from the movements involved in these protests to the governments faced with the daunting task of responding to them. The emergence of anti-austerity protests also throws up a series of questions which have been hotly debated among scholars:

First of all, is this indeed a cycle or wave of protest? Are the protests related to each other or just superficially similar? What is the connection between the emergence of movements making similar claims in such disparate geographic, political, economic, social and cultural settings? To what extent are globalizing processes responsible for their emergence?

Protest waves have been of interest to scholars since at least 1848, when contemporary observers spoke of a "springtime of peoples", while Palmer's groundbreaking work on the "Atlantic revolutions" of the late eighteenth century added to the idea. Over time, new "waves" such as that from 1916–1924, European anti-fascism, de-colonization movements in the majority world, 1968, post-Soviet transition, the alterglobalization movement and Latin America's "pink tide" have come under scrutiny.

However, most studies have either simply acknowledged the empirical reality of such waves or have described their internal relations in terms of quantitative macro-indicators, to the detriment of inter- and intra-organizational dynamics, collective identity processes, and the diffusion of protest frames and strategies. This descriptive choice constrains theoretical questions as to why such waves occur at all and what factors explain their timing, geography and characteristics.

Marxist and world-systems analyses such as Arrighi, Hopkins and Wallerstein, and Halperin redress this balance with attention towards the changing balances of power between popular and elite forces. Others such as Skocpol focus on the breakdown of particular forms of state power. By contrast, Katsiaficas, Castells and Linebaugh, and Rediker focus on cross-boundary diffusion, communication tools, and mobile social agents. Nonetheless there is clearly still much work to be done in order to understand what has been a recurrent feature of the modern world for the past quarter-millennium.

Currently, the question of the relationship between "Arab spring", the post-2008 European anti-austerity movements, and the "Occupy Wall Street" movement is unclear, both conceptually and empirically. Moreover, the relationship of any of these with the wider "Global Justice Movement" since 1999 (whose organizations and networks certainly flowed into the latter two), or with opposition to neo-liberal IFI (International Financial Institutions) policies in Africa and Latin America, is also an open question, both theoretically and empirically. Which brings us to the next set of questions: Are these protests new and unprecedented, or do they in fact represent continuity with previous cycles of contention, namely the Global Justice Movement? New versus old debates are popular in the literature, but are often quite sterile. A more fruitful line of inquiry, and one adopted by many of the contributors to this volume, asks which elements are new and which can be seen as developments of previous movements and networks.

The contributions to this book would urge us to approach radical claims for newness with caution. Nevertheless, there are clearly some features of these current protests that *are* new, whether in degree, scope, or actual innovation. One area that has been much discussed in this regard is the use of ICTs and social media and their impact upon the emergence, dynamics, and extension of the mobilizations: What is the importance of ICTs and social media in mobilizing protest? Is the use of ICTs qualitatively and quantitatively different from previous cycles of contention?

Within the European context the use of social media (such as Facebook) has increased since the early 2000s, as has its acceptability among social movement actors. Yet the ways this use actually shapes the speed, scale and form of mobilization is still unclear and therefore more research is needed in this area. While some scholars outside the social movement studies field call for a conceptual reworking of collective action on the basis of increased ICT use, ethnographic work on social movements has demonstrated that such claims overlook the actual ways in which collective actors use ICTs in physical (face-to-face) social movement settings, and that the interconnection between virtual and physical space and its impact upon mobilization needs to be more fully understood.

The question of continuity or rupture from the Global Justice Movement is salient in discussions of movements' use of ICTs, with strong claims for the importance of social media in the rapidity and scope of the 15-M protests being noted as novel or distinctive. However, the 13-M protests in 2004 were also convoked and spread in a matter of hours, by movement actors firmly located within the Global Justice Movement network in a highly unfavourable political context which involved risk taking and low expectations of success by the organizers (Flesher Fominaya 2011). The difference, of course, is that 13-M emerged from existing networks but did not coalesce into a sustained movement.

Qualitative research, and ethnographic research in particular, is crucial to critically examine claims for the radical transformative impact of ICTs on protest activity. For example, Bennett's (2012) claims that 15-M represents a radical departure from traditional forms and logics of social movement organizing display a lack of awareness of the history, development, and actual practices of social movement networks in Spain and of autonomous movements more broadly. If social movement studies is often a self-referential subfield that needs to reach out beyond its boundaries, as we have argued in this book, it must also be said that scholars outside the field would do well to familiarize themselves with the large body of research on social movements over the past decades before making authoritative claims about social movement dynamics. When faced with a lack of clearly visible formal organization, some scholars (including some social movement scholars) mistakenly assume that there *is* no organization or coordination, a conclusion easily refuted by qualitative primary data on autonomous movement networks by engaged social movement scholars. Nevertheless, more research *is* needed to understand the way ICT use alters and impacts upon contentious mobilization; there *is* evidence for significant changes over the past decade, and surely an engagement with experts in digital communication and new information technologies will yield important insights.

In particular, we might consider a re-engagement with the crucial point made by Linebaugh and Rediker (2001), which is that, at any period in the development of global capitalism, it is in essence those *same* social actors, production processes, means of communication and transport, and cultural orientations necessary to the construction and maintenance of the system which are also used to undermine it. "Capitalism creates its own gravediggers", or at least its own resistance, in very literal ways – from the *détournement* of Atlantic capitalism to piracy, the spread of revolutionary ideas and the creation of alternative societies in the eighteenth century to the *détournement* of contemporary social media and Maffesoli's "society of tribes" to generate new kinds of political mass mobilization – on Wall Street, in Reykjavik, or at Puerta del Sol. Following Hardt and Negri (2001), we might also note that Web 2.0 is itself a commodification of new interactive uses of IT, pioneered most notably by the creation of Indymedia for the Seattle protests: the creativity of capitalism and that of its opponents are not separate, but a cycle of commodification and creative resistance.

What should be clear from this book is that these processes do not operate in the kind of ahistorical, culture-free, technologically determined vacuum that is often presented not only by journalists but also by some researchers who should know better. Social actors – even transnational squatters, cyberactivists or global organizations – are nonetheless deeply *situated*, their wider connections, historical perspectives and attempts at generalization profoundly structured by the specificities of their own networks. City-specific, regional, national and European histories shape social movements: not for all time, but providing the "circumstances not of their own choosing" which they work with (or against) to create new activist identities, organizational and movement cultures, political strategies, and alliances.

This most recent wave illustrates this neatly: if in Europe Occupy overlapped with other anti-austerity movements, its core was nevertheless in North America and shaped by the particular US defeat of the alterglobalization movement following 9/11, while European anti-austerity movements drew on the very different history of that movement there to shape new responses to EU fiscal policies. If European movements looked to the Arab Spring for inspiration, and there was communication in both directions, this does not make the two become as one – rather, they are very differently shaped responses to the particular movement histories and locations of these regions within the capitalist and geopolitical order.

As this book shows, we have to understand locally-situated processes across time with their continuities and ruptures, together with transnational waves which articulate very different national and regional realities, if we want to arrive at an accurate understanding of how social movements continue to be both universal *and* particular, specific to their time and place yet also reaching beyond it and attempting to transform it.

As struggles over austerity seem set to continue and deepen in the EU's long-running financial crisis, journalistic impressions and commentaries by specialists on state actors are no substitute for serious ethnographic and archival research by engaged scholars who can explain why it is that popular movements do *not* accept the wisdom of EU, state and media actors and instead set their own agendas which not only overturn those official realities at times (as in Iceland), but are also more broadly reshaping Europe's political landscape in the latest assertion of democracy from below.

References

Bennett, L. 2012. "The logic of connective action", paper presented to ECPR Conference, Reykjavik.

Fishman, R.M. 2012. "Anomalies of Spain's Economy and Economic Policy-making", *Contributions to Political Economy* 31, 67–76.

Flesher Fominaya, C. 2011. "The Madrid bombings and popular protest", *Contemporary Social Science* 6, 289–307.

Hardt, M. and Negri, A. 2001. *Empire*, Cambridge, Mass.: Harvard University Press.

Krugman, P. 2012. *End This Depression Now!* New York: W.W. Norton & Co.

Linebaugh, P. and Rediker, M. (2001) *The Many-Headed Hydra*, New York: Beacon Press.

Shihade, M., Flesher Fominaya, C. and Cox, L. 2012. "The season of revolution: the Arab Spring and European mobilizations", *Interface: a journal for and about social movements* 4, 1–16.

Index

An environmentally friendly book printed and bound in England by www.printondemand-worldwide.com

This book is made entirely of sustainable materials; FSC paper for the cover and PEFC paper for the text pages.

#0287 - 210515 - C0 - 234/156/16 - PB - 9781138025462